Margaret Mead

Made Me Gay

Edited by Michèle Aina Barale,

Jonathan Goldberg, Michael Moon,

and Eve Kosofsky Sedgwick

Margaret Mead Made Me Gay

PERSONAL ESSAYS, PUBLIC IDEAS

Esther Newton

Forewords by

Judith Halberstam

and William L. Leap

Duke University Press

Durham and London

2000

© 2000 Duke University Press
All rights reserved
Printed in the United States of
America on acid-free paper ⊗
Typeset in Scala by Tseng
Information Systems, Inc.
Library of Congress Cataloging-in-
Publication Data appear on the last
printed page of this book.

To the memory

of my mentor,

David M. Schneider,

and of my father,

Saul Bernard Newton

CONTENTS

FOREWORD

The Butch Anthropologist Out in the Field

Judith Halberstam

In this century of speed and simultaneity, it is rare that scholarly work can stand the test of time. Works written yesterday can look dated by the time they appear in print, and many of the feminist and lesbian texts from the 1970s simply do not translate in the present. But, as *Margaret Mead Made Me Gay* shows, Newton's older work remains relevant for a new generation of queer scholars and her newer work continues to build on her own legacy but also responds carefully and methodically to new concerns and research agendas.

Newton has clearly been one of the most important figures in gay, lesbian, and transgender studies over the past two decades, and her work on drag, camp, gender performances, and lesbian masculinities, which dates back to 1972, has been foundational and fundamental to the development of an interdisciplinary project of tracking and identifying lesbian genders. Some fifteen years after the publication of her essay on Radclyffe Hall's "mythic mannish lesbian," Newton's formulations of inversion and the butch have still not been eclipsed. More than twenty-five years after the publication of her study *Mother Camp: Female Impersonators in America* (1972), Newton's insights about drag and camp, role playing and gender impersonation still constitute some of the most important considerations of gender variance available. Indeed, contemporary queer theory, especially queer theory under the influence of Judith Butler's work, has come to circulate endlessly around problems of drag and performance, the very problems, in fact, raised initially by *Mother Camp*.

Judith Butler carefully and significantly relates her debt to *Mother Camp* in an essay titled "Imitation and Gender Insubordination," when she provides her readers with an uncharacteristic moment of personal confession: "As a young person," she tells us, "I suffered for a long time from being told that what I 'am' is a copy, an imitation, a derivative example, a shadow of the real" (1991:20). Butler foregrounds her confession by saying that it "thematize[s] the impossibility of confession" and she follows up on the confession by adding that she found a defense against the accusation of inauthenticity through her reading of Newton's book: "I remember quite distinctly when I first read in Esther Newton's *Mother Camp* that drag is not an imitation or a copy of some true and prior gender; according to Newton, drag enacts the very structure of impersonation by which any gender is assumed" (21). This moment of what we might call "reluctant butch disclosure" suggests the ways in which the personal and the theoretical come together in all projects about queer belonging, queer dislocation, and queer identity. Most queer theorists, whether they deploy a personal voice or not, pick their way to theoretical understandings through their own histories of unbelonging. We embrace our personal memories of dislocation and dysphoria through theoretical rewritings of moments of shame and embarrassment.

As I was working on my book *Female Masculinity*, I found my scholarly preoccupations criss-crossing time and again with Newton's "butch career." An interest in *The Well of Loneliness* led me to her essay on Radclyffe Hall; struggling to make the pleasures of the stone butch viable, I found my way to her essay on "sexual vocabularies"; and more recently, working on contemporary drag king scenes, I returned, of course, to *Mother Camp* and she shared with me her "Dick Tracy" essay. My work at every instance has been informed by Newton's, my understanding of butch embodiment has been shaped by hers, the sense of the viability and importance of a butch project has been handed down from Newton's work to mine. Many times as I was at work on this topic, I reflected on my own butch history and I felt the way it echoed the fragments of personal history that I found in Newton's. When Newton became a reader for *Female Masculinity* during its production, I felt that we struck up a most productive mentoring relation. Newton has been a generous, meticulous, and precise interlocutor—where I am sloppy, she is accurate; where I am rash and grandiose, she is methodical and tempered; where my project faltered, she gave it equilibrium. I have looked, I realize, to Newton, both in my work and in my life, for a model of how to be in the world.

But Newton's work has done much more than simply enable other butch scholars like me to find theoretical meaning in their memories of rejection; she also injects her own work with these moments of laconic butch self-revelation. Indeed, Newton has a particularly subtle and deft touch when it comes to personal voice revelations. In the appendix to *Mother Camp*, she offers us this gem of a story: While working with some female impersonators in Kansas City, Newton comments: "I considered my own role to include a great deal of participation . . . I not only listened and questioned, I also answered questions and argued. I helped out with shows whenever I could, pulling curtains, running messages for the performers, and bringing in drinks and french fries from the restaurant across the street" (1972:134). Here Newton quietly introduces her role as participant-observer to the drag queen scenes she studies, but she also draws a strict line between being helpful backstage and participating onstage: "When the performers half-jokingly suggested that I should stand in for an absent stripper, however, I drew the line." But, Newton continues, she was finally granted the kind of acceptance she sought in this backstage life when a drag queen responded to a visiting impersonator who had asked what Newton was doing there: "He replied casually, 'Oh she's my husband'" (134–35 n.3).

This anecdote provides a lovely insight into Newton's investment in the world of female impersonators. It illustrates precisely the way she refuses to distance herself from the "stigma" of the drag queens and how she understands her own gender identity as a role; furthermore, Newton carefully marks the boundaries of her role in this personal confession and distances herself from normative femininity. The queens, after all, are teasing Newton about her own performances by including her in their backstage banter and pulling her into the business of running a show. Her disjuncture from the role of stripper and her obvious pleasure at being called the drag queen's "husband" mark Newton's butchness in clear terms and make obvious her own gendered investments in this theatrical world of camp and drag impersonation.

Although some may feel that the entire project of lesbian history has been an excavation of the butch and her habits, her troubles, her lifestyles, her lovers, it is also clear that we have only just begun the long task of unraveling the meaning of female masculinity and its relation to queerness. However, reading through Newton's theoretical preoccupations over the past twenty years, as this rich volume allows, gives us some idea about how long it takes to properly formulate and produce butch history. In 1972, for example, Newton provided an interesting footnote to *Mother Camp*. She wrote: "There are also women who perform as men: male impersonators ('drag butches'). They are a recognized part of the profession but there are very few of them. I saw only one male impersonator perform during field work, but heard of several others. The relative scarcity of male impersonation presents important theoretical problems" (5). In an essay that appeared in print twenty-six years later called "Dick(less) Tracy and the Homecoming Queen" (1996a), Newton finally returns to these important theoretical problems and begins to navigate the complicated terrain of butch camp and drag king theater. Newton's own publishing history, this particular lag between recognizing herself as the drag queen's husband, noting the absence of a comparable world of male impersonators, and then finally picking up the threads of a butch camp project, shows the break in continuity between gay history and lesbian history, and shows, simply, how long it takes to construct the complicated archaeology of gender-deviant lives. We have to confront medical opinion and mainstream doctrines of pathology and only then can we identify the vibrant vernaculars and inventive subcultures of queer lives. Butch history, far from being a completed project, has so far only filled in the barest details of the lives of a few extraordinary women.

While butch history, then, remains an ongoing and vital project, Esther Newton, perhaps more than any other scholar of her generation, has shown us how to think through the complex relations among erotic behavior, community formation, gender variance, and embodiment. Newton has always taken risks, big risks, in her work: she was an ethnographer of sexual subcultures in America at a time when anthropology still focused on so-called exotic cultures, and she was a chronicler of gender variance at a time when lesbian history still searched the past for "romantic friendships" between women. Newton was "queer" before the word had been reclaimed and dusted off for a new generation, and she identified her butchness at the very moment that lesbian feminism designated butch-femme as an outlaw, outmoded, outlandish category. The misleading perspective of hindsight, perhaps, prevents us from fully recognizing the boldness of Newton's research decisions on the one hand, and the costliness of them on the other. She asked questions that others did not think of asking ("Did the doctors invent or merely describe the mannish lesbian?") and she pursued projects that other researchers avoided because they feared it might cost them their jobs. Hindsight has also rendered certain Newtonian paradigms inevitable when in fact they are the consequence of enormous intellectual labor. For example, though while now, in the 1990s, we seem to have unhinged butch-femme from the anxious formulation of "role playing," in 1984 a defense of the "mythic mannish lesbian" in terms of the power of her masculinity would have seemed counterintuitive. Again, a decade before a transgender movement, before a butch-femme revival, before current theories of performativity, Newton dared to suggest that Radclyffe Hall's "equation of lesbianism with masculinity needs not condemnation, but expansion."

Newton's work remains vital and central to the fields in which it participates. One of Newton's very best essays, for instance, is a gorgeous piece on "the erotic equation in fieldwork." Published originally in 1996 and included here as one of the real jewels in Newton's collected work, this essay, titled "My Best Informant's Dress," places Newton at the forefront of new queer and feminist anthropology; it also provides a great example of the combination of humor, vulnerability, and lucidity that makes Newton's work consistently compelling, relevant and, in the end, necessary. In "My Best Infor-mant's Dress," Newton comments on the self-reflexive turn in anthropology and produces her own self-reflexive meditation on the motivations of the anthropologist and the potentially erotic relationship between researcher and informant. Newton remarks that in graduate school she had been taught that erotic interest between fieldworker and informant did not exist; moreover, when the topic of erotic interaction did finally enter into discourse, Newton notes, it was all too often accompanied by confessions in the form of con-quest narratives by straight male anthropologists or narratives about missed sexual opportunities by straight female anthropologists. Newton, character-istically, cuts to the chase and asserts, "My fieldwork has been fraught with sexual dangers and attractions that were much more like leitmotifs than light distractions" (1996b:220). Newton qualifies this statement by saying, "I was not looking for sexual adventure in the field" but she confirms that as a gay anthropologist studying gay research subjects, "my key informants and spon-sors have usually been more to me than just an expedient way of getting in-formation and something different than 'just' friends" (221).

The confession that follows is a rich story about Newton's erotic admira-tion for an old woman, Kay, who became her "best informant" for her book on Cherry Grove. In *Mother Camp,* we recall, Newton reveled in the moment that her drag queen informant dubbed her his "husband." A similar moment occurs in "My Best Informant's Dress" when Newton tries to solicit Kay's help in setting up an interview with someone in the Grove. Newton asks Kay to tell the resistant interviewee that she is "a good guy." Kay responds mis-chievously, "Oh I tell that to everybody" (225). There is a remarkable parallel between being named the drag queen husband and then being dubbed the older lesbian's "good guy," and in both instances we can see precisely how Newton forges a bond with her best informants that consists of much more than mere professional trust: these bonds are erotic in both instances and, in both cases, Newton positions herself and is recognized as a masculine suitor. In both relations, furthermore, the relationships are satisfyingly eccentric and cross many more boundaries than just the one that is supposed to distance the anthropologist from his or her object of study.

Newton cites from her field notes throughout "My Best Informant's Dress"; they themselves make fascinating reading and suggest that one of Newton's real skills is her ability to keep records and diaries; she literally makes her own archives. This skill, of course, is closely linked to the talent for sorting through the notes and journal entries later on and knowing what should be published, what may hold a general interest, and what is too idiosyncratic for public consumption. With surgical precision, Newton seems to extract just

With Kay in Cherry Grove, 1988. Photo by Diane Quero

the right episodes and quotes from what must amount to a mountain of re-search. She is also, one imagines, an enormously gifted interviewer, able to listen carefully and solicit information without prying, leading, or imposing. In 1996–1997 when I tried my hand at interviewing for a drag king ethnogra-phy, I discovered firsthand how profoundly difficult it is to encourage people to talk in a way that leads them to the topics of concern to you. After tripping and stumbling a few times and consistently soliciting one-line answers or else endless and pointless anecdotes from my informants, I went to Newton to try to discover the secret of the ethnographic interview. She gave me two pieces of advice: first, craft the question in terms of hows rather than whys ("How did you first start doing drag?" and not "Why did you first start doing drag?"), and second, listen to the response. Simple advice but truly effective. Newton is, ultimately, an active listener, and by listening closely she pays her informants the highest compliment possible; her attention lets them know that they are not simply useful but also desirable and admirable. For Newton, the best informants, in the end, are not simply those people who give her the most information; they are loved ones with whom she constructs worlds and creates knowledge. "If Kay had not existed," writes Newton, "I would have had to invent her." And in a way she did.

Newton does small things to insert herself into her ethnographic narra-tives; inevitably, for instance, she includes pictures of herself with her in-formants and these photo documents place her within rather than outside the frame of analysis. The more usual photograph of the ethnographer situ-ates him or her to one side of the action, writing or watching. As James Clif-ford says of the picture of Stephen Tyler in India that serves as the cover art for Writing Culture, "In this image the ethnographer hovers at the edge of the frame—faceless, almost extraterrestrial, a hand that writes" (1986:1). Newton is no hand that writes and never faceless, but neither is she the tradi-tional participant-observer who immerses herself in another culture in order to "learn" it and represent it. Newton is always of and in the cultures she studies. In the photograph of Newton in Mother Camp, she stands slightly be-hind her "best informant," Skip Arnold, who is made up but not yet in drag. The caption reads: "Skip Arnold with the author between shows." The photo-graph very effectively places Newton in relation to the drag cultures she docu-ments. The young and masculine-looking woman has short hair and wears a bulky sweater; the face is handsome and serious; she looks down and away from the camera but inclines her head toward Skip, listening intently. Skip has obviously been caught mid-sentence by the photographer and his mouth is open in conversation. He has the heavy eye makeup of the drag queen and a lipsticked mouth; his gender indeterminacy actually emphasizes hers, espe-

Skip Arnold with the author between shows, 1965. Photo by Sherry Ortner

cially because as the caption tells us, he is between shows, not on stage and not off. Newton joins him precisely in this in between space: between genders, between shows, between subject and object, between the university and the drag club.

In the photograph that accompanies "My Best Informant's Dress," Newton again stands behind her informant. Kay is in a wheelchair, centered in the photograph and smiling coyly at the camera. In this shot, however, Newton leans forward, now stares into the camera with a seductive and bold glare. In both this shot and the photograph with Skip Arnold, Newton appears as a face without a body and the body of the informant covers her own. These images suggest again the intimacy that Newton cultivates with her subjects, an intimacy that stops short of sexual involvement but goes far beyond the role of participant-observer. By appearing as a face without a female body, Newton presents herself not as androgynous or hidden but as resolutely butch, and she puts on display not her own body but the beautiful body of the drag queen or the magisterial body of the older lesbian. These photographs encourage the viewer to read the relationship between Newton and her informants as collaborative, erotic, and motivated. While Skip Arnold's made-up face forces us to consider the remarkably bare and unfeminine face of his ethnographer, so too Kay's femme grace allows us to read the butch's courtliness.

Another photograph of Newton accompanies her essay on the infiltration of a drag queen contest in Cherry Grove by a dyke (p. 165). This essay, "Dick(less) Tracy and the Homecoming Queen" is in many ways Newton's attempt to survey the relation of camp and drag queen cultures to lesbian public cultures in the 1990s. There are obvious echoes in this essay of her earlier work in *Mother Camp* but it is the photograph of Newton that most clearly demonstrates the connection between the ethnography of drag queens from the 1970s and her history of Cherry Grove in the 1980s. As if to illustrate the changing conditions of visibility for gays and lesbians from 1972 to 1996, this photo reprises Newton's earlier photo of herself and Skip Arnold. Here she is accompanied by drag queen Ann Miller and dressed in a smart and handsome white tuxedo. Newton wears shades and a rakish grin and looks directly at the drag queen on her arm. Once again the circuit of the gaze includes Newton looking at her informant while her informant boldly stares into the camera lens. But now Newton is not hidden behind her feminine partner nor is she in the background. Here she comes out into the full glare of visibility and accepts her active and explicit role as the drag queen's husband.

Esther Newton's work, I boldly assert here, has changed anthropology, feminist studies, and queer studies in remarkable ways. And her intervention into all three fields occurs as much at the level of methodology as it does in terms of subject matter. As I have tried to outline here, Newton's methodological innovation has less to do with crafting new empirical tools than with a creative and inspired mode of listening and participating in the cultures she studies. Newton performs an anthropology of self that is neither narcissistic nor alienated. She explores cultures that reflect her own difficult rites of passage and that place her in relation to stigma and deviance but also in the way of contempt. Commenting on her facility with establishing a rapport with the drag queens in *Mother Camp*, Newton comments: "My status as a bookish female enabled me to present myself as a relatively asexual being, which was helpful. Although my own background is middle-class, alienated perspectives are congenial to me . . . however the respect and liking which I had for the performers may have been decisive. Impersonators, like members of other stigmatized groups, are extraordinarily sensitive to contempt (1972: 135).*

"Alienated perspectives are congenial to me." Despite the passive voice and the lack of a referent for her own alienated perspective, in moments like this,

---

* In personal communication with me, Newton commented: "I cringe reading my first sentence, which was a lie, or at least a partial lie. I presented myself to them (drag queens) as gay from day one (and also bookish), and the only reason I didn't say so was fear of coming out within academia or anywhere in straightsville."

Newton does much more than try to empathize with the impersonators; indeed, she links her fate and her psychology to theirs. By the last sentence we can include Newton in the category "impersonators" and understand that she shares with the performers a sensitivity to contempt. Once we locate Newton within her various ethnographic texts, we realize the courage of her projects new and old. Once we realize how carefully and delicately she has placed herself in the company of so-called deviants, impersonators, and mythic mannish lesbians, we recognize the skill of the ethnographer who wants to be in the picture without engulfing it with her presence. Once we discern the personal narratives of desire and erotic admiration that infuse Newton's relations to her subjects, we understand that the stories of drag queens have been the stories of butches and femmes all along. Margaret Mead may well have made Newton a gay anthropologist, but the drag queens and the femmes have made her queer, butch, and resolutely *out* in the field.

On Being Different: An Appreciation

William L. Leap

Esther Newton is one of the first anthropologists who actively disrupted the divisions between professional and personal life that otherwise define the academic "closet." Building an anthropological career in these terms may have limited Esther's opportunities for career advancement and restricted her access to professional support networks. Even so, she has produced a series of scholarly works that have become foundation material in today's lesbian/gay anthropology, including *Mother Camp,* the essay "The Mythic Mannish Lesbian," and *Cherry Grove, Fire Island.*

Esther describes herself as *different* in her introduction to this volume. And her research and writing have been deeply concerned with issues of difference—particularly with how people come to distinguish themselves as gendered persons in everyday life. She shows us how drag queens and Fire Island society matrons use clothing, hairstyle, makeup, jewelry, posture, gesture, tone of voice, and other forms of self-presentation to create a sense of public presence, to establish claims to social space, and to maintain a sense of dignity, even when surrounded by adversity and oppression. In *Mother Camp,* it is through their judicious use of clothing, hairstyle, and the like that men become female impersonators, female impersonators become drag queens, and drag queens become constructions that in some ways are more original and accessible than their intended target. Similarly, in "My Best Informant's Dress," Kay's carefully cultivated, commanding style enabled her to transform the physicality of a visually, respiratorily, and mobility challenged eighty-six-year-old woman into the vibrant social doyenne of Cherry Grove, a status she had long enjoyed in this community (and on the mainland), and a status she was delighted to retain.

Read in terms of today's theory making in lesbian/gay/bisexual/transgendered studies, these claims about performative masquerade are hardly original. But remember that Esther Newton developed the basic form of this argument more than twenty-five years ago—long before it was safe for lesbian/

gay/bisexual/transgendered academics to be out of the closet, long before les-
bian/gay/bisexual/transgendered studies was one trajectory a scholarly career
could take. And by doing so, Esther Newton helped initiate a critique of more
conventional research paradigms that habitually positioned the foundations
of gay experience within the confines of arrested psychological development,
misplaced and misshaped desires, or impersonal, anonymous sex. *Mother
Camp* showed us that gay culture was also about being true to ourselves,
whomever "we" identifies and whatever we understand "selfhood" (or "truth")
to mean. Continuing this tradition, "My Best Informant's Dress" shows us
that gay culture is still about transcending who we are, about adding glamour and style to our lives when confronted by adversity and oppression, and
about working out our own ways to be fabulous.

Lesbian/gay anthropologists really needed to hear this message in the
1970s. *Mother Camp* predated the institutionalized emergence of lesbian/
gay/bisexual/transgendered networking and public credibility making within
our profession. It was published several years before the formation of the
Anthropological Research Group on Homosexuality, the organization that
became today's Society for Lesbian, Gay, Bisexual and Transgendered Anthropologists (SOLGA). At the time, many of us did not understand how to incorporate Esther's analysis of sexual/gendered differences into our own research interests, or even how to find anthropological colleagues with similar
research/personal interests. But *Mother Camp* showed us that ethnographic
research could contribute richly to the understanding of homosexuality. Indeed, if Esther could present the lived experiences of female impersonators
with such clarity, beauty, and power, maybe some of us could do the same for
other areas of lesbian/gay culture.

And thus emerged one of the defining characteristics of anthropological study of same-sex identities, desires, and practices: exploration of these
themes in site-specific, people-centered, ethnographic terms. *Mother Camp*
was a study of homosexuality "here at home," at a time when doing fieldwork
in exotic, overseas locations was still the anthropological norm. Once again,
Esther was being different — and the extent to which her choice of a "different"
fieldwork location contributed to the emergence of U.S.-based ethnographic
inquiry in the 1970s is also worth exploring. Esther's work was successful
in these regards because she developed and maintained close, respectful relationships with her "research subjects." For Esther, these "subjects" were
people, and their differences mattered. She writes, for example: "The men
whom I knew in Kansas City were tough; they knew how to fight and suffer
with comic grace. They had the simple dignity of those who have nothing else

but their refusal to be crushed" (1972:xiv). Part of documenting their courage was documenting their antagonistic relationships with theater managers, technicians—and with each other. There is no effort here to idealize or sanitize these conditions of lived experience, and that makes Esther's description all the more believable and appealing.

A similar believability underlies Esther's presentation of Kay, the "best informant" wearing the "best informant's dress." Esther describes how her relationship with Kay gradually evolved from respectful strangers, to friends, to close friends, and almost to the point of physical intimacy. "Someday, I'm going to surprise the hell out of you and really kiss you back" (1996b:224), Kay said to Esther one afternoon. And later in the essay, after describing how Kay commanded the cloudy sky to clear so that the sunshine could pour down on a deserted beach (and, at her words, that's exactly what happened), Esther notes, "In another culture, Kay would have been some kind of priestess" (226).

Today, of course, it is not unusual for anthropologists to develop strong feelings of closeness, intimacy, and respect toward their informants (or for informants to respond in kind). But using such feelings as the centerpiece for data analysis, and integrating those feelings so explicitly into the write-up of the research findings, as Esther did in *Mother Camp*, was most unusual in the anthropology of the early 1970s. Indeed, the ethnographic sensitivity displayed in this monograph predates by several years the emergence of the interpretivist anthropology of James Clifford and associates. And though these interpretive scholars have much to tell us about the value of subjectivity and emotion in ethnographic research settings, they still say very little about the "erotic equation" between researcher and informant. "My Best Informant's Dress" reminds us that such equations often guide researchers and informants as they coconstruct the richness of the ethnographic moment; here again, Esther Newton's ethnographic work remains ahead of her time.

Not so apparent in *Mother Camp* or the Cherry Grove study, but certainly important for these remarks (and this anthropologist) has been Esther Newton's sexuality/gender-related political activism within our profession. Esther was one of the first chairs of the Anthropological Research Group on Homosexuality, and one of the first women to serve in a leadership position within that organization. Her mentoring of younger women anthropologists has been instrumental in bringing greater visibility to solga—and to the work in lesbian/gay anthropology that sustains it. She was one of the original cochairs of the American Anthropological Association's Commission on Lesbian and Gay Issues in Anthropology, and—documenting difference yet again—she was instrumental in urging commission members to collect life-story narratives from lesbian, gay, bisexual, and transgendered anthropologists and to use that testimony as the focus for COLGIA's write-up of its fact finding.

The incentives for such professional networking can be traced to the isolation that has haunted Esther throughout so much of her academic career and which she describes powerfully in "Too Queer for College," reprinted below. But it also reflects the vision of anthropology that first attracted her to the profession, and which she has helped to build and sustain: "Anarchism, I read once, is an ideology of permanent rebellion. Anthropology, by refuting any one culture's claims to absolute authority, offers a permanent critique" (p. 1, this volume).

It has taken some years for lesbian/gay studies to become a part of anthropology's "permanent critique," and Esther Newton has been one of the vanguard figures in this struggle. The essays in this collection show how effectively she has incorporated this critique into her studies of lesbian/gay experience and how greatly anthropology has been enriched because she never lost sight of that greater vision.

ACKNOWLEDGMENTS

Each of the essays in this book has its own history. But for the existence of the overall project, to those who supported the big picture, I owe special thanks. Starting with graduate school in the Department of Anthropology at the University of Chicago, I was sustained personally and intellectually by a group I called the "Albanian Conspirators" (perhaps because of Ben Apfelbaum's and Bobby Paul's big black beards), whose other members at our smoky poker games and cheapo dinners included Sherry Ortner and Harriet Whitehead. Three other friends, Chuck Palson, Charley Keil, and the late Cal Cottrell, were always up for the fun and games along with endless anthropology discussions that made graduate school more bearable.

In 1973 a group of feminist faculty, students, and staff at Purchase College led by colleagues Evelyn Keller and the late great Mary Edwards waged a successful battle to convince Abbot Kaplan, then the president of Purchase College, to give me tenure. Without these folks at Purchase who believed in my potential despite the nasty things my enemies were saying, I would have had no career in higher education and most likely would have written nothing after my first book. More recently, a Professional Development/Quality of Working Life Award granted by our union, the United University Professions of the State University of New York, and a President's Research Support Grant from Purchase College have helped defray some expenses of publication.

During the 1980s a network of gay, lesbian, and feminist intellectuals inspired and encouraged me after a period when I had turned away from scholarship. I would especially like to acknowledge the pioneering scholarship and/or personal support of Allan Bérubé, John D'Emilio, Martin Duberman, Lisa Duggan, Larry Gross, Jonathan Ned Katz, Liz Kennedy, Ellen Lewin, Joan Nestle, Gayle Rubin, and Carroll Smith-Rosenberg. In particular, another scholar and friend, Jeffrey Escoffier, and my former partner, Amber Hollibaugh, believed in me implicitly and energetically, encouraging me to think of a book of essays before anyone else did.

The essays having to do with gays and lesbians in anthropology would not have come about without a network of other anthropologists active in the Society of Lesbian and Gay Anthropologists; among the many dedicated people who provided leadership in SOLGA, I am particularly indebted to Deb

Amory, Evie Blackwood, Jeffrey Dickemann, Sue-Ellen Jacobs, Liz Kennedy, Bill Leap, Ellen Lewin, and Martin Manalansan.

As always, I am grateful to my literary agent, the incomparable and splendidly maternal Frances Goldin. Ann Miller, editor at Columbia University Press, made me think this book could matter by her continuing interest over a period of years. Thanks to the anonymous readers at different presses whose constructive criticism helped me improve the individual essays, and especially to Liz Kennedy, whose insightful nagging forced me among other revisions to expand the introduction. At Duke University Press I thank everyone and especially Richard Morrison, formerly assistant editor; Leigh Anne Couch, senior editorial assistant; Judith Hoover, copy editor; Jean Brady, managing editor, and especially Ken Wissoker, editor in chief, for their respectful and flattering enthusiasm for my work. Mei-Mei Sanford and Roanna Judelson helped with typing and reformatting some of the essays. Thanks to Kay Wosewick for the index.

I must mention four special people in my life: Jane Rosett, who shares my taste for electronic gadgets and a good laugh, gave me technical and editorial advice on assembling the photographs; Judith Halberstam, just for being her inimitable self and for her all-around good example that pushes my middle-aged envelope; Julie Mutti, for twenty-five years of steadfast and intuitive friendship; and my friend of forty-one years, the coauthor of three of these essays, who's been through all the ups and downs with my *mishegas,* Shirley Walton Fischler.

And finally, I thank my partner, Holly Hughes, my companion and solace during the six months of never-ending snow at Kalamazoo College in Michigan during the winter/spring of 1997 when this book (whose final title she came up with) took its current shape. For her wit, creativity, intelligence, and amazing courage, my deepest gratitude and love.

INTRODUCTION

Reading Margaret Mead's *Coming of Age in Samoa* was my introduction, not only to the concept of culture, but to the critique of culture — ours. Before 1961, when I read *Coming of Age* in an Introduction to Anthropology course at the University of Michigan, Mead had already done a great deal to popularize the concept of cultural relativity. Her voice had reached into my teenage hell, to whisper my comforting first mantra, "Everything is relative; everything is relative," meaning: There are other worlds, possibilities than suburban California in the 1950s. I was a scholarly minded half-Jew from New York (where I had spent my childhood) and a red diaper baby. I was athletic, hated dating boys, and resented pretending I was less of everything than they were. Neither girls' clothes nor girlish attitudes felt "right" to me. And I was attracted — in some sweaty way that had at first no name — to girls and women.

College in Ann Arbor was better, but still found me unhappily struggling to fit into a slightly more sophisticated workup of American womanhood. I was looking for any way out, some Mad Hatter to lead me down a rabbit hole into a world where I didn't have to carry a clutch purse and want to be dominated by some guy with a crew cut and no neck. Having these thoughts was, however inchoately, a critique. Acting on them constituted rebellion. Calling myself gay, which I had done tentatively and with self-loathing at sixteen, moved opposition to a higher level. Anarchism, I read once, is an ideology of permanent rebellion. Anthropology, by refuting any one culture's claims to absolute authority, offers a permanent critique. So when I read *Coming of Age in Samoa* my senior year in college, I was, to put it mildly, receptive.

Through Margaret Mead I grasped that my adolescent torments over sex, gender, and the life of the mind could have been avoided by different social arrangements. It's not that I imagined a better life in the South Seas. I was far from fancying myself in a grass skirt (despite becoming an anthropologist, I am a homebody; the rigors of long lonely stays in places without electricity and flush toilets only appealed to me, as it turned out, in books). Even though Mead's Samoan girls were happily exercising a heterosexual openness that I had found unsatisfying, the setup was so radically different — multiple parenting, sexual freedom — from what I had been convinced was normal and

With Majestic Errol Flynn, C.D.,
C.G.C. Photo by Robert Giard

right. Mead's work taught me that the smug high school peacocks whose dating/popularity values had rated me so low, reduced me to such a *nothing*, were not lords of the world but only of one nasty barnyard.

The kind of cosmopolitanism that is anthropological knowledge is a dangerous thing to tyrants. I once heard a German woman say that the worst damage the Nazis did to young people in the 1930s was to censor knowledge of alternatives, so that young Germans had no point of comparison. I knew nothing about Margaret Mead's being bisexual, in fact nothing about her, period. (I would not meet her until years later, and then my contacts with her, though significant to me, were fleeting.) Nor is *Coming of Age in Samoa* an overt defense of homosexuality. But it *is* a defense of cultural and temperamental difference, and that, despite my desperate attempts to go with the flow, described me: different.

If Margaret Mead opened the world of anthropology to me, the sheer fact that she was a woman and chose women as subjects was just as important. I first encountered versions of the other worlds that anthropologists explored in the science fiction of such writers as Robert Heinlein and Isaac Asimov (there are strong resemblances between the two genres, made most explicit in the work of Ursula LeGuin, the daughter of an anthropologist). But Heinlein's and Asimov's universes were male and straight. I could only imagine myself into their settings as the macho guy I'd always been ashamed of wanting to be. Though their books were wonderfully escapist, they didn't provide the scripts in which I could star as any kind of woman. (Something similar could be said of the philosopher Spinoza, about whose work I wrote an admiring high school paper.)

I had come to college with the intention of becoming a psychologist like my father, but reading Margaret Mead and Ruth Benedict's *Patterns of Culture* reset my course. Perhaps, in retrospect, the examples of such intellectually powerful women gave me the courage to strike out on my own. I studied and was deeply influenced by literature and then European history. But as a graduate field of study, history promised a life of isolation in the library. I was a misfit whose relationships were troubled because intellectuals are not popular or respected, because women intellectuals back then were weird, and because I was a tormented, closeted queer. Anthropology, I thought, would force me to get out and interact with people, as Margaret Mead had done. And as it turned out, through anthropology I became an activist intellectual, like Mead, dedicated to education and reform. My chosen life work, as these essays show, has been to chronicle and champion the lesbian and gay cultures in which I have found both a home and ever-compelling subject matter.

However, my relationship to the organized profession has never run smoothly for a number of reasons, not least among them the entrenched homophobia of academic anthropology. "Go into anthropology," I was told as a college student. "You can study anything you want." As it turned out, I took that advice further than anyone, including me, expected, further certainly than the majority of anthropologists approved. As explained in several of these essays, notably in "Too Queer for College," my academic career almost foundered early on and has been blocked both indirectly and at times aggressively at every stage of advancement. Without the organized support of feminists at Purchase College, where I have taught since 1971, I would have been expelled from academia in 1973. So I looked instead to lesbian-feminism for support and later to the gay community, or more specifically, the growing network of lesbian and gay intellectuals. Yet my true vocation as a writer has been nurtured and sustained by anthropological ideas, and this collection records the intellectual journey into which I was seduced, not by Margaret Mead in person, but figuratively by her, in every lovely sense of the word figurative.

The excerpts and essays here constitute an intellectual autobiography. They begin with sections from *Mother Camp* (1972), my first published work, based on my dissertation on drag queens, and continue until the present. Frustrated by how little of my writing had been published—until the mid-1980s, neither academic nor popular venues were receptive—I first conceived of putting together a book of my essays in about 1988. At that time fewer essays than at present were organized chronologically, including some fiction that I had written in the 1970s. My all-consuming focus on the book that became *Cherry Grove, Fire Island* (1993) precluded further progress on this collection, and I didn't come back to it seriously until 1994, after the Grove book and several essays derived from the Grove fieldwork had been published.

My longtime friend Jeffrey Escoffier, who had edited the journals *Socialist Review* and *Outlook,* agreed to go over the essays and suggest some form of organization other than just chronological. Looking for distinctive themes in my work, he suggested three alternative schemas that ranged from combining essays with a lot of new autobiographical writing to a minimalist collection of perhaps ten essays. The current organization into four broad topics is derived from one of Jeff's outlines and is a hybrid of chronological and thematic principles of organization. I did begin the autobiographical writing that Jeff had proposed in 1996 after an invitation from the Center for Lesbian and Gay Studies at the City University of New York to give the annual David R. Kessler lecture, which became the essay included here, "My Butch Career." By then there were so many essays that setting them in a memoirist frame seemed too unwieldy. (I have decided to expand the material in "My Butch Career" into a separate, book-length memoir.)

The four broad topics of drag and camp, lesbian-feminism, butch, and queer anthropology do not all correspond to periods in my career that came and went. Rather, they represent the constellations by which I have steered my intellectual life through the currents of time and the phosphorescence of personal experience. They signify my preoccupation with the theatrical and political symbols that designate and shape queer American life, albeit in very different ways, for both gay men and lesbians, including myself, as some of these essays show.

The reasons I write anything, why I chose to write about Cherry Grove, for instance, are the same as those for any human action: to be found in culture, history, personality, and chance. Some factors are imposed externally, as when my then-partner and I were harassed by young boys during a Catskills vacation and so sought safety in the gay beach resort. Others well up from a deep internal aquifer. Drag and camp dramatize the "gender trouble" that has shaped me from the first; theatricality delights and excites me, period.

PART 1, DRAG AND CAMP

Gay theatrical cross-dressing and the sensibility that usually accompanies it were the subjects of my first big anthropological project. *Mother Camp* was based on several months of fieldwork in American cities, as described in its appendix. "Role Models," the best-known chapter from that work, has been reprinted several times, and my reason for including it here is its foundational position in my own work and in that of a number of other scholars. *Mother Camp* itself laid the groundwork for the anthropology of homosexuality, especially the branch that is the study of the cultures of queer people. In the melancholy preface to the 1979 reprinting of *Mother Camp* (included here hesitantly, because it takes an unnecessary swipe at practitioners of s/M, about whom I then knew little) I publicly swear off drag and camp, obliquely reflecting my disappointment over my book's lack of recognition within anthropology. Yet, after taking up residence in Cherry Grove in the mid-1980s, I fell for gay men and their dominant cultural forms all over again. "Theater: Gay Anti-Church" was originally to be a chapter of the Cherry Grove book, which it outgrew. Another Grove-based essay, "Dick(less) Tracy," explores the relationship of lesbians to drag and camp, an issue I had mentioned only in a footnote in *Mother Camp*.

PART 2, LESBIAN-FEMINISM

My climb up the academic ladder was disrupted not only by the unconventionality of my first book on female impersonators and the gay subculture, but also by the historical intervention of the Vietnam War and second-wave feminism. All but the last of these essays were written in the period between 1971 and 1973, when the feminist firestorm was crackling through my mind and heart. Although I had been changed forever by the time the fire died down, part of the transformation was burnout and partial disillusionment with ideology and social movements.

The first four essays in this section reflect a revolutionary feminist rethinking of my life to that point. I could have called the section "Feminism and Lesbian-Feminism," but that seemed awkward. I became a feminist during the winter of 1968; certainly by 1971, when "The Personal Is Political" was written, I had become a lesbian-feminist. That essay, though in an "objective" mode, is a collective portrait of my middle-class generation's tumultuous experience in consciousness-raising groups. The excerpt from *Womenfriends,* a joint journal written with Shirley Walton, who was and remains my chosen sister, records painful attempts to integrate the lesbian-feminist I had become with the rest of my life.

Lesbian-feminist separatism, which I had once ardently supported, had evolved by the late 1970s into something too much like a cult, and finally degenerated into the antipornography movement, whose alliances with the

Christian Right were utterly repugnant. This disillusionment is most strongly reflected in "Will the Real Lesbian Community Please Stand Up?"; the first draft was written for the annual anthropology meetings in 1984. This essay was among those that marked my return to social science work after more than a decade of disaffection.

PART 3, BUTCH

Beginning in 1981, I attempted to deal personally and intellectually with my lack of femininity (to that point having shied away from calling it "masculinity"). "The Misunderstanding" came out of a talk that Shirley Walton and I had given at the famous 1981 Barnard Conference on Women's Sexuality, a watershed confrontation between the "pro-sex" feminists I sided with and the antipornography feminists that marked my decisive rejection of lesbian-feminism. In the years after the conference I set to work on the essay that eventually became "The Mythic Mannish Lesbian," a reappraisal and rehabilitation of Radclyffe Hall's *The Well of Loneliness,* and the first of my work to be published by an academic, albeit feminist, journal. Its positive reception encouraged me to take up scholarly work once more.

I would also like to think that "Mythic" built on whatever influence *Mother Camp* has had in encouraging the emerging transgender movement composed of transsexuals, the intersexed (hermaphrodites), cross-dressers, nelly queens, and butches and femmes that grew from and intersects with the gay and lesbian movement. Lesbian-feminism, despite its (by now quaintly refreshing) militant opposition to capitalist "patriarchy," had submerged sexual and gender nonconformity into one big proposition: women are oppressed by men. But even an idea as momentous as that one can't explain everything; the world is just too complicated and there are too many vectors of domination going at once. My own experience and the research on *Mother Camp* taught me that not everyone lines up obediently on the boy/girl grid. During the 1980s I reflected more deeply about the gender grid itself, as the book review reprinted here, "Beyond Freud, Ken, and Barbie," in which I evaluate some of the social science literature on gender, attests.

My enduring involvement with butch issues is the flip side of my love of drag and camp, except that the butch essays track how I came to identify myself as butch and to become slowly but steadily more public about it. The third-person voice in "The Mythic Mannish Lesbian" is still separate from the first-person voice in "The Misunderstanding," published the same year; "My Butch Career" makes my lifelong relationship to issues of gender dissidence personal and explicit.

PART 4, QUEER ANTHROPOLOGY

About 1980 I became active in the Anthropological Research Group on Homosexuality (now the Society of Lesbian and Gay Anthropologists in the American Anthropological Association); our goal was to provide a safe space for queer anthropology and anthropologists and to challenge the entrenched homophobia we had encountered. After becoming more active professionally I came to write what I consider one of my strongest essays—"My Best Informant's Dress," the first to be published in an anthropological journal—in which the personal and analytical perspectives that are both intrinsic to my thinking are fully integrated. The essays in this final section are diverse, but they all deal with broadly defined anthropological issues, either intellectual or institutional, in relation to homosexuality or, if you prefer, the reverse.

In putting the essays together, my general rule was that (unless otherwise noted) writing that had already been published was left as is. The significant number of previously unpublished essays posed a bigger problem. However embarrassing I found some earlier ideas, I left them alone as having historical value, but in some cases I streamlined whole sections considerably and made sentences more felicitous (this also applies to the joint paper written with Shirley Walton, "The Personal Is Political," which we have shortened and worked to clarify, but not essentially alter). Two unpublished essays, "Theater: Gay Anti-Church" and "Will the Real Lesbian Community Please Stand Up?" were substantially revised for this collection. The particular history of each essay can be found in the Notes section.

Although this book amply documents my career, a few essays that I still consider worthy and let go of with regret were not included because of space or time considerations. The writing I clung to longest was a chapter of which I am very proud from *Cherry Grove, Fire Island,* that dealt with ethnic and racial prejudice in that gay seaside resort. This collection is already long, however, and the Cherry Grove book is easy to find. Many of the other essays either were never published or were published in places that are difficult for the general reader to access, for reasons that are discussed in "Too Queer for College."

Coming of age politically during the antiwar movement, I had a jaundiced view of capitalism, but as Gayle Rubin once pointed out to me, despite its terrible injustices, capitalism is not all bad, and the one institution that has changed more than any other in response to the demand created by a queer reading public and queer students is publishing. Never will I take for granted how gratifying it is to be published and to have people read and respond to my work!

Which brings me back to Margaret Mead and to Ruth Benedict. Both of these brainy women (in common with Gertrude Stein, who, as "My Butch Career" reveals, was the third of my idols) were not only good writers, they were versatile writers. They aimed to engage both the cognoscenti in their fields *and* a general literate readership. They went where their interests and talents took them rather than sticking to the academic straight and narrow. Mead even wrote in the mass media and appeared on television; Benedict was a poet. As women and as sexual iconoclasts, Mead and Benedict were partial outsiders to the insular world of professional anthropology, and they both believed in influencing public opinion to promote social justice. It is to this tradition that I aspire in the hope that both the general reader and the student of anthropology will find pleasure, interest, and inspiration in these pages.

October 22, 1999
New York City

PART I: DRAG AND CAMP

Writing my dissertation on a typewriter!

From the Appendix to *Mother Camp:*

Field Methods

1972

  The research for this book was traditional anthropological fieldwork, with certain qualifications imposed by time, resources, and the special constitution of the "community" under study. There is to date no full ethnography of the homosexual community, much less of the drag world, so that from the beginning I was "flying blind." Moreover, very few ethnographies (except for the early community studies) have been attempted in America, so that my model of fieldwork procedure was largely based on non-urban precedents.

  A female impersonator show or "drag show" generally consists of a number of short acts or routines performed sequentially by the same or different performers. The shows often open and close with routines by all the performers together, called production numbers. The number of performers in the cast of a particular show can range from one to twenty-six (this was the largest cast I ever saw, although in theory a cast could be larger), but the majority of drag shows have casts of about five or six. The shows take place in bars, nightclubs, and theaters for paying audiences, and last about an hour each. Performers generally do three shows an evening.

  The first drag show I saw was in a small bar on Chicago's Near North Side. I did not understand about half of the performance, and my reaction was one of mingled shock and fascination. The audience clearly found the performance exceedingly funny. Never having seen a man dressed in full female attire before, I was astounded to find performer and audience joined through laughter in the commission and witnessing of a taboo act. At the same time I was struck by the effectiveness of the impersonation, by the highly charged nature of the symbol being presented dramatically, and by the intensely familiar interaction between the performer and the audience. The closest analogue I had seen was a Negro Gospel show in Chicago, in which the performers came down off the stage and mingled with the audience in a "laying-on of hands," and members of the audience "got the spirit." On the basis of that observation

I hypothesized that I had witnessed a "cultural performance" (Singer 1955) and decided to attempt to analyze it in much the same way that Keil (1966) had analyzed the blues show in relation to Negro audiences.

At this early stage the practical problem was to see more drag shows and to establish contact with a female impersonator to see if the study was feasible. At that time (August–September 1965) there were five drag shows in Chicago, and I very shortly got around to see four of them. This convinced me that drag shows did indeed follow predictable conventions that indicated ritual or cultural performance. At the same time, I approached a female impersonator between shows in the bar in which he was working. I explained that I was an anthropologist at the University of Chicago and that I would like to interview him. I stated that I was impressed with his performance and with the enthusiasm of the audience and that I wanted to question him about the profession of female impersonation. To my amazement, he replied that he had majored in anthropology in college and that he would willingly talk to me. Thereafter I interviewed this man seven times, at first in the bar and later at his home with a tape recorder. He turned out to be my entrée into the drag world and my best informant. He was a highly articulate, intelligent man who from the first was at least as dedicated to the study as I was. He had been performing professionally for about twelve years in several different parts of the country, and he knew the history and structure of the profession.

Between August and November 1965, I interviewed four other female impersonators in their apartments. These interviews were set up for me by my original informant. In addition, I spent many evenings "hanging around" Chicago drag bars, seeing shows, and getting to know performers and audiences. The problem at this stage was getting impersonators to talk to me at all. Above all they did not wish to be confronted by an unsympathetic person who would ask insensitive questions or show a condescending attitude. The fact that most of them did not really know what an anthropologist was was helpful in avoiding preconceived hostility. But it is doubtful that they would have consented to talk to me without the enthusiastic endorsement of my original informant, who was a respected figure in the group. Second, in speaking with the potential informant to set up the interview, I made it plain that I had some familiarity with drag (that I was "wise," in Goffman's terminology) and that I was not interested in psychological problems.

I continued to find the taped interview a very useful tool throughout the fieldwork. However, it was not possible to interview many impersonators in this way.

Such interviews were done only with the "stage" impersonators who were verbally oriented and articulate and who felt relatively comfortable with the interview situation. All in all, I interviewed ten of them: six in Chicago, three in New York City, and one in Kansas City. All were interviewed in two-hour or longer sessions from one to seven times in their own apartments. But my tentative attempts to interview "street" impersonators convinced me immediately that this would not be a useful approach with them. Many of them perceived me as a complete outsider and were appalled at the idea of spending several hours alone with me. In addition, their apartments were too chaotic to permit the requisite privacy and concentration. Even given good will, they were unwilling or unable to respond thoughtfully to sustained verbal interaction. Some more informal approach was called for, and I needed a chance to observe interaction rather than to ask questions about it.

These problems were solved when my original informant left Chicago to take a job in Kansas City. He suggested that I come to Kansas City and that in his capacity as "boss" of the show, he would give me admittance to the backstage, where I could meet the performers on a more sustained and less formal basis and could actually observe them in their natural habitat. Accordingly, between December 1965 and December 1966 I made three trips to Kansas City. The first two times (December 1965 and August 1966), I stayed about a month each; the third time I stayed one week. Once the performers had accepted me as a fixture backstage and rapport had been established, I proceeded more or less as a fieldworker might. I lived in two different cheap hotels where performers lived. I spent time during the day with impersonators, both singly and in groups, and participated in their activities, including parties and outings. Most important, I spent every night in the two bars where the impersonators worked, either backstage, watching the show, or talking to the bar personnel and generally observing the bar life. I considered my own role to include a great deal of participation that would have been difficult to avoid in any case. I not only listened and questioned, I also answered questions and argued. I helped out with the shows whenever I could, pulling curtains, running messages for the performers, and bringing in drinks and french fries from the restaurant across the street. When the performers half jokingly suggested I should stand in for an absent stripper, however, I drew the line.[1]

There is no reason, in theory, why a fieldworker actually could not have stayed in Kansas City (or any city in which rapport has been established) for a full year, and in this way approximate conventional fieldwork. The ethnography of such a small and specialized group as female impersonators did not seem to demand such a commitment. However, ethnography of the homosexual community in even one city, or of the various "street" groups, would certainly require such an effort.

Role Models

1972

THE ACTRESS

Female impersonators, particularly the stage impersonators, identify strongly with professional performers. Their special, but not exclusive, idols are female entertainers. Street impersonators usually try to model themselves on movie stars rather than on stage actresses and nightclub performers. Stage impersonators are quite conversant with the language of the theaters and nightclubs, while the street impersonators are not. In Kansas City, the stage impersonators frequently talked with avid interest about stage and nightclub "personalities." The street impersonators could not join in these discussions for lack of knowledge.

Stage impersonators very often told me that they considered themselves to be nightclub performers or to be in the nightclub business, "just like other [straight] performers."

When impersonators criticized each other's on- or offstage conduct as "unprofessional," this was a direct appeal to norms of show business. Certain show business phrases such as "Break a leg" (for good luck) were used routinely, and I was admonished not to whistle backstage. The following response of a stage impersonator shows this emphasis in response to my question, "What's the difference between professionals and street fairies?" This impersonator was a "headliner" (had top billing) at a club in New York:

> Well [laughs], simply saying . . . well, I can leave that up to you. You have seen the show. You see the difference between *me* and some of these other people [his voice makes it sound as if this point is utterly self-evident] who are working in this left field of show business, and I'm quite sure that you see a *distinct* difference. I am more conscious of being a performer, and I think generally speaking, most, or a lot, of other people who are appearing in the same show are just doing it not as a lark—we won't say that it's a lark—but they're doing it because it's something they can drop in and out of. They have fun, they laugh, have drinks, and play around, and just have a good time. But to *me*, now, playing around and

having a good time is important to me also; but primarily my interest from the time I arrive at the club till the end of the evening—I am there as a performer, as an entertainer, and this to me is the most important thing. And I dare say that if needs be, I probably could do it, and be just as good an entertainer . . . I don't know if I would be any more success-ful if I were working in men's clothes than I am working as a woman. But comparing myself to some of the people that I would consider real professional entertainers—people who are genuinely interested in the show as a show, and not just, as I say, a street fairy, who wants to put on a dress and a pair of high heels to be seen and show off in public.

The stage impersonators are interested in "billings" and publicity, in light-ing and makeup and stage effects, in "timing" and "stage presence." The quality by which they measure performers and performances is "talent." Their models in these matters are established performers, both in their perfor-mances and in their offstage lives, insofar as the impersonators are familiar with the latter. The practice of doing "impressions" is, of course, a very direct expression of this role modeling.

From this perspective, female impersonators are simply nightclub per-formers who happen to use impersonation as a medium. Many stage imper-sonators are drab in appearance (and sometimes in manner) offstage. These men often say that drag is simply a medium or mask that allows them to perform. The mask is borrowed from female performers, the ethos of perfor-mance from show business norms in general.

The stated aspiration of almost all stage impersonators is to "go legit," that is, to play in movies, television, and on stage or in respectable nightclubs, either in drag *or* (some say) in men's clothes. Failing this, they would like to see the whole profession "upgraded," made more legitimate and profes-sional (and to this end they would like to see all street impersonators barred from working, for they claim that the street performers downgrade the profes-sion). T. C. Jones is universally accorded highest status among impersonators because he has appeared on Broadway (*New Faces of 1956*) and on television (*Alfred Hitchcock*) and plays only high-status nightclubs.

THE DRAG QUEEN

Professionally, impersonators place themselves as a group at the bottom of the show business world. But socially, their self-image can be represented (with-out the moral implications) in its simplest form as three concentric circles: the impersonators, or drag queens, are the inner circle. Surrounding them

Skip Arnold performing, 1965. Collection of Esther Newton

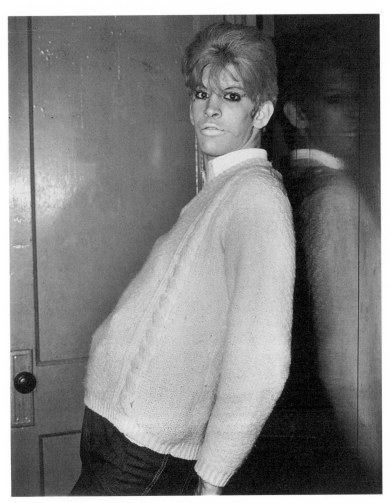

"Street fairy" in Kansas City, 1965. Photo by Esther Newton

are the queens, ordinary gay men. The straights are the outer circle. In this way, impersonators are "a society within a society within a society," as one impersonator told me.

A few impersonators deny publicly that they are gay. These impersonators are married, and some have children. Of course, being married and having children constitute no barrier to participation in the homosexual subculture. But whatever may be the actual case with these few, the impersonators I knew universally described such public statements as "cover." One impersonator's statement was particularly revealing. He said that "in practice" perhaps some impersonators were straight, but "in theory" they could not be. "How can a man perform in female attire and not have something wrong with him?" he asked.

The role of the female impersonator is directly related to both the drag queen and camp roles in the homosexual subculture. In gay life, the two roles are strongly associated. In homosexual terminology, a drag queen is a homo-sexual man who often, or habitually, dresses in female attire. (A drag butch is a lesbian who often, or habitually, dresses in male attire.) Drag and camp are the most representative and widely used symbols of homosexuality in the English-speaking world. This is true even though many homosexuals would never wear drag or go to a drag party and even though most homosexuals who do wear drag do so only in special contexts, such as private parties and Halloween balls.[1] At the middle-class level, it is common to give "costume" parties at which those who want to wear drag can do so, and the others can wear a costume appropriate to their gender.

The principal opposition around which the gay world revolves is masculine-feminine. There are a number of ways of presenting this opposition through one's own person, where it becomes also an opposition of "inside" = "out-side" or "underneath" = "outside." Ultimately, all drag symbolism opposes the "inner" or "real" self (subjective self) to the "outer" self (social self). For the great majority of homosexuals, the social self is often a calculated respectability and the subjective or real self is stigmatized. The "inner" = "outer" opposition is almost parallel to "back" = "front." In fact, the social self is usually described as "front" and social relationships (especially with women) designed to support the veracity of the "front" are called "cover." The "front" = "back" opposition also has a direct tie-in with the body: "front" = "face"; "back" = "ass."

There are two different levels on which the opposition can be played out. One is *within* the sartorial system itself,[2] that is, wearing feminine clothing "underneath" and masculine clothing "outside." (This method seems to be used more by heterosexual transvestites.) It symbolizes that the visible, social, masculine clothing is a costume, which in turn symbolizes that the entire sex-role behavior is a role—an act. Conversely, stage impersonators sometimes wear jockey shorts underneath full stage drag, symbolizing that the feminine clothing is a costume.

A second "internal" method is to mix sex-role referents *within* the visible sartorial system. This generally involves some "outside" items from the feminine sartorial system such as earrings, lipstick, high-heeled shoes, a necklace, and so on, worn with masculine clothing. This kind of opposition is used very frequently in informal camping by homosexuals. The feminine item stands out so glaringly by incongruity that it "undermines" the masculine system and proclaims that the inner identification is feminine.[3] When this method is used on stage, it is called "working with (feminine) pieces." The performer generally works in a tuxedo or business suit and a woman's large hat and earrings.

The second level poses an opposition between one sex-role sartorial system and the "self," whose identity has to be indicated in some other way. Thus when impersonators are performing, the oppositional play is between "appearance," which is female, and "reality" or "essence," which is male. One way to do this is to show that the appearance is an illusion; for instance, a standard impersonation maneuver is to pull out one "breast" and show it to the audience. A more drastic step is taking off the wig. Strippers actually routinize the progression from "outside" to "inside" visually, by starting in a full stripping costume and ending by taking off the bra and showing the audience the flat chest. Another method is to demonstrate "maleness" verbally or vocally by suddenly dropping the vocal level or by some direct reference. One impersonator routinely tells the audience: "Have a ball. I have two." (But genitals must *never* be seen.) Another tells unruly members of the audience that he will "put on my men's clothes and beat you up."

Impersonators play on the opposition to varying extents, but most experienced stage impersonators have a characteristic method of doing it. Generally speaking, the desire and ability to break the illusion of femininity is the mark of an experienced impersonator who has freed himself from other impersonators as the immediate reference group and is working fully to the audience. Even so, some stage impersonators admitted that it is difficult to break the unity of the feminine sartorial system. For instance, they said that it is difficult, subjectively, to speak in a deep tone of voice while on stage and especially while wearing a wig. The "breasts" especially seem to symbolize the entire feminine sartorial system and role. This is shown not only by the very common device of removing them in order to break the illusion, but in the command "Tits up!" meaning "get into the role" or "get into feminine character."

The tension between the masculine-feminine and inside-outside oppositions pervades the homosexual subculture at all class and status levels. In a
sense, the different class and status levels consist of different ways of bal-
ancing these oppositions. Low-status homosexuals (both male and female)
characteristically insist on very strong dichotomization between masculine-
feminine so that people must play out one principle or the other exclusively.
Low-status queens are expected to be very nellie, always, and low-status butch
men are so "masculine" that they very often consider themselves straight[4]
(although the queens say in private that "today's butch is tomorrow's sister").
Nevertheless, in the most nellie queen the opposition is still implicitly there,
because to participate in the male homosexual subculture as a peer, one must
be male inside (physiologically).

Recently, this principle has begun to be challenged by hormone use and by
the sex-changing operation. The use of these techniques as a final resolution
of the masculine-feminine opposition is hotly discussed in the homosexual
subculture. A very significant proportion of the impersonators, and especially
the street impersonators, have used or are using hormone shots or plastic
inserts to create artificial breasts and change the shape of their bodies. This
development is strongly deplored by the stage impersonators, who say that
the whole point of female impersonation depends on maleness. They further
say that these "hormone queens" are placing themselves out of the homosexual subculture, because, by definition, a homosexual man wants to sleep
with other men (i.e., no gay man would want to sleep with these "hormone
queens").

Carrying the transformation even further, to "become a woman" is approved by the stage impersonators, with the provision that the "sex changes"
should get out of gay life altogether and go straight. The "sex changes" do not
always comply, however. One quite successful impersonator in Chicago had
the operation but continued to perform in a straight club with other impersonators. Some impersonators in Chicago told me that this person was now
considered "out of gay life" by the homosexuals and could not perform in a
gay club. I also heard a persistent rumor that "she" now liked to sleep with
lesbians!

It should be readily apparent why drag is such an effective symbol of both
the outside-inside and masculine-feminine oppositions. There are relatively
few ascribed roles in American culture and sex role is one of them; sex role
radiates a complex and ubiquitous system of typing achieved roles. Obvious
examples are in the kinship system (wife, mother, etc.), but sex typing also ex-
tends far out into the occupational-role system (airline stewardess, waitress,
policeman, etc.). The effect of the drag system is to wrench the sex roles loose

from that which supposedly determines them, that is, genital sex. Gay people know that sex-typed behavior can be achieved, contrary to what is popularly believed. They know that the possession of one type of genital equipment by no means guarantees the "naturally appropriate" behavior.

Thus drag in the homosexual subculture symbolizes two somewhat conflicting statements concerning the sex-role system. The first statement symbolized by drag is that the sex-role system really is natural; therefore, homosexuals are unnatural (typical responses: "I am physically abnormal"; "I can't help it, I was born with the wrong hormone balance"; "I am really a woman who was born with the wrong equipment"; "I am psychologically sick").

The second symbolic statement of drag questions the "naturalness" of the sex-role system in toto; if sex-role behavior can be achieved by the "wrong" sex, it logically follows that it is in reality also achieved, not inherited, by the "right" sex. Anthropologists say that sex-role behavior is learned. The gay world, via drag, says that sex-role behavior is an appearance; it is "outside." It can be manipulated at will.

Drag symbolizes both these assertions in a very complex way. At the simplest level, drag signifies that the person wearing it is a homosexual, that he is a male who is behaving in a specifically inappropriate way, that he is a male who places himself as a woman in relation to other men. In this sense it signifies stigma. At the most complex, it is a double inversion that says "Appearance is an illusion." Drag says, "My 'outside' appearance is feminine, but my essence 'inside' [the body] is masculine." At the same time, it symbolizes the opposite inversion: "My appearance 'outside' [my body, my gender] is masculine but my essence 'inside' [myself] is feminine."

In the context of the homosexual subculture, all professional female impersonators are "drag queens." Drag is always worn for performance in any case; the female impersonator has simply professionalized this subcultural role. Among themselves and in conversation with other homosexuals, female impersonators usually call themselves and are called drag queens. In the same way, their performances are referred to by themselves and others as drag shows.

But when the varied meanings of drag are taken into consideration, it should be obvious why the drag queen is an ambivalent figure in the gay world. The drag queen symbolizes all that homosexuals say they fear the most in themselves, all that they say they feel guilty about; he symbolizes, in fact, *the* stigma. In this way, the term "drag queen" is comparable to "nigger." And like that word, it may be all right in an in-group context but not in an out-group one. Those who do not want to think of themselves or be identified as drag queens under any circumstances attempt to disassociate themselves from drag completely. These homosexuals deplore drag shows and profess total lack of interest in them. Their attitude toward drag queens is one of condemnation combined with the expression of vast social distance between themselves and the drag queen.

Other homosexuals enjoy being queers among themselves, but do not want to be stigmatized by the heterosexual culture. These homosexuals admire drag and drag queens in homosexual contexts, but deplore female impersonators and street queens for "giving us a bad name" or "projecting the wrong image" to the heterosexual culture. The drag queen is definitely a marked man in the subculture.

Homosexuality consists of sex-role deviation made up of two related but distinct parts: "wrong" sexual object choices and "wrong" sex-role presentation of self.[5] The first deviation is shared by all homosexuals, but it can be hidden best. The second deviation logically (in this culture) corresponds with the first, which it symbolizes. But it cannot be hidden, and it actually compounds the stigma.

Thus, insofar as female impersonators are professional drag queens, they are evaluated positively by gay people to the extent that they have perfected a subcultural skill and to the extent that gay people are willing to oppose the heterosexual culture directly (in much the same way that Negroes now call themselves Blacks). On the other hand, they are despised because they symbolize and embody the stigma. At present, the balance is weighted on the negative side, although this varies by context and by the position of the observer (relative to the stigma). This explains the impersonators' negative identification with the term drag queen when it is used by outsiders. (In this way, they at first used masculine pronouns of address and reference toward each other in my presence, but reverted to feminine pronouns when I became more or less integrated into the system.)

THE CAMP

Although all female impersonators are drag queens in the gay world, by no means are all of them "camps." Both the drag queen and the camp are expressive performing roles, and both specialize in transformation. But the drag queen is concerned with masculine-feminine transformation, whereas the camp is concerned with what might be called a philosophy of transformations and incongruity. Certainly the two roles are intimately related, because to be a feminine man is by definition incongruous. But strictly speaking, the drag queen simply expresses the incongruity; the camp actually uses it to achieve a higher synthesis. To the extent that a drag queen does this, he is called "campy." The drag queen role is emotionally charged and connotes low status for most homosexuals because it bears the visible stigmata of homosexuality; camps, however, are found at all status levels in the homosexual subculture and are very often the center of primary group organization.[6]

The camp is the central role figure in the subcultural ideology of camp. The camp ethos or style plays a role analogous to "soul" in the Negro subculture (Keil 1966:164–90). Like soul, camp is a "strategy for a situation."[7] The special perspective of the female impersonators is a case of a broader homosexual ethos. This is the perspective of moral deviance and, consequently, of a "spoiled identity," in Goffman's (1963) terms. Like the Negro problem, the homosexual problem centers on self-hatred and the lack of self-esteem.[8] But if "the soul ideology ministers to the needs for identity" (Keil 1966:165), the camp ideology ministers to the needs for dealing with an identity that is well defined but loaded with contempt. As one impersonator who was also a well-known camp told me, "No one is more miserable about homosexuality than the homosexual."

Camp is not a thing. Most broadly, it signifies a *relationship between* things, people, and activities or qualities, and homosexuality. In this sense, "camp taste," for instance, is synonymous with homosexual taste. Informants stressed that even between individuals there is very little agreement on what is camp because camp is in the eye of the beholder; that is, different homosexuals like different things, and because of the spontaneity and individuality of camp, camp taste is always changing. This has the advantage, recognized by some informants, that a clear division can always be maintained between homosexual and "straight" taste:

> He said Susan Sontag was wrong about camp's being a cult,[9] and the moment it becomes a public cult, you watch the queens stop it. Because if it becomes the squares', it doesn't belong to them any more. And what will be "camp art," no queen will own. It's like taking off the work clothes and putting on the home clothes. When the queen is coming home, she wants to come home to a campy apartment that's hers — it's very queer — because all day long she's been very straight. So when it all of a sudden becomes very straight — to come home to an apartment that any square could have — she's not going to have it any more.[10]

Although camp is in the eye of the homosexual beholder, it is assumed that there is an underlying unity of perspective among homosexuals that gives any particular campy thing its special flavor. It is possible to discern strong themes in any particular campy thing or event. The three that seemed most recurrent and characteristic to me were *incongruity, theatricality,* and *humor.*

All three are intimately related to the homosexual situation and strategy. Incongruity is the subject matter of camp, theatricality its style, and humor its strategy.

Camp usually depends on the perception or creation of *incongruous juxtapositions*. Either way, the homosexual "creates" the camp by pointing out the incongruity or by devising it. For instance, one informant said that the campiest thing he had seen recently was a Midwestern football player in high drag at a Halloween ball. He pointed out that the football player was seriously trying to be a lady, and so his intent was not camp, but that the *effect* to the observer was campy. (The informant went on to say that it would have been even campier if the football player had been picked up by the police and had his picture published in the paper the next day.) This an example of unintentional camp, in that the campy person or thing does not perceive the incongruity.

Created camp also depends on transformation and juxtaposition, but here the effect is intentional. The most concrete examples can be seen in the apartments of campy queens, for instance, in the idea of growing plants in the toilet tank. One queen said the *TV Guide* had described a little Mexican horse statue as campy. He said there was nothing campy about this at all, but if you put a nude cut-out of Bette Davis on it, it would be campy. Masculine-feminine juxtapositions are, of course, the most characteristic kind of camp, but any very incongruous contact can be campy. For instance, juxtaposition of high and low status, youth and old age, profane and sacred functions or symbols, or cheap and expensive articles is frequently used for camp purposes. Objects or people are often said to be campy, but the camp inheres not in the person or thing itself but in the tension between that person or thing and the context or association. For instance, I was told by impersonators that a homosexual clothes designer made himself a beautiful Halloween ball gown. After the ball he sold it to a wealthy society lady. It was said that when he wore it, it was very campy, but when she wore it, it was just an expensive gown, unless she had run around her ball saying she was really not herself but her faggot dress designer.

The nexus of this perception by incongruity lies in the basic homosexual experience that is squarely on the moral deviation. One informant said, "Camp is all based on homosexual thought. It is all based on the idea of two men or two women in bed. It's incongruous and it's funny." If moral deviation is the locus of the perception of incongruity, it is more specifically role deviation and role manipulation that are at the core of the second property of camp, *theatricality*.

Camp is theatrical in three interlocking ways. First of all, camp is style. Importance tends to shift from what a thing is to how it *looks*, from *what* is done to *how* it is done. It has been remarked that homosexuals excel in the decorative arts. The kind of incongruities that are campy are very often created by adornment or stylization of a well-defined thing or symbol. But the emphasis on style goes further than this in that camp is also exaggerated, consciously "stagy," specifically theatrical. This is especially true of *the* camp, who is definitely a performer.

The second aspect of theatricality in camp is its dramatic form. Camp, like drag, always involves a performer or performers and an audience. This is its structure. It is only stretching the point a little to say that even in unintentional camp, this interaction is maintained. In the case of the football player, his behavior was transformed by his audience into a performance. In many cases of unintentional camp, the camp performs to his audience by commenting on the behavior or appearance of "the scene," which is then described as "campy." In intentional camp, the structure of performer and audience is almost always clearly defined. This point will be elaborated below.

Third, camp is suffused with the perception of "being as playing a role" and "life as theater" (Sontag 1964:529). It is at this point that drag and camp merge and augment each other. I was led to an appreciation of this while reading Parker Tyler's (1963) appraisal of Greta Garbo. Garbo is generally regarded in the homosexual community as "high camp." Tyler stated, "'Drag acts,' I believe, are not confined to the declassed sexes. Garbo 'got in drag' whenever she took some heavy glamour part, whenever she melted in or out of a man's arms, whenever she simply let that heavenly-flexed neck . . . bear the weight of her thrown-back head" (12). He concludes, "How resplendent seems the art of acting! It is all *impersonation,* whether the sex underneath is true or not" (28).

We have to take the long way around to get at the real relationship between Garbo and camp. The homosexual is stigmatized, but his stigma can be hidden. In Goffman's terminology, information about his stigma can be managed. Therefore, of crucial importance to homosexuals themselves and to nonhomosexuals is whether the stigma is displayed so that one is immediately recognizable or is hidden so that he can pass to the world at large as a respectable citizen. The covert half (conceptually, not necessarily numerically) of the homosexual community is engaged in "impersonating" respectable citizenry, at least some of the time. What is being impersonated?

The stigma essentially lies in being less than a man and doing something that is unnatural (wrong) for a man to do. Surrounding this essence is a halo effect: violation of culturally standardized canons of taste, behavior, speech, and so on rigorously associated with (prescribed for) the male role (e.g., fanciful or decorative clothing styles, "effeminate" speech and manner, expressed disinterest in women as sexual objects, expressed interest in men as sexual objects, unseemly concern with personal appearance, etc.). The covert homosexual must therefore do two things: first, he must conceal the fact that he sleeps with men. But concealing this *fact* is far less difficult than his second problem, which is controlling the *halo effect* or signals that would announce that he sleeps with men. The covert homosexual must in fact impersonate a *man*, that is, he must *appear* to the "straight" world to be fulfilling (or not violating) all the requisites of the male role as defined by the "straight" world.

The immediate relationship between Tyler's point about Garbo and camp/ drag is this: if Garbo playing women is drag, then homosexuals "passing" are playing men; they are in drag. This is the larger implication of drag/camp. In fact, gay people often use the word "drag" in this broader sense, even to include role playing that most people simply take for granted: role playing in school, at the office, at parties, and so on. In fact, all of life is role and theater — appearance.

But granted that all acting is impersonation, what moved Tyler to designate Garbo's acting specifically as "drag"? Drag means, first of all, role playing. The way in which it defines role playing contains its implicit attitude. The word "drag" attaches specifically to the outward, visible appurtenances of a role. In the type case, sex role, drag primarily refers to the wearing of apparel and accessories that designate a human being as male or female when worn by the opposite sex. By focusing on the outward appearances of role, drag implies that sex role and, by extension, role in general is something superficial, that can be manipulated, put on and off again at will. The drag concept implies *distance* between the actor and the role or "act." But drag also means "costume." This theatrical referent is the key to the attitude toward role playing embodied in drag as camp. Role playing is *play;* it is an act or show. The necessity to play at life, living role after superficial role, should not be the cause of bitterness or despair. Most of the sex-role and other impersonations that male homosexuals do are done with ease, grace, and especially humor. The actor should throw himself into it; he should put on a good show; he should view the whole experience as fun, as a camp.[11]

The double stance toward role, putting on a good show while indicating distance (showing that it is a show), is the heart of drag as camp. Garbo's acting was thought to be "drag" because it was considered markedly androgynous, and because she played (even overplayed) the role of femme fatale with style. No man (in her movies) and very few audiences (judging by her success) could resist her allure. And yet most of the men she seduced were her victims because she was only playing at love — only acting. This is made quite explicit in her film *Mata Hari,* in which Garbo the spy seduces men to get information from them.

The third quality of camp is its *humor.* Camp is for fun; the aim of camp is to make an audience laugh. In fact, it is a *system* of humor. Camp humor is a system of laughing at one's incongruous position instead of crying.[12] That is, the humor does not cover up, it transforms. I saw the reverse transformation — from laughter to pathos — often enough, and it is axiomatic among the impersonators that when the camp cannot laugh, he dissolves into a maudlin bundle of self-pity.

One of the most confounding aspects of my interaction with the impersonators was their tendency to laugh at situations that to me were horrifying or tragic. I was amazed, for instance, when an impersonator described to me as "very campy" the scene in *Whatever Happened to Baby Jane* in which Bette Davis served Joan Crawford a rat, or the scene in which Bette Davis makes her "comeback" in the parlor with the piano player.

Of course, not all impersonators and not all homosexuals are campy. *The* camp is a homosexual wit and clown; his campy productions are a continuous creative strategy for dealing with the homosexual situation and, in the process, defining a positive homosexual identity. As one performer summed it up for me, "Homosexuality is a way of life that is against all ways of life, including nature's. And no one is more aware of it than the homosexual. The camp accepts his role as a homosexual and flaunts his homosexuality. He makes the other homosexuals laugh; he makes life a little brighter for them. And he builds a bridge to the straight people by getting them to laugh with him." The same man described the role of the camp more concretely in an interview:

> Well, "to camp" actually means "to sit in front of a group of people" . . . not on stage, but you *can* camp on stage . . . I think that I do that when I talk to the audience. I think I'm camping with 'em. But a "camp" herself is a queen who sits and starts entertaining a group of people at a bar around her. They all start listening to what she's got to say. And she says campy things. Oh, somebody smarts off at her and she gives 'em a very flip answer. A camp is a flip person who has declared emotional freedom. She is going to say to the world, "I'm queer." Although she may not do this all the time, but most of the time a camp queen will. She'll walk down the street and she'll see you and say, "Hi, Mary, how are you?" right in the busiest part of town . . . she'll actually camp, right there. And she'll swish down the street. And she may be in a business suit; she doesn't have to be dressed outlandishly. Even at work the people figure that she's a camp. They don't know what to *call* her, but they hire

her 'cause she's a good kid, keeps the office laughing, doesn't bother anybody, and everyone'll say, "Oh, running around with Georgie's more fun! He's just more fun!" The squares are saying this. And the other ones [homosexuals] are saying, "Oh, you've got to know George, she's a camp." Because the whole time she's light-hearted. Very seldom is camp sad. Camp has got to flip. A camp queen's got to think faster than other queens. *This* makes her camp. She's got to have an answer to anything that's put to her. . . .[13]

Now, *homosexuality* is *not* camp. But you take a camp, and she turns around and she makes homosexuality funny, but not ludicrous; funny but not ridiculous . . . this is a great, great art. This is a fine thing. . . . Now when it suddenly became the word . . . because like . . . it's like the word "Mary." Everybody's "Mary": "Hi, Mary. How are you, Mary!" And like "girl." You may be talking to one of the butchiest queens in the world, but you still say, "Oh, girl." And sometimes they say, "Well, don't call me 'she' and don't call me 'girl.' I don't feel like a girl. I'm a *man*. I just like to go to bed with you *girls*. I don't want to go to bed with another man." And you say, "Oh, girl, get you. Now she's turned butch." And so you camp about it. It's sort of laughing at yourself instead of crying. And a good camp will make you laugh along with her, to where you suddenly feel . . . you don't feel like she's made fun of you. She's sort of made light of a bad situation.

The camp queen makes no bones about it; to him the gay world is the "sisterhood." By accepting his homosexuality and flaunting it, the camp undercuts all homosexuals who won't accept the stigmatized identity. Only by fully embracing the stigma itself can one neutralize the sting and make it laughable.[14] Not all references to the stigma are campy, however. Only if it is pointed out as a joke is it camp, although there is no requirement that the jokes be gentle or friendly. A lot of camping is extremely hostile; it is almost always sarcastic. But its intent is humorous as well. Campy queens are very often said to be "bitches" just as camp humor is said to be "bitchy."[15] The campy queen who can "read" (put down) all challengers and cut everyone down to size is admired. Humor is the campy queen's weapon. A camp queen in good form can come out on top (by group consensus) against all the competition.

Female impersonators who use drag in a comic way or are themselves comics are considered camps by gay people. (Serious glamour drag is considered campy by many homosexuals, but it is unintentional camp. Those who see glamour drag as a serious business do not consider it to be campy. Those who think it is ludicrous for drag queens to take themselves seriously see the whole business as a campy incongruity.) Because the camp role is a positive one, many impersonators take pride in being camps, at least on stage.[16] Because the camp role depends to such a large extent on verbal agility, it reinforces the superiority of the live performers over record performers, who, even if they are comic, must depend wholly on visual effects.

Preface to the Phoenix Edition of *Mother Camp*

1979

Scrutinizing one's past work is like meeting a former lover: evocative, disconcerting, perhaps saddening. This book was written in the late sixties, and our affair is over. I had no desire to revise it for this second edition, not only because it belongs to my past, but also because it strikes me still as an accurate analysis of its subject: drag queens as gay male culture "heroes" in the mid-sixties. Nor do I think that the contradictions that gave rise to female impersonation have changed in essentials, so that the analysis in *Mother Camp* is still valid. New fieldwork on the current state of the drag world would certainly be desirable, but I am not the one to do it, having been severed from that world by my own evolution and the brute passage of time. Those who would bring things up to date will find in *Mother Camp* a solid baseline for their own explorations.

Still, I follow female impersonators and the gay male world from afar, and seize the opportunity to offer some thoughts about the changes of the past ten years. These fall into two categories: various cracks appearing in the straight world's relentless wall of hostility, and the transformations wrought in the gay community by the gay pride movement.[1]

The gay pride movement has challenged the traditional stance of the dominant culture: that homosexuals are a shameful group of pariahs to be erased, if possible, or passed over in silence, if not. In the mid-sixties, and, as new historical research indicates, probably long before that, drag queens both defied and upheld societal attitudes toward "queers." The dominant culture, which has its own internal divisions—the constituency represented by Anita Bryant is not the same as that represented by the *New York Times*, for example—has not been able to prevent gays from becoming visible and clamoring for rights and toleration. But the structural underpinnings of heterosexual domination are still very much intact. What few legal gains have been made in the areas of decriminalization and discrimination are being vigorously attacked by the organized sexual reactionaries. Yet gay books and films appear at a rate undreamed of in the sixties; the business world, having discovered that gay people spend money, is taking advantage of the new openness to direct products toward the "gay market."

Not only that, but recent movies point to a co-optation of drag symbols and camp sensibility by the mass media. In *Outrageous* a female impersonator of the type described in this book is portrayed sympathetically; indeed, he is seen as a kind of counterculture Everyman, who invites the admiration of both gay and straight. The surrealistic figures in *The Rocky Horror Picture Show* are not female impersonators per se, but the symbolic elements in this latter-day Frankenstein *cum* Dracula story will be familiar to readers of this book. Though Dr. Frank N. Furter's drag is drawn more from pornography (black garter belt, tight corset) than from gay drag, and though he is represented as an androgynous bisexual, his creation of a witless muscle man as an ideal lover puts us back on familiar ground. The muscle man and the drag queen are true Gemini: the make-believe man and the make-believe woman. But if the symbolism of the film is familiar, the fact that it was made, and that apparently thousands of American adolescents flocked to see it at midnight showings, is not.

At a further remove, the immensely popular film *Star Wars* is saturated with drag ("powers-of-darkness" drag, "princess" drag, "terrestrial alien" drag, "robot" drag, etc.) and camp sensibility. I'm sure the queens loved it, but then so did millions of other people. The gay sensibility, like that of other minorities before it, is finding, in watered-down form, a larger audience.[2] I would guess that masses of people are finding themselves torn, as drag queens are, between traditional values and an acquired but profound cynicism. The campy way of expressing and playing with this tension is becoming presentable.

Yet just as gay sensibility and even real live drag queens are making their way into mass culture, the conditions that nourished them are changing. Although camp humor was an assertion of gay existence, much of its content was self-hating, denigrating, and incompatible with the assertions of gay pride, whose aim is perhaps not the end of drag, but at least the transformation of the ethos described in *Mother Camp.*

The gay pride struggle revolves around the issue of coming out, which the conservatives have correctly seen would lead to the toleration of gays as a minority. Why this is the key issue will be clear to any reader of *Mother Camp.* The overwhelming concern of the premovement gay community was disclosure, and the resulting overt/covert distinction referred to throughout this book. In chapter 1 I refer to "baroque systems of personal and territorial avoidance," which had resulted from the fact that the stigma of homosexuality, unlike blackness or femaleness, could be hidden. If more and more gays come out, and get away with it, the most dramatic forms of shame and suffering imposed on drag queens, who previously were among the very few visible, aggressive homosexuals, would fade.

However, gay men are kidding themselves if they think the deeper stigma of homosexuality can be eliminated while the antagonistic and asymmetrical relations between men and women persist. It is true that legitimized male homosexuality and male domination have coexisted in some cultures (for instance, ancient Greece and tribal New Guinea), but never exclusive homosexuality, and besides, these men were not Judeo-Christians. So long as women are degraded yet powerful enough to constitute a threat, gay men will always be traitors in the "battle of the sexes." So long as current models of sexuality persist and predominate, gay men will always be "like" women.

In the past ten years there has been an enormous struggle within the gay male community to come to terms with the stigma of effeminacy.[3] The most striking result has been a shift from effeminate to masculine styles. Underline the word *styles*. Where ten years ago the streets of Greenwich Village abounded with limp wrists and eye makeup, now you see an interchangeable parade of young men with cropped hair, leather jackets, and well-trimmed mustaches. "Sissies" are out. Inevitably, and sadly, the desire to be manly, pursued uncritically — only a few souls in the wilderness cried out for a feminist analysis — has led to a proliferation of ersatz cowboys, phony lumberjacks, and (most sinister) imitation Hell's Angels, police, and even storm troopers. The s&m crowd, once a small and marginal subgroup, are now trendsetters; their style and, to a lesser degree, their sexuality have captured the gay male imagination.[4] This is playing with shadows, not substance. John Rechy, himself a "butch" gay, exposes "those who put down 'queens' and 'sisters' (and most leather gays do so, loudly) for hurting our image. (Ironically, it is a notorious truth that mass arrests of transvestites almost inevitably result in rough, heavy punching out of the cops, whereas a mass raid in a leather bar will result in meek surrender, by both 'm's and 's's)" (1977:258).

Rechy, whose admirably honest and thought-provoking book *The Sexual Outlaw* confronts (and approves of) promiscuity and male worship among gays, condemns the s&m trend as self-hating and destructive (his own model is Charles Atlas, which is surely more benign). But he stops short of saying that, without new models of manhood, its glorification can lead only to dead-end dramas of domination and submission.

I much preferred drag queens. What will happen to them amid the conflicting pressures of the gay pride movement, the s&m trend, feminism, con-

tinued homophobia, and a limited mass acceptance of gay sensibility is difficult to predict. But even if female impersonation and all it stands for were
to disappear tomorrow (which seems most unlikely), *Mother Camp* now has
the virtue of being an invaluable historical document, at once photograph and
x-ray of the male gay world on the edge of historic changes.

I would never do this work again, though having done it immeasurably
enriched my twenties. The men whom I knew in Kansas City and Chicago
were tough; they knew how to fight and suffer with comic grace. They had the
simple dignity of those who have nothing else but their refusal to be crushed.
I bid them farewell with a bittersweet regret, and leave it to others to carry on
the work of illuminating their past and chronicling their future.

Theater: Gay Anti-Church—More Notes on Camp

1992/1999

The most talented gay theatre people have traditionally assimilated themselves into the heterosexual theatre as writers, directors, composers, librettists, and actors. Under pressure to sublimate their drives in parodies of "true" romance, these artists have created an unchartably furtive history. (Mordden 1981)

I think we're so sick in our real lives of fighting . . . of pushing against things, that out here [Cherry Grove], it's more like a stage, more like theater, more like a bracketed reality that keeps it free and transcendent. (Edrie Ferdun, interview with author)

The notorious, primary relationship of gays and lesbians with theater has always been anecdotal. (Dolan 1998)

In her famous 1964 essay "Notes on Camp," critic Susan Sontag was the first to publicly suggest the power of "camp sensibility" in modern culture, a point that now seems prescient and indisputable; the plays of Oscar Wilde and Noël Coward, the films of George Cukor, Busby Berkeley, and Andy Warhol, Halston's designs, and *Other Voices, Other Rooms,* are only a few obvious exemplars. Yet Sontag made a serious mistake in ascribing camp to a vaporous and elusive "modernism." It is groups of people in social networks, not abstractions like "modernism," that still create and use what Andrew Ross called "cultural technologies."[1] The fondness of postmodern approaches for treating symbolic systems as "texts," though interesting as a mode of analysis, has falsely divided coherent sensibilities from the social groups that have generated them. Though camp is, as Sontag saw, an integral aspect of twentieth-century culture, it cannot be understood as a disembodied mechanism for the creation of elite taste in a mass society; if camp is a "cultural technology," the question remains, whose?

One of the first to write about camp, Christopher Isherwood, caught its essence perfectly in his account of meeting Truman Capote at Random House: "When this extraordinary little figure came into the room with his hand raised rather high, possibly indicating that one should kiss it, my first reaction was 'My God! He's not kidding!' But then I realized that though he was putting on an act, it was an act that represented something very deliberate and quite genuine. Something happened which one wishes occurred far more often in life: I loved him immediately." [2]

Back in 1968 I argued that it is gay sensibility that has been "camp" and that camp's necessary elements were incongruity, humor, and theatricality, just as exemplified in Isherwood's narrative.[3] Twenty years later I had the pleasure of living surrounded by camp theatricality while doing fieldwork in Cherry Grove, an island resort community in the New York metropolitan area, and home of the world's first exclusively and explicitly gay theater. Floated over from the mainland on barges in 1948, this theater, originally an old barn, was and still is the community center. Not only was the Arts Project the first institution to be founded by Grovers, but the whole Cherry Grove way of doing things was, and, to a lesser extent still is, theatrical: the beach, the boardwalks, the cottages were all stages upon which people played to sympathetic and appreciative (but discerning) "audiences." [4]

Attaining freedom under the protection of the impersonal real estate market—queer money proved a powerful equalizer—residents of the resort were mostly untroubled by the apparent contradiction between bourgeois ideals and what seemed a frothy and frivolous camp domain. The concerned gay citizen-homeowner, fanatical about maintaining the height of the dunes and the cleanliness of the beach, set up a queenly republic under the sign of light and witty parody, or broad and vulgar clowning. Determined to endure, Grovers turned away oppression *and* introspection with a flip laugh.

This essay explores two themes: the larger relationship of gay men and lesbians to Anglo-American theater—a topic that has intrigued me for over thirty years—and the emergence of explicitly gay theater in the Grove. I have concluded that the affinity between gays and lesbians and the particular forms of theatricality that were so boisterous and pervasive in the Grove is not a fluke or accident. To understand the emergence of Grove theater from American theatrical forms developed on and off Broadway, I had to look even further back toward a deep opposition between theater and Christianity. For centuries, homosexuals and theater have been silent partners in their conflict with churches.[5]

By saying theater is a gay anti-church, I point to its social functions of affiliation and solidarity, and to the way theater has provided an iconography and sensibility for homoeroticism, in opposition to the way churches have worked for reproductively oriented society. And I also mean this: because of the biblically justified enmity toward sodomy, gays have been alienated from

Christianity and persecuted by it; they have sought both alternatives and re-sistance in theatricality as an ethos, and theaters as institutions, which is why I call theater a gay "anti-church"—a queer Noah's Ark against the flood of domi-nation. Yet the ark was always under surveillance by God's self-appointed rep-resentatives, often allied with state power, and so never truly seaworthy. The Grove's camp theatricality was *limited to* and also prodigiously *rich in* parody and light wit on the one hand and low farce on the other because gay expres-sion and its protest against the "heterosexual dictatorship"[6] were trivialized and contained within these modes by the authorities *and* by fearful theatrical people.

Beginning with an overview of how and why these elements might be con-nected, I go on to review aspects of the long and contentious relationship between homosexual signifiers and their repression on stage. After a more de-tailed look at gay expression and puritanical censorship in twentieth-century Broadway and Off-Broadway shows, I trace the theatrical forms on which the world's first explicitly gay and lesbian stage productions were based.

In my retelling of the relationship between gays and theater, I argue that the "theatrical/parodic" perspective inherent in camp is Anglo-French in ori-gin, springing from the anti-Puritanism of the Elizabethan and Restoration London theatrical scene and the underground world of prostitution, descend-ing through the late-nineteenth-century Symbolist and Aesthetic movements as represented, especially in the English-speaking world, by the life and work of Oscar Wilde. Associated with the greater dramatism and more segregated gender roles of the upper and lower classes, with antibourgeois royalism and also with the demimonde, the "theatrical/parodic" perspective pervades gay male campiness and, to a lesser degree, lesbian butch-femme identity sys-tems.[7]

By contrast, the "egalitarian/authentic"[8] gay perspective is rooted in demo-cratic and bourgeois ideology. It shaped the nineteenth-century institution of "romantic friendship" and the feminist movement, was given expression in the writings of English socialist Edward Carpenter and the poetry of Walt Whitman, and is more comfortably congruent with homegrown American ideals.[9]

Life was experienced and expressed theatrically by Grovers because under-ground gay culture had descended from the theater world and continued to find a haven from its enemies there in both the power of dramatic representa-tion and in everyday theatrical life. Because only the performing arts offered the conjunction of a relatively safe social space with the power of "make-believe," the camp strategy for building gay community predominated over the egalitarian until the 1950s, when powerful poetry, drama, new forms of bar life, and the homophile political movement all demonstrated the growing power and diversity of the gay community.

The homophile movement that led to Stonewall was made up not only of political movements but also of cultural developments. Because this tiny resort was the first, and for years the *only* gay-controlled geography, in the years after 1938 thousands and thousands of gays and lesbians around the country and the world came for the day or the summer to ask, What would it be like to be free? Because of this, and the cultural power of New York–based Grovers, the Grove and its theatricalism played a major part in transforming the furtive invisibility preceding World War II into the gay nationalism that began building after the war and culminated in the Stonewall Riots in 1969.[10]

GAY HISTORY/THEATER HISTORY

The attraction of performing arts such as opera, dance, burlesque, theater, and the circus for many gay men and lesbians is made of a magic beyond simple explanation. With the exception of drama scholar Laurence Senelick, to be discussed below, those who have noted the connection have tended to take gay presence as a given, a starting point to examine gay themes, or the lack of them, on the stage.[11] But *why* are gays and lesbians so present in theater? The question of whether gays may or may not be found just as frequently among corporate lawyers, auto mechanics, salespeople, secretaries, and domestic workers is unanswered and at present unanswerable.[12] What is certain is that gays and lesbians in other walks of life have remained more invisible, both to the outside world and within their work niches, than in show business.

There is a fundamental attraction and interaction between performing arts and gays that has shaped the arts themselves and the evolving gay subculture and whose causes are to be found in broad modernizing historical processes.[13] My discussion here is limited to the theater (as opposed to circus or dance, for instance) because its history is well documented and because it was so central in the Grove. But in what follows I look at high and low theater, if only because, as will become apparent, a variety of venues gave birth to Grove theater; aesthetic questions are beyond my scope, although the differing status accorded to performers and performances, depending on venue and theme, and the lesser theatrical access that low status guaranteed, is a theme that will recur.

Gays have been drawn to all the arts, but the sociability of the performing arts distinguishes them from the solitary disciplines of painting, composing, and writing. Writers may form networks and even communities, but in theater the art itself is inherently interactive and collaborative. How attractive the theatrical life must have been to outcasts whose chief difficulty was finding each other! Broadway, as Michael Bronski (1984:110) observed, was "where the threat and the promise of toleration for homosexuals found a sort of social truce: the theater was the circumscribed playground for 'artistic types,'" a legal and legitimate arena within which gays could lead a normal—by which I mean social and sociable—life.[14]

The theater had an inherent resonance with the gay situation. Gay men and lesbians escaped from their hometowns, families, and local expectations to big cities or to traveling shows, where they found a foothold on the margins of society and a degree of anonymity.[15] Even urban gays, like the young Irving Drutman (later to be a drama critic, publicist, and Grove homeowner), were swept up in its promise of another, more welcoming world:

> My introduction to the "legitimate theater" began with the show business trade paper *Variety*, a discarded copy of which I picked up on the sidewalk.... In a box on the front page was a bit of raffish dialogue which, because of its audacity (1923 and I was thirteen), I can still remember.
>
> *1st Chorus Boy:* Do you know Nance O'Neill?[16]
> *2nd Chorus Boy:* Maybe. What's his first name?
>
> I wasn't aware that Nance O'Neill was a ranking female star of the serious drama but of course, as a son of the city pavements, the irreverent word play didn't escape me.... I must have gone through every page, held captive by the columns reeking of show biz. (1976:5)

Gays were "held captive" by show biz not only because of the social freedom promised there, but because in the art of acting itself gays escaped from their everyday difficulties and dangers by turning their lifelong experience of deception and passing into a socially legitimate career. If actors are "shape-changers by vocation," as Senelick (1990:41) observed while thinking about the same relation, gays and lesbians are shape-changers by necessity, and this became all the truer as homosexual desire became the basis for identity.[17] As former Grover Bob Adams put it from a slightly different perspective, "You can't change the fact that you're gay and that's your private life, but you can play any role you want to on stage" (interview with author).

Although gays were not allowed to "act gay" on stage by displaying either homoeroticism or gender deviation ("butch" for women or "nellie" for men) —ballet and opera are hyperheterosexual and the vast majority of plays featured heterosexual characters and revolved around a "romance plot"—the possibility of "openness" does not exhaust theater's deeper appeal to gays and lesbians, which is situated in its "competition with . . . the doctrines espoused in schools and churches" (Barish 1981:79) and, in our own day, its potential challenge to the reigning ideology of bourgeois realism.[18]

Thoughtful Grovers like Bob Adams were well aware of the reasons for the profound appeal of theater and for its predominance in Grove life. Yes, he had met writers and painters in the 1950s Grove, but above all, everyone loved "the theater, the theater":

> *EN:* Now, why was it the theater?
>
> *BA:* Gee. Well it's make-believe, isn't it?—number one.
>
> *EN:* But so is fiction.
>
> *BA:* Yes, yes but you are *It*. The writer is invisible. You don't meet as many friends writing a novel as appearing in a play (laughs) . . . I think it was the community feeling of play that is the theater, and the laughter and fantasy world and costumes.

Working purely deductively from the overwhelming importance of theater and theatricality in Cherry Grove, I looked back for its causes almost five hundred years to the infancy of English drama. Some scholars had written about antitheatricalism, some about theater, some about homosexuality, and others about female impersonation, but none had tied these together with the conviction the evidence warrants.

Because women were excluded from all public roles in the medieval Church, men alone acted in Church-sponsored Mystery plays. It is also likely that the rough life of early traveling troupes was all-male, and that in both venues, female parts were played by boys or young men (R. Baker 1968:52). When the first English theater companies were formed during the sixteenth century, the all-male tradition continued.[19] The boy actors of the public theaters were "beautifully dressed. It was a familiar practice for the players to inherit the dresses worn by ladies of the court, so one may justly imagine that Beatrice, Hermione, the Duchess of Malfi and the rest gave the groundlings good value in fashionable display" (R. Baker 1968:61). The boys were trained in female impersonation, and records from the end of the seventeenth century indicate that they "developed special voices and a feminine way of walking. It was an intensive training and there seems no reason why a boy should not have continued to play women after puberty" (60–61).

Although boys were accepted by the public as representing women, not sodomites, as plays became increasingly secular during the sixteenth century the authorities took alarm. The Christian order had been represented in medieval morality plays by players *personifying* concepts such as Virtue and

Chastity. *Impersonation*, not just of women but sui generis, the portrayal of historical characters and secular people, was seen as inimical to Christian belief. According to theater sociologist Elizabeth Burns, "The difference of the two modes lay in their frames of reference. *Personification* referred always to man in his relationship with the unseen, inferred world of spiritual reality or to universals or to spiritual beings, *impersonation* to the known social world" (1973:163).

Mark Booth's speculative history looks for the origins of camp sensibility in the sixteenth-century "breakdown of the agriculture-based social hierarchy" and the growth of the bourgeoisie which created the conditions for the birth of secular theater. Complex city life required a person to "adapt his personality to the values of the different social groups he might meet . . . [and] encouraged man to stand outside his personality and to see it as something of a put-on, something artificial. . . . It is but a short step from this experience of alienation to the exploration of its ironic possibilities that lies at the heart of camp" (1983:45–46).

It was its use of impersonation, *acting* in the modern sense, and portrayal of the "known social world" that, as Jonas Barish observes, put the secular theater "in unwelcome competition with the everyday realm and with the doctrines espoused in schools and churches. Moreover, by the element of freedom implicitly claimed in it, it threatens at any moment to depart from the fabric of received belief" (1981:79).

Rightly fearing their possible use as "instruments of blasphemy or sedition," churches and the state repeatedly tried to control the plays and players (Burns 1973:152–53). When Henry VIII announced his intention to get rid of "ruffians, vagabonds, masterless men and common players" (152–53) by impressing them into the Navy, the players sought refuge from the king's persecution in the patronage of wealthy nobles, establishing an imaginative and economic connection between theater and powerful aristocracies. There may or may not have been a homosexual implication to the boy actors' representation of women onstage.[20] But behind the scenes, homosexual relations with overtones of prostitution between noble sponsors and actors, and actors and boy apprentices were likely widespread. There were also separate troupes of boy players—reputedly very lewd—who had begun as royal choir boys before degenerating into common players.[21]

It is not that homosexuality occurred only in London or only in the theater. On the contrary, European men and boys of varied classes and from different regions had sex with each other; Alan Bray notes that homosexual incidents frequently took place in patriarchal households and schools and universities.[22] But in England, at any rate, it was in the linked domains of theater and prostitution that homosexuality first took root as a "continuous sexual subculture."[23]

My assumption is that lesbians gained access to performing arts after gay men were already well established, perhaps not until the nineteenth century. Lesbian culture in general partly modeled itself on an already formed gay male life. Three scholars of homosexuality have somewhat different views on lesbianism during the Renaissance. Bray (1982:17) thinks that female homosexuality "was rarely linked in popular thought with male homosexuality, if indeed it was recognised at all. Its history is, I believe, best to be understood as part of the developing recognition of a specifically female sexuality." James Saslow (1989:95–96) gives more credence to a separate concept of lesbianism in Europe generally, but the documentation is very fragmented. Judith Brown (1989) sees almost a will to "disbelieve" in the possibility of lesbianism on the part of smug and phallocentric medieval and Renaissance men.[24]

In a groundbreaking essay, historian Randolph Trumbach (1991) finds evidence for the emergence of the modern role of the Sapphist in England in the last quarter of the eighteenth century, about seventy-five years later than the male "molly" or sodomite. Trumbach's archtypal sapphist, Mrs. Damer, dressed partly in male attire and had suspect relations, significantly, with an actress (131).[25] I suspect that as more research is done we will find that lesbian subcultures developed later and were modeled on those of gay men in significant ways, including a very important role for theatrical institutions.

Because censorship and repression always publicize "vice," persistent Puritan attacks singling out the theater world as a favorite "haunt of sodomites" must have stimulated the concentration of homosexual experience (Bray 1982:54).[26] It was Burbage's opening of the first public theater in London in 1576 that "served to mobilize the forces of a growing religious conservatism in England, and a series of sermons at Paul's Cross by Thomas Wilcox and others opened the campaign with all the fervor of a new crusade" (Carlson 1984:79).

The actors and playwrights resisted. In particular, the playwright Christopher Marlowe (1564–1593) created homoerotic scenes in his poetry and plays and was accused of having said both that "they who loved not tobacco and boys were fools"[27] and "that the first beginning of religion was only to keep men in awe." "Heresy, homosexuality and treason," observes Bray, "are blended in the famous allegations made against [him]" (1982:20, 63–66).[28]

Thus, the struggle between the Puritan forces—for whom, as Jeremy Collier wrote in 1698, the only legitimate purpose of drama is "to recommend Virtue, and discountenance Vice"[29]—currently led by Jesse Helms, and the arts, represented by blasphemy and homosexuality, is the legacy of four hundred years of bitter emnity.[30] Early Puritan attacks were not limited to the fact that homosexuality was more freely practiced behind the scenes; if anything, the charge of homosexuality was at first a weapon against the larger enemies, the Renaissance court and the theater (Bray 1982:37). But the antagonism between Christianity and the practice of nonprocreative sexualities amounts to (unequal) warfare; each almost negatively defines the other. It is no accident, then, that secular theater and the gay subculture emerged together; they are both, potentially, despite determined attempts to domesticate the theater (and current indigenous efforts to domesticate gays), historic forms of anti-Christian protest.[31]

During the reign of the Long Parliament (1642–1660), the Puritans succeeded in closing the London theaters and the actors scattered, though many, understandably, identified with and sought protection within the Royalist cause (R. Baker 1968:94). When King Charles II was restored to the throne in 1660, he assembled around him a "glamourous, permissive court" (62) and allowed the theaters to reopen. It is in Restoration comedy that the outlines of camp sensibility first emerged: "Of the arts, the theatre played a dominant role in glamourising insincerity, an essential ingredient of camp. . . . The Comedy of Manners then emerging, shifted the emphasis from moral dilemmas to stylistic ones—not 'What shall I do?' but 'What shall I wear?'" (Booth 1983:52).

Women began to play the female parts in Restoration theater, slowly supplanting the boy female impersonators. By 1690 the drag tradition in legitimate theater was "vanquished" (R. Baker 1968:62–63).

Underlying economic and ideological forces began generating the modern world at this historical moment, around 1700, and the gay community is an integral part of that creation. Just when, as Bray and Trumbach have shown, a marginal and clandestine but organized male homosexual subculture was born in London's "molly houses," female impersonation became "a comic curiosity and soon separated from the straight theatre to take its place in the music hall, the comic show, the cabaret and pantomime" (R. Baker 1968:62–63).

This separation was very convenient for the theater world, whose vital function in the gay subculture could more easily be disguised. Just as the outcry against the spread of sodomy throughout society intensified, "similar attacks on stage sodomy die down" (Senelick 1990:39). Those who were attacked were usually the former boy players, such as Edward Kynaston. Senelick thinks theatrical sodomites took advantage of their greater ease in finding like-minded men within their professional world and the long-standing protection of powerful elites to avoid the arrests and abuse suffered by "small tradesmen" and "parsons" who were caught in "molly houses" during the eighteenth century (40–41).

In their clandestine meeting places, the "mollies"—the word previously had meant female prostitute (Trumbach 1989:137)—met to have sex with each other. They used "drag"—the term probably derives from "the petticoat or skirt used by actors when playing female parts"[32]—embedded in a nascent theatrical camp sensibility to represent their relationships and their distinct existence. Despite the intervening centuries, what Grover would not recognize kinship with this (hostile) description of a ball at an eighteenth-century molly house? "The men calling one another 'my dear' and hugging, kissing, and tickling each other as if they were a mixture of wanton males and females, and assuming effeminate voices and airs. . . . Some were completely rigged in gowns, petticoats, headcloths, fine laced shoes, furbelowed scarves, and masks; some had riding hoods; some were dressed like milkmaids."[33]

Theatrical impersonation, driven underground, became the core symbol of an alternative and subversive atmosphere. Under the situational aegis of the "Queen," class distinctions tended to dissolve; a distinctive secret language based on "heterosexual terms turned to new and ironic applications" was elaborated in conjunction with an "extravagant effeminacy and transvestism," not as an incidental feature but "at the root of the way they [molly houses] worked" (Bray 1982:86). "There had begun to appear a new kind of sodomite who was identified principally by his effeminate manner," Trumbach writes in his aptly named essay, "The Birth of the Queen" (1989:135–36). As the eighteenth century went on, the authorities and theatrical advocates of respectability, such as the actor/producer David Garrick, had to work hard to disguise and deny the vital connection between theater and gay subculture. Garrick himself was attacked as a sodomite after the disgrace of his actor colleague Bickerstaff's arrest for giving presents to a soldier.[34]

The 1730s, a period of intensive legislation against the theater's outspokenness, also happened to be a high-water mark of English newspaper reporting on arrests for sodomy and on the Dutch executions of seventy men for sodomy. In collaboration with changes in taste, the mechanisms of social control were being applied concurrently in the sexual sphere and the theatrical (Senelick 1990:42).

The growing public identification of homosexuality with molly houses probably suited the theater world, which knew itself to be vulnerable. By the late 1700s, the molly was so despised and feared that respectable men could not even kiss each other lest they be tainted, but had to shake hands, and on stage even the "fop" or effeminate man was exiled from high comedy and relegated to "low farce," as the female impersonators themselves had been

one hundred years before (Trumbach 1989:134). And yet the immediate efflo-
rescence of theater and theatricality in the Grove strongly indicates that the
affinity between the gay world and the theater still held fast below the surface.

That theatrical companies began as all-male units removed from family
life and local controls, that they featured female impersonation—the Old Tes-
tament strictly enjoined no crossing over of genders and likened "passive"
sodomy to acting like a woman—that both theater and nonprocreative sexuality were attacked by Puritans because they gave pleasure, and that secular
drama posed an inherent threat to "the fabric of received belief," all these
overdetermined the interweaving of theater and homosexuality in England.

AMERICAN THEATER

During the seventeenth century, when England as a nation-state and English
national culture were taking shape, religious discontent and England's rising
economic power led to substantial emigration. Between 1630 and 1640 about
twenty thousand Puritans settled in New England (Palmer 1960:143). Their
fanatical antitheatricalism shaped the policies of their new homeland. Over a
century later, in 1778, the Congress of the new United States passed a resolution "condemning all theatrical representations, along with gambling, horse
racing, and cock fighting, as sinful and intolerable; with the result that theatrical activity, for the next decade or two, retreated into the universities, where
even so it could fall under the lash of precisians like Timothy Dwight, who
warned his students at Yale that to frequent the theater was to lose their souls"
(Barish 1981:296).

During the nineteenth century, American theater was allowed a certain
legitimacy so long as it remained bland enough not to offend. Drama became
so middle class, in fact, that it was regarded as a "useful" art, "subservient to
popular taste in all things, especially moral content" (Mordden 1981:viii). The
"two prime requirements" for popular drama before the twentieth century,
wrote one nostalgic critic, had been "cleanliness and happy endings."[35]

The challenge to these vapid norms came from the same tradition that had
long infuriated the puritanically minded, for modern American theater de-
scends from the ideas of the Anglo-French Aesthetic movement—of which,
in the English-speaking world, gay playwright and intellectual Oscar Wilde
was the exemplar and leading exponent. Wilde's celebrated lecture tour introduced and promoted the ideas of the Aesthetic movement to America in
the 1880s. In 1905 the New York cultural scene was turned upside down
by *The Art of the Theatre*, whose author, Englishman Gordon Craig, was a
Wilde admirer.[36] Craig's "art movement," a direct offshoot of camp gay sensi-

bility in England, was daring, sensual, and in full revolt against nineteenth-century bourgeois realism (Mordden 1981:59–60). The antirealist, antibourgeois transformation happened in New York City, where "almost everyone of any standing in the theatre was living," and the innovations spread at the parties theatrical people gave and where they went to socialize, exchange ideas, and "read plays aloud" (57). The art movement strengthened the position of theater in American life. By the 1920s Broadway was booming alongside a flourishing "advanced" theater in Greenwich Village, as well as touring and regional productions.[37]

GAY IDENTITY AND THEATER CENSORSHIP

Not only was early-twentieth-century Broadway theater *not* marginal to dominant culture either commercially or artistically, but gays were not marginal within theater either. The very fact that the public did not know this—whatever they may have suspected—allowed lesbians and gay men to hold jobs in the theater world (and other performing arts) from top to bottom. Some of the very biggest stars of the 1920s and 1930s formed "the most exclusive club in New York"[38] and were known to be gay or bisexual by theater habitués: stars like Katherine Cornell, "the first lady of the American theater," and her husband Guthrie McClintic, Alfred Lunt and Lynn Fontanne, Eva Le Gallienne, Jeanne Eagles, and Clifton Webb; among playwrights and composers, Noël Coward, Cole Porter, and Lorenz Hart.[39] Willingness to employ people who were openly and obviously gay behind the scenes or offstage extended to many of the ancillary jobs and businesses—managers, drama critics, publicists, costumers—connected with the performing arts.[40] Grover Stephan Cole, who held various backstage theater jobs and ultimately managed Tallulah Bankhead, Hume Cronyn, and Jessica Tandy,[41] told me being gay was "no problem, ever. Who cared?"

As gay networks and the New York theater flourished during the prosperous 1920s, tremendous pressure built for more explicit expression of gay themes, characters, and sensibility both backstage and onstage. After all, the art movement had called for "imagination" and "honesty" on stage, and America was moving into a twentieth century that would value self-expression and authenticity. These longings for gay expression, whether realistic or campy, were largely frustrated both on and off Broadway by state censorship, self-censorship, and commercialism. Because of the Puritan legacy of antitheatricalism, American traditions of free speech remained weak in the theater: "Neither theatre people nor the nation as a whole recognized drama's part in the development—if nothing else the maintenance—of free expression as a universal right" (Mordden 1981:86). Complicating the picture was the pervasive influence of commercialism, which would later virtually gut television of controversial, difficult, or contrarian perspectives. Theater historian Ethan Mordden pointed out the circular relationship between commercialism and censorship: "An emphasis on popular taste—on a theatre meant to please—virtually invites state censorship: writers who reinforce rather than challenge pop attitudes make themselves hostage to those attitudes, and to the state that presumably passes and enforces the popular law. Art had to teach pop a significant lesson: freedom is won by defiance, not propitiation" (88).

In what follows I summarize the tension between gay and lesbian longing to signify and be signified on stage and the complex effects of censorship and fear.

Broadway

The more open and daring gay presence in mainstream theater prompted more vigorous efforts to control and repress it during the 1920s. A female star of a musical comedy playing in Chicago remembered: "I was doing a show with an obnoxious leading man who was hated by everyone in the company. 'We'll put the bitches' curse on him,' one of the chorus boys told me. One night after the performance, the ingenue and I were invited to join the boys backstage after the theater was empty. By candlelight they danced and carried on in outrageous drag. The stage manager walked in on us and in a fury broke it up with the warning that the chorus boys better not camp it up again."[42]

When plays began appearing on Broadway with explicit gay themes, none of the authors were identified as gay, and the point of view was always society's, that is, homosexuality was presented, whether sympathetically or not, as a problem with which "decent citizens" must deal. The gay authors wouldn't or couldn't treat the subject explicitly. As W. Somerset Maugham later explained to a gay nephew, "Why do you suppose that Noël [Coward] or I have never stuck our personal predilections down the public's throats? Because we know it would outrage them. Believe me, I know what I'm talking about. Don't put your head in a noose."[43]

The first Broadway play with a gay character was *The God of Vengeance*, a Yiddish play set in a Polish house of prostitution, which had been first produced in English in an "art movement" theater in Greenwich Village, where it played to full houses without incident. But when the play was moved to Broadway in 1923, the whole cast was arrested—whether on the complaint of the Society for the Suppression of Vice or from a prominant rabbi is not clear—because of a lesbian love scene.[44] The theater world and theater critics were sharply divided over the censorship. There was to be no automatic defense of free expression where homosexuality was concerned.

In 1926 *The Captive*, a French "problem play" about lesbianism, became a Broadway sensation, but no legal moves were made against it until word reached Broadway of Mae West's planned sensational play, *The Drag*. Despite the fig leaves proposed by West and other financial backers that *The Drag* was a "problem play" like *The Captive*, dealing with a serious "medical problem," it was actually "an *extremely* serious melodrama that borders on a plea for tolerance of homosexuals."[45] It was full of gay characters and gay slang and featured a "sensational, amusing, and very theatrical drag party scene" (Curtin 1987:72). To prevent the Broadway opening of the even more threatening West play, *The Captive*—which had previously been okayed by the "play jury," Broadway's internal censorship body—was raided in 1927 by New York City police. They arrested the actors, including Helen Menken (then Humphrey Bogart's wife) and Basil Rathbone. West herself and the cast of her earlier production, *Sex*, were also arrested and harassed.

Although the cast and a few others strongly defended *The Captive*, Actors' Equity stood cravenly by without protest and most critics applauded the state action. The *Post* noted optimistically that "the subject of sex perversion has been prevented from establishing itself in the theater."[46] Later that year the New York State Legislature passed the Wales Padlock Law, prohibiting plays "depicting or dealing with, the subject of sex degeneracy, or sex perversion," and threatened theater owners who rented to producers of "corrupting" plays with a year-long closing (Curtin 1987:100). Although plays with gay characters and even gay themes were never entirely banned during the 1930s, 1940s, and 1950s, the atmosphere was certainly chilling. For almost half a century after *The Drag* and *The Captive* were forced to close, a penal code prohibition inhibited the emergence of lesbians and gay men in Broadway dramas. Consequently, their real-life counterparts bore the stigma of being the only citizens of the United States adjudged too loathsome and morally infectious to be seen even in fictitious characterizations in legitimate theater productions (102).

Despite the moralists and censors, there was a frustrated audience longing to see both gay themes and camp sensibility. The audience for *The Captive* was 60 percent women, many of whom were young, "unescorted girls in twos and threes."[47] When *The Drag* opened in Paterson, New Jersey, a reporter observed that about a third of the largely male audience were New Yorkers: "The audience seemed to have been divided into two groups—those who fully understood the subject under discussion and those to whom the whole theme was a puzzle."[48] At Mae West's 1928 play, *Pleasure Man*, one critic was disgusted by "the laughter of the audience, or at least that part of it which howled and snickered and let out degenerate shrieks from the balcony" when some female impersonators were onstage. Complaining presciently of how difficult it would be to curb gay themes as long as audiences not only tolerated but encouraged them, he concluded, "The real culprits are on the other side of the footlights."[49] Gay men in theater had become adept at working this kind of legerdemain. Sophisticated dramas, ostensibly heterosexual, Noël Coward's *Design for Living* and Mordaunt Shairp's *The Green Bay Tree* were smash Broadway hits in the 1930s. Both were full of dialogue and themes which read "gay" to audiences in the balcony even though they had received approval from censorious critics.[50]

Throughout the repressive 1950s, the Grove retained connections to the legitimate Broadway stage and to ballet. Even though the theater world did nothing to publicly oppose the McCarthy witch-hunts (see Mordden 1981; Navasky 1980), de facto toleration of gays continued. When Bob "Rose" Levine needed a gown, wig, and fur stole to sing "The Hostess with the Mostest on the Ball" in a 1956 Grove show, there was "no hassle" when director Frank Bradley took him to New York City theatrical outfitter Brooks Costume. "There were all queens running around, you know, working there. So it was no big deal" (interview with author). Unlike most Grovers, Jack Sonshine received personal mail and telephone calls at his office in the late fifties because his employer was Capezio Shoes: "Salvatore Capezio, who founded the company, had a shoe shop across the street from the Metropolitan Opera and started supplying dance slippers for the members of the chorus. And since . . . dance people and theater people, especially dance I suppose, the vast majority of the men were gay, there was never any problem in the company about anyone being homosexual, male or female. It just meant nothing. You did your job? Fine, that's what counted" (interview with author).

Theatrical gay men and lesbians were important anchors for New York social networks. There were "fast friendships" between gay and straight show people, Bob Adams said, recalling how the straights came to the Grove to see and even appear in the "wonderful" Grove shows of the fifties. The connection between gays and the theater was so expected that he would jokingly introduce himself in gay circles by saying, "Hi. I'm so-and-so, but I'm not in the theater now." Indeed, young and attractive gay men could find acceptance in theatrical circles via the democratic principles of social and sexual attraction, said Adams: "It didn't really matter. I mean, you could be a butcher or work in Macy's or whatever and if you were likable and so forth, friendships occur whenever, wherever."

The performing arts played an equally important role in the social lives of the privileged lesbians who came to the Grove in the 1930s through the

1950s.[51] Peggy Fears and Dottie Justin had been show girls from Ziegfeld's Follies. When the fifties crowd gathered around Charles Clawson playing the piano at Duffy's Hotel, what they mostly sang were Broadway show tunes. Cris knew torch singer Libby Holman and her circle through her "best friend for many years," Louisa Carpenter, Holman's sometime lover.[52] Although Cris owned a textile factory, "a great number of our friends were show— involved in show business, sure. Either directors, writers, stage managers, actors and actresses, you name it, and they were here" (interview with author). The New York City Ballet came out and practiced lifts using the open beams in Duffy's barroom. While sneaking a beer (he was underage) in 1956, Don Hester from Sayville saw "the better part of the dance group from *My Fair Lady,* which had just opened, they were in there doing the routine of the races at Ascot—and it was right there, except they were all dressed in cut-offs—it was really neat" (interview with author). Whole sets of costumes and props from closing shows and operas found their way to parties and Arts Project revues: "When Cole Porter's show *Out of This World* closed in New York, a trunkful of original costumes from the musical mysteriously appeared at the Grove" (D. Lewis 1989).

Rose Levine, one of those amateur Grove performers who was an "admitted ham," explained that most directors of Arts Project shows *were* in show business, but usually they were dancers and actors. The woman who was the second lead in *Me and My Girl* was Rose's dance director for *Dames at Sea;* people in the production number took tap dancing lessons in town "for weeks." Another time, a choreographer who worked with Jerry Herman gave Rose lessons during his lunch break in Manhattan. Working with a gay theater was a "release" for these people, although the old compromises obtained and held. Audrey Hartmann heard from the oldtimers that theater people like Hermione Gingold, Bea Lilly, and Billy deWolf would come out from Manhattan, "just for that day, you name them, all theater people would come out just to see the shows, there was so much talent in the shows." But the talent was local, nonprofessional talent, because as Rose Levine understood, no matter how comfortable the Manhattan theater closet, it still had a thick door: "The people who really made it—big—never stayed here. The people who were here never made it big on Broadway. But they worked here cause they loved it and they were gay and they worked with us. But the people who really made it, like Ralph Burns was here, he left, he never came back. Jane ———, she's not here. Jerry Herman still is part of the island, not that he comes to Cherry Grove, but . . . he's still part of the old roots. . . . If they made it on Broadway they didn't come here—after—they didn't come back. . . . Oliver Smith was living here in the early days, he didn't come back. You know, Cherry Grove had a name that was very gay, and—people didn't want to be associated with it" (interview with author).[53]

Off-Broadway

By 1920 theatrical people had founded "little theaters" that formed a "scattered secondary theater district dedicated to the principles of the art movement: imagination, honesty, unity of conception, and Craig's "inner beauty and meaning of life."[54] Producer Harold Clurman even conflated the serious theater that Off-Broadway aspired to be with homosexuality by calling the former the "art which dares not speak its name" (1983:272). Yet Off-Broadway was far from providing consistent representation of gays, much less offering them a voice.

In 1916 a group of theater-loving friends who had discussed their dissatisfaction with the commercialism of Broadway during summer vacations at Provincetown on Cape Cod founded the Provincetown Players.[55] As the Grove's Arts Project would be, the Players were at first "essentially an amateur group" supported by subscription from private citizens, but they immediately moved into the MacDougal Street Playhouse in Greenwich Village and began to produce plays in the season of 1916–1917, which shows that the "serious" plays they had in mind—they were known principally for their introduction of the work of Eugene O'Neill—were not as taboo as the light revues the Arts Project was to do thirty years later on the safety of an island. They did produce the controversial Yiddish play *God of Vengeance* and the lesbian-theme play *Winter Bound,* something of a knockoff of *The Well of Loneliness,* in 1929 (see Curtin 1987:140–53). But for the most part, Off-Broadway production companies did not use their greater leeway to deal with "difficult" subjects by representing homosexuality.

After wwi, members of the Washington Square Players formed "one of the most influential theatre companies in American history," the Theatre Guild, where many founders of the gay Grove first met each other (Mordden 1981: 61). Grove impresario George Freedley, Arts Project founder Cheryl Crawford, Natalia Danesi Murray, Tom Farrar, the designer and owner of Pride House, and Hallye Cannon, eccentric heterosexual and wardrobe mistress— all these Grove pioneers of the 1930s were employed and nurtured by the Theatre Guild.[56]

The Guild was progressive in theatrical terms—strongly influenced by the art movement and highly democratic in structure. But it was elitist culturally, and as time went on it concentrated on producing "serious" European plays (Mordden 1981:69). In 1927 the Guild put on Eugene O'Neill's *Strange Interlude,* featuring a character who was a composite of two gay painters O'Neill had known in Greenwich Village, Charles Demuth and Marsden Hartley. O'Neill's intention to portray a closeted gay man was so successful that the critics never noticed that the character was intended to be gay (Curtin 1987: 115).

Looking back in his memoirs, the great Off-Broadway producer Harold Clurman remarked on the increasing conventionality of the Theatre Guild, which allowed it, he thought, to survive the economic hardships of the Depression: "It stands for a policy that is guided by an adaptability to the trend of the times on the level of average good taste. It was a truer reflection of the middle current of American theatre-goers in that it borrowed from everywhere and used everything to sell to the broadest Broadway market for buyers of honest wares" (1983:293). "Average good taste" and the requirements of commercialism excluded gay representation, so that the many gay and lesbian members of the Theatre Guild were left virtually invisible in theater— on Broadway and off.

In 1929, young Theatre Guild veterans Clurman, Cheryl Crawford, and Lee Strasberg formed the Group Theater (Mordden 1981:178–79). Far more of a radical alternative to Broadway than its parent the Guild, the Group's philosophy was egalitarian and homegrown. The founders wanted to encourage the development of American plays about "American character as we saw it depicted in plays or as we knew it from our own experience" (Clurman 1983:34), to be performed by a repertory company that would get away from the emphasis on stars and profits. Clurman had a clear vision of what transcendent American theater should be about: "The artist to be of value in any capacity must always proceed from what is—from what he is in the first instance—rather than from what he believes should be. . . . It is more than dangerous for him to force his vision to fit a preconceived pattern (no matter how 'correct' that pattern may appear to his intellect)" (295). How could such sentiments have been received by his gay peers in the theater world: coproducer Cheryl Crawford, *New Yorker* critic John Mosher, critic and publicist Irving Drutman, and designer Thomas Farrar? They knew from the fate of *The God of Vengeance* and *The Captive* that realist presentation of homosexuality, no matter how serious and tasteful, would be subject to severe censorship. Indeed, the Group, despite Clurman's intent to develop an approach "that might be common to all the members," did not even try to produce gay-theme plays. Instead, their province became the "protest" or social play. The subject of "serious" drama was to be left-wing politics and class conflict.

Both Clurman's and Crawford's memoirs show how deeply closeted Crawford must have been, not only for public consumption but even to a degree within the intense and intimate Group company. Although Clurman makes clear that he and Strasberg were heterosexual, he leaves Crawford's personal life a blank. As late as the forties Clurman wrote naïvely that when he and Crawford returned from a trip to the Soviet Union in 1935 they were given "a gay reception" by Group members, completely ignoring the association—known in theatrical circles—of the word "gay" with homosexuality (1983: 162).

Writing her own memoir in the more "liberated" seventies, Crawford did not invent a spurious heterosexuality, but either could not find the courage to come out or preferred to remain with the old compromises, even though the curious title of her memoir is *One Naked Individual,* and by her own account, the business of the theater is to tell truth: "Ideally, my business or profession or art—and it is all of these—is to make it possible for people to see themselves as they are, as they wish to be, as they might be" (1977:5).[57] Writing that she was too busy to have a personal life—"the theatre has been my life" (ix)—Crawford does admit to "an intermittent love life" during the Group Theater years (61), but ultimately, she writes, her higher commitment to the theater and lack of time left her solitary: "It was a high price to pay. . . . Man's best friend became this woman's best friend" (112).

Contrary to this account, Crawford shared a busy social life with her companion, Ruth Norman, with whom she rented Pride House, then one of the most imposing Grove houses, and shared the Connecticut summer home she bought in 1948 with the profits from her hit play *One Touch of Venus.*[58] Only the Connecticut home is mentioned in her memoir, where she entertained the same friends—Janet Flanner, Natalia Murray, Thornton Wilder, Tennessee Williams—whom she had seen in Pride House (1977:170).[59] And of all her theatrical endeavors, her involvement in founding the Arts Project of Cherry Grove passes in total silence.

MODELS FOR GROVE THEATER

Because "legitimate" theater could not be openly gay, it is no wonder that gays and lesbians in this and other theatrical circles of the thirties were looking for "a little hideaway" where they could "quote unquote be themselves" just as the progressive political wave was cresting between 1935 and 1938.[60] The theatrical mode flourished from the beginning of the gay Grove, from the first theme parties that were attended by show-offs dressed as the Statue of Liberty to the first performances upstairs in Beatrice and Thom Farrar's Pride House, lit by lanterns. Prevented from responding directly to the call for authenticity and political and social action of Off-Broadway, gay expression on even the most painful topics flowed in the same camp direction it had for nearly three hundred years, toward theatrical forms that were considered light, trivial, or informal and so escaped the notice of censors.

The direct formal and thematic antecedents of Arts Project productions are to be found in "revues." A number of song-and-dance acts loosely strung together under a common theme, the revue burlesqued and highlighted the "follies" of the day by giving individual performers a few action-packed moments in the spotlight.[61] Apparently, the revue originated in the music halls and early cafés of France (about 1880), where entertainers mocked politicians and current foibles.[62] Brought to New York in 1907 by theatrical entrepreneur Florenz Ziegfeld and his wife Anna Held, a former entertainer, the "Follies" were soon imitated by other cabarets, all trying to attract the carriage trade with lavish atmosphere, drinks, dinner, dancing, and "beautifully mounted productions, each featuring gorgeous scenery, snappy comedians, and, most important, beautiful women, beautifully presented" (Erenberg 1981:206). Designed as a late-evening escape from the business world for the husband, and from the isolation of the home for the affluent housewife, reviews like *Follies of the Moment, Spice of Life,* and *Cut Ups,* "created an image of vitality, good cheer, and sparkling urban enjoyment" (211). Revues were far more spontaneous than "book shows," which followed written scripts. Each comedian out of burlesque and vaudeville could perform his or her own shtick. The emphasis on women's clothing that would prove to have enduring appeal to Grovers was there in the revue format from the beginning: "Just about every revue had at least one gorgeously gowned number. . . . For the patrons, undeniably, 'it's women and clothes. Why try to make it anything else?' "[63]

Many of the follies were performed not on a stage but at floor level, and there was a determined effort to involve the audience, another feature that appealed to the intimate community of the Grove. Patrons "reveled in the world of 'Keep Smiling,' where the serious constraints of time, place, and class were absent" (Erenberg 1981:212).

Because they were closed by Prohibition in 1922, Erenberg argues, cabarets and revues, already associated with freedom from traditional conservative roles, came even more to represent "individual rebellion from society" (1981:236). None of the affluent urban young had a bigger stake in leisure-time escape from the business world, exploring new gender roles, and individual rebellion against conservative values than gays and lesbians.

In 1925, junior members of the Theater Guild presented *The Garrick Gaieties,* the first of the "intimate" onstage revues. These downplayed the gaudily or skimpily dressed show girls in favor of "amusing, irreverent skits": "The satyric gave way to the satiric, so to speak, with the intimate revue increasingly favored by audiences who preferred wit to window dressing" (Drutman 1976:64).[64]

The postwar urban sophisticates who had flocked to New York from all over the country founded *The New Yorker* magazine the same year, 1925, and the hit song of *The Garrick Gaieties* was "Manhattan." Almost entirely apolitical in the usual sense—the only political spoof twitted President and Mrs. Coolidge as dullards whose idea of an enjoyable evening was listening silently to the radio and falling asleep by ten—the show burlesqued "Michael Arlen's novel *The Green Hat* ('The Green Derby'); Sydney Howard's hit play *They Knew What They Wanted* ('They Didn't Know What They Were Getting'). . . . 'The Scopes Monkey Trial' was staged with a jury in monkey suits. . . . Then came a rapid succession of hilarious skits, sparkling parodies and freshly conceived songs and dances" (Bradshaw 1985:49).

New classes need their own cultural vehicles. Just as the Yuppies of the 1980s had their comedy clubs, the "literate" and "civilized" revue was the vehicle of a modernizing class that was not entirely or explicitly gay and lesbian, but in which gays played a central and major though unspoken role (Bradshaw 1985). It was no accident that Lorenz Hart the librettist was gay, that *The Green Hat*, made into a hit Broadway play that year, dealt somewhat covertly with homosexuality, and that gay critic Alexander Woollcott touted *The Garrick Gaieties* as "fresh and spirited and engaging, bright with the brightness of something newly-minted."[65]

The revue tradition caught hold, both on stage and among theater people for their own pleasure and amusement.[66] In the summer of 1932 the Group Theater company displayed a "lighter side" in "a series of house entertainments—shows the actors put on for themselves and their visitors. A sketch in doggerel represented the three directors in outlandish caricature. Margaret Barker as Cheryl Crawford was a kind of female cowboy, addressing herself with laconic shrewdness to her two quixotic partners" (Clurman 1983:97). This was to be the form of gay theater. All that was needed was a way to make revues "read" indisputably gay, and that signifier was drag.

Someone would *have* to know that Grove revues were gay, Ray Mann told me, because of "all the drag, first of all, and all the suggestive things." Revues had been racy since Ziegfeld, probably since Paris. But of course what was suggested was women displaying themselves to men to invite a male response: "The 1915 Midnight Frolics featuring a number called 'Balloon Girls,' men in the audience being encouraged to burst these balloons with cigars or cigarettes, and other variations soon followed, always the climactic number of the revue" (Erenberg 1981:217).

The "intimate" revues like *The Garrick Gaeities* were suggestive too. Ridiculing the Coolidges' nighttime lack of activity implied there were more pleasurable ways for men and women to spend the evenings. But it was not so easy as it may seem for Grovers to make the suggestions homosexual. Censorship by the property owners and Grovers' own ideas of good taste inhibited explicit sexual representation. Founding Grovers never seem to have thought in terms of what is often considered gay theater today: skits or realist narratives *about* gays.[67] Homosexual desire and sensibility were expressed by parodying heterosexual situations and plots, and the fundamental signifier was drag, the wearing of men's clothes by women and, more frequently, women's clothes by men.

Since the earliest days of an identifiable "continuous (homo)sexual subculture," male homosexuality in England was associated with effeminacy, symbolized above all in the cross-dressing figure of the "molly," who became the "queen." This symbolism and the social network of avowed homosexuals crossed the Atlantic. The "queen" was the key figure in identifiable gay Navy groups in Newport around 1920, where in the unsubtle view of Navy officials, "perverts were men who behaved like women."[68] "She" was central to the social organization of gay men in a Canadian city, and to gay men in the Midwest during the 1960s (Leznoff and Westley 1956; Newton 1972, 1979). The identification of masculinity with lesbianism had perhaps a shorter history, but certainly the writings of the sexologists and the 1928 publication of *The Well of Loneliness* stressed this notion to the virtual exclusion of the competing models: romantic friendship and sapphic decadence.[69]

Meanwhile, female impersonation was an established part of the performing arts, especially in vaudeville, where it was "a form of family entertainment that was ostensibly about women and men, not deviant sexuality" (Bérubé 1990:73). During the twenties some of the racier follies featured female impersonators whose performances did straddle the line between reading "female" and reading "gay." Grover Irving Drutman very much enjoyed the female impersonators Jimmy Watts and Bert Savoy, who played in the bawdy *Greenwich Village Follies*. Watts sent up female opera stars, and Savoy specialized in a "profane delineation of a Broadway tart."[70] But as movies began to usurp vaudeville's role as entertainment for the masses, female impersonation declined along with it, especially after the first talkies in 1927: "Out-of-work female impersonators flocked to Hollywood looking for off-screen jobs in sound pictures as makeup men and costume designers or found work elsewhere as fashion designers, milliners, dressmakers, and hairdressers" (Bérubé 1990:73).

Though she probably exaggerated more than a bit, Mae West's experience in casting *The Drag* in 1926 indicated the desperation of out-of-work female impersonators: "Five thousand perverts applied for only fifty parts when we were casting for *Drag* because there only could he do what he was starving for—act like a woman and wear expensive, beautiful gowns."[71] Her defense of using five female impersonators in her 1928 show *Pleasure Man* was a bit more pragmatic: "If they are going to close up the play and prevent these people from making a living because they take the part of female impersonators, then they should stop other female impersonators from appearing on the Keith Circuit [vaudeville]. . . . How many thousand female impersonators do you think there are in the country? Are they going to put them all out of business?"[72] But because they were not allowed to perform in the new medium, movies, especially after the stricter Hayes Office code in 1934, most female impersonators *were* out of business. Those who remained were called "pansy impersonators" and developed a bawdier style based on double entendres and explicit caricatures of effeminate homosexuals (Bérubé 1990:73). By the 1930s professional drag had been driven back into the demimonde.[73]

Grovers from the 1930s through the 1950s were almost all upper and middle class. Professional female impersonators did not appear in Grove productions until the 1960s, but cross-dressing and female impersonation, in a reprise of their banishment from the legitimate stage during the Restoration, was held more and more to represent gayness and nothing else. As Bérubé observes, "Pansy drag shows in nightclubs and gala drag balls publicly linked the artistic styles of female impersonation even more closely with homosexuality" (1990:74).

During World War II female impersonation was given a new lease on life by the respectful reviews accorded Irving Berlin's soldier variety show, *This Is the Army,* which eventually toured the world.[74] *This Is the Army* established "the three basic wartime styles of GI drag. These were the comic routines, chorus lines or 'pony ballets' of husky men in dresses playing for laughs; the skilled 'female' dancers or singers; and the illusionists or caricaturists, who did artistic and convincing impersonations of female stars" (Bérubé 1990:71). Taking off from *This Is the Army,* many gays within Army units got involved in creating their own shows. Bérubé interviewed a New York fashion designer who told him, "A lot of the guys from the theater world in New York were in the outfit . . . and we decided to write our own musical comedy. . . . There wasn't a woman in the show. . . . We made all our own costumes and sets" (67).

Although any attempt to represent homosexuality for the amusement of the troops—"when performers impersonated queers or seemed queer themselves" (Bérubé 1990:72)—was harshly reprimanded as "obscene" by critics and punished by the Army, the drag shows "inadvertently opened up a social

A scene from "Dismembering the Wedding," a spoof of Carson McCullers's hit play in the Grove Production *Berthe of a Nation*, 1950. Collection of Esther Newton

space in which gay men expanded their own secret culture. The joke was on the unaware members of the audience—a subplot about homosexuality was being created right before their eyes and they didn't even know it" (72).

Meanwhile, Broadway theater had actually begun to decline in the 1930s because of the Depression and competition from movies. From 207 Broadway productions in 1931–1932 the number had dropped forty years later to 58.[75] According to theater historian Ethan Mordden, as early as 1930 the acting profession had begun to split into film and theater branches. It would have boded ill for the future of the Grove had it been utterly dependent on the health of New York theater, for gay freedoms in the theater did not translate directly into the newer mass media, which were even more pressured by censors than theater precisely because they reached so many more people. The movie industry, which had already relocated to California, would play much less of a role in the economic and cultural life of the Grove, much as the elements of fantasy and drama in films continued to attract gay people. After the stricter Hayes Office code was imposed in 1934, movies became almost devoid of homosexual reference (Russo 1987:31, 40).[76]

During the ten years after World War II, Broadway theater declined still further. The number of productions and theaters fell each year, "road" and touring companies went out of business, many members of Actors' Equity were unemployed, and flops generated big losses (Clurman 1983:301–2). But the decline of Broadway opened the field for the growth of Off-Broadway and regional theaters, which began to receive critical attention (316).

In a typescript dated May 4, 1948, called "The Community Theatre," Grover George Freedley surveyed the regional movement, from which the Arts Project was about to spring. Taking note of summer theaters as an outgrowth of the "little theater" movement, Freedley found that though many of them performed scripted book shows for "the community," by which he meant the mainstream, "pure" community theater consisted of amateur actors who "in many instances [are] concerned primarily with their own pleasure and with the therapeutical effect of the drama rather than providing cultural entertainment for the community" (1948a:n.p.). Yet despite the fact that Grovers must have been brewing their plans to start a community theater in the very months when Freedley was writing "The Community Theatre," he didn't mention the Arts Project as an example of the theatrical renaissance he extolled either in his manuscript or later in his published work on theater (Freedley and Reeves 1968).

BERTHE OF A NATION

The main impetus for the founding of the Arts Project did not come from professional actors or playwrights, but from women and men in the gay world—including participating heterosexuals like Helen and Howard Ely and Beatrice Farrar (whose husband Tom was gay)—whose gay and theatrical sensibilities were all of a piece. These people were producers, designers, critics, theatergoers: committed first-nighters. Part of the eager but frustrated audiences who had flocked to *Design for Living, The Green Hat,* and *The Garrick Gaeities,* they were "just a group of hams," their friend Ray Mann understood. "A lot of them were not actors. A lot of them were just having fun and they went on stage and they did it," Bob Adams said. Grover Audrey Hartmann was told by participants that the Arts Project was founded "because there were so many talented people that wanted to put on shows." What most of these talented people wanted to have fun doing was representing their forbidden homosexuality.

In 1948 the first Cherry Grove production mounted in the new community theater featured the Broadway actress Bertha Belmore backed by a chorus line of Grove "boys" in tuxes. But by 1950 the productions became frankly and aggressively gay, thus breaching the compromises that had allowed the 1930s and 1940s Grove to represent itself to the outside world as simply theatrical.

The 1950s show that marked a turning point in gay and theatrical history was written by Ed Burke, directed by his companion George Freedley, and titled aptly and momentously *Berthe of a Nation*.[77]

Although *Berthe of a Nation* was meant to be funny, there can be no doubt about the seriousness of Burke and Freedley's intentions. Burke frequently directed Grove shows and was, so I was told, always trying to get around the censorship practiced by (heterosexual though gay-friendly) president of the Arts Project, Helen Ely. Freedley, the first director of the Lincoln Center Library of the Performing Arts, was a daring and committed gay man. In 1951 he took on repressive sex laws in his *New York Morning Telegraph* column. Reviewing a book called *Sex and the Law*, Freedley wrote that its author, a judge, "finds himself sickened by the hypocrisy of the laws dealing with sexual matters because he knows from practical experience how unreasonable they are. . . . Judge Plascoe calls for a reform of the existing laws, though he knows how unlikely it is that it will ever be attained. Prejudices and special interests will probably always prohibit a sensible or a scientific approach to the subject. Apparently only virgins of both sexes are safe under the law and they are not too safe" (1951a).

Freedley championed the work of the "great" T. C. Jones in laudatory notices of *New Faces of '56*, placing him in the legitimate theatrical tradition of female impersonation.[78] Ignoring the Grove's growing reputation as a gay haven, Freedley blithely praised the community in a 1954 column as "the most theatre-minded community on the eastern coast of the U.S.A." (1954a). And on the kind of light note that turned up in Grove revues, Freedley headlined one column "Gay Book about Cats Authored by Miss Gay." In case readers missed the point, Freedley continued, "Miss Gay has compiled a revised edition of her famous book which was as amusing and gay (no pun intended) as it is useful" (1954b:n.p.).

Modeled on the revue format, *Berthe of a Nation* was "a very light book" and "the production numbers were just musical numbers, thrown in," and not necessarily related to the story. The theme, drawn from D. W. Griffith's epic movie about the South's defeat in the Civil War,[79] was based on the conceit that Broadway character actress Bertha Belmore, then a prominent Grove hostess and homeowner, "supposedly was the one that founded this nation here. They got lost in the fog out in the Great South Bay and they came upon this magical place . . . and they gave birth to the nation of Cherry Grove."[80]

Belmore herself did not star in *Berthe of a Nation*, appearing only as one performer in a mock "Board Meeting," probably of the Cherry Grove Property Owners. The role of Queen Berthe I in the "Coronation" and "Presentation at Court" numbers was taken by one of the "girls." It should come as no surprise that *Berthe of a Nation* had nothing to do with a realistic or authentic presentation of gay topics, characters, or themes. Instead, it built on the theatrical traditions discussed above—camp, revue, and drag—to *signify* rather than *realistically represent* a sophisticated Manhattan version of gayness. There was no contradiction in the nation's being founded by a heterosexual married queen, not if she was an older hostess with an outsize personality and sharp sense of humor.

The players were about evenly divided between men and women. Photographs show that in rehearsals, and in some numbers, people wore the clothing of their own gender. But in "Floradora," the men dressed in gowns and heels and the women led them in couple dancing wearing morning trousers and cutaway coats. In "Dismembering the Wedding," a send-up of *Member of the Wedding* (author Carson McCullers was a frequent visitor to the Grove), a butch-looking woman played the housekeeper Bernice Brown in a gingham apron and an eye patch; a woman played the tomboy Frankie Adams in loafers and socks topped by a silver lamé dress and chiffon scarves; and a barelegged man played the boy John Henry West in a T-shirt and tutu. Although somewhat handicapped by being seated, John Henry strikes a decidedly fey pose and Frankie's hands are firmly planted on her hips.

Judging by their recollections, many people most enjoyed the number called "All Girl Orchestra" by Bill Ronin, a take-off on Phil Spatolomne's all-girl orchestra of the 1930s. A group of thirteen Grove "girls" conducted by Ed Burke dressed in black skirts and ruffled white blouses—Maggie Mac-Corkle described the look as "Vassar prom women"—with wreaths in their hair. The genteel aura of the girls' "playing" was deconstructed at the climactic moment. Grover Peter Worth recalled how, at the end of the number, Mary Ronin, "who had been sitting very primly through the whole thing suddenly opened her legs and she had two cymbals there she clashed together. It brought the house down!" (interview with author).

Photos of the larger production numbers show Queen Berthe I center stage costumed in a flowing robe and tiara, holding aloft a torch and looking unmistakably like the Statue of Liberty. Surrounding Queen Berthe I/Lady Liberty, her subjects, a swirl of smiling young cast members, energetically wave tiny American flags.[81]

Despite the presence of large gay populations in European countries, the gay liberation movement—Stonewall—erupted in America because as early as 1950 the idea of gays as a distinct and oppressed minority group deserving of equal rights found both cultural and political form. In the same year that Grovers celebrated the birth of gay nationalism in a campy burst of clever songs and tap dancing, a group of men in Los Angeles began a discussion

With my partner, performance artist Holly Hughes, who carries on the queer theatrical tradition.

group that would become the Mattachine Society. Although the "theatrical/ parodic" and "realistic/authentic" gay perspectives to which I referred at the beginning of this essay have different histories and can differ widely or even be opposed at the extremes, the theater still provided a common venue from which all gays could draw strength. Drama critic and theater librarian George Freedley had the courage to speak out publicly against sex laws in a 1950 newspaper column, and Harry Hay, the founder of the politically activist Mattachine, met his first recruit in Los Angeles at the Lester Horton Dance Theatre (D'Emilio 1983b:62).

A sequel to this essay might trace the emergence of more modern gay and lesbian theater from the fusion of and tension between the camp style practiced in the Grove and the avant-garde represented by Off-Broadway and especially nonunion, low-budget Off-Off Broadway, which spun off by the late 1950s and became "theatre[s] of the outcast viewpoint and topics."[82] I believe that the Grove theater will prove to have been not only a very important manifestation of growing gay nationalism, but also a direct influence on Off-Off-Broadway productions and performances (perhaps via performers such as Jack Smith).

By the 1970s the parodic/theatrical style of gay representation was having to contend with realistic/authentic gay plays, whose proponents decried the former as old hat and outmoded by liberation. Camp sensibility was just a symptom of victimhood, these people argued. Although it is true that camp was born of oppression, so were many robust traditions, such as blues and even Christianity. Camp is still the preeminent sensibility of queer people, especially gay men, still a supple and witty aesthetic, a potent weapon in the everyday battle for survival, and a rich tradition in the gay anti-church that is theater.

Dick(less) Tracy and the Homecoming Queen:

Lesbian Power and Representation

in Gay Male Cherry Grove

1996

Dedicated to our young artists and intellectuals:
breathless, beautiful, and brilliant

Sometimes our theatre is really rough. But the audience we play for needs us. Lesbians never see themselves represented. And seeing yourself represented is what makes you feel you have a place in the world. (Lisa Kron, professionally trained actress and longtime wow director and performer, quoted in Chansky 1990)

1

In the twenty-three years since the publication of my work on professional female impersonators, I have often been asked if lesbians also did drag, and if not, why not?[1] The drag show scene I had written about in the 1960s was a world of gay men, in which the ten or so lesbian "drag kings" competing against each other in a Chicago drag ball seemed almost an oddity among hundreds of drag queen contestants. When the touring *Jewel Box Review* advertised twenty-five men and a girl, I spent the evening checking out the gowned and feathered female impersonators to find out who the "real girl" was without ever considering that the self-assured tuxedo-clad male emcee would turn out to be Stormé DeLarverie, a lesbian performer.[2] The general gasps of wonder that greeted Stormé's revelation of her gender at the finale were certainly a tribute to her adept drag performance but also exposed a certain void of expectation. Did lesbians do drag? Yes, but not as often as gay men did, and with far less impact.[3] Two stimulating essays and a controversial event in the recent community life of Cherry Grove, a gay and lesbian resort, got me to thinking again about why this might be.

While doing a book tour in the summer of 1993, I met a young graduate student in anthropology at Berkeley who was doubling as a reporter for the *Seattle Gay News*. In exchange for an interview, Sarah Murray shyly gave me a paper she had written on "lesbians and drag." "Drag has not developed into an autonomous theatrical genre within the lesbian community," Murray argued, pointing toward "the heart of the differences between lesbian and gay male subcultures in the United States" for answers why (1994:343–44).[4]

Murray's (and my own) sense of a profound and significant asymmetry between gay men's and lesbians' relation to drag clashed with the audacious proposition put forward by Sue-Ellen Case in "Toward a Butch/Femme Aesthetic" (1993). "The butch-femme couple," she writes, ". . . [are] playfully inhabiting the camp space of irony and wit, free from biological determinism, elitist essentialism, and the heterosexist cleavage of sexual difference" (305). Case's association of butch-femme with camp seems predicated on the assumption that butch clothing, whether onstage or off, equals drag, in her reference to "the cross-dressed butch" and assertion that the butch represents and bears the stigma of lesbian desire because of her (masculine?) clothing (302).[5]

Butch-femme as camp? Case's notion was an irritant: exciting and disturbing, suggestive but hard to pin down. What butch-femme couple was she talking about, and just where exactly, beyond the printed page, was to be found this "camp space" they inhabited? On the stage, apparently, as Case's only exemplars are lesbian performers Lois Weaver and Peggy Shaw, who played Beauty and the Beast, respectively, in the Split Britches production. "The portrayal is faithful to the historical situation of the butch role" (1993:302), Case adds, but nothing in Joan Nestle's appended statement indicates that butch-femme was ever a camp in the fifties and sixties. The significance of Weaver's and Shaw's performances, it seems to me, has much more to do with the recent past and the future, and despite Case's proviso that to recuperate butch-femme for a feminist aesthetic one would have to "[develop] an understanding of the function of roles in the homosexual lifestyle . . . particularly in relation to the historical class and racial relations embedded in such a project" (295), her construction of butch-femme as a form of drag/camp seemed a provocative and flip abstraction, ungrounded in history—the opposite of Sarah Murray's judicious social theories exploring the marginal role of theatrical drag in lesbian culture.

Gay male camp culture of the 1960s, I had argued, was self-consciously theatrical, played on incongruity, and had to be funny (Newton 1979:106–11). My own experience of butch-femme bar culture in the late fifties and sixties told me that butch-femme was not, as Case asserted, ironic, not a camp, and certainly not, as Judith Butler (1990:146; 1993b:314)had suggested, a parody, at least not then. It was utterly serious, always "for real," completely different in feeling and tone from the fabulous and bittersweet excesses of the camp drag queen. But before I could send Case's argument packing, I had to agree with certain implications of her essay. First, bar life *had* had a dramatic side: fist and knife fights, jealous passions, the erotic bravura of "the fish" (a coupled slow dance), and the striking entrances that certain lesbians achieved. In 1959 my juvenile brain was imprinted by the panache of a curly haired blond butch, debonair and assured in beautifully cut men's sports wear, who dismounted from an ordinary yellow cab as if from a chauffeured Cadillac, sweeping into a smoky New York City dive called the Seven Steps and intentionally turning every head. And yes, the spectacular gender effects and contrasts achieved by many butch-femme couples, then as now, seem more related, certainly aesthetically, to gay male drag/camp than to the plain and androgynous lesbian-feminist look that displaced it in the 1970s and 1980s.

But is the assimilation of butch-femme with gay male drag/camp an accurate description, or rather a cultural manifesto and political maneuver? In my view there have been two major themes of gay male sensibility and political action: one is drag queen-centered camp that highlights theatricality and humor, and the other is an egalitarian anarchism that foregrounds authenticity and realism. That lesbians, like gay men, have been drawn to egalitarianism is obvious, from the days of the Daughters of Bilitis (the first lesbian rights organization) in the 1950s through lesbian-feminism and 12-step programs. But the other gay male sensibility, camp style, has always centered around the figure of the queen; as such, it is not easily appropriated by lesbians.[6] And until the performance theorists came along, no one positioned lesbian butch-femme as comparable to drag queen–centered camp, primarily because it had so lacked the element of humor and light theatricality, the self-conscious play with which Case endowed it.[7]

Conflations of butch with drag (queen) and butch-femme with camp obliterate several critical distinctions.[8] From the perspective of cultural history, the lesbian relationship to drag and to camp sensibility has been and continues to be mediated through the fact of its primary production in the particular suffering, creativity, and social networks of gay men. The tendency of some male and female queer theorists and writers to describe "queers" (Case reverts to the older term "homosexual") as if gender were no longer a relevant or important difference deletes just what, in my view, we should be highlighting: the appropriation of gay male practices and culture by lesbians.[9]

Drag and camp are not simply anti-essentialist performances that some-how undermine traditional gender dichotomy, nor are they to be diluted into the broader concept of transvestism or cross-dressing without first specifying how they function ethnographically.[10] (Not coincidentally, drag's detractors commit the opposite error, that drag per se reinforces traditional gender.) For one thing, it is not even clear when and under what conditions lesbians con-sider butch appearance and clothing to *be* drag.[11] Most drag performances I have seen, and I have seen many, usually build on and even reinforce what are taken to be stable (essential) selves and concepts of authenticity rather than destabilizing or abolishing them, even as they may flirt with such possi-bilities.

Both mundane and theatrical drag and camp are signification practices that cannot be separated from material conditions or from the intentions of actors and audiences who embody and interpret them.[12] They are always what phi-losopher Kenneth Burke called "a [symbolic] strategy for a situation"; that is, drag as performance and camp as a sensibility are cultural schema used by individuals and by collectivities to signify, constitute, and advance particular agendas in specific situations. This is not to advocate observation *instead* of social theory, but rather to insist that social theory emerge from and be con-sidered in the frame of social behavior and belief, not just in relation to other theories.

The most important historical situation in which drag and camp have been implicated has been the greater power of gay men than lesbians within every socioeconomic class and ethnic group. After a brief review of this power im-balance, I will show how lesbians have (and have not) been able to use drag and camp in a dense site of gay and lesbian culture production. In the resort community of Cherry Grove, lesbians have attempted to modify or interrupt the customary deployment of traditional symbols—not to destabilize gender categories as such, but rather to destabilize male monopolies and to symbol-ize and constitute the power of the lesbian minority. Finally, I suggest that the proposition that lesbian butch-femme and female impersonation have an equivalent relation to the drag/camp system should itself be understood as a sign and a strategy of emerging lesbian empowerment rather than as his-tory or social theory. Drag and camp are embedded in histories and power relations, including when they are deployed in the theatrical venues so be-loved in Cherry Grove, in the lesbian theatrical and film productions studied by performance theorists, or on the pages of academic journals.

2

I think of myself as a queer first, a woman second. ACT UP New York is my political home. Despite gay male sexism, I could not survive without gay male camp, aesthetics, humor and sexuality. I would go crazy. To me, gay men are family, straight feminists merely allies. (Stroud 1994)

Since the early 1980s there has been an apparent convergence between lesbians and gay men that is reflected in the revalorization of the genderless term "queer." I write "apparent convergence" because much of the movement has resulted from lesbians moving closer to gay men and gay male culture than the reverse. Widespread dissatisfaction with the excesses of lesbian-feminism and heterosexism in mainstream feminism caused many lesbians to look toward gay male culture for alternatives and to be attracted to male-dominated groups like ACT UP.[13] Indeed, Sue-Ellen Case's stated purpose in revalorizing the concept of the butch-femme couple was to chastise both straight feminism (for its homophobic theories) and lesbian-feminism (for its class prejudice, "antipornography crusade and its alliance with the right" [1993:297]).

But lesbians who swallow the queer concept whole, without qualification, risk indigestion. When Maria Maggenti worked with ACT UP and Queer Nation, she "believe[d], like many women before me, that with hard work, enthusiasm, knowledge, and skill, not to mention the sheer force of personality, I [would] somehow be exempted from my status as girl, outsider, woman, bitch, cunt, other . . . [although] . . . in fact, it is nearly impossible to cross the million-year-old canyons that make men men and women women. I avoid my own late-night questions about what it means to be a lesbian in a gay male universe and prefer to believe in the united colors of the Queer Nation" (1993:249).

No matter how much distinctions between lesbians and gay men remain unproblematized, they cannot remain unproblematic because gay men belong to the dominant gender. Holding race and class constant, gay men have more power and money than lesbians do.[14] Their history as a distinct social entity is longer, their institutions are more numerous and developed, and they take up much more symbolic and actual public space, both in relation to dominant society and within most, if not all, institutions termed "gay and lesbian."

Turn to the Stonewall issue of the *Advocate*. In a long article on the Stonewall celebrations of June 1994 in New York City, Chris Bull allots only one phrase to the Dyke March organized by the direct-action group Lesbian

Avengers. A large, boisterous, and highly successful takeover of Fifth Avenue, it was likely the largest public gathering of lesbians in history, but one would never know that from the *Advocate*. Bull writes, "The proliferation of splinter marches mirrored larger disagreement over the political significance of the Stonewall riots" (1994:19). Almost as if responding, the lesbian magazine *Deneuve* writes in its Stonewall issue: "Why should a woman read today's *Advocate?* Well, as the mag's *woman-oriented* pitch letter puts it, it's 'significantly redefined and expanded to include better coverage of lesbian news and interests than ever before.' Translation: They axed or alienated most of their female staff. But the mag also features 'a new balance in our coverage of lesbian and gay men's issues.' From here that looks a lot like the old 'balance.' Boys, boys, boys—and the occasional fag hag" (Lesbofile 1994:48).

In citing the resentment of some lesbians all of the time and many lesbians some of the time toward gay male power and entitlement, my intent is not to provoke, much less enlarge that anger. Both before and after my separatist mood in the 1970s, gay men have been near and usually dear to me—as subjects of inquiry, as friends, and as political allies. In fact, the lesbian relation to gay men, both within gay life and through gay men to the dominant culture, has been underdescribed and undertheorized. As a group, and often as individuals, they are there on our lesbian horizon, and because of their historic predominance, gay men occupy both object (as *other* to straight America) and subject positions in American life whenever homosexuality comes up, a near hegemony that, despite the efforts and effects of separatism, lesbians have not been able to elude or entirely escape anywhere.[15]

What do these generalizations mean in people's lives? How do lesbians use drag and camp in the context of gay male predominance? Events I witnessed during the summer of 1994 in Cherry Grove surrounding the election of the first-ever lesbian Homecoming Queen, the most important ceremonial role in Grove life, provide some answers.

3

A "camp" *herself* is a queen who sits and starts entertaining a group of people at a bar around her. They all start listening to what she's got to say. . . . A camp is a flip person who has declared emotional freedom. She is going to say to the world, "I'm queer." (Skip Arnold, female impersonator, 1966)[16]

In Cherry Grove, a summer resort community of about 275 houses in the New York metropolitan area, gay men used their greater socioeconomic power as *men* (not as patriarchs or lovers) to discriminate against lesbians (for example, in buying and renting houses and in access to leading community roles). They also assumed a hegemonic subject position in which both straight people and lesbians, albeit for different reasons, were cast as the *other*. Gay men's subject position was effected through that central Grove persona, the queen, embedded in a camp sensibility.[17]

The early years of Grove history, from about 1932 to 1960, were dominated by what might be called queenly figures, who most often were middle-aged heterosexual or bisexual women of a definite flamboyance, referred to by gay men as "fag hags" (Newton 1993:81).[18] Mrs. Helen Ely, the alpha of the species, used her ample liquor cabinet and big beach house to host theme parties (at which she would appear in her own grand dresses and costumes), helped found and dominated the most important community organization, the Arts Project, and frequently represented Grove interests to the outside world when legal and political issues arose.

The term "queen," however, was usually restricted to gay men, some of whom hosted theme parties, but whose principal roles were played out in everyday social interaction, at parties, and on the stage of the Community Theater. They didn't need wealth: theatrical flair, quick repartee, and a talent for campy drag performance were enough. Designer Arthur Brill came to one of the first gay parties in the mid-1930s as the Statue of Liberty. Drag queen Dicki Martini wowed Grove audiences in gay revues featuring female impersonation that signified the gay (and lesbian) collectivity. Men dressed as men were relegated to escorting or supporting these larger-than-life figures. Even when male "beauties" were of great erotic interest to other men, they were not often center stage. When the Queen of the Night made her grand entrance from the ocean to the Heavenly Bodies Party of 1957, she was carried by muscular bearers in loincloths in that recurring and central trope of Grove celebrations: young men elevating her royal highness, a drag Salomé, Cleopatra, or Marilyn Monroe, figuratively (and sometimes literally) over their heads.

During the 1960s and 1970s, gay men gradually appropriated and inhabited all the queenly roles. On stage, Irish, Jewish, and Italian gay men such as Thom *Panzi* Hansen, Dickie Addison, and *Rose* Levine brought a new glamour and dedication to queenly performances.[19] *Teri* Warren, a hairdresser from the Bronx who rose to be not only a star Grove performer but also president of the Arts Project, told me frankly, "I want to be the Helen Ely of my generation." In 1976 the Grove formalized the position of the queen by instituting the Homecoming Queen contest, the winner being picked by a panel of local notables. The Homecoming Queen had no formal power. *Her* duty was to represent the Grove at Arts Project events such as fundraisers, bingo night, and elections, but her most visible and important ceremonial moment occurred as leader of the Invasion of the neighboring upscale gay resort, Fire Island Pines. On Fourth of July weekend every year, cross-dressed Grovers—mostly men, with always a sprinkling of women—ferried down the Great South Bay to bless the glitzy Pines harbor, thereby reasserting both gay (male) commonality and gay (male) conflicts over class and age differences. The requirement to cross-dress for getting on the ferry provided a very loose community standard as to what could constitute drag for both women and men.

The idea of wearing one of Martin's dresses to compete in the Homecoming Queen contest as Scarlet Ooh came to Joan Van Ness as she woke up on the morning of May 30, 1994. She was missing her *sister* Martin, who had died of AIDS two years before: "I was feeling sort of campy, you know, in the mood to do something outrageous." Though two friends, Donald and Evan, "were immediately excited by the idea," they were not impressed by how Joan looked in Martin's dress. Known locally themselves as *the Shapiro Sisters,* Donald and Evan offered to dress Joan and make her up for the contest to be held that night as a benefit for the Arts Project of Cherry Grove. She accepted gladly, even though "according to Van Ness, those who would have thought of her in drag, would have imagined her in butch-drag tux, not as the unlikely female-female impersonator complete with bouffant blond wig, and feather boa that she donned to compete."[20] Actually, Joan, dressed in a tux, had accompanied her late "sister" Martin on the Invasion of the Pines several times, once as a groom to Martin's bride.

By the time the ten drag queen contestants took the stage that night, word had spread through the excited crowd that among them was Joan in a dress, heels, wig, and pancake makeup. According to Panzi and *Bella,* two former winners who monitored the applause for each contestant, Joan was the clear winner, elected Queen Scarlet Ooh, symbolic representative for the 1994 season.

Taken out of context, Joan's election might appear to validate theories that treat lesbian and gay male drag as equivalent forms of camp. Joan, embodying in herself a butch/femme gemini, if not the butch-femme couple invoked by Case, since she was a butch in drag queen's (if not exactly femme's) clothing, certainly could be described as "playfully inhabiting the camp space of irony and wit, free from biological determinism" (Case 1993:305).[21] But in fact, it is impossible to understand what Joan's candidacy or victory meant to Grovers without knowing the history of lesbian/gay male relations in the community and beyond. If the goal is to theorize how representational strategies work, how can intellectuals skip over this ethnographic step to broad abstractions and generalities without being guilty of a misleading (and reprehensible) imperialism ("Who cares what you think your representations mean, they mean

Joan as "Queen Scarlett Ooh" escorted by two prominent Grove lesbians at the Invasion of the Pines, July 4, 1994. Photo by Esther Newton

what we say they do")? There is a balance to be struck between accepting the "natives'" accounts at face value with no analysis, and discounting them completely as "fictions" or useful only to our already determined theoretical agenda. In any case, many queer theorists never even consider ethnography or history. Are academic intellectuals only interested in theorizing each others' representations?

4

While presenting a slide history of the Grove in the community theater I showed a picture of a former resident, a lesbian private detective. Panzi shouted out, "Oh yes, we used to call her 'Dickless Tracy.'"

Lesbian numbers and power in the gay Grove had fluctuated. From the 1930s to the 1960s a distinguished and well-off group of lesbians known as "ladies" were outnumbered by men of similar upper-middle-class backgrounds by at least five to one, yet still played important roles as hostesses and in the community theater. Both genders shared a common identification with the theater, but women were jokingly referred to (and referred to themselves) as "Lithuanians," suggesting an exotic group from some faraway land.

As capital and infrastructure made the Grove a more accessible resort, a diverse population of gay men flooded in. The "ladies" retreated, and a new group of working-class "dykes" and their femmes constituted a small and rather beleaguered minority from 1960 to about 1973. During this period of growing gay nationalism, promiscuous and ubiquitous male-male sexual desire was increasingly seen as the common bond between gays, a formulation that excluded lesbians far more than their being "Lithuanians" had done. Yet during the 1970s and 1980s lesbians gained footholds, and by 1987, in a gritty, gradual, and individual process, they had become business owners and homeowners, theater technicians and actors, and leaders in the volunteer fire department—without, as a group, ever directly challenging gay male predominance as expressed through queen-centered camp.

For instance, in Amelia Migliaccio's recounting of a "fabulous" story that "just kind of depicts what Cherry Grove is," all the parts were played by men. Back in the early 1970s, in the period of greatest male hegemony, Amelia lived in a mixed-gender household that became friendly with an all-male "royal family" living next door. When a man in Amelia's household named Eric was tapped to become a viscount, Amelia got into the spirit by baking ziti and all kinds of Italian food for the coronation ceremony. The day of the coronation, "We thought, well, we really should dress for the occasion. So I wore a gown and [her butch lover] Babe wore a tuxedo. And of course we had to dress Eric, who was now going to be the new viscount, so I put a wig and makeup and eyelashes and a dress on him." After a public procession led by the central figure—a large man known as the Infanta dressed in red velvet robes and red velvet hat and sporting a huge papal-type ring—the begowned Eric was subjected to various tests to see "if he was truly gay," including taking "a sample from his toenail to see if it was really Meat Rack soil," that is, soil from the outdoor male cruising area.

Amelia made food for the protagonists, dressed the prospective gay viscount (as a femme, she was perfectly capable of using makeup), and helped arrange the mise-en-scene. She and her butch lover dressed as extras and didn't question the exclusionary criteria for being "truly gay" (e.g., soil from the Meat Rack, which lesbians never frequented). Amelia assessed the lesbian situation at the end of her narrative matter-of-factly, stressing, "It was an all-male family. I want you to understand that."

EN: Were there any duchesses?
Amelia: Well, there may have been, but they were still of the male gender.

EN: There were no women at all?

Amelia: No women at all. In fact, Babe was invited to become a baron or a baroness, I'm not sure, and that never happened. It never happened, but she was being considered.

As queens, gay men assumed the subject position in a coherent camp sensibility that acted to marginalize, or even obliterate, lesbians as iconic. By this I mean both that lesbians were rarely allowed any representation as a group within the community, and that lesbians were virtually never allowed to represent the community as a whole. This exclusion was effected by gay men's far greater numbers and power, by social pressure, and by outright discrimination. Given the overwhelming hostility of the surrounding straight world and, during the 1970s and 1980s, of lesbian-feminism toward the butch-femme system that predominated in the Grove, lesbians were glad to be tolerated in a physically safe space that supported the existence of same-gender love, and accepted playing second fiddle.

Although the camp system helped lesbians imagine other narratives about gender, elements of its internal logic also marginalized them. First, because drag was defined in the first instance as the clothing of the "other" gender, lesbians, as women, could not easily embody queens. (Even the word "drag" has its probable historical origin in the long gowns males wore playing female parts on stage.) Though a few of the "ladies" had been wealthy and confident enough to be queenly hostesses, or even portray queenly figures on stage, they were considered to be dressing grandly or in costume rather than to be in drag.[22] By the 1960s lesbian femmes were implicitly barred from dressing up in any context that could be interpreted as competing with gay male queens.[23] Amelia could dress up in a gown to witness Eric's rite de passage, but she could not be part of it.

Second, by its overwhelming emphasis on the queen, the camp system has acted to disempower the "king" role that butch gay men or lesbians might have logically played (in this key respect, camp is deliberately and devastatingly subversive of masculine power). As Babe's bit part in Amelia's narrative implies, the role of drag butch was not well defined.

In narrators' accounts of the past or in daily life during the 1980s, I hardly ever heard the term "drag butch" much less "drag king," and there was no distinction between "real boys" and drag butches to parallel the well-known one of r.g. (real girl) and drag queen. In the exception that proved the rule, a Jock of the Year contest was held in the late 1970s to pick a consort for the Homecoming Queen. Most of the lesbian contestants dressed in black leather pants, jackets, and caps (the insignia of gay male leathermen), but the judges picked a very butch woman who was wearing a black T-shirt with the words "Keep Cherry Grove Gay," bright red shorts rolled up to reveal a girdle, and a tiara. The lesbians present were strongly divided over this representation—some found it trivializing, others said it was an appropriate camp—and the contest was not repeated. (Years later, a Grove man dismissed the jock contest as having excited "less interest than an outdoor barbecue in January.")

However, by the early 1980s, leading butch Lyn Hutton, dressed one year in black leather pants, jacket, and motorcycle cap, and the next in a tux, became the customary though titleless escort of the Queen during the Invasion of the Pines. (In the late 1980s, I asked Hutton why, although she had dressed splendidly in a tux and red bow tie to attend an "Italian wedding," she wasn't playing a part in the ceremony. "No, I've spent ten years clearing the aisles," she said with mild bitterness. "That's my role.")

Although lesbians were severely limited in how they could participate in drag events, which meant virtually all Grove events, through the medium of camp they could imaginatively enter the system, especially on less formal levels. All Grovers were familiar with camp humor, and some lesbians could employ it, as in this boardwalk exchange on a summer morning in the 1980s. I was chatting with Lynne, a feminine lesbian with long curly hair, who was wearing a mismatched outfit of flowered Bermuda shorts, socks of a different color, and sneakers of yet another:

> Lynne: [taking my arm]: I love these butch numbers!
> EN: You pretend like you don't, but I knew.
> Lynne: Oh, exposed!
> Passing gay man to Lynne: Love your outfit.
> Lynne: Like it? $2.99 on 14th St.
> Man: Liar. You paid at least $3.99.
> Lynne: I see you know my routine.
>> Ted Drach approaches, wrapped in a sheet like a toga. A wreath in his hair, drink in a plastic glass; obviously returning from an all-night party.
> Ted: They stole my underwear.
> Lynne: Now here comes a real man.
> Ted: Oh God, what I wouldn't give for a real man.
> Lynne: [taking his arm and walking off]: Let's go, honey.

Of particular significance for understanding Joan as the Homecoming Queen is the interplay between and among dominant gender categories (man/woman) and gay gender categories (queen/butch, "real" man, femme/butch). Lynne contrasts the "real man," Ted Drach, with the clothes-conscious queen who inquired about her outfit and with my (butch) self. Ted demurs. He is a queen, not a "real" man, because he *wants* a "real" man. Lynne trumps us all on exiting: she, the femme, is the "real" man.

Years before Joan's exploits, others had experimented successfully with what I have referred to as "compound drag": representations of conventional masculinity by a "nellie" gay man or femme lesbian or of femininity or nellie-ness by a "butch" lesbian. A butch lesbian named Cris described how, back in the fifties, she tried to impersonate a gay man on stage by doing a "real drag number": "I played Carol Channing. I got in drag, fell down the steps in my high heels [she laughs], the whole place broke up. . . . Oh, I was trying to be so [makes a feminine gesture of twirling her hair] you know, cause I didn't want them to know who I was, and I had this wig, I really did it, and I thought, 'Now I'm really going to get away with this, they're gonna think I'm one of the guys.' And the guys of course can walk in heels, and I couldn't."

In the 1970s a fondly remembered production of *Little Mary Sunshine* in the Grove theater had featured a chorus of the butchest lesbians, including Lyn Hutton, in gowns and makeup that had been a big hit, and had also successfully featured nellie queens as princes and bandits. As lesbians were gradually becoming more of a presence in the Grove, a group of dykes and femmes entered the Arts Project's thirtieth-anniversary ball as "Sisters of the Sand." The central figure, played by Grove homeowner Jan Felshin, was the "sheiksa" dressed as a sultan, carried by solemn butch litter-bearers and surrounded by skimpily clad dancing girls, thus refiguring the central trope of the queen and splitting her erotic bearers/admirers into butch and femme elements. In contrast to the jock contest, this representation was universally applauded; yet like the jock contest, it was not repeated. The women felt they had proved their point, they could bend the rules just enough to play by them. None of these representations took root to grow into recurring traditions.

By the mid-1980s, the representational possibilities had not changed that much, even though the lesbian presence was increasing. Revues in the Grove's theater from that period featured a parade of older but flashy drag queens, so well-known they were referred to affectionately year after year as "the Golden Girls." The lesbians who ventured on stage were usually dressed in tuxes as male-looking props to escort the Golden Girls to center stage. Lesbians never sang sexy or funny love songs to each other or to drag queens, whereas straight women and gay men together often represented hetero-sexual couples in singing duets.[24] When I questioned the lack of lesbian representation in the revues, other lesbians professed not to have noticed. Butch-femme duos were not represented, in part because only butches seemed to want to participate. No femmes volunteer, I was also told, in a reference to the implicit ban on femme performance that might upstage drag queens. But in any case, all the shows of the era were written by gay men, who apparently had little or no interest in giving lesbians onstage roles.

Only on one evening in 1986 at Drag Search, an open talent night at the hotel disco modeled after *Star Search,* the Ed McMahon TV talent show of the era, did I see an indication of the more daring and confident lesbian attitude that was to emerge later. (Significantly, this popular commercial event never had the symbolic weight of theatrical productions or even theme parties, and most contestants were from outside the Grove.)[25] The drag queen emcee, *Electra,* explained that he'd always encouraged people to perform and had been disturbed all summer that no "ladies" were performing. The girls liked to get out and shake their tits by the pool in the wet T-shirt contest, he remarked dryly, but this afternoon three girls had approached him and said they wanted to perform, and here they were, the "Jersey Girls."

The three "girls," in their twenties, wearing shorts and no makeup, proceeded to lip-synch an upbeat neo–Andrews Sisters–style song with the recurring line, "It's not the meat, it's the motion." Their coordinated dance steps showed they had taken their performance seriously enough to rehearse a bit. "It's not the meat"—they pointed to their crotches—"it's the motion"—they swiveled their hips energetically. Each performer took a turn in the spotlight. When the most butch of the three came forward, the crowd went wild. After admonishing, "It *is* the meat *and* the motion," Electra came out and let them do an encore. When he said the Jersey Girls couldn't compete in the *Miss* Ice Palace competition, their pals, a claque of energetic young lesbians, set up a prolonged howl. "I'm glad they don't know where I live," quipped Electra. "Miss Ice Palace has to be a male in drag," he continued over the hoots of the lesbians. "But listen, maybe next year we'll have a new category, 'Mr. Ice Palace.' Let's have an *Elvis Presley* up here, a *Frank Sinatra,* why not?" But it didn't happen.[26]

As a rule, lesbians either found a way to participate on the edges of queen-centered camp or they could appreciate it as spectators; they could not alter the basic schema. The more public the event, the more central to Grove self-definition, the more lesbians were relegated to walk-on parts or pushed backstage.

In retrospect, 1988 was the year when, as one older Grove lesbian said with a sly grin, "they [gay men] first began to get real nervous." At the same time that gay male predominance was being undermined by illnesses and deaths from aging and from AIDS, lesbians began going there in very large numbers.[27] The word was out, another lesbian told me then, that the Grove was a good place for lesbians. In general, these newer arrivals were younger and took certain 1970s attitude changes for granted; I refer to them as postfeminists in this sense.

More and more comments were heard from gay men about "those pushy dykes" who made too much noise, hogged the boardwalks, and generally took up too much space. At the annual Art Show, the 1988 Homecoming Queen, *Vera*, out of drag and rather drab, wore a black T-shirt emblazoned with the crisp white letters "What Becomes a Lesbian Most?" across his chest. When Lynne commented on it he said, laughing sarcastically, "You notice there's nothing written on the back." Lynne and other lesbians all made disapproving faces, which Vera ignored.

At Bella's Dish, a weekly late-night event at the hotel, a group of visiting queens from the Pines put on a "fashion show" wearing trampish outfits they apparently thought appropriate for a Grove venue. As the lead queen mounted the stage she declaimed, "My name is Tawana Schwartz, and this is what I was wearing the night I was raped by six white lesbians in Cherry Grove" (a reference to an infamous New York case in which a young black woman named Tawana Brawley claimed she was raped by some white men). My (white) lesbian friends were looking at each other and I made a slitting motion across my throat. As in the Vera incident, we just sat there fuming. We all knew that the Grove, like America, had a history of sexist, racist, and anti-Semitic representations, but did that excuse doing them in 1988?[28]

In 1991 tensions surfaced again over gender, race, and representation issues. A lesbian named April (who is black) objected to *Miss Stephanie* from the Pines (who is white) doing a blackface version of Diana Ross in one of the Grove theatrical revues. April "was not any kind of revolutionary," I was told, but she quietly went to the director and said that if Stephanie did blackface, she, April, couldn't participate. The director held a meeting with Stephanie and some others from the cast, all of whom tried to talk April out of her objections: It didn't mean anything, wasn't racist, just for fun, etc., etc. Meanwhile, some of the men were heard to say, "If we let these dykes tell us not to do blackface, next they'll be telling us not to do drag, and we can't let them tell us what to do." The women involved split on the issue, vaguely along dyke versus postfeminist lines. In the end, Stephanie did Diana Ross in "brown face" and April and other feminists silently boycotted the show. The director let it be known that if lesbians didn't like the shows they could damn well write their own (a challenge that was taken up in 1993 by a woman who produced a mildly successful first-ever lesbian-written revue in the light, campy Grove style).

At the very end of the 1991 season, people began to see publicity for a planned "Women's Weekend" in the Grove in September, organized by a Long Island lesbian newspaper. Someone made and distributed a leaflet to every house in the Grove and Pines with the bold words "Do We Need This?" printed across the Women's Weekend ads. Local lesbians were upset, but nothing came of it. Every succeeding year the number of lesbians grew. By 1994 Grovers generally agreed that though gay men and straight people together still owned around 75 percent of the houses, lesbian home ownership was slowly growing and—most dramatically and visibly—lesbians constituted over half of day-trippers and renters.

Alongside the grousing and resentment, some male Grovers were trying accommodation. At a meeting of the Property Owners Association at the beginning of the 1994 season, someone proposed putting two benches at the end of the walk leading to the Meat Rack, the gay male outdoor cruising area. The head of the newly established memorial fund, a highly respected elder male homeowner, objected that it would be inappropriate to pay for something from the memorial fund that would not be used by the whole community. Apparently it was understood that it was women who don't use the Meat Rack and so shouldn't have their contributions used to pay for Meat Rack amenities. In the event, another prominent male Grover raised the money privately, that is, only among men. It was in this precarious balance of changing demographics and power that Joan ran for and won the Homecoming Queen contest.

5

Lesbians . . . suffer from an odd invisibility in our society. This invisibility allows us to see both how the masculine and the feminine are defined in opposition to each other, and how relationships to men function as the critical factor in gaining social visibility and cultural power. (Sarah Murray 1994)

Reaction to Joan's victory was immediate. Thom Hansen (Panzi) joked next morning, "I'm afraid to walk down to my house." As president of the Arts Project, he, aided by Bella, had judged the applause meter and Joan had clearly won. (Sometime around 1990 the old system of picking the Queen by local notables had been replaced by an applause meter, because there had been many complaints of cronyism—another barrier to lesbians). Panzi had thought Joan's entry was funny (though he told a newspaper interviewer he had not approved of having a woman Homecoming Queen), but he was amazed at not only the hurt egos but "also, I'm afraid, the outright misogyny of some of these queens." Some had turned in their Arts Project membership cards and others were flying their Arts Project flags upside down. And, he added, "We all said too bad Esther's already written her book, this would have been a great chapter." After Panzi, who was clearly both ruffled and amused, had walked off, a lesbian friend with whom I was sitting remarked, "This is a terrible year for some of these guys. First a lesbian writes the definitive book on the Grove's history, then a lesbian becomes Homecoming Queen," jarring me into a consideration of how my recent book might have figured into the tensions.[29]

Considering the number of young lesbians I was seeing all around me, the queens might have considered themselves lucky that some lesbians cared enough to crash the contest on gay male terms, for Joan's victory was both subversive of *and* submissive to male power. As such, though, it was the perfect challenge to the "old boy" system of the Grove. The contest was rarely about "beauty"; usually, the Queen was a middle-aged community booster. Joan had been around since 1979. She had appeared in numerous Arts Project shows, gone on the Invasion in a tux, and volunteered for every cause and committee: the Dunes project, the memorial fund, the doctor's fund had all received her checks. A volunteer firefighter for over a decade, she owned a house that she was constantly improving, encircled by a well-tended garden. She was the perfect soldier of the year, Boy Scout of the decade. There was only one reason why Joan should not be Homecoming Queen, and everybody knew it: she was an r.g., a real girl.

In the first days after Joan's election, the dyke versus postfeminist split among community-involved lesbians evident in the April/Miss Stephanie affair surfaced again. Indeed, my most feminist Grove friends decried Joan's having entered the contest, which one described as "patriarchal stuff," adding, "She wants to be accepted by the men so badly she'll do anything." In contrast, most dykes professed to be shocked by the male reaction, because it was all just a camp and in fun, while obviously relishing Joan's victory. Lynne gloated that "the dykes elected [Joan]" by clapping extra loud at the contest, and added that Joan's new lover, Lorraine, who was quite butch, was going to make a great (cross-dressed) escort for Queen Scarlet Ooh at the Invasion.[30] Joan left no doubt she was utterly determined to exercise her queenship. When I later asked her if it was a real pain to dress up like this, she said "No, because the community elected me and I'm very proud of it. It's an honor. And there's no question but that I won. Sure, the dykes clapped loudest, but without the men I couldn't have won." "It wasn't even close," Lorraine added. "And so of course I'm going to do it," Joan said. Lyn Hutton looked me straight in the eye and deadpanned, "It's a camp. That's my only comment." Meanwhile, Panzi was advising Joan that if she was going to be the Homecoming Queen she had to appear at every public event every weekend.

The controversy neared its peak the weekend of June 11–12, with Joan's first scheduled public appearance as Queen to hostess tea at Cherry's bar.[31] On the appointed day a couple of fliers proclaiming "Boycott Dyke Tea" were quickly torn down. Initially sparse attendance ultimately swelled to a good-size crowd, with a much larger than usual lesbian presence. "Joan looked great" in drag, one lesbian acquaintance who had initially scoffed said, and watching the normally short-haired, no-makeup, preppie-looking Joan on videotape later, I would never have recognized her, so heavy was her drag queen makeup, so voluminous her gown, so Hello-Dollyish her wig. Adding to the theatrical effect was Lorraine at her side—taller, butch, and good-looking—wearing a well-fitting suit and tie.

Fred, an older male friend, told me that the Joan affair was the talk of the Grove from the moment he got on the ferry that weekend until he left. He couldn't understand why Joan would do such a thing, she seemed "such a sensitive person." A charming man with many female friends, Fred seemed impervious to my argument that Joan was the victim of unreasoning prejudice. Other men insinuated that Donald and Evan, the Shapiro Sisters, had put Joan up to it to get revenge on the Arts Project because Donald had lost the contest the previous year. Or that Panzi had fixed the contest somehow, because he had been heard to remark before Joan came onstage, "History will be made tonight." There were male slurs against Joan: How could she fulfill the Queen role? She had no personality and didn't know how to pose for a camera; she must have been put up to it, she didn't have the brains to think it up herself, and so on.

The next weekend the controversy overflowed the Grove. Two big New York City newspapers wrote features on it, without taking sides.[32] But the boil burst with the publication of *Patti Ann's* weekly "Talk of the Grove" column in the local *Fire Island Tide:* "Joan Van Ness accepted the 'Cat calls' or whatever and allowed herself to become 'Homecoming' for 1994. I would like to add that this was a 25 year tradition of males cross dressing as a female that was swept aside, and pushed into the sewer. . . . I had thought Joan was more sophisticated than to embroil herself into this controversy. However! On with the 'Invasion in Exile'" (P.A. 1994:34).

Not only did Patti Ann call for an alternative Invasion to be led by *Vicki,* whom he referred to as "the real 'Queen,'" he appealed traitorously to the men of the Pines ("Do you want a woman 'Queen' blessing your harbor?") and to "the intelligent, sophisticated women of Cherry Grove thank you for your support of the tradition. You know who you are and hopefully you'll make your voices heard." Finally, he shot his most poisonous arrow past the signifier of Joan's victory toward the signified—the social change sweeping Cherry Grove: "(Quote from a former professional 'Drag Queen') 'First the boys got sick, they died, their houses sold and now kicked in the ass and their tradition is taken away. P.A. it is time to sell.'"

Patti Ann's article backfired. All the lesbians and many men joined in opposition to this divisive provocation. Calls for unity, references to the lesbian contributions in the AIDS crisis, and appeals to the camp tradition flew thick and fast. One prominent lesbian wrote in response: "P.A., How dare you? It was evil and cruel. I know I speak for myself and all of the so called unintelligent and unsophisticated women of the Grove in saying to you, unequivocally, 'take it back'" (Bozzone 1994:12). Another long-time lesbian homeowner, arguing that it was the American way to accept changing values, went so far as appealing to our revolutionary history that was indirectly commemorated by the July 4 Invasion, and observing pointedly, "[Lesbians] can not (and should not) be relegated to the permanent role of supporting and applauding the men. Joan Van Ness won the title in a fair election, cheered by members of both sexes. Perhaps her victory represents the evolution of a new tradition—one that allows men and women to share equally in all that this wonderful community has to offer. What a great tradition that would be!" (Schwartz 1994:12). One of the few remaining "ladies" weighed in, too, writing a letter to the rival local paper decrying Patti Ann's column in the most sarcastic terms and reminding readers that in the old days, men and women had gotten along. Echoing Lyn Hutton's remark, she asserted that the Homecoming Queen was about camp, not about drag per se, a point to which I will return later. Privately, she castigated Patti Ann and his followers as "illiterates" and "not the most popular in Cherry Grove," a reference to lingering class resentment toward the working-class parvenus like Patti Ann who had come to dominate the Grove in the 1970s.

Even feminist lesbians fell in line, though one remarked (probably accurately) that the younger lesbian renters we were seeing all around us "didn't give a rat's ass" about the Homecoming Queen contest. When I mentioned that Joan's Queendom had united all the community-involved women for the first time in an explicitly feminist cause, this friend commented, "At least half the women on the island think drag is disgusting. . . . Drag is a men's thing, and there are areas that we are concerned with that we don't want them mixing into, and women shouldn't mix into this. But then when there was such immediate opposition from some men, then everybody had to swing behind Joan. Otherwise it would never have been a feminist issue."

Most of the male establishment also firmed up against Patti Ann and his band of naysayers. Rose Levine, who had once gotten himself in trouble with disparaging remarks in his gossip column about "chubby lesbians" taking over the fire department, wrote an approving and supportive article about Joan in the rival *Fire Island News*. Thom's long-time friend Max said that although the head of the Grove could not be a "king," Joan's drag was high camp, and he couldn't understand what all the fuss was about. Max wasn't going to go on the Invasion itself (in the end he did), but he would go down to support "the Empress" who would lead the procession to the boat. I had never heard of an Empress, so he explained that Thom (Panzi) was the Empress of the Invasion, that Thom thought he owned it. (I wondered then if Thom as the Empress could be seen to trump Joan as the Queen, and I was later to witness a number of attempts to upstage Joan.)

David, the owner of one of the Grove's most beautiful houses on the bay, explained that he had decided to be more open toward women after his lover's death. He approved of Joan as Queen. Why shouldn't she be Queen? Only the men who just couldn't change were still disgruntled. And it was only for one year, after all. If those men didn't like it, they could go down and try to win it back next year. Joan had breathed life into what was perhaps a dying institution. And it *was* camp. David and his new lover were the only men I talked to who suggested, hesitantly, that Joan's being Queen was appropriate because there were more women in the Grove now.

The day of the Invasion a crowd ten deep lined all approaches to the deck of the Ice Palace and all the way down to the ferry, including a large number of women, perhaps a third of the total of several thousand spectators—not only Grovers but many visitors from Long Island. By noon the usual kinds of mostly middle-aged Grove drag queens—trampish, showy, French maids, queens with gowns made cleverly out of garbage bags, and one who was wearing and showing a large realistic dildo under his dress—were being introduced by Sal the emcee and milling around having their photos taken. There were fewer male group entries and more women entrants (though not even a quarter of the total) than in the past, including a campy and confident Elvis imitator with a drag queen showgirl on *his* arm who did a funny little well-rehearsed song-and-dance number together. Sal made quite a few references to there being a woman Queen this year, lightly sarcastic, but nothing really mean. One contestant who was wearing fishnet stockings but also a leather motorcycle cap announced that he didn't know what his drag name was, that his drag was confused: "Since this year our drag queen is a woman, this proves we are all confused in Cherry Grove."

Several people remarked that as usual Panzi's drag was cleverest of all. He had always led the Invasion in glamour drag, but this year he came as a "firedyke" (lesbians had long been prominent in the volunteer fire department), complete with big rubber boots, official lettered firefighting coat, and black fire hat. His makeup was relatively understated, and he wore an earlobe-length red wig—nothing glamorous but not ugly, either—thus avoiding the stereotype of lesbians being ugly that Queen Vera had invoked. He announced over his bullhorn that if a dyke could be the Queen then he could be in the fire department. From time to time to the delight of the crowd, he flipped up his short skirt to show his "vagina," represented by false pubic hair (he later explained sheepishly that after shortening the wig he needed something to do with the leftover hair).

Aiding Panzi in maintaining order and "in keeping with the theme," as Grovers say, there were two male marshals dressed in short wigs and black leather pants, jackets, and caps. For the knowledgeable Grove audience, these two were impersonating the two lesbians who for years had served as marshals in male leather drag. Grove regulars and the public roles they play are so well-known among residents that it is easy to portray them through several transformations of gender. From this perspective, people understood that Joan, as Queen Scarlet Ooh, was also portraying her dead friend Martin.

Finally some coronation music began blaring over the loudspeakers. Preceded by the marshals and then by an honor guard of two socially prominent Grove lesbians dressed as naval officers came Queen Scarlet Ooh, smiling and waving to the crowd, escorted by Lyn Hutton in dazzling white tails. Bullhorn blaring, Panzi urged the spectators to welcome the new Queen, who was making history for Cherry Grove—the first Homecoming Queen ever to be a woman! There was applause and ooohs and ahhs. Joan, Lyn, and their dyke naval escorts willingly posed for lots of photographs, and then Joan was escorted to the boat by Lyn, followed by all the other queens and dykes through the excited crowd. As the cross-dressers embarked, Panzi shouted through his bullhorn, "Ladies and gentlemen, I am proud to announce that this is the most successful Invasion, ever!"[33]

Nevertheless, I did overhear male grumblings in the crowd that faded to murmurs as soon as they realized I could hear—"It's just unbelievable" in an aggrieved, complaining tone—but there was no sign of any protest or alternative invasion, and several people said there were only three men who went over by water taxi, in what was effectively an invisible protest.

Every boat in the Pines harbor was decorated in welcome, including one yacht filled with cheering women that sported a banner reading "Women of the Pines Welcome the Grove's First Woman Queen." The gay rainbow flag was flying everywhere, as it had during the Gay Games and Stonewall 25 celebrations that just the month before had brought millions of gays and lesbians to New York. Panzi had draped the prow of our ferry with a piece of the mile-long flag that had been carried by hundreds in the official Stonewall 25 march, and I marveled again at his clever leadership in making such a prominent appeal to gay and lesbian unity.

Queen Scarlet Ooh and her naval escort were first off the boat. There was polite applause from the overwhelmingly young, white, male crowd. Then, one by one, other queens and dykes got off, the showiest eliciting the biggest cheers, as usual. Again I overheard a few fragments of complaints about Joan, such as, "They should have said it had to be a female *impersonator*."

Back in the Grove at Cherry's bar, Queen Scarlet Ooh was holding court in her platinum wig and low-cut red gown slit up the side, now escorted by Lorraine (who had said that her job in the public sector precluded participation in the Invasion) in a man's suit and mustache. In response to my friendly "How's it goin'?" Joan said firmly, "Great. There is no controversy. The only controversy is those sour grapes over there," pointing toward four or five middle-aged drag queens sitting glumly across the bar. "You know what it is, they're all sour old drunks. Everyone else has been very supportive."

A month later my friend Fred told me that Joan doing the Homecoming Queen was "incredibly campy" and completely okay. I reminded him how he had said she shouldn't have run for Queen because it was "insensitive" to the feelings of the boys. He said he'd changed his mind after thinking it over and almost didn't own up to his original position, stressing how, the previous season, when Fred's ailing companion had to be taken by fire department wagon to the police helicopter, Joan was the one who came, and she was "absolutely marvelous" with them both.

Through the medium of such long-standing personal and professional interdependency, the Grove's wounds began to close. My feminist friend Lucy was running into male opposition to her authority over an important local committee. Some women sitting around Lucy's house commented that the men just hated dykes, you felt it all the time. But even if the men hated you, they were not going to hit you or hit on you. Lucy sighed that the Grove was like family. She couldn't believe the support of *everyone* in the Grove at the time of her son's premature death. People just hung out, they brought food, whatever they could do or contribute. But just like family, too, you can't scratch too deep below the surface, Lucy laughed.

Meanwhile, Patti Ann, the leader of the male resisters, had bought into one of the Grove's most successful restaurants, which was owned by a powerful local lesbian. Lesbians thought he would have to mute his male supremacist stance to get along with his new co-owner and not alienate the many women patrons. The whole controversy died down, but behind the scenes Arts Project membership for the summer of 1994 dropped by almost a third. Panzi and others thought disgruntled men were "voting with their feet."

At the opening of the 1995 season, one of the Shapiro Sisters was elected Homecoming Queen. But the changes signaled by Joan's Queenship were still at work. Of the three shows scheduled for the theater, one was written and directed by Lynne Tunderman, and Panzi had convinced the leadership of the Arts Project to break with almost a half century of precedent, that all talent must be local, by hiring Lea Delaria, a prominent lesbian comic from outside the Grove, to perform for the second show. In spite of this, membership in the Arts Project was back up over three hundred, to levels before the rumpus over Queen Scarlet Ooh.

6

This notion of being "locked out" is a compelling one; it signals the lesbian's socio-symbolic status as one of not being in the game or even in the room where the game repeatedly and perpetually plays itself out. The lesbian's distance from the symbolic order is so great, her status as empty signifier so decisive, that she is effectively erased in the psychosocial register of the visible. (Davy 1993) [34]

Cherry Grove is too white, too middle class, and too middle aged to be a microcosm of America's diverse lesbian and gay communities. In any case, it is more of a hothouse than a laboratory, with gays and lesbians living in unusual proximity and interdependence, a situation that made lesbian erasure from "the register of the visible" both more acute and perhaps more changeable than in America's big cities or rural areas. It is just this hothouse closeness that magnifies and reveals the fundamental asymmetry between lesbians and gay men, and thus of lesbians to drag and camp. As a group, Grove men always had more money than lesbians, owned more houses, took up more public space, and wielded hegemonic (though usually comically inflected) symbolic power through the system of queen-centered camp. Although lesbians could and did deploy camp humor informally, they could not be queens and so could never have center stage. Lesbian butches, the queens' theoretical complement, were not persecuted, but they were not celebrated either, and played only marginal roles in Grove public life.

This is a version of the problem of lesbian "visibility" that lesbian performance theorists are now so usefully preoccupied with.[35] Certainly, Grove lesbians were "empty signifiers," lacking social power to be instruments of representation. It was only in the context of the larger and more powerful lesbian presence, hence audience, of the 1990s that Joan Van Ness was able to re-dress the lack of lesbian visibility brilliantly (though unconsciously, because she maintained in private that had she known what a furor her candidacy would cause she would never have competed) by executing three strategic moves. First, she placed herself squarely in the Grove male tradition by ap-pealing to the memory of her dead sister, Martin, who had died of AIDS (from one perspective, she *became* Martin), and she went to the local drag queens, the Shapiro Sisters, to have herself transformed into a queen.[36] Second, she framed her Queendom within the more gender-neutral category of camp, rather than the more male-specific drag. This framing of Joan's intervention as camp or even high camp, and so irreproachable, was repeated and validated by influential Grovers like Lyn Hutton, Max Killingsworth, and Panzi. Third, Joan reached back to a secondary but legitimate possibility within what can only be called gay gender (because through historical elaboration it has estab-lished partial autonomy from the heterosexual system)—that of compound drag, whereby queens could parody (an appropriate word here, because it was always done for laughs) "real men" or butches, and butches could parody either "real women" or drag queens.[37]

Contrary to assertions that drag subverts any gender position, or gender as a system, for many Grovers, certainly for the major actors in this narrative, drag becomes a performance in relation to what is subjectively experienced and socially accepted as an authentic self, defined by more or less coherent gay gender positions: butch (for masculine gay women and men), femme (primarily for feminine gay women), and queen (only for effeminate men).[38]

Lyn told me she had felt "awkward as hell" going to a relative's wedding in a dress to please her mother. "Well, that *was* drag for me. This [her tux and tie] isn't drag for me, it's getting dressed up." For Lyn, the clothing of her gay (true/butch) gender, the tux, is not a costume, but a sign of her true self. At the same time, on July 4 she wears the tux to comply with the rules of the Invasion, that participants must show both gay and straight spectators that they are gay by wearing drag. Does drag cover or reveal the true self, ex-press or obscure it? That depends, but without concepts of authenticity, the transformations drag performs are meaningless.

What made Joan's portrayal of Queen Scarlet Ooh drag? For one thing, because she looked like a drag queen (rather than, say, a housewife or a wait-ress). But for another, because she wore the clothes of her opposite gay gen-der. When I asked Joan what made her performance drag she looked at me blankly, and so I rephrased, "Is being on the butch side what makes what you are doing 'drag'? Like, if you were more feminine," I explained, when she still seemed uncomprehending, "and got into this gown, would people accept it?" "No," she replied, seemingly on firm ground. "My being the way I am is what makes the whole thing camp." This simple statement contains the proposition that her "real self" is butch, that therefore her wearing a dress is a drag performance, a "camp." Or, as the Jersey Girls had put it eight years before, "It's not the meat, it's the motion"; that is, lesbians don't need a penis to be sexy, campy performers, to wear drag, to hold the attention of an audience, to be as gay as a gay man and so represent gayness—in short, to be what the performance theorists call "phallic."

Performance theorists are on to something about the decentering of gender, including gay gender, in postmodern society, but they are wrong to propose that gay male or lesbian representations are taking place in a hypothetical "camp space of irony and wit, free from biological determinism, elitist essentialism, and the heterosexist cleavage of sexual difference." Even if we ignore the differences between performance spaces—the WOW Café (the all-women theater space and company that nurtured many of the lesbian performers mentioned here), the Cherry Grove theater, or the Invasion—and mundane gay life, even in these creative spaces performers are working under material conditions to specific audiences. Both camp and butch-femme do tend to dislodge gender from biology, but the purpose and effect is not to eliminate gender—a hopeless project, in any case—but rather to multiply and elaborate gender's meanings. Butch-femme and camp are not demolishing essentialism and the idea that there is an authentic (gay) self; rather, that is their foundation.[39] Nor are these creative spaces at all free from the many power imbalances between gay men and lesbians that the term *queer* papers over; quite the contrary. Grovers *are* redeploying elements of gay gender, but less in the service of shifting and self-reflective styles than in that of shifting collective power.

Joan's victory in the Homecoming Queen contest, the burgeoning of camp in lesbian theater, and the work of the performance theorists are situated ethnographically within the historical frame of (gay) male dominance, in Cherry Grove, in Off-Broadway theater, and in academia. Everyone in the Grove accepted that Joan Van Ness's running for and winning the title of Homecoming Queen in a male-dominated public venue and arguably within the queen-centered camp tradition constituted a subversive bid for inclusion and for lesbian visibility within the landscape of gay male symbolic and social power.[40]

Although nineties butch drag has its own tradition in butch-femme sensibility and practice, and queer theory likewise has roots in feminism, for lesbians to name themselves as bearers and creators of camp on the stages of drag contests or Off-Broadway theaters and in the pages of academic journals *constitutes and reflects* a significant and wide-ranging change in lesbian/gay life, a change in which lesbians are aspiring to more power and representation through gay men and through the appropriation of gay male culture. Camille Paglia credits three gay men with helping create "the campy, semimythic diva and deranged gender-neutral entity" she proclaims herself to be.[41] The same process is evident in the Off-Broadway lesbian theater originating in the wow Café, such as the plays of Split Britches, the Five Lesbian Brothers, Holly Hughes, and Carmelita Tropicana, that have inspired performance theorists. Kate Davy cites Holly Hughes as locating her inspiration in "the queer theatrical tradition in the gay male drag performances of Charles Ludlam, Jack Smith, and Ethyl Eichelberger" (1993:84).[42] Lynda Hart recounts the story, enacted in Peggy Shaw and Lois Weaver's performance piece "Anniversary Waltz," of how the two actors who figure so centrally in Case's butch-femme camp scenario met:

> Shaw was traveling with "Hot Peaches," a gay theater group consisting mostly of drag queens. Weaver was traveling with the feminist theater group Spiderwoman. They met on tour in Berlin. Spiderwoman had arrived without their costumes; feminists at the time were busy, as Weaver says, "deconstructing the feminine image," hence they were accustomed to wearing old clothes, "rags with baby's toys tied around their belts." That night, however, they went on stage wearing the resplendent gowns and sequined accessories of the drag queens, and Weaver knew that "somehow they would never be the same again." And, indeed, before the tour was over Weaver would be transformed from a drab feminist into a sexy femme, playing to Shaw's butch. (1993:129)

Hart concludes, "This representation points to sexual preference as a choice that is not bound to a gendered object"; in other words, drag/camp can serve lesbians as well as gay men. Kate Davy has a more ambivalent attitude toward the fact that "as the notion of camp has circulated among wow practitioners in recent years, it has garnered a certain currency that has noticeably influenced the Work" (1992:234).[43] It has done so because camp as a representational system is more developed than butch-femme and *also* because of the social and economic successes of gay male theater. wow performers were sick of being poor and performing only in a lesbian ghetto while gay male theater was gaining acceptance and success in mainstream venues.[44]

When Peggy Shaw, Lois Weaver, Holly Hughes, Carmelita Tropicana, and the women at the wow Café were looking for theatrical alternatives to the earnestness of lesbian-feminist political theater and the realism of Jane

Chambers, they reached back into the gendered and dramatic world of butch-femme and across to the camp theater of artists like Charles Ludlam with which butch-femme was most compatible. Why hadn't lesbians developed a theatrical drag tradition? Sarah Murray's essay asked. Alongside her sophisticated arguments about psychological and symbolic differences between gay men and lesbians, she should have placed more emphasis on the lack of opportunity, confidence, and clout that goes a long long way toward explaining why "the power of women, lesbian and straight, to create distinctive and persuasive images of women that break with conventional mainstream images *and are taken up by others and culturally reproduced* has been and continues to be weak, despite our abundance of creative expression" (1994:344; emphasis in original).[45] It is a sign of change that Case's essay was able to do just that: take up and culturally reproduce a butch-femme image based on her reading of Lois Weaver and Peggy Shaw's performance of *Beauty and the Beast.* That is why "Toward a Butch-Femme Aesthetic" is more of a cultural manifesto than a cultural analysis, much more of a "historical reenactment" than a history.

What I see happening, at least among white urban lesbians (whose influence among lesbians in general is not to be lightly dismissed), is a creative ferment arising from the synthesis of lesbian traditions—butch-femme and feminism—with gay male culture (queer identity, camp theatricality, and modes of sexual behavior and imagery) in the context of *modestly expanding lesbian power.* Can it be a coincidence that this unprecedented outpouring of sophisticated work on lesbian signification and visibility that focuses, whether wholeheartedly or with reservations, on butch-femme as camp or queer, comes at the same time that Judith Butler, Teresa de Lauretis, Sue-Ellen Case, Lynda Hart, Jill Dolan, Peggy Phelan, and others have ascended to tenured positions at research universities and attained a critical mass within the queer theory or performance studies domains unheard of for lesbians in other intellectual disciplines? (Perhaps we need our own *Patti Ann* to make us appreciate the significance of these accomplishments.) My purpose is not to denounce successful lesbian intellectuals—quite the opposite—but to issue this cautionary note on behalf of ethnographically grounded social theory: in the long run, what we see in the mirror we hold up to lesbian signification practices will be distorted, unless it shows us the tangle of power and precedent in which even our own faces will be seen, acting in and on our moment in history.

PART II: LESBIAN-FEMINISM

Reading Germaine Greer, with feminist big hair, about 1972.
Photo by Barbara Towar

High School Crack-up

1973

This paper grew out of an odd discomfort which several women friends and I experienced while reading *Zelda*, the biography of Zelda Fitzgerald (Milford 1970).[1] Zelda was diagnosed as mentally ill and confined for many years in various institutions. But her letters seemed coherent and insightful, rather than what we thought of as crazy (confused, deluded) ravings. The fact that a supposedly hopeless schizophrenic was writing clear, if angry letters, let alone a novel, was very unsettling to us.

As I was puzzling over Zelda's life, I was reading *The Four-Gated City* by Doris Lessing (1969). Lynda Coldridge, one of the central characters, went insane shortly after her marriage and was hospitalized. Later, she lived in the same house with her husband, but insisted she was too "ill" to be touched by him. Whenever her husband suggested that Lynda should become his wife again, her response was another "psychotic" episode, and back to the hospital.

When I counted up female characters (created by women authors) and women authors or artists who went insane and/or attempted suicide, besides the two mentioned above, my list included Sylvia Plath (insanity, suicide); Virginia Woolf (insanity, suicide); *The Snake Pit* (Ward 1946; insanity); *I Never Promised You a Rose Garden* (Green 1964; insanity); Jill Johnston (insanity); Edna Pontellier in *The Awakening* (Chopin 1972 [1899]; suicide); Marilyn Monroe, Janis Joplin, Diane Arbus (the photographer) (all suicide); Yvonne Rainer (the choreographer and dancer) and Dorothy Parker (suicide attempts).

There were also some exceptions: Anaïs Nin (although she suffered from serious depressions), Gertrude Stein, whose case is suggestive and needs further thinking out, and Valerie Solanis. Some of my women students said that *The Scum Manifesto* (Solanis 1971) sounded crazy to them, but we all agreed it was coherent. It is this kind of craziness that I want to talk about: craziness that sounds lucid. *The Scum Manifesto* is like a flaming descendent of Zelda's letters to Scott, so I'm back where I started.

I found a suggestive interpretation of insanity in *Sanity, Madness and the Family* by Laing and Esterson (1970). The book opens with the same question I had been asking: "Are the experience and behavior that psychiatrists take as symptoms and signs of schizophrenia more socially intelligible than has come to be supposed?" (13). The authors explore the problem by interviewing eleven schizophrenic hospitalized women with their families. Simply, the authors concluded that much of so-called schizophrenic behavior is a predictable and purposeful response to certain techniques of mental torture. The families keep saying over and over to the interviewers: "I don't know what happened to her. She used to be, before her illness, happy, cheerful, no trouble to anyone, obeyed all our commands" and so on. This is normality. To be ill is to be miserable, unhappy, quarrelsome, disobedient, have sexual fantasies, to blame, reproach, want to get away from family-husband, try to kill herself, and so on.

Laing and Esterson suggest that the schizophrenic women are most crushed when considered most normal by their families, and most alive when considered most "crazy." Caught in an intolerable, frozen normality, these women resorted to behavior that was then labeled insane, basically an attempt to leave the scene of the action, the "real" world, and retreat to an interior monologue. By the time I finished the book my head was spinning, not with the supposed insanity of the women, but with the insanity of their families, any family, *my* family.

Perhaps the women artists are symbolizing, and living out, the general condition of women, except that the artists tend to be crazy-suicidal rather than crushed-normal for two reasons. The first has to do with the occupational hazards of writing and creating. To write authentically, a person has to look inside herself, set up an interior monologue similar to that of the schizophrenic women. Perhaps what they find is their ground-up rage and confusion. Second, becoming an artist, becoming recognized, separates women from the "normal" world of other women. When you read the lives of women artists, you see a variety of ways, some more successful than others, in which these women tried to adapt to their special status. (For instance, Gertrude Stein wrote in her early novel, *Q.E.D.* [1971], "Thank god I was not born a woman.")

I don't want to be what parents, men, the "real" world say I am or should be. But I don't want to be "crazy" or kill myself, either. This means accepting all my past selves: the me who tried and failed to be "normal," the me who went "crazy" and came back. We women want to define ourselves, and change the "real" world to our world. The craziness in my own past is not so painful to me as it was, and writing about it may speak to the experience of other women.

For two months before and after my sixteenth birthday, I kept a journal. When the journal began, I was functioning "normally" in the "real" world:

I was dating boys, eating dinner with my family, going to school, getting good grades, and doing my homework. In the journal I recorded my inner thoughts and daily concerns. My secrets included increasing signs of "madness": outbursts of rage, staying more and more in my room, self-hatred, self-mutilation, and confusion. In the last entries I was no longer able to keep my "madness" secret.

I grew up in New York City during the 1940s. My environment was upper middle class, Jewish, and liberal to radical. I was sent to a small progressive school that pushed the latest techniques in education, among them a less rigid notion of sex-role stereotyping than was then common.

When I was twelve, my mother, for reasons of her own, took me out to Palo Alto, an upper-middle-class suburb of San Francisco, where we both lived with her mother.[2] By the time I was sixteen, I had suffered through four years of public schooling and had arrived in the junior year of Palo Alto High School. "Paly" seemed to me like a concentration camp, yet I had internalized most of its values and blamed myself mercilessly for my inability to "really" fit in. My mother, too involved in her own troubles and fearful that I would move back East with my father, did not encourage my feeble efforts at rebellion. My girl friends, never having known anything different, were more effectively resigned, that is, more "normal" than I.

My high school offered basic training in oppression: child oppression (all teachers were superior to all students), sex oppression (all males were better than all females), popularity oppression (a student caste system modeled after but different from the class oppression in the adult world), and race oppression (blacks and Mexicans were simply not social persons).

Child oppression: The school was compulsory, regimented, competitive, and effective. Children were at the mercy of teachers, whose rule, however, was disguised as benign, "in our interests," and so on. Student government was a puppet popularity poll with no power; this may have been just as well, considering the values of the students. And of course all children (but girls more than boys) were controlled by their parents, on whom they were financially and emotionally dependent.

Sex oppression: As far as the school was concerned, boys and girls were technically equal. However, sex-role differences were strictly enforced in toilets, dress regulations, athletics, shop versus cooking, and so on. From the student viewpoint, boys and girls lived in two completely separate worlds. Male domination was unquestioned. Inter- and intrasex behavior were endlessly discussed and rigidly controlled down to the smallest and most personal detail. Heterosexuality was the only acceptable sex (although some boys, I now suspect, exploited others homosexually). From the girls' perspective, boys inhabited a mysterious, glamorous, free, and of course superior world. To gain access to this world, via a boyfriend, was *the* goal of existence. Not to have a boyfriend was the worst possible fate.

Popularity oppression: The caste system was an outgrowth of male domination, for it was based on a hierarchy among boys; a girl was ranked according to which caste of boy she dated. Beyond the pale were those girls who were said to fuck "anybody." Fucking even a popular boy made a girl lose her reputation. Most girls who were said to fuck, whom we discussed in giggly whispers, were working-class or Mexican girls.

The upper caste of most popular boys consisted of the good athletes, who were also "handsome" and "good dressers." The middle caste was made up of the majority of boys who weren't popular but who didn't stick out either. The lower caste were called the "queers": these boys were physically handicapped, grossly "emotionally disturbed," the overly studious, the antisocial and obvious sex-role deviants. The black and Mexican boys were not categorized at all.

The girls' hierarchy was exactly parallel, except that membership in the popular caste was not based on any form of achievement, but on dating the popular boys. This depended on clothes, looks, and a mysterious something called "personality." A girl's "reputation" was her assessed value in the caste hierarchy.

When I say caste, I mean just that. There was no *open* dating or socializing between the castes, and it was extremely difficult to change your caste position. The lower castes were required to avoid and defer to the upper ones. The system was enforced by a sadistic system of social control, involving restriction of information, the power, through student government and influence, to define who was who and what was what, ridicule, gossip, and occasionally physical force.

The dating system embodied the miserable status of the female students. To begin with, boys did not need to date; they could maintain respect and even be popular without dating at all. Dating for girls was mandatory; a girl had no social personality if she did not date, she was simply a social reject. So most girls were obsessed with dating and crushes, that is, were "boy crazy." But girls could take no initiative in getting dates. They strove to be "attractive" to boys, but the boy had to make the first move. Girls were not supposed to phone boys or ask boys for dates. Even the power to refuse boys who asked them was limited by the need to date anyone. Once on a date, girls were supposed to "keep a boy interested," that is, to be sexually available, but not to "go too far." A girl who did this got a bad reputation. On the other hand, a girl who would not "put out" at all, who was "frigid," also got a bad reputation.

"Normal" behavior for me meant being who the school wanted me to be:

bright, obedient female student; who the other students thought I was: a big, awkward, badly dressed, too studious girl hanging desperately onto the tag end of the middle caste. And who my mother and grandmother thought I should be but wasn't: a bright, charming, helpful, cooperative daughter and granddaughter. My family, like most, had many of the elements that are supposed to produce the "normal"/ "crazy" woman. Mine, however, was also culturally deviant, because I lived with my mother and grandmother and there were never any men in the house. My father, long divorced from my mother, lived far away in New York. I was entangled in a power struggle between them and terribly mystified as to what was going on and where my loyalties should lie.

Who did I think I was, in the middle of all this? I didn't know. I kept referring to my other life in the East, where I returned each summer and where I was more respected. I was almost – but not totally – overwhelmed by the negative judgments that were imposed on me. The only sources of support were good grades, occasional comfort from one or two girl friends, and extensive help from one woman teacher. In short, like the families of the schizophrenic women, the "real" world insisted that *I* was the bad one, *they* were all fine.

The journal, although the only ear I trusted completely, showed my secrets to be full of mystifications, obsessions, confusions, and fantasies, as well as many authentic insights about which I wasn't any too confident.

School, where I got good grades, was even so a source of confusion:

> I didn't do one lick of homework this weekend, and it was a great mistake, I'll really be sorry. What's the matter with me?? Have I no will power? I wish I could quit school. It seems so unrealistic, so far from life.

The journal is mainly concerned with boys, the power struggle with my mother, and girl friends. My fantasies about boys were obsessive. I listed over and over again my various crushes on boys I hardly knew, against a background of my current crush on another boy I hardly knew:

> I knew it. It turned out that John was at Performers on Friday. He played a big old solo. I probably could have had him all evening. Of course he won't show up again for months. And I was at Miss White's! Oh well, It's probably just as well. There is no doubt that I am attracted to him, and there's no sense fanning the flames that can only lead to hopelessness. Poor John, he doesn't realize what a little love could do for him. I guess it's not my problem. I wish it was.[3]

In between this kind of thing are wistful references to relationships with boys in the East, some of which seemed more "real" to me. As to the boys I actually dated, I was sadly analytic, but had no answers to the questions raised by my experience. Notice how many "guesses" I had to make:

> In the middle of the 8th grade I met Paul at [dancing school]. From the moment I met him I was out to get him. I liked him at first I guess. But I guess for my ego I was just determined to get him. And I certainly did. For a year we went together, and for the last two months of it we went steady. I knew I didn't like him when I accepted his offer to go steady. I mean I liked him but not sexually. He bored me, for my mind outstripped his by about fifty miles. He was smart, but I was smarter. Furthermore, my personality was much stronger and more forceful. I gave in to him a lot to try to hide this, but it really was pathetically obvious.
>
> Also, he never kissed me. We held hands and danced close, but he never kissed me. I guess he would have gotten around to it eventually, but he was scared I guess. And I don't think the match was too popular with his friends. He was really pretty cute, and I guess everyone wondered why he was going with me. The only reason that I went steady with him was that I wanted to find out what it was like to go steady, and there was so much security in it. Also going with him brought my reputation up a lot.

And again:

> I have just spent a more or less enjoyable evening with Ed. Ed really is a nice boy . . . but for some reason I don't go for Ed in a romantic way. I feel sorry for him, because he really likes me.
>
> I wonder if he dreams about me the way I dream about boys I like? It is a rather frightening thought. With Ed, everything is so false. That's the way it has been with almost all the boys I have ever known. There have been damned few exceptions. . . . I never really fell for Paul, and he was one of the first on my list of lies. Poor boy, I fooled him so shamefully. I am such a sham, and why they don't realize it I'll never know. . . . Bob was and still is the best example of sham. Now I am beginning to think that he was fooling me as much as I was fooling him. Isn't it ridiculous. But he wanted something, sex. That isn't what I wanted, but it's what I wound up with.

I had moments of painful clarity about the popularity caste system, and how angry I was about it. But I had largely accepted its negative view of me. Nor did I question male superiority, confining myself, consciously, to envy of the popular *girls*.

Palo Alto misfit, about 1954.

Fighting with my mother reached a peak. I was striving for a degree of autonomy that threatened her need to keep me with her. At the same time, I felt terribly guilty and confused about our fights. The events in the drama were complicated. Mothers, it seems, have more power to make us "normal"/"crazy" than any other person. I think I see better now what the "real" world had done to her. I can afford this luxury because she no longer has the power (or burden) of being responsible for my life. One fight may give some of the flavor, if not the substance. One of the issues was the use of her car. In California it is impossible to get anywhere without a car, but bicycles were socially taboo:

> Last night the car only set it off. The spark was: I said rather cuttingly that there was nothing to do around here but brood. At this point my mother started fooling around with her wispy hair, and looking very smug. "You are much too given to brooding," says she in her most superior. I cannot really explain why this made me so furious.

I could not have managed without my girl friends, but some of my friendships were not so friendly:

This deal with Anne is really beginning to reach the ridiculous stage. And I am beginning to hate myself more than Anne or anyone else. I am acting like a first class hypocrite. And I can't really figure her out. I don't know how much she likes me, or if she does at all, or if she is completely out for herself. One thing is sure, she hurts often, and with an apparently clear conscience. She makes an ass out of me with John. I think the only real solution is to try to keep away from both of them.

But:

Actually it's a good thing for me that she is there, because she is the only one I can go around with during lunch. Of course she's in the same predicament, but she can always cup it up to ["brown-nose"] someone. And I hate myself for cutting her so much to Cassandra while still being friendly with her. I am doing just what I hate and complain of in others. I wish I could get out of this mess. But I don't quite know how.

At the same time, I sometimes felt attracted to my girl friends, which scared me to my roots. This subject was absolutely taboo, so whatever I felt was *my fault*. There was no way to find out what others felt. After a fight with Anne, mentioned above, I wrote:

Either she adores me, or she needs a friend or she admires me. I suspect it's a little of all three. I don't think she will stay mad. If I were a boy she would go ape over me. I have just come to an important point. She knows, and I know, that something is sort of odd about our relationship. I wonder sometimes if I am a homosexual. If I am, then why do I get crushes on boys?

Later on, a crush on an older girl was rationalized away:

I have figured out my "thing" about Judy. I don't really think of her as a person, but as an impersonal symbol of the kind of intellectual, intelligent person I wish I were. She is just a symbol to me, and I don't think of her in terms of reality, but in terms of an idea or ideal. I feel better now that I have it straightened out in my mind.

The shadow fell in secret, on November 29, 1956, the day after my sixteenth birthday, a month after I began the journal:

After school I went to the dentist and got lots of Novocain. When I came home my jaw was completely out. I decided to take a razor blade and find out how much I couldn't feel. . . . I gashed myself quite deliberately in the chin. In fact, I carved it quite carefully. I passed it off pretty well as an accident with my mother and others. And I satisfied all my desires . . . after dinner my mother and I went to see *The Desk Set* which was very good.

During the Christmas vacation, the power struggle between my mother and me climaxed. I wanted to fly back East to visit my New York friends and my father, a distant and forbidding figure who nonetheless financed my summer and holiday trips out of Palo Alto. My mother, for reasons she would not discuss, tried to prevent me from going, perhaps she sensed that in spinning out of control I would pull away from her orbit. In the end, my father sent me the money and I went against my mother's wishes, having what I thought was a wonderful time with both male and female friends. When I got back, I found I could no longer live in the "real" world of Paly High. I wrote that "everything hurts," that there was nothing real in me but a "small shrine at the center, very small and very strong."

> Tonight I sat down on the couch and as I sat back I accidentally leaned against the dog. I turned around to say "excuse me" and out of a clear blue sky she bit me on the nose (that was what was sticking out I guess). I grabbed her neck and started to shake her. Suddenly I let go as tears came to my eyes. I don't know why. She didn't hurt me much. All of a sudden I felt terrible. I staggered upstairs and fell on the floor crying and sobbing. I guess the dam just broke or something. I cry pretty often alone, but I die when I cry in front of people. I even feel guilty crying alone. I keep wanting to drive my fist through a window. I have a very strong wish to do it. Partly for attention and partly to hurt myself. I wish I wasn't so God damn alone and confused and crazy.

That night I dreamed a long and terrible dream, of chasing and being chased, and in the dream I had a beard. For a moment when I woke up, I wasn't sure whether I was a boy or a girl. In the last paragraph of the journal, I reflected on an appointment with the hairdresser the next day:

> My hair gives me a sense of camouflage and protection. I am torn between a desire to have it cut short, and a desire to keep up pretenses as much as possible. I don't know how I'll have it cut. I am feeling so defiant, I feel like having it all cut off as short as possible, just to show that I don't give a damn. There's more to say, but to hell with it.

In the next few days I began to break windows in the house, threaten my mother, drink to unconsciousness, fly into uncontrollable rages and tears, and more. My mother threatened to commit me to a local hospital. If she had, perhaps I would have wound up like the schizophrenic women in *Sanity, Madness and the Family*. Luckily, through the intervention of a sympathetic woman teacher, I was sent to an analyst instead. With the help of the analyst and the teacher, I was able somehow to get through the rest of the school year, although there were frequent outbursts of my "sickness."

At the end of the year, I went back East and never lived in California again. My father sent me to a boarding school, where the "real" world was less destructive. Things were better for me then, but there is no happy ending. There will never be peace between me and the "real" world until the "real" world makes more space for me and for all other women.

Marginal Woman/

Marginal Academic

1973

Since the age of three, I have spent—wasted?—my life in schools. Although both my parents are intellectuals of sorts, neither is an academic. But I was good at school and soon realized that it was one of the few places where I could compete with boys on what seemed an equal basis. My father, an ex–labor organizer and former communist, had advanced theories on women and was willing and able to pay for my education indefinitely, so in spite of a certain incoherent anger and a lot of boredom, I just kept climbing up the academic ladder.

In the fall of 1962, after four undergraduate years at the University of Michigan, I entered graduate school in anthropology at the University of Chicago. Instead of the hothouse dormitory life where all my physical needs were met, I lived alone for the first time, learning to cook, go to the laundromat, and deal with the telephone company, though I was almost too broke to have a phone. My father sent me a hundred dollars a month, and apart from that, my fellowship was under three thousand dollars a year. Even this small sum could be withdrawn by the department at any time. I had no sense that I was earning the money, but rather it was mine if the gods smiled on me, if I played my cards right . . . and always in fierce competition with my peers. Graduate school teaches future academics to be insecurely grateful for favors.

Little groups of us students huddled together for survival and comfort. Night after night we met for dinner to exchange the latest departmental gossip, to play chess, checkers, Monopoly, poker, and, rarely, to discuss our work. We were the lost astronauts, POWs, but who were our jailers? Our feelings of isolation were overwhelming. How we made friendships in such a competitive, barren atmosphere I am not sure, because we learned, if necessary the hard way, that our goal in life was to advance ourselves as rapidly and single-mindedly as possible. Cooperation among students, or even among faculty, was almost accidental. If there was any sense of social responsibility, it was to the profession of anthropology, though at Chicago perhaps the "higher" goals

"The Albanian Conspirators," graduate school friends, 1966; (l. to r.) Bobby Paul, Ben Apfelbaum, and Sherry Ortner. Photo by Esther Newton

More "Albanian Conspirators" at the University of Chicago, (l. to r.) Ben Apfelbaum, Harriet Whitehead, and the author. Photo by Sherry Ortner were stressed more than elsewhere: the defense of the academy against hostile higher-ups above and the anti-intellectual "slobs" below; the advancement of anthropology as a discipline and the maintenance of its high standards; and the well-being of its representatives on earth, the professional anthropologists. We learned to project our future along a set course from graduate school (the more elite the better) to first job, to tenure, invitations to learned conventions, numbers of papers given, publications (not to be too popular with the general public), graduate students trained, books dedicated to us, a stack of reprints, and, most optimistically, a distinguished professorship at Chicago, Harvard, or Yale, with minimal teaching duties.

Of all that I learned during the long and complex process that was graduate school, what was really of value, and what am I trying to unlearn and undo?

On the positive side, I learned an intellectual skill, discipline, and perspective that is still personally and socially useful. I learned how to describe and compare cultures, shared systems of understanding, and something, at least theoretically, about how people work. I learned the ropes of my profession, the ways to get along, the contacts that would enable me, even as a woman, to support myself outside the family doing relatively high-prestige work. I got the confidence to avoid what would have been, for me, a disastrous marriage. I also learned how to survive in a man's world, and this brings me to the darker side of my accounting.

To say that my higher education was male-dominated is not a figure of speech. Since high school I had had no woman teacher. The rewards, values, punishments, all were coming from men, and one had to know how to please them. One way was to be traditionally feminine, but logically this meant giving up one's career and losing men's respect, becoming a sex object or a wife. The other way was to become as "manly" as possible. We women worked out combinations of these tactics that let some of us survive, just barely. To the extent that we could make ourselves into men, we were accorded "special woman" status. But this left us in the limbo of being better than and separate from other women, yet never truly accepted by men as peers. The academic woman was, and is, a marginal woman and a marginal academic.

One of the hardest lessons for me was to separate my personal life from my professional life. By this I mean that the links between one's experience and one's research were not openly discussed, and that details of one's biography or feelings were never supposed to enter into a professional context. (As a result, they became gossip.) The ideal was to present a bland, controlled, impersonal, invulnerable exterior. Ideas seemingly floated in the air, disembodied.

Distrust was everywhere. Anything personal could be used against you.

Our values were individualism, competition, "commitment" to the profession, and elitism. By elitism I mean we anthropology students thought there were absolute standards of thought and conduct and that our job was to learn these and then enforce them in others. These standards were supposed to be difficult, almost impossible for ordinary people to attain or even to understand. We were proud to be in the elite, yet I did not think in political terms. I was an expert, or tried to act like one. I knew something about the politics of individual advancement within a prescribed system of rules and hierarchies, nothing about collective political action.

I'm not saying that we graduate students were worse than other people. We adapted ourselves to a system for which college had prepared us and over which we seemed to have no control. We learned how to do what worked. And we learned much that was really useful, embedded in a destructive and conservative context.

I also learned how to rebel, to preserve some autonomy and integrity, some private vision, without being ejected by the system. This was a fine art that, in all honesty, I still practice. I had, and continue to have, many close and hurtful scrapes, at times major, lasting wounds, pushing too close to rebellion. Since high school I had cultivated what was called a "bad attitude" and survived with the counterbalance of good grades. My master's research, on black ghetto women, was acceptable because it was framed within a traditional anthropological problem (why poor black people in the Caribbean and United States had a "deviant" family form called "matriarchal"), but my doctoral research, on homosexual female impersonators (recently published as a book called *Mother Camp*), got me in more trouble. To most of my teachers at the University of Chicago, this was not a legitimate area of anthropological study. I won an important victory over their resistance with the indispensable help of several more progressive male faculty.[1]

My first job, at Queens College of the City of New York, made it painfully clear to me why academics want to get jobs in elite institutions. I was confronted with anonymous masses of students who, for the most part, cared nothing for books, much less lofty standards of intellectual pursuit. I had never learned to teach. Most professors at Chicago had no idea how to teach; they just read things at us or rambled on. There had been no teaching assistantships, so at Queens College I learned how to teach by trying to interest aspiring young accountants who were snoozing off last night's frat party in the back rows of an auditorium.

This was the grubby "real world" they had warned us about at Chicago. We teachers were there to keep the institution running and to process students through it so they would be hirable. Our mission was to distinguish among the A students who might go on to graduate school and become like us, the B and C students who were destined for mediocre jobs in business and city bureaucracies, and the failures. We were administrators of the class society, supposed to give out just so many AS, so many BS, not too many FS, just enough to show we were tough. This is called the bell curve, and grades were supposed to fall on it naturally. If they didn't, we had to make it come out that way. After all, there were just so many places in graduate and professional schools. Anyone who tried to give too many AS (or too many FS) might pay for it, in the end, with his or her job. On the side, we were supposed to advance our careers and build the prestige of our department in the profession by publishing research.

Even during my first year at Queens (1968–1969) I was upset enough to begin experimenting on the side with some other disgruntled academics in a small scheme of alternative education. Some of these people had political experience in the civil rights and student movements of the sixties, and I began to question traditional education, careerism, and capitalism.

In this uneasy frame of mind, the two student revolts that disrupted the campus in the spring of 1969 turned me around completely. There were two separate movements: one of black students in the SEEK program (an educational opportunity program designed to help disadvantaged students) and one of white students in SDS (Students for a Democratic Society) with an allied group of young, radical faculty. Stunned by the arrogant, racist, violent, yet weirdly lifeless response of the senior faculty and administration (some of whom likened the protesting students to Hitler Youth), I felt the bottom drop out of the academic world for me. Was this what I was knocking myself out to become?

The energy, creativeness, and idealism of the students in the revolt, in contrast to the zombies they became in the classroom, impressed me as no theory could have. At the same time, I saw that the university, which had always seemed as fixed as breakfast, lunch, and dinner, could be stopped, shut down. The black students won important gains for the SEEK program, but the white students and faculty failed to effect a single change in the college. This convinced me that the college as a whole could not be changed in any radical way. I now try to get as much out of the university as I can for myself, my students, and the women's movement.

The student revolts of 1969 taught me one other lesson that changed my life: that as a woman I had no more prestige or power in the radical left than I had as a dutiful academic. And so, in the summer of 1969, I joined a women's group, made up mostly of young, white, college-educated dropouts from the radical left. I was the only professional, and the oldest member. The group

lasted for two years, and I learned as much there as I had in six years of graduate school. Every week we thrashed out issues of sexuality, elitism, competi-
tiveness, class, racism, socialism, political tactics, and personal growth. For
the first time in my life I was proud to be a woman, and my total commitment
to the women's movement came out of my love for the group.[2]

On the other hand, I was attacked in my group as a "heavy" because I was
an academic and had a Ph.D., and this confused me. What was to be gained
by quitting my job and driving a taxi or going on welfare? The women in my
group, who were bitter about their college experience, felt, rightly, that I was
helping to perpetuate a system that had hurt them. Yet I couldn't see any
alternatives.

In the middle of this confused period, in the fall of 1970, one of the worst
things that can happen to an academic happened to me: I came up for tenure
(I was only two years past my Ph.D.) and didn't get it.[3] In the prior months,
I had become known in the department as a militant feminist. At that time
there was no organized women's movement at Queens. I had no allies, and
the other faculty made my life miserable. The price I paid for abandoning the
survival tactics I had learned in graduate school was a heavy one, one that
feminists in academia are still paying and will continue to pay. Here are some
excerpts from the letter I wrote to the tenure committee when they asked me
to explain why I should get tenure:

> For those of you who are trying to say you don't know where I stand,
> here it is:
>
> It has been said that the department cannot be sure of me, that it is
> not clear what direction I'm going in. I should make a clear statement of
> my next research project. I can't do that. That's the position. Itself. Any-
> one who knows what direction he or she will take over the next five years
> is in trouble. Not knowing should be a requirement for all academics at
> this time. There are two areas in which academics should not know their
> direction.
>
> Research: Anthropologists should be confused about the relationship
> of traditional concerns to fruitful directions for future anthropology. We
> should be questioning what it means to be a "professional."
>
> Teaching: If we are honest with ourselves, we have to say that we
> don't know how to successfully teach about 97% of our students. The
> lack of intellectual or other kind of curiosity which students consistently
> present in spite of my best efforts has been a source of serious frustra-
> tion and concern to me. This has led me to question the entire structure
> of the teaching situation. . . .

. . . We have applied anthropological thought to the whole world except ourselves. . . . We can't get away with it any more. Everyone who isn't totally committed to the status quo is having to question his or her involvement, both personal and collective, in our present state of affairs.

We shouldn't wait until we can precisely legitimate all the reasons why it's bad for our work and ourselves and our students to be like capitalists and politicians. We should follow our instincts, our heads or whatever we can toward the roots of the matter. That will be somewhere in our categories of work and play, of subordinates and authorities; where we draw lines and how we get ahead.

My statement was not an effective political move, and it was not overtly feminist (I noted in my journal that I was too frightened to criticize their chauvinism). But it represented my growing feminist political consciousness and my disillusionment with the anthropological profession and the university. And, on a gut level, it was a statement of rage about having to sit up and beg one more time, to jump through the hoop to prove I was a good loyal girl. There's no resting place on the academic ladder.

The department's answer to my impassioned criticisms reached me formally about a month later, via this letter from the president of the college: "I regret to inform you that the Committee on Personnel has not recommended your re-appointment with tenure as of September 1, 1971. Your current Appointment, therefore, is terminal."[4]

This was a rude jolt. My belligerent appeal to my fellow professionals was rejected, and I was out of a job. My emotional ties with anthropology were all but severed, yet I didn't have a new identity or an alternative way to make a middle-class salary. All during that year I looked for a job, and found just one. The State University of New York at Purchase stresses interdisciplinary studies and has a less repressive, pass/fail grading system. Working with other professional women, I began to reorient my work and teaching toward the women's movement rather than toward anthropology and getting ahead. I don't mean that I've given up on getting ahead, even within the academic world. A certain amount of getting ahead is good for the soul, and anyhow, if you don't get ahead, you don't keep your job. In general, as long as universities are paying us and, to a large extent therefore controlling us, women academics will never be among the most extreme, daring, or visionary leaders or spokeswomen of the women's movement.

A great number of academic women have tried to resolve the kinds of conflicts I'm talking about by banding together in collectives and consciousness-raising groups. These groups try to build trust and friendship among academic women and sometimes become a fertile environment for thinking out women-oriented research and teaching. With such goals in mind, a small group of women anthropologists formed what came to be known as the Ruth Benedict Collective in New York City.[5] From the beginning we have had great difficulty trusting each other because of our competitive backgrounds and because, although some of us want to rise to the top of our profession and get all the power and recognition that women have been denied, others feel that careerism in anthropology cannot go along with a true commitment to the liberation of women.

Nevertheless, the Ruth Benedict Collective was an important step for us. We attempted, through a mixture of consciousness raising, discussion of intellectual problems, sponsorship of women's symposia at the national convention, and a national newsletter, to sort out our heads about being women anthropologists and to support each other as professionals. We tried to help each other get jobs and to be in touch with women graduate students who needed jobs. I believe that every member of the collective has written at least one paper on women, and many of us have gotten involved in teaching women's courses.

[After summarizing the then-current state of feminist anthropology, I continued presciently:] Anthropology as a discipline can teach us something else. Culture, that system of language, symbols, shared understandings, and traditions that is learned from one generation to the next, divides one group from another. The tie to one's group and one's culture is one of the deepest that a human being knows. Although it would benefit women to unite worldwide, it's not going to happen soon, as communists found out about workers. Women are divided from each other by men, by class, and by culture.

A corollary is the difficulty we feel in disentangling ourselves from our own cultural system and traditional ways of doing things, even though that tradition devalues and harms us. In our culture, a few white men get most of the rewards, and we have been brought up to believe in a system of ideas and values that legitimizes and even glorifies the domination of women by men, and of the many by the few. What can we do about this in an academic situation?

There are basic contradictions facing academic feminists: the university is a part of the system and values that we should be trying to change and replace; the majority of college women are white, middle class, and heterosexual; the students are always under the pressure of grades; and the faculty and staff are afraid of losing their jobs and are pulled by obligations to the school and to their professions. With those limitations in mind, there are still three domains where we can effect feminist change: personal freedom, campus feminist organizations, and alternatives to the university.

My ideology had been reshaped in the furnace of my first women's group, Upper West Side WITCH. I no longer believe in male domination or capitalism or imperialism or racism. As a faculty member, I think of myself as a woman rather than as some weird kind of man, and as a worker rather than as a member of an exclusive elite. At the same time I have tried to regain control of my own ego. After I was fired, two and a half years ago, I began to work with my friend, Shirley Walton Fischler, on a book made up of our parallel journals. I never believed that it would get me any credit in the academic world; rather, I have used it as a place to untangle my writing style and my thoughts from the academic lockstep. One of my first entries reads, "I'm tired of precision and professionalism. I'm tired of being an uptight, objective, write-up-your-grant-proposal-with-3/4" margins-type person (woman?), so I'm going to goof off."

Our book turned into a serious project, but an artistic project, not an academic one. I need time to make art and even time to goof off in order to feel good about myself, for myself. And almost all of my friends, people I see off campus, are women.

On campus, I have reoriented my work and teaching as much as I could toward the needs of women. We feminists have an organized group on campus with an office and a little money, and are trying to get good health care for women, day care, to offer more women's courses and a women's studies curriculum, to support women faculty and the hiring of more women faculty.

But we are troubled by issues of power. How can we get things done without duplicating the destructive divisions and hierarchies of the university? Should we go for power within the university, or stay aloof? One of us wants to get a woman dean hired. Others feel that a woman dean might wind up controlling us instead of promoting our agenda. Some of us feel an aversion to going after or exercising open power ourselves, and others find that aversion a copout. I find these issues confusing.

Because of the contradictions inherent in the university, there is a pressing need for independent feminist schools. They shouldn't be four-year colleges offering B.A.s because accredited schools have to submit to too much state control. So women should use accredited higher education, but have the option of teaching and learning in a feminist school at night, for one course, or in the summer. I know many women who would be interested in such schools if only they could support themselves while teaching or learning there. A group of women artists I work with have been thinking about making a start on this on land we use collectively in Massachusetts, and certainly there should be urban schools, too.[6]

Finally, as painful and confusing as these past four years have been, they've been a hell of a lot better than those depressing years in graduate school. But if you go to graduate school knowing that you are there to make it as a woman and for other women, even graduate school will be bearable. It is worth committing your life to the struggle to free women all over the world and to work for women's power.

The Personal Is Political:

Consciousness Raising and Personal Change

in the Women's Liberation Movement

with Shirley Walton, 1971

PROLOGUE 1971

We are able to write this essay because of the Women's Movement. We have been close friends for thirteen years, since the beginning of college, yet never before thought of working together. We saw ourselves through traditional grids, separated by our professions and our other relationships. But the movement enabled us to generate this new and productive dimension to our friendship, using our skills in writing and anthropology.

Yet this essay departs from much of traditional anthropology: we are both committed to the ideological system we are writing about, and one of us is not an anthropologist by training. Our own transformations convinced us that committed feminists had experienced something equivalent to religious conversion. Although we look here at the process and outcome of conversion without relation to the truth or falsehood of the assertions that are the content of the conversions, we do in fact believe in the truth of feminist ideology and don't accept the academic proposition that by definition, ideology is false and science true. In other words, we are not detached and "objective"; we are "natives" studying ourselves.

Of course, we see that many people, both women and men, have converted to movements with quite different ideological content but with conviction equal to our own. How can all these ideologies be true? We had to ask ourselves if content were irrelevant, if only the process counted. Based on our own experience, we answer that content *is* crucial, that ideologies and religions are successful because they contain important truths about the lives of *their* potential converts. Religions and ideologies always spring from and explain particular historical situations.

We are not simply propagandists for the Women's Movement. Our commitment makes us more, not less, interested in the truth. Were our analysis of consciousness-raising groups wrong, it would not help the movement; we hope this essay can be of some use to other women. Theory is important to us because it is a model of and for action. We now see anthropology as a body of accumulated skills and knowledge to be used by us, rather than as an institution to which we are committed.

The Women's Liberation Movement surfaced publicly when a small group of women picketed the Miss America Pageant in Atlantic City in August 1968. Most early members were either discontented professional women involved in the more reformist National Organization for Women or disenchanted female members of the New Left. The movement quickly grew to become a potentially powerful agent of social and political change. Broadly, the movement demanded full equality for women, but the more radical sections of the movement were also concerned with profound social and psychological change, involving the development of a women's culture, the possible destruction of the nuclear family, and ultimately the end of ascribed sex roles. The movement centered largely in urban areas and university campuses, and was overwhelmingly young and white, although feminists looked to alliances with such groups as the Welfare Rights Organization and the Young Lord Party, a radical group of New York Puerto Ricans.

This is a study of seventeen women who were in consciousness-raising groups and became committed feminists, and of the groups themselves. It is based on lengthy interviews with each of the women, structured to determine how consciousness raising affected their lives.[1]

In trying to describe the social organization of the Women's Movement, we found a correspondence with the descriptive concepts in *People, Power and Change* (Gerlach and Hine 1970:33–63). Gerlach and Hine describe the Pentecostal, Black Power, and other movements in complex societies as "decentralized," "segmented," and "reticulate." Decentralization means primarily that a movement has no leader or leadership hierarchy. Although the Women's Movement had many prominent literary and political figures, both those who were primarily media "stars" and those who were known largely inside the movement as "political heavies," not one of them had any formal or informal power beyond the influence of the personal "charisma" they could exert.

Segmentation is the composition "of a great variety of localized groups or cells which are essentially independent, but which can combine to form larger configurations or divide to form smaller units" (Gerlach and Hine 1970:41). This is an apt description of the basic unit, or cell, of the Women's Liberation Movement, the consciousness-raising (c-r) group. These groups formed without any central decision making, they often united into large groups for major meetings, demonstrations, and conferences; and they sometimes divided to form new, smaller cells. Each cell determined its own style or method of c-r, although there were suggested modes of conduct offered by the original "model" groups, such as Redstockings or WITCH (Women's International Terrorist Conspiracy from Hell).

Finally, Gerlach and Hine employ Webster's definition of reticulation as "something . . . weblike resembling a network—with crossing and intercrossing lines," and further, "an organization in which the cells, or nodes, are tied together, not through any central point, but rather through intersecting sets of personal relationships and other intergroup linkages" (1970:55).

The network in the Women's Movement was one of close personal ties among members of individual groups and between groups, with continuous communication among the various movement "stars" and "heavies," as well as relationships between those "leaders" and the movement in general. Furthermore, the movement was characterized by "ritual activities" (Gerlach and Hine 1970:57–58), such as demonstrations, marches, and rallies.

Ideology and movement rhetoric further defined the cell structure, despite social and/or past political differences. A surprising number of publications arose within the movement, maintaining a degree of communication and unity among major regions of the country.

CONVERSION EXPERIENCE

Active in Women's Liberation ourselves, we observed many women in c-r groups profoundly changing themselves and their personal lives. The changes we saw and experienced were similar, we thought, to religious conversion experiences. To understand religious conversion, we looked primarily at *The Varieties of Religious Experience*, where William James defined it as "the process, gradual or sudden, by which a self hitherto divided, and consciously wrong, inferior and unhappy, becomes unified and consciously right, superior and happy, in consequence of its firmer hold upon religious realities. . . . What is attained is often an altogether new level of spiritual vitality, a relatively heroic level, in which impossible things have become possible, and new energies and endurances are shown. The personality is changed, the man *is* born anew" (1902:189, 241).

Despite the absence of religious references, women we interviewed described their c-r experiences in similar terms:[2]

> I feel my whole life has been changed. I think that there are two aspects to that which are related. One, for the first time in my life, I feel authen-

tic as a woman. Two, there's been a whole revamping of my entire life, in which I was able to see my problems in the context of being a woman and in commonality with other women. My whole concept of the world changed.

*   *   *

[My group] made me realize many things; it was a great, devastating group. All my assumptions were questioned. Particularly, [the group] made me realize that I could live without a man. It sounds absurd now, but it changed my whole world.

According to James, conversion mends a previously "divided and consciously wrong, inferior and unhappy self":

I don't know [exactly what has happened to me] but I know I'd never go back. I don't know what I am now, but what I was, was lousy. I don't know how I lived through it.

*   *   *

No . . . this feeling of a pervasive head and attitude change about where I stand as a person, a woman . . . wouldn't have happened [without c-r]. I would still be sitting in therapy . . . feeling that my pain was wrong, irrational, unjustified, evil, hopeless, and all my fault.

There are two concepts that parallel "conversion" but include *both* religious and sociopolitical personal change. These are "the commitment process" (Gerlach and Hine 1970:158) and Berger and Luckmann's (1967) concept of "alteration." Unlike James, both sets of authors deal with nonreligious movements and with the social contexts of conversion.

Alteration is a process of resocialization. The most important social condition for alteration is an effective plausibility structure, conveyed to the individual by means of "significant others" with whom a strong, affective identification is established and who serve as guides to the new reality. In simple terms, this means that the individual undergoing alteration must interact intensely with the new group of "significant others," ideally in a physically segregated situation, separate from her old life (Berger and Luckmann 1967:157–59).

The concepts of conversion, commitment process, and alteration refer broadly to the same phenomena resulting from a dialectic between an individual and a primary group. The synthesis is a new "consciousness" or reality structure, a changed identity, a new set of reference groups, and an altered system of personal interactions.[3]

Nonparticipants or observers of a new social or religious movement often describe converts as "misfits," people who "just can't make it."[4] Members of the Women's Liberation Movement were often described as women "who just can't get a man." These comments, however off-target, do imply a "discontent" or "maladjustment" theory of the rise of social movements, though most social scientists have looked to broader causes. Anthony F. C. Wallace (1961: 146–48) theorizes that social movements arise in response to "social distortions." Vittorio Lanternari, in his comprehensive study of nativistic religious movements, *Religions of the Oppressed* (1963), concludes that these movements in the Third World arise as a disguised political reaction to massive dislocations imposed by imperialism.

Other writers have focused on manifestations of "strain" and "dislocation" in the individual. Berger and Luckmann (1967) maintain that the precondition for alteration is a failure of socialization. When too many areas of individual experience are unsocialized, they are subjectively perceived as isolated, crazy, unexplained, and so on. Alteration functions to socialize the previously isolated areas of consciousness. According to James (1902), the preconvert is a "sick soul" who suffers from a profound "melancholy." In conversion, areas of consciousness that were formerly "cold" and "peripheral" (read: "isolated, unsocialized") come to the center of consciousness in a "new and energizing synthesis" (196).[5]

Both the social and the individual analyses of conversion experiences are relevant to the rebirth of feminism in the 1960s. The end of the farm economy with its extended families and productive roles for women, the emergence of the isolated urban nuclear family with the wife as a helpless dependent, the rise of education for women coupled with barriers to jobs and professions, the limitation of women's reproductivity by birth control, and many other factors point to cultural strain. The official ideology of this country, stressing equality and equal opportunity, conflicted with the subordinate status of women and other minorities. The delegitimation of official institutions brought about by the social and political upheavals of the 1960s left a vacuum that numerous political and religious movements attempted to fill. The ideology of the Women's Movement amounted, in its most radical form, to a profound challenge to the Establishment.

A number of our informants were active in the New Left prior to joining a c-r group, itself a measure of discontent with the status quo. Nearly all the informants volunteered that they had been aware of discontent with some aspect of their lives as women for a time previous to the movement:

My cousins could wear pants with pockets, and I had to wear dresses. Later they were allowed to go to movies alone, and I never was. I was very conscious of those things. . . . In 1964, -5 and -6, I used the word "sexist" when I taught at the ——— University. . . . I remember my sociology teachers told me it was not a meaningful word; now of course, it's accepted.

*   *   *

My oppression struck me at the birth of my child. At that time there was no feedback from society or other women. . . . I wasn't fulfilled. . . . I became depressed, let down and disappointed.

*   *   *

In college I became very aware of the ways I was being discriminated against because I was a woman . . . it became very obvious, and I got very angry.

*   *   *

[In the group] was the first time I was able to relate my problems to something other than just personal hang-ups. The vaginal orgasm thing, for one. Little inadequacies. I always knew from lesbianism that's not where orgasms take place, but I was affected by the myth. My analyst would ask me about orgasms and he never corrected me in my ideas about vaginal orgasms. Why isn't it publicized? There seemed to be a lot of heavy questions for me around maturity and identity. I'd been asking myself these things, and not getting any answers. So I decided I had to get into the movement.

Although discontent was a necessary condition for entering a c-r group, our data did not support the folk wisdom that women's liberationists were "misfits," failures, or ugly women who couldn't get a man. In spite of their discontent, before the movement, every woman was functioning adequately or even outstandingly in her job and daily life. All the women were attractive in conventional terms, some exceptionally so. Not one woman reported difficulty attracting men. All but one of the heterosexual women were living with a man at the time of joining the first c-r group, and even after c-r, only two of the heterosexual women were not living with men.

Certainly the fact that all but three of the women had been in psychotherapy at one time or another is evidence of role strain and some personal "maladjustment," but only four reported any serious or potentially debilitating disturbance, and two of these were in the remote past. Therapy was a common recourse for members of the upper middle class, male and female. Although discontent was a predisposing factor, or necessary condition, it was not the "sufficient" condition for joining the Women's Liberation Movement. The majority of informants offered the fact that they were finally moved to join a c-r group because of positive contact with a friend or colleague who described her experience in glowing terms. For instance:

> A colleague I met one day [where the informant worked] was going to the Jeannette Rankin Brigade and told me that they were forming a women's movement and it was the only thing she looked forward to. She said it was the only place in her life she felt respected. That's how I found out about Women's Liberation, 1968.

Another informant spent a year in Italy, where she found herself isolated by "Italian machismo":

> At that time I had a friend who joined Redstockings and she sent me all this literature [to Italy]. When I came back she invited me to a meeting. She was so militant that I was terrified to go. . . . I just knew it was necessary to do, because I had to find out about myself.

In some cases, the first contact did not immediately lead to the informant's joining a group, in fact, there was often a high degree of resistance. But several contacts with significant acquaintances over a period of time ultimately resulted in the decision to join:

> I met Ellen, a minor star in the movement. She lived with a guy who was a friend of mine. She was one of the founders of Redstockings and she began pressuring me to come to meetings. I agreed with the principle, but was very chary of doing anything with women only; I disliked women. . . . I promised Ellen I'd go to a lot of actions with her and then never went. Then I went to Europe that summer . . . [and] I kept hearing from friends about Women's Liberation and I decided that when I got back I'd join a group.

For different reasons, a lesbian informant was also resistant. When asked if she had known any feminists before becoming one, she said:

> Nobody I thought of as a feminist . . . this kept me away from the movement before. In fact, I thought lesbians weren't welcome, were put down. I felt bitter and frustrated about it. But when I realized that there were lesbians in the movement . . . it opened a path for me personally.

Next, the potential convert began to redefine her discontents in terms of movement ideology through initial contacts, feminist literature, feminist meetings, feminists in the media, and early meetings of the c-r group.

Many women recall media influence (several watched the first and/or second Miss America Pageant demonstrations in 1968 and 1969 on TV); a majority began to read feminist literature that contained a great deal of testimony to change; several heard "media stars" in the movement speak. Also, just prior to or just after joining a c-r group several informants began to attend mass women's meetings, with films and speeches. Several new groups also had women from older, founding c-r groups, such as Redstockings, or from the Women's Center, come to their initial meetings to focus their attention on the c-r process and the ideology of the movement.

Group members learned to reinterpret their personal experiences as manifestations of their oppression as women. Early topics of successful groups nearly always pertained to personal and intimate subjects: "marriage, children, jobs, sex, how we felt about life, how we were oppressed as women."

Women sometimes dropped out of or were ejected from groups when they were unable to identify with the ideological assertion that women are oppressed:

> Our first meeting was to get acquainted. Most of the women previously had been in other groups. They discussed what they wanted [from the group]. My sensibilities were compatible with those who had a raised consciousness. . . . The second meeting verified serious division within the group. The youngest woman was not keen on the movement—"I can't understand why you women feel oppressed." This provoked hostile response, arguments exchanged, she was lambasted . . . and finally left, making a hostile remark.

After the initial decision to join and the refocusing of the women's discontent as feminist issues, many women described a definite stage in the development of groups that one informant termed the "sisterhood period." This stage, lasting six months or more, was one of intense trust and intimacy among a now stabilized membership:

> We met at K.'s house for one whole year, really cozy—really important. Then at one point we decided to meet earlier and had dinner with each other each week. I think this was the year of sisterhood, a microcosm of what was happening all over the movement.

This "sisterhood period" could be likened to what William James describes, in religious terms, as the surrender to a higher power, the giving up of individual will,[6] which corresponded in our data to informants' descriptions of feeling solidarity with all other women, and an acceptance that "there are no personal solutions," during the sisterhood period. Only women acting collectively would be able to significantly change an individual woman's life situation:

> The loving stage. We were fascinated with each other. it was great for me; here all of the women were doing something with their lives . . . we seemed to be peers. I felt really good.
>
> We were a lot more into learning from each other's experiences— we felt tremendously released for some reason. All of a sudden politics meant something totally different to us.

Often this period of sisterhood coincided with a period of great energy release and/or activity on the part of a group:

> That period between the end of January and July of that year was really the high point of the group—enormously productive.
>
> *   *   *
>
> Lots of things happened then; this was the sisterhood period—we felt good toward each other and all women . . . we went away for a weekend together. R began making a movie with the whole group involved somehow. We were very politically active.

A woman who was in a c-r group dealing with weight issues told us:

> We fed each other pieces of raw vegetables to get into really trusting and testing it, with our eyes closed. . . . We've done portraits, self-portraits . . . we all drew ourselves nude and put them in the middle of the room without identifying them—getting in touch with our body images.

PERSONAL CHANGE IN THE LIVES OF INFORMANTS

Observers of movements, as well as converts themselves, describe profound personal change as one of the most impressive effects of the conversion process. Because of the way we structured our questions and because we did the interviews sometimes long after the sisterhood period, we do not have data describing the conversion process per se. What we have are the manifestations, the aftereffects of conversion experience, which fall into five general categories: altered worldview/cognitive reorientation, changed identity, lessening of guilt, changes in reference group and interpersonal situation (including family), and changes in job/career orientation.

Altered Worldview/Cognitive Reorientation

Informants stated that c-r had given them a heightened understanding of the world and their own experience; a sense of new clarity, a sense that through "consciousness" about themselves as women, the whole world looked different and less mysterious. In many instances this altered or enriched worldview was only vaguely expressed. Several women assured us, "I feel as though my whole life has changed," or simply, "The pieces all fit together differently." Even those women with grave doubts and confusion resulting from the c-r experience expressed those doubts in terms of cognitive reorientation, or altered worldview:

> One thing I never knew before was that change was so painful. This has been the most painful year I've ever had. I feel like I'm in a very uncomfortable position as a social being. It's become impossible for me to be like other people. I notice things that other people seem to think are crazy if I notice them.

Our informants' perceptions of themselves in relation to their gender, race, politics, and class had changed dramatically after c-r. On gender:

> It's important now to be less competitive. It's hard for me now to ignore women, like old women or the women behind the food counter, or those I have no social connections with, who are not my peers. I think now they *all* are my peers, or I want to feel that. . . . Before, I wasn't aware of women. I had no conscious attitude. . . . Now I understand better why and how women accept oppression. I thought, if I can see it, why can't they? I still get angry at the real male-identified woman.

* * *

> I feel *now* that women have been treated as a class, and that we really are a natural class, and that I'm glad to be a part of that *natural* category. I no longer want to erase the differences. . . . When I used to see a Playboy bunny, I'd think, how disgusting. Now I start from an assumption that most women's behavior is the outcome of oppression. I have more choices than most other women because of my class background, that's all.

None of these women had previously thought of women as a group with certain definitive characteristics. Rather, before c-r they saw women in strictly individual terms or as part of a race or class without respect to sex. Now society was divided into two sharply distinguished classes of people: men and women. Conceptual differences among types of women or types of men faded in importance.

On race:

> At one point [before c-r] I could see that we were going to eventually do away with all of our separatist differences. Now I see them more clearly and am more aware of the depth of those differences. . . . I'm much more aware of the white woman/black man seductive thing . . . and understand more how black people have accepted their oppressors, since I see now how we accept ours.
>
> *   *   *
>
> I consider myself more privileged than blacks. I identify with black women as much as possible. I support autonomy for black women to do what they need. Their problems are more complex and serious, but we are all oppressed together. I do not see blacks any more as people under my kindly protectorate.

Views on race changed in c-r, but white informants found there was no mechanism for confronting racism in themselves or in society. There was, however, a major shift from patronizing attitudes toward identification:

> [Racism] hasn't been dealt with. I'm more conscious of my racism. I haven't been confronted by it and I don't know how to do it. There is no organization to deal with it and I can understand why—tedious—I wouldn't want to be in an organization confronting men continuously with their chauvinism.
>
> *   *   *
>
> I'm more understanding about the problems of being nonwhite. There are parallels between women and third world people . . . you're taught to shuffle by your family—if you didn't shuffle you'd never survive. Third world people learn all their lives to be subservient, then they, too, can survive.

The other change was the perception of a "seductive" relationship between black men and white women. Several informants had had relationships with black men; some had several such relationships. They all indicated that these relationships were artificial "bridges" over their inherent racism, and basically sexist. They reported enhanced or new hostility toward black men, with greater sympathy toward black women.

> I was one of the world's great "nigger-lovers"—I mean that in insidious, liberal terms. Because of a series of muggings by blacks and Puerto Ricans, just previous to getting into Women's Liberation, and becoming sensitive to my anger at sexists on the street, which is rife in my neigh-

borhood—I've gotten in touch with a lot of angry feelings toward black and Puerto Rican *men*. I've also discovered my guilt toward black sisters because I was in a series of relationships with black men.

On class:

> I'm more aware of how I've been oppressed by upper-class people—economically and psychologically. . . . In the group I saw that you had to start from the interests of the most downtrodden women, not the most pampered. That has had a profound effect on my thinking about class, and to a lesser extent, in my *feeling* about class.
>
> *   *   *
>
> I think now that women have been treated as a class, that class is a totally artificial, totally cultural, categorization. . . . Classes are perpetuated through personal identities as much as through hard cash. For example, the academic life is an elite life, and if you treat it that way, you are putting yourself in a class others aren't in. You may want to do that, but you should at least realize that you're doing this. You see that all the time in men's politics, where power elites always develop. . . . The good thing about Women's Liberation is that we're conscious and watching out for this kind of mechanism. . . . If we can keep it from happening, it'll be the first time in history. It'll be the revolution itself.

Although several of our informants altered their ideas on the subject of class, there was less change in this area than in any other. Many women expressed a confusion about class and its implications.

On politics:

> Politics has come to mean in a way *everything* to me, as in another way it doesn't mean anything. It's as personal as the way I feel about my body— I consider that a political concern now—not only political, but the political level has become pervasive—who's on top when we fuck has become a political question. But I'm not in any political theorizing group—that's phony to me now.
>
> *   *   *
>
> By the time I went into the group I had a class analysis and basically felt that reform wasn't possible—we needed a whole new system, but I was thinking mostly in terms of economic system. Now I feel that political change, meaningful change in classic Marxist-Leninist terms isn't possible [either]. It's going to be something none of us even knows. . . . The family is the classic institution of political oppression. . . . I'm suspi-

cious of any political solution that doesn't talk about the elimination of hierarchy.

The above statement shows the defection of women who came to the Women's Movement from the New Left:

> I'm disgusted with the form politics takes in this country; the very form of the movement [New Left] takes [the same] power coloration that conventional politics does.

Women who had not come from the New Left were equally or even more extremely alienated from "male" politics:

> No theory of revolution conceived so far in this history of *man*kind does anything for me as an oppressed woman. . . . There's something basically fucked-up about the radical left in this country. For instance, many of my woman friends had an emotional reaction to the Attica prison riot, but I saw it as two groups of males in a power struggle, using the same power tactics that men have always used. Both sides knew that the hostages were going to be sacrificed like lambs. I see this in the tactics and strategy of the Panthers or SDS versus the Rockefellers—like union versus management, or any male-dominated situation. I don't see me. Politically, I think that women have got to find a new way of thinking.

Changed Identity

One of the most profound and liberating changes experienced by many women was in their body image, often symbolized by concrete changes in cosmetics and clothing. The direction of change depended on the woman's starting point. Women who had been elegant and obsessive dressers now often wore simple or inexpensive clothing; women who had been dowdy now dressed more flamboyantly. All of them felt liberated from having to dress to please men or to live up to a media glamour standard. Many experienced their bodies as more active and competent in everyday life and/or sexually:

> After the first session [of the group] I said, now I'm going to ask for what I want [sexually]. This permanently solved all my sexual problems. Since that day I never made love when I didn't want to, and I always have an orgasm. . . . I make love less than before—I do it now out of feeling for another person, out of my *own* will and feeling.

The same woman also made great changes in her self-image and dress:

I don't buy any clothing anymore except essentials. . . . I'm careful not to reveal my body [around the office]. I've gone to pains not to dress as a sex object—I felt too feminine before . . . I dress more simply—old jeans, etc., I don't wear makeup anymore. My attitude toward my body has changed. Before, I never went a day without feeling fat and ugly. Now I have a day sometimes. I always made love in the dark because I was ashamed of my body. Now I never read fashion magazines; I look after my body more—eat better, try to get a little exercise. At 25 I felt old; at 31, for the first time, I don't feel old. I don't worry about wrinkles on my face. I see the rest of my life as an improvement now. It has to do with other women. I'm not afraid any more.

*   *   *

I wouldn't get something I wanted because it seemed too masculine; instead I'd pick out something feminine 'cause I wanted people to relate to me that way. But I sent all of those feminine things to the Salvation Army. Now I select clothes on the basis of strength—I no longer see them in terms of masculine/feminine, but as what I want. I hardly ever wear skirts, I wouldn't wear a bra, a girdle, or stockings unless I had to be in disguise.

*   *   *

Big change in body image. At first in my group, my physical style was extremely different from anyone else's. They all had long hair, and I had short. I thought I looked dykey . . . but as a result of being in that group, I modeled myself on them to some extent. I'm much more "zaftig" [fleshy], which I never would have allowed before.

*   *   *

I don't need to look like Marilyn Monroe any more. I'm more concerned with looking like me. . . . I used to go on binges of fluffy femininity, but I'll never be five-foot-two. I never set my hair or paint my fingernails any more. I feel good about it.

*   *   *

I haven't worn a bra for a year and a half, although I'm still conscious of it on the street. I stopped shaving my legs recently and also under my arms. I feel good about it, it's an aggressive sexuality. I also like my pubic hair. But I had a dream recently that I lifted my arms up and the hair looked disgusting to me. I also have hair on my breasts, this has been traumatic to me. They never show pictures of hair when you see photographs of naked women. I felt it was masculine, [but after talking about it in c-r] it turned out a lot of other women did too, and I felt much better. . . . I wear more traditionally feminine clothing now than I did before, clothing I didn't feel good enough about myself to wear.

And finally, from a woman who declared that she never used to think she had breasts: "Oh, I really like my breasts. They're so nice—they're fantastic!"

Sexual identity changed for a number of women. Many "straight" women now included homosexual feelings as part of their identity, while gay women identified themselves as women first and gay second:

> [Speaker is straight]: I was in love with a woman in college and I wanted to sleep with her, but . . . the word "lesbian" never fitted into my head . . . I never thought being gay was relevant to my life. Now I think about it all the time, and it's totally clear that it's relevant.
>
>   * * *
>
> [Speaker is straight]: Relating to women sexually is an option to me now, whereas it wasn't before c-r. I realize now that part of the weirdness and anger with close female friends in college had to do with sexual feelings for each other.
>
>   * * *
>
> [Speaker is gay]: I'm still gay, but I don't think of myself as a dyke any more. . . . Everyone has homosexual feelings, and I never realized that before . . . before, if I saw myself as a woman at all, I saw myself as a gay woman. Now I see myself as a woman first.

Lessening of Guilt

If there was one subtle yet pervasive theme in the interviews, it was an enhanced sense of self-acceptance and worth, a lessening of guilt and self-doubt throughout informants' lives:

> I feel good about knowing what I want—less hung up about what other people want me to believe. I always thought being a Zionist was a guilty secret; now I see it as one way of being Jewish. If I get attacked about my kind of Zionism, fuck it! I do have reasons for what I am saying. I have validity.
>
>   * * *
>
> Interviewer: Did you have bad feelings toward straight women?
> Informant [who is gay]: Yes, and I still do. This has altered slightly. I have affection for them, but I still have a lot of resentment for gay . . . I mean straight women.
> Interviewer: Why do you think you made that slip?
> Informant: Actually, I think I used to like straight women. I wanted their

approval, their acceptance. I don't need their acceptance now . . . well, that's my goal.

The same woman expressed confident feelings about a completely different area of her life:

> *Interviewer:* What do you think of the class struggle, Marxism-Leninism?
>
> *Informant:* Sounds like a piece of the pie to me. I don't know anything about Marx and Lenin, but I feel less guilty about that now. . . . I'm confident . . . that I'm analyzing things from a pretty real basis. . . . I'm not trashing Marxism-Leninism, but I don't *have* to know them to participate. Some women are calling themselves post-Marxists now. It's new thinking, and women are doing it. But no more "required reading" (laughs).

*   *   *

I'm not upwardly mobile any more. I do not aspire to wealth, fame, or being with the upper classes. I was intimidated by rich people, because they have status, money. I mistrust rich people now—I don't like them. I don't want to hang around with them. If I do, I go on my terms.

*   *   *

[The group] made me feel okay about being vulnerable, about thinking and relating personally and concretely, which my whole academic training had made me ashamed of; about showing the feelings that I have. . . . I realized I had been denying this strenuously. [The group] even made me feel okay about denying these feelings, and about not feeling guilty for having done it. I saw my whole past in a completely new way, as a woman caught in an impossible situation making semisuccessful personal adaptations, instead of as a freak.

Change in Reference Group and Interpersonal Relations

All informants now saw women, rather than a man or men, as their primary reference group. All reported they had fewer men friends than before, talked to women instead of men at parties and other social situations, cared less about what men thought of them, and so on. Marital relationships (legal or consensual) came under a great deal of strain. But of fourteen straight women we interviewed, only one married woman divorced and only two single women ended relationships they had had on entering the Women's Movement. Two of the three gay women gave up former claims to bisexuality:

> *Informant:* I've given up men (laughs). I used to be bisexual, but relating to men sexually now would be difficult. I'd feel disoriented, out of place.

Interviewer: Have you slept with men since you joined the group?
Informant: Yes.
Interviewer: What was wrong with it?
Informant: Nothing. It was irrelevant, a waste of time.
Interviewer: What do you mean?
Informant: I didn't want any more power positions in bed, and I'm still
 trying to make that change in my life as a whole.

However, informants told us about other feminists with broken marriages, separations, changed heterosexual relationships, and of several women who became gay. For instance, in one group of eight women, the group actually became a support group for four women to end marriages. In another group of twelve women, half ended "bad" relationships with men. The Older Women's Liberation group originally had a membership of twelve, and by the end of that group's life, all but two of the women were divorced.

Even informants who remained in relationships with men, whether married or consensual, made significant steps toward more egalitarian practices:

My marriage is more egalitarian—[my husband] shares more household
responsibilities and we have a much more even-handed relationship.

*   *   *

I used to think it was necessary to have a man, that it would be the only
thing to keep from being lonely. I no longer have to live with a man and
it's okay. I have no need to get hung up in projected fantasies—my future
doesn't rest in his love for me, or mine for him.

*   *   *

With [my boyfriend] I started out with the myths. When we started living
with each other I used to cook every night and laugh at all of his jokes. . . .
We've really worked out all of these blindnesses and it wasn't easy, but
some of it was fun and I'm glad we did it. We wouldn't have the understanding of each other today if we hadn't been through this. We split
everything down the middle.

Other married women and single women living with men shared the same sentiments, with one or two notable exceptions. Where the man in the relationship resisted change, the relationship became strained to the breaking point:

My husband still wants me to organize myself around his needs. I'm
the photographer, writer, chef, and doer of household chores. It's still a
power struggle. He does some things, but not as much as he should. My
husband has been inconvenienced by my liberation, although he liked
it intellectually. He became more and more hostile to the women in my

life. . . . I don't know if our relationship can survive. I feel cheated. If my marriage breaks up, I'll never marry again.

Informants' attitudes toward their family of origin also changed. More sympathy and understanding were expressed toward mothers, with a heightened ambivalence toward fathers. Many said it was too late to make drastic changes in the way they related to their family, but that they understood them better:

My father controlled every inch of my life and now I am struggling to get control of every inch of my life—it's like a muddy swamp . . . I began to break the bubble of my happy family. It's one of the more important things that happened to me, because my family was abnormally disguised as happy . . . I can't even talk to them anymore. I'm really in touch with being angry.

* * *

I am more sympathetic with my mother. I have much more admiration for her because she was before her time in ways—very self-reliant and rebellious. . . . I have much less respect for my father than I had and am more aware of his contemptuous and hateful feelings toward women and how he played those feelings out on my mother.

* * *

My father's threatened by women and hasn't been able to look me in the eye since I got breasts. I used to take it personally, but I'm not so vulnerable anymore. My mother waits on my father hand and foot and the only gesture I've been able to make to her is to help her around the house when I'm there, so she can get some rest. My mother is actually very strong and I feel sorry for her—she's just doing what her mother told her to do and it's really too bad for them they didn't know any better.

* * *

It hasn't made me closer to my parents; it has made me closer to my brother, who's a homosexual. He and I have been able to talk intimately with one another where we hadn't before—it's the issues of Women's Liberation and homosexuality that brought us together.

Finally, informants report more and/or warmer relationships with women, both physically and emotionally, and "straighter," more honest relationships with men—with less game-playing and seductiveness.

Changes in Job/Career Orientation

Two changes occurred in job/career orientation. First, many women felt more ambivalence toward professionalism, careerism, and the "male-dominated" institutions in which some of them worked. Second, there was a tendency to realign occupational and/or avocational interests toward the Women's Movement:

> [From a freelance writer]: I only write to and for women now. I won't take work oriented to preserving sex roles as they are.
>
> *   *   *
>
> [From an academic]: "My whole teaching style has loosened up—it's less authoritarian, more personal. I am less career-oriented, climb-up-the-academic-ladder-oriented. I became aware of the elitism and how it isolated me from other women. There has been a shift away from identifying with the academic world, which I see as male, to identifying with the Women's Liberation Movement and all women.
>
> *   *   *
>
> *[From an architect]:* Oh, boy! I've been thinking about my profession. I see the possibility of it becoming secondary instead of primary. But that hasn't happened yet.
> *Interviewer:* What would be primary?
> *Informant:* Politics, doing things for the movement, making feminist films. I would feel much closer to it than making buildings.
>
> *   *   *
>
> [From an architect/executive]: The group *did* affect me in business relationships. I was a cipher on the job. The job was unbearable in contrast to the warm relationships in the group. . . . I don't want to spend my life in unnourishing relationships. I have a desire to take a long, maybe permanent, leave of absence.
>
> *   *   *
>
> [From a former teacher]: I know I'm not going to find a job that'll be satisfying and fulfilling. Now I look at jobs as a way of earning money and I do things I like to do outside of earning money. I can't bear to be in a position where I'm lording it over people—I'm too conscious now that I'm lording it.

The seventeen women who joined c-r groups and became committed feminists experienced deep, pervasive changes in their worldview, personal relationships, personalities, jobs, and goals. However, as in the literature on conversion and its effects, we found that the more striking and extreme feminist conversions drove the convert to a "bridge-burning act," some symbolic action that separated her from her past life. Extreme religious and political conversion resulted in a kind of "social suicide" and rebirth into a totally new life, such as entering a convent, undertaking missionary work, or committing some act that sends the initiate to prison. In contrast, although some of our informants did perform bridge-burning acts, with one exception (to be discussed below), these were not dramatic enough to be called social suicide. For sixteen of these women, heads may have changed totally, daily lives altered in innumerable small ways; but from the outside, their lives looked very much the same as before c-r.

CONCLUSIONS

We define feminist alternative institutions as groups composed exclusively of women that were committed to feminist goals, such as the generalized c-r group. There were also specialized c-r groups, many of which were committed to changing specific institutional sectors: a women's social science group, a women's Christian group committed to changing a particular church, a women's guerrilla theater, a women's film collective, a women's health collective, a women's abortion project, a radical women therapists group, and women's centers.

Another, somewhat different example, was the women's institutions sponsored by or within the gay women's community. They were clearly built on premovement traditions within the gay community, but had been transformed by feminism: women's dances and parties, a lesbian center, gay women's communes, and lesbian "marriages" of two feminists.

The most important factors in conversion maintenance, and therefore the continuity of a movement, are "support and segregation" (Gerlach and Hine 1970). The convert was supported when she had institutions that gave her a place where her cognitive reorientation and changed identity were reinforced and where the behavior patterns resulting from conversion could be acted out. This obviously took place best in institutions that consisted only of believers, secure from the doubting Thomases and participants in old behavior patterns. Support activities were group activities, group interaction, and recruitment.

All the alternative women's institutions mentioned above were segregated from nonfeminists and performed support functions. Many of the specialized c-r groups and also larger groups (e.g., the women's abortion project) committed to changing specific sectors of the institutional establishment were the groups our coupled heterosexual women and the highly professional single women went into after being in general c-r. These groups, though clearly segregated and supportive, did not provide *consistent* segregation in the lives of the women. Most of them met once a week and were more instrumental than social and intimate. On the other hand, women's guerrilla theater, film collective, ongoing creative or research projects, and activities of the gay women offered more intensive and continuous segregation and support, because they met more often and were more diffuse and less instrumental. These were the kinds of groups that the gay women and single women with less professional commitment joined after general c-r. These women more often committed bridge-burning acts; membership in the group sometimes constituted a bridge-burning act in itself.

The lesser commitment of the married women, manifested by membership in less segregated and supportive alternative institutions, derived from their greater commitment to men and the absence of alternative support institutions in the area of intimacy and interpersonal needs. This conclusion is not original with us, but was widely discussed within the movement. One widely circulated paper, "The Woman-Identified Woman" (Radicalesbians 1973), blamed heterosexual women for seeking an "individual solution" with their men, directing energies toward them that otherwise might go into the Women's Movement. At the other pole, a paper by Eunice Lipton, "The Invisible Woman" (1971), was the testimony of a heterosexual woman who blamed her fear of making personal changes and a strong commitment to the movement on the fear of losing her man.

The most significant exception to the generalizations above really proves our point. One of our informants was a woman in her middle thirties who had been married for years and had three children. She was also far advanced in a prestigious career, although she had been a New Left radical before the Women's Movement. She joined a c-r group early, in October 1968, and left her second group in about spring 1970, so she was active in the movement for about a year and a half. She described her conversion as profound: "It shook me to the roots." She realized in the groups that she could live without a man, and stated that "it changed my whole world." She also said that during her membership in the second group, "I hated men, all men, for about a year. I didn't want to work with them or even talk to them."

Toward the end of her tenure in the second group, this woman left her husband and began to drop out of her profession completely. Over a year after dropping out of her last group, she described herself as declassed because she took welfare and "ripped off" (shoplifted), was completely divorced from all "straight" institutions, cut off from her parents, and committed to the "acid" or Yippie Left. Her dress and behavior were completely unconventional. She lived in a consensual relationship with a bisexual man younger than she, and they engaged in some group sex. She described herself as "trying very hard to be bisexual."

This woman's bridge-burning acts took place almost entirely outside the context of the Women's Movement. After she left her husband, she felt ready to make moves in life that she had desired or believed in before but had felt unable to take. But she found herself isolated. Where were the institutions in the Women's Movement that could support her through this difficult time? For only a week she survived without a man, before finding one in the Yippie Left who gave her support while she burned her bridges to conventional society.

Though she still had a feminist consciousness, she described despairingly the gap between her ideology and her behavior. She was afraid to join another c-r group, for then she would have to break up her current relationship and what would she do? Her break with conventional society was supported by him and the institutions to which they both belonged by virtue of his affiliations, rather than by the Women's Movement. The extent to which this was true and the conflict it caused with her feminist ideology is shown in the following interchange:

> *Interviewer:* Have you been involved in any alternative institutions to your former profession?
>
> *Informant:* This is not a priority. I just want to get by. I might go back on welfare, or I could go into prostitution.
>
> *Interviewer:* What!
>
> *Informant:* Why not?
>
> *Interviewer:* It's degrading to women.
>
> *Informant:* I consider prostitution less degrading than having to go back to a connection with the straight [conventional] world.

Two other informants testified to the lack of alternative institutions within the Women's Movement that would offer support and segregation for complete life change (bridge-burning acts). One of the women was married with children, and the other was a gay woman with a prestigious career. The mother was married to a man resistant to the kinds of adjustments that the other married feminists demanded. She felt pressure because of her feminist consciousness to break out of her situation, and yet described no concrete alternatives:

> I don't know if our relationship can survive. I feel cheated. I don't know, unless he's willing to support me. The only way I can feel good about it is he'd have to let me do anything I wanted—extramarital sex, leave the kid . . . restless energy . . . I may abandon the whole bag . . . I'm boxed in by wifehood and motherhood . . . I'm willing to risk it all, I can't go back. But I have a lot of baggage.

This woman sounded as if she would like to put her husband in the same position as the male lover of the first woman – as a support for profound life change—which again points up the perception that the Women's Movement could not perform that function. There was no institution yet within the movement that equaled the support potential of married heterosexuality. Marriage not only took time and energy, it posed a barrier to movement activities if the woman feared they would threaten the shaky marital relationship. If she had children, the movement provided few secure, continuous alternatives for aiding her in parental functions.

Another informant pointed up the lack of a women's economy and alternative institutions around professions and work. This woman had attained high status in a profession and was considering dropping out. Strongly committed to the Women's Movement, she was the only informant who posed the desirability of female supremacy:

> We have to take over, because men need to go through such far-reaching changes. . . . Obviously we have a long way to go before we could take over, in terms of power. But maybe it's necessary. Let them play second fiddle. Let them feel what it's like. Maybe that's the only way they'll learn.

This woman was gay, but like the woman who had dropped out of the conventional world, she was fed up with monogamy, even of the gay type. She was currently involved in a part-time living and sexual arrangement with a married couple. This appeared to be the only personal institution to support her in her projected change from monogamy and a career into another lifestyle.

The general c-r groups have offered a highly effective matrix for feminist conversion. But the groups have broken up when their function, conversion, was accomplished. After general c-r the women sought to join or create other ongoing support institutions, and even the least committed persistently attempted to remain in touch with the movement and to find some activity-oriented way of staying within it.

A tendency developed in the Women's Movement to describe first the radical feminists and then the radical lesbians as the "vanguard" of the movement, using the masculine analogy to a military formation. Instead, we conceived of the Women's Movement as concentric circles, with a core and a "buffer zone." The core consisted of radical lesbians and radical feminists existing in a milieu of high support and segregation, surrounded by a buffer zone of women less able to act on their commitment, many of whom were married/mothers or women who were invested in conventional professionalism. We must look for other ongoing institutions to carry the majority of feminists from their new perception of reality into a new way of life.[7]

Research Methods

SELECTION PRINCIPLES We knew from our personal experience that many c-r groups had been formed through friendship and professional networks, so we used these networks in looking for informants. We began by announcing to our respective c-r groups that we needed the names of women who would be willing to be interviewed.

We approached the search for informants with two main goals in mind, which were seemingly contradictory. We wished to get data on at least two different groups by interviewing several women belonging to each; the reason for this will be discussed below. Simultaneously we wanted as wide a variety of women and groups as possible. We hoped originally that we would be able to determine the class, age, occupational, homosexual-heterosexual, marital, racial, and ethnic spread in the movement's metropolitan-area population. We stipulated that the prospective informant had to have been in at least one group that had lasted more than a few months.

One obvious limitation in our selection was that, of the women who heard about our study or whom we contacted, only those who wanted to participate were interviewed. The probable effect of this self-selection was that we interviewed women who were more committed and who had more positive experiences in their c-r groups. Also, because we stated that we hoped this project would be of benefit to the movement and that the interview would take at least four to eight hours of the informant's time, self-selection was a kind of commitment in itself.

C-r groups by definition were leaderless; however, there were many women in the movement who were well-known. No effort was made to include either the "political heavies" or the "media stars" of the movement, and none were selected.

Another limitation resulted directly from searching out our own networks. We discovered that our friends, our friends' friends, and our colleagues' colleagues and friends were all women with very much the same class and educational background as our own, and that the entire selection of informants was white. And although we had originally hoped to reach women in all the boroughs of New York City, most of the women we ultimately interviewed were residents of Manhattan.

It is important, therefore, to state that this project was an in-depth study of only seventeen women who were committed feminists. Although our sample may be suggestive, our range of informants may not reflect the spread ethnically, racially, by class, or by occupation of the metropolitan Women's Movement.

INTERVIEWING To save time, we interviewed separately, although we stuck closely to the same questionnaire. Many of the strengths and weaknesses of our data derived from the fact that we were committed feminists interviewing our peers. It is doubtful that any of the women would have consented to be interviewed by men, or even by uncommitted women. Once they were assured that we were feminists, they responded with remarkable trust and openness to our questions, with apparent faith that our intentions were benign. The interviews tended to be relaxed, informal, and intimate, and with one exception, took place in our homes or theirs. Rapport was so great and the peer aura so strong that informants felt freer to question *us* than perhaps is usual in such situations. This added to the lengthiness of our interviews (as long as ten hours in some cases). It also put us on the spot, and led to semiconfrontations in some cases, where we were led to reveal personal or political differences with the informants.

We were so committed to working with peers that we decided to start by interviewing some of the members of our respective groups. After the first of these interviews we concluded that the degree of intimacy the interviewer had with the group-mate and the amount of inside knowledge she had, caused the interviewee to block. She obviously could not reminisce freely about the group. To correct this problem, we thereafter interviewed members of each other's groups. We wanted to get sets of interviews with several members of the same group for two reasons: to provide some kind of check on the reported changes in an individual's life, and to get differing perspectives on the development of a single group. We wound up with three such sets, our own two groups and a third group that we stumbled into by accident. Of our seventeen women, four had belonged to the same group and three each had belonged to the two other groups. Although our sample seems small, we have data on a total of twenty-eight groups because many informants had been in more than one group, and indirect data on a total of 222 group members.

Because we were doing a peer group study, it seemed perfectly plausible, even indispensable, to include ourselves in the data. We interviewed each other rather than answer the questionnaire privately. This procedure showed beyond question how limiting an interview, even an intensive one such as ours, necessarily is. When we looked at the data against the backdrop of intensive knowledge we had of each other, the interview was revealed for the still photograph it is. Perhaps we were satisfied with our other interviews merely because we didn't know enough not to be.

The Informants

The informants were mobile and independent, young, educated, predominantly self-supporting, and for the most part childless.

AGE The age ranged from twenty-three to thirty-nine, with most in their mid-twenties to early thirties.

EDUCATION The range was from junior college degree to Ph.D.; specifically, one associate degree, three bachelor's degrees, eleven master's degrees or some advanced training, and two with either a Ph.D. or other advanced professional degree.

OCCUPATION No one described herself primarily as a housewife. Occupations ranged from waitress to corporate executive. Specifically: one waitress; one part-time primary teacher involved in women's guerrilla theater; three graduate students, of whom one was a teacher/consultant/writer/researcher (also in guerrilla theater), one was an unpaid full-time researcher, and one did part-time primary teaching; two part-time college teachers; two social workers and lay analysts; two freelance writers; one sculptor who also taught privately; two architects, one of whom was a corporate executive; one museum curator; and one college professor. One woman was living on a small, private income from inheritance and doing unpublished, woman-oriented creative writing.

In some cases it was difficult to assign a single occupation. The women had more occupational flexibility than most men of their class. For instance, one of the part-time college teachers described herself alternately as a poet-revolutionary and a housewife. Even the museum curator was engaged in teaching and writing that were not directly connected with her main occupation.

RACE/ETHNICITY/RELIGION All informants were white. Two were Catholics; nine were Jews, one by conversion (ex-WASP); five were WASPs; and one was half-WASP, half-Jewish.

CLASS All informants described themselves as middle to upper-middle class, although five reported lower-middle-class backgrounds and one described a working-class childhood.

FAMILY OF ORIENTATION All but two were from "stable" homes, those two reporting divorce between parents. Seven informants said their mothers were housewives.

GEOGRAPHIC ORIGINS All but one informant came from urban or suburban backgrounds; nine from the East, four from the Midwest, and one from the West. Three backgrounds showed significant geographical discontinuities. With the exception of one graduate student who was a student at a Midwestern school, all the women lived in New York City.

MARITAL STATUS Nine of the informants had been married; eight were single. Of the women who had ever been married, one was separated and two were divorced. Both the separated and divorced informants were currently living in heterosexual consensual unions; the other six were married and described themselves as heterosexuals.

Of the ever married, two women had one child each, one woman had two children, and one woman was pregnant; a low number of children for the total sample, yet every informant was of childbearing age.

Of our eight single women, three were living with men. Of the remaining five, two described themselves as historically heterosexual, currently unattached, and with doubts about their heterosexuality (directly derived from the movement). The other three described themselves as homosexuals. None of the single women had children.

Significantly, only four informants expressed no doubts concerning their heterosexuality. The doubts of the other informants in most cases came directly out of their experiences in c-r groups, with the exceptions of the three homosexual women.

LIVING SITUATION In line with the relatively high occupational status of the women, all but two of our sample were either totally self-supporting or contributed significantly to the household income.

THERAPY Fourteen women told us they had been in therapy at one time; six were currently in therapy. Four women disclosed that they had had serious, potentially debilitating psychological problems in the past; two had had difficulties in the remote past; two, just prior to joining the movement.

POLITICS Our sample broke down into three main political categories previous to joining the movement, and only one woman had been completely apolitical before Women's Liberation. Liberal (liberal political views, little or no political activities): four women. Liberal/Left: six women with Liberal or Left views and moderate Left activities. Left: six women who had radical views and were very active in the New Left.

The Groups
The seventeen informants had been in a total of twenty-eight groups that they described as c-r groups. This includes one group, a local chapter of NOW, that consisted of thirty-five women and men, the only group that included men. We did not include the thirty-five in our total of 222 women, but did include it as a group because the informant stated that the group, though not intended to do c-r, in fact did so in small subcommittees composed entirely of women. This group was therefore the exception that proved the rule that c-r groups were small and entirely female. A second exception was a profes-

sional women's group with a membership fluctuating between fifteen and twenty-five. In this case, the informant complained that not much c-r was going on.

SIZE With the exception of the NOW chapter and the professional women's group mentioned above, the initial membership of the groups ranged from six to fifteen. After an initial deselection process, lasting for about six months in some cases, stable memberships of from four to twelve women emerged, showing a pattern of c-r groups as small, relatively intimate, face-to-face groups.

STRUCTURE No group had formal leaders or leadership, and all had a strong ideological commitment to a peer structure. Although power struggles developed in some groups, these were seen as conflicts between personalities or as unfortunate developments to be resolved.

CLASS AND ETHNICITY Using the informants' class descriptions, membership in nineteen groups varied from middle to upper-middle class. There were seven groups that ranged from lower or working class to upper-middle class or higher (including one "millionairess"). This gives us a complete class spread, but with a heavy center of gravity in the middle to upper-middle class.

The composition of the groups was entirely white, except for one black woman whom the informant clearly stated was middle class. We did not gather consistent data on the ethnicity of the group members. We have an impression of something like a 50–50 split between Jewish and Gentile. One group was specifically for Jewish women, and another was specifically for Christian women.

AGE The age spread was from twenty-eight to over sixty. The large majority were in their late twenties or early thirties. Only two of the women were under twenty, and only a few were over fifty. Most of the older women came from one group specifically for "older women."

SELECTION PRINCIPLES The stated purpose of all groups was to do c-r about being women. However, nine of the groups were limited in membership to achieve slightly more specific purposes: two groups were for gay women only; two were related to women in the arts; one group was for women over thirty; one dealt with overweight problems; one was for Jewish women, and another for Christian women; one consisted of professional women in one of the social sciences. All the functionally specific groups were the second or third to which the informant belonged. All informants first joined groups with no explicit membership limitations (except gender) and no function except generalized c-r.

The generalized groups were formed in two different ways. In the majority of cases, a small (two to four) nucleus of friends or colleagues in a political group or job organization decided to form a group. This nucleus then contacted friends and colleagues and a group formed from interested women. The second pattern was more random: a large public meeting concerning Women's Liberation was held at some center or institution; smaller groups then formed from the mass by geographical location or random selection (picking names out of a hat).

Of the functionally specific groups, the two gay groups were formed through a personal contact network. Of the two art groups, one was through personal contact in the art world; one was open to all women in the art world and publicly announced. The older women's group was formed through friendship networks, mainly in the old left political world, which eventually led to the formation of twelve such groups. The social science group was formed through a personal contact network. Both the weight group and the Jewish group developed out of classes on these subjects at a radical educational institution. The Christian group was formed from the membership of a radical New York church.

LOCATION Only three of our twenty-eight groups met outside of the New York metropolitan area, one in Princeton, New Jersey, and two in St. Louis, Missouri. The rest were basically Manhattan groups, rotating on a weekly basis among members' homes. Because some groups had members who lived in Brooklyn or the Bronx, they occasionally met in those boroughs.

DURATION The groups that had terminated at the time of the interviews ranged in duration from a brief two months to a long two and a half years (members of this group stated that it was one of the longest groups they had heard of). Ten groups were still functioning at the time of the interview, but the longest of these had been in existence for only one year.

Excerpt from *Womenfriends*

with Shirley Walton, 1976

[E.N.]   June 8, 1971

Gay is angry! gay is squished; gay is invisible.

Why haven't I talked about gay more in this journal? I think it's hard for us "old" gay women (we're the ones who have done the complete gay oppression trip, unaided or abetted by gay liberation, women's liberation, the "leniency" of the sixties, or anything else) to come out. I try to hide or ignore it, then I explode furiously, then I retreat again.

I write in the context of Rebecca's pregnancy and the rotten Ruth Benedict Collective (RBC) meeting at Rebecca's house. Almost every woman there felt it necessary to present as part of her credentials that she had "her" man and kids, while I sat in stony silence. In contrast, at a recent meeting of gay professional women, none of whom had the slightest "political" consciousness, some of whom were not even feminists, I felt more "we-ness" than with those sophisticated social science women. Lots of gay women are sellouts to the class system (which is a male form of domination, all right), but none of them are sellouts to direct male domination in their beds, homes, hearts, where it really starts and ends.

There were also several comments made at the meeting about "mannish" women professors, or "old spinster" types . . . "Why, you couldn't even tell if they had a cunt or a womb." And the way we can tell that you have a cunt, bitch, is that some man fucks it and nine months later you get a kid. Big deal! But, it is a big deal. I am so angry, and don't know where to start . . .

It's finally time, because of the pregnancy, to confront Rebecca, and through that, myself. I must stop thinking and acting like a second-class human being, stop accepting that treatment. Anyone called my friend must put herself on the line; where does she stand?

Rebecca, at this moment I feel like ending our friendship. You've finally done an act I can't follow. (Why not? Is it because I wouldn't do it without the protection of a man? This is not clear.) Rebecca, I'm tired of being insulted by your boyfriend while you stand there. Tired of your slumming in gay bars. Tired of having to be explained to your men friends; tired of hearing you say you would have been gay, but you couldn't stand the social condemnation.

With Shirley Walton, reading from *Womenfriends* at the feminist bookstore Womanbooks in New York City, late 1970s.

When you married Sid, I felt I had to do it too, like that was maturity. But my "marriage" makes me an outcast, yours sets you up as a card-carrying member of the human race. I have outsider problems, you have insider problems. Are they comparable? Is it worth the struggle anymore? Maybe not.

And my anger; I didn't give you permission to have a baby while we were working together. I can't give up on the book now; I'm trapped. I didn't bargain for this, and it never was suggested that I had any say. Yet the intimacy, the demands of working on the book, make it hard for me to cool it with you for a while, much less abandon you. If I were on an equal footing with you, as a woman (or human being), this wouldn't be so hard. We were precariously balanced. Now you've pushed me off the edge, and I want to punish you for it.

[REVENGE] COLLAPSE

June 13, 1971

There, Rebecca, I had my revenge on you. I haven't written anything since last week. I collapsed, indulged myself. Truthfully, I blew a fuse and needed time to think things over. Well, a few days, a couple of bad dreams, and two shrink sessions later, I am calmer.

Why was I so passive about the possibility of your getting pregnant? We both acted like it was purely your decision, or yours and Sid's, because heterosexual monogamy is a sacred, personal relationship, and by comparison our friend-workship is not legitimate. I resent that assumption. Now I must put up with your pregnancy whether I want to work on the book around it or not. And partly it's my own fault.

I have just reread "Woman-Identified Woman" to clear my head; it helped. Both Laura and the shrink helped me to see that I was projecting the implication of my inferiority into your pregnancy. Rebecca is a good girl; she will get approval. I had accepted that my relationship with Laura was a second-class, socially illegitimate version of your relationship with Sid. Nature overwhelms me. NATURE has this day RATIFIED your marriage, casting me and Laura into the void of perversion, nonexistence, invisibility and insignificance. Pitiful, perhaps, two women together. What do you suppose they do in bed? . . . har . . . har . . . har! When will this rage, this pain stop? Not here, not yet. This competitive stage isn't nice, but I've got to face it.

Righting It

Contrary to my fears, your marriage with Sid is devoid of social significance. It is part of the history of our oppression. You are wasting energy; reformist energy.

> Our energies must flow toward our sisters, not backwards toward our oppressors. As long as women's liberation tries to free women without facing the basic heterosexual structure that binds us in one-to-one relationships with our oppressors, tremendous energies will continue to flow into trying to straighten up each particular relationship with a man, how to get better sex, how to turn his head around—into trying to make the "new man" out of him, in the delusion that this will allow us to be the "new woman." . . . It is the primacy of women relating to women, of women creating a new consciousness of and with each other which is at the heart of women's liberation, and the basis for the cultural revolution. (Radicalesbians 1973:242)

I realize that you are not trying to make a new man out of Sid because it is a goal of women's liberation, but because you "love" him. To the extent you were afraid to be gay, you "love" him because he has a cock. You can say I "love" Laura simply because she has a cunt. Maybe, and therein lies the difference.

As I write these things and fear writing them, it becomes clearer how I have shuffled and rolled my eyes all these years, eaten watermelon, not until the seeds come out of my ears, for I always maintained a defensive measure of rage against the straight world, but biting delicate ladylike bites. Sometimes you stuffed the watermelon in my face, but more often I brought my own along.

This is not an orgy of self-blame: if you and I stood before the world together, 98 percent of it would say you're a good, normal woman, and I'm a twisted, perverted woman, if I'm a woman at all. Ninety-eight million Frenchmen can't be wrong. I believed them and kept busy apologizing for my existence.

Now the worms are turning, or is it the tables? When Laura and I go to visit women friends, they are a little in awe of us. Their husbands or boyfriends resent and fear us. Instead of hiding, shuffling, and eating watermelon, it is up to us to affirm ourselves. Because we do make space, we are free women.

The other day we went to visit a woman artist who knew of us through several friends. She is married and has a two-year-old boy. She said that Laura and I had been part of her new sense of excitement about women and the direction her art was taking! Is that fantastic? How? Simply because we exist.

The problem goes deeper into my own head. Laura and I are free. We have enough leverage, given current conditions, to live more or less the way we decide to. The next struggle is in our own heads, against our self-hatred. You are in no such fortunate condition. However, and this is a big however, you have always been more self-affirming than me, in one way. It goes back to the conversation we had so long ago; a key one for me. You said that no matter what attitude a male had toward fucking, even if he leapt up and called you a whore and slammed out, there was no way he could degrade you if you knew you fucked for your own benefit and your own enjoyment. I could never, never pull that off. I was so stifled by men that living without them became a viable option. This is a paradox. You have maintained more of your integrity in relationships with men than I could have done. And so you've wound up with certain privileges and a big vested interest in the system as it now stands, that is, heterosexual relationships.

This brings me to the pregnancy and what it means to me. What is a woman-defined pregnancy? Pregnancy exists in relation to men; to hold a man, to create a bond with one, to please one. Or, you are passive and victimized by men-pregnancy. Or pregnancy is something to *prove* you're a woman, biologically and as a mother. In the process you immobilize yourself, both physically by being big and unwieldy, and after the child is born. Pregnancy has been a symbol to me, just like fucking men was, of womanliness. I envied it, and yet always rejected it. Pregnancy disgusts, repulses, and fascinates me. It represents the cop-out, the easy answer, which I long for but cannot accept. Maybe you have a better vision of a woman-identified pregnancy than I do.

A large part of the struggle around our book (and I do not mean just your struggle) has got to be over this point: that pregnancy is something only a woman can do, that only a woman should decide on, that it must be an act of affirmation that we control, for our own purposes and pleasure. If it were true, I'd have children myself, and our future as friends would be safe. If not . . . slavery to men, through pregnancy and children, has caused our downfall. To be free of this slavery and subjection is the highest priority, and here you are choosing it. Then there's all the conventional problems . . . it goes so deep.

I have to sign off now. I'm having fantasies of how angry you'll be when you read this, how you will refuse to go on with the book, toss me out of the house, etc. But my head says that won't happen, that we can survive this and grow with it; no matter what, I've got to dig up what's been buried so many years and air it out, try it on: my buried self.

[S.W.]   *June 14, 1971*

Well, the shit has really hit the fan, hasn't it, Pauline? First I want to say, that no matter how angry and defensive I may get as this diatribe, or whatever it turns out to be, goes on, I love you; I think we will survive this.

Mind you, I also want never to speak to you again. I am sick to death of your hounding me about standing up shoulder to shoulder with you over being gay, about putting demands on me that I don't want to face, about affirming your relationship with Laura by putting me in my lowly, conventional, unsocially significant place.

I'm relieved to realize that you, too, have wanted to chuck the whole thing. Behind my desire to chuck the journal and to chuck you in the process has been the knowledge that our negative history was still at work. You were lurking somewhere, waiting to point the finger at me and say, "You see? You, Rebecca, have finally proven conclusively to me that you are not worthy of my friendship; you're not hip enough, large enough, cool enough, smart enough, or way out enough."

Your point about my not leaping into the fray at the "Rotten Women's Meeting" is a good place to see what's happening. We talked more than a year ago about how I had never stuck up for you publicly. Isn't it interesting that after that long discussion we never settled how I could show solidarity, support, or reassurance? And why is it, that after last week's meeting, when we, oh, so tenderly, accused each other of not understanding the state each of us was in respectively, we still didn't talk about what we can do about it, at least for us, if not for all women?

What is it you want? Why won't you get off my fucking back, or at least tell me what I'm supposed to do? OK, *I could have come down hard on the women at that meeting, right? But I thought we were not divulging your gayness, so why was it my place to defend you? You might well have gotten angry with me for being presumptuous.*

Last week there was a class thing between the academic and nonacademic women in our work group, and I was stuck in that struggle. Could I expect you to leap to my side and forgo your prestige position as a bona fide, certified, licensed professional college professor? I mean, you talk about anger! I think your ability to tolerate those academic snobs is a complete crock of rationalized shit.

Because of our friendship you can single me out as your oppressor, your betrayer. What am I, a fucking tool? What do you mean confront yourself through me? Why don't you just confront yourself and stop beating the shit out of me? I refuse to let you finally admit yourself to the human race by dehumanizing me. I will fight with you tooth and nail; I cannot let you bury me so that you can finally like yourself.

I think you have asserted yourself, made yourself at least tolerable, if not OK, by being outside the norm, untouchable, secret, extra special. But the price of setting yourself in that position is to simultaneously feel monstrous to yourself privately. I have not created you a monster, so I will not be wiped out nor negated nor ripped off, simply so you can reaffirm your life. Nor will I bear the burden of your anger at society, alone. I can't bear it. I will only be defensive and angry and hateful if I get it all dumped on my head.

Do you think I like knowing you are in a special category compared to other people in my life? Sid and I are comfortable and warm with regard to you and Laura; we like it. But you have a mystification thing going about how I relate you to the larger world. I wouldn't hesitate for a minute to tell the whole world that my oldest and closest friend is a lesbian: but I don't recall that we have ever attempted between us to resolve this.

If you're saying there are problems that would be simpler if you ended our friendship, that you would no longer have a straight friend who complicated how you were presented to the larger world, that's not my problem. That has to do with your own decision to be committed to the gay world, and whether straight people are worth bothering with. You must decide that, and if I spent the next ten years trying to prove to you that I may live straight, but I am human, too, it would still be your decision.

I always feel so hopeless when you cast me back into all of the stereotypes you hate so well. You're always sitting in harsh judgment of me. I'm forever not making it, but you condescend to take pity on me anyway. Besides, it's kind of quaint to have a straight friend. It's real generosity on your part, isn't it? You can sit and watch me flounder my way through my nasty, petty, insignificant, little conventional life and breathe a big sigh of relief that, there but for a good hearty push from your upper-class WASP mother and your upwardly mobile, highly invested-in-achieving Jewish father, and a good drive for an ivory tower away from all the sordid, everyday mundane realities of normal people (meaning middle class, not necessarily straight—

there are so many "straights"), would go you. Don't trash me with your oppressed shit—you've been holding me up as a model of what you would rather die than be for thirteen years.

Do you truly think I am pregnant because nature and society have now ratified my existence as married, straight woman? Or am I pregnant because I want to be, and have wanted to for more than a decade? I am pregnant because I like it, I feel good, I want to hold a baby, I want you to love me doing it, I want Sid to love me doing it.

I think you resent me because you know I do many things because I want to, and I resent you because you have always done the safe thing; always finishing what you were told to do, even if you did act out a little along the way, protected by education and professionalism and a publicly acknowledged IQ; I call it a lot of smarts and a fair dose of reluctant ass-kissing. A Ph.D. by necessity means loss of integrity by playing the system, and I have always resented the fact that you did it. That's right! Furthermore, while you were waiting for me to fall on my face in my nice, conventional marriage, I was delighted to see that you were not comfortable in your "ivory tower" (which doesn't exist, does it?) once you got there. For me it was the biggest reaffirmation of why I love you, despite your predilection for snobby, upper-class, controlling intellectual, academic shit. I think you are going to make it, why in the fucking, goddamn, cuntlicking (I am trying to be impartial in my obscenities . . .) hell can't you ever, just a little bit, have faith in me?

Why am I here? Why have I been here? Why did I write a paper on the status of women over ten years ago, and poetry about women eight years ago, and why have I dreamed of a philosophy for women since childhood, and why am I always agonizing, miserable, questioning, and fighting, sick and scared and mean and nasty and defensive and threatened?

Where were you? If I'm not mistaken you were out in the big world playing budding professional in academia and settling into what was self-admittedly a very nearly male-identified homosexual role. Okay, I won't "hock" you for your former shortcomings, if you will cease and desist in reviving all of mine, continuously.

Let's start working from now. There are so many things I need so desperately to sort out, to face, to confront; or to discover I cannot face. And when you have trust in me, you are one of the few people in my life I can trust to care, to support, and even to help, sometimes without understanding what's going on.

I'm angry and frightened and hurt, yet relieved that this all came out, and hopeful that we can work with it. If your humanity has not been reflected in me, then let's find out why not. Because one of the greatest things about you as my friend, when you feel all right about me, is that you reaffirm my humanity.

Maybe these bad spots come about because there are parts of our inhumanity, the

secretmost places, which we have not shown each other. So I can only—sometimes
deliberately and sometimes unwittingly—react as a squish, to invisible you.

[E.N.]   June 15, 1971

The bastille of the whole monster is the structured secrecy of social etiquette.
Islands of secrecy . . . (Jill Johnston, "Lois Lane is a Lesbian, part 3")[1]

Last night at the RBC meeting, Sandra said that she kept her politics separate
from her life and work. I countered that how I live my life is the strongest
possible political commitment/statement I can make. Something clicked in;
I *am* living my politics, because I have no choice. But there is still this matter
of the closet at work; a bigger matter, closer to me and less abstract, than all
the other questions about academia like hierarchy, grades, and so on.

The "closet" stands for everything legislated out of academic life. The closet
contains not only my homosexuality but also my aliveness, my integrity, my
rebelliousness, and everyone else's too. The musak plays on: Do what you're
told, don't make waves and you'll wind up with respect, a little power, and a
secure pension plan.

During dinner today I started humming a little tune to myself, and the
words went like this: "tarpaulin, . . . tar——paulin, tar*paulin* . . . tarpaulin."
Of course, I was thinking about the land I'm buying, and putting the tarpaulin up on it. It was a happy, silly little tune reminding me of Pooh Bear and
Piglet. This silly happy part of me has been stuffed in the closet, huddled on
the closet floor, and it sits there humming little tunes in secret to women I
love, including me. People in the academic world think that when they get
tenure (or whatever goal of their fond fantasy), they will be able to sit in their
office or be in faculty meetings and hum some little tune out loud, but it
doesn't work that way. You never stop dancing on your hind legs at command;
hastily stuffing your homosexuality and the silly tune into the closet. It's only
that the stakes get bigger. I mean to reunite with myself and the women I
love. I've apologized for so long, refused to see the truth, buried my head in
self-hate. I'm going to break out of this closet . . . tune, women and all.

A FRIED-EGG BELT

June 16, 1971

Last night's dream: Pamela and Nora (former lovers of each other and me) and
Laura and I are sitting around Pamela's country house having a social visit.
Laura has never met Pamela. Pamela is telling Nora funny stories about her

parents and some kids that she had visited at an orphanage. She had taken them food or picnic baskets or some such charity thing appropriate to her upperclassness. But the disturbing thing was how she looked, wearing a floor-length granny dress with some ditsy pattern and a bodice(!); also she had grown her hair long and it fell on both sides in front. She looked like the queen of a small town high school dance crossed with some kid playing a princess in a fairy tale. I was fretting and anxious that Laura was getting the wrong impression, as it was unclear what any sane lesbian would find interesting in such a person. Just at this point Pamela pulled out a cigarette, and with one bold gesture she struck a wooden kitchen match on her belt and lit her cigarette. The belt was a plastic fried egg; the yolk where she lit the match was brilliant yellow-orange. I dug my elbow into Laura's ribs; I was reassured. The lesbian in Pamela was showing through the bizarre princess drag at last!

(Wonder woman! Mother! I used to light wooden kitchen matches on my zipper fly; a trick I learned from male classmates at boarding school. The dream is about me and "phallic mothers," but their real name is lesbian mother, mama/dyke, wonder/woman.)

June 17, 1971

Dear Rebecca:

My c-r group met last night, and I told them the fried-egg belt dream. They don't know Pamela, but they pointed out (correctly) that the dream is also about you, and that it makes a hopeful statement about your pregnancy (the fried-egg-belt being your baby. Maybe it isn't so complimentary to the kid). I frequently overlook the nose on a dream's face. The dream says I could be pregnant without losing my independence and self-determination.

I wanted to call you today, but then didn't. I'm worried about what is happening with us, but maybe we need some time and space to sort things out. I know it must be hard for you to have me breathing down your neck.

[S.W.]   *June 18, 1971*

(Excerpt from a letter to a friend and former roommate of both Pauline and me)

Dear Hester:

. . . Something has come up; the main reason why I have not written or called. I have been afraid to tell you this news.

I am pregnant.

Sid and I talked around this subject for nearly a year, with a long interruption due to the ovarian cyst. Last fall, when the cyst first appeared, I thought I was pregnant for a bit, and Sid and Pauline and I began half-assedly to relate to the problem (and it is a problem). When we found that I had a cyst instead, we all promptly dropped the subject. Sid and I dropped it after both admitting we felt ready to try parenthood. Pauline and I, however, never straightened the thing out between us.

The day I found my test was positive, I went home to tell Sid, elated and excited. He slammed me with every iota of resentment he had about our relationship, my "abdication of responsibility," my "rampant princess" act (you can imagine how that term, supposedly accusatory, appeals to me!), his inability to communicate, his abdicatory tendencies. This painful argument went on for several days and I sank into my old desire to flee, permanently, something I had never felt toward Sid.

Pauline and I also began to act out threatened emotions toward each other. I thought she would desert me, since I was voluntarily doing the ultimate conventional "married woman act." She felt I was deserting her and our book, to become Super Mama.

All of this took place as she was beginning to feel positive about being gay, about being in the vanguard of the women's movement, and she began to confront me over not supporting her as gay. I have been feeling wiped out. I try to understand that the two people closest to me are threatened by the pregnancy, but mostly I feel angry, hurt, defensive, put out and upon, deprived, unsupported, unloved, attacked, and so sorry for myself. I want to absolve myself of any responsibility for this action, by rationalizing that I act only from the pressures around me (as Flip Wilson says, "The Devil made me do it!"). You know, the much-maligned, long-suffering little goody-goody tied to the tracks by the villain. Or Wonder Woman fighting the evils of the world.

I have been afraid to tell you for similar reasons—fear that you would be angry or hurt. But what I really think is: whether you get angry, hurt, threatened, excited, bored, indifferent—just continue to love me. This is excruciatingly embarrassing for me to say.

There are so many things going on in my head, so confusing. It's wrapped up in thinking of you and Pauline as integral parts of my life (friends were always something nice to have around, but not something you regarded as highly as a man, a marriage, a heterosexual relationship, monogamy . . .). Yesterday I went to a new shrink, a woman. And though she seems to be very straight, I felt immediately that I would relate to her more honestly than I ever did with male shrinks. Really disagreeing with a shrink has always been impossible for me, largely because they were male. My feelings were invalid, nonexistent, if they didn't coincide with the "father-shrinks." But with this woman, even though she is highly trained, I feel an equal.

It was a relief to see her, because I have been so boxed in by Sid and Pauline, and hope the new shrink will help me away from the wall.

It won't be easy, though. Last week Pauline wrote a long and angry statement to me about my "slumming with gay," about not standing up with her on the issue, about not facing my status as privileged, married, pregnant, male-defined woman, and about my social insignificance as this kind of woman. I responded angrily, but later sank into sullen hurt. This morning, for the first time since Pauline and I began our journal, I showed Sid the entry she made last week. He agreed with Pauline, entirely!

And amazingly, I was relieved. Not because the "man in my life" condescended to agree with us little women. But because he wasn't hurt by the social insignificance part, which had torn me up. My fondness for Sid comes in large part from his indifference to what people think of him, his disinterest in playing social catch-up, being hip, with it. He's the squarest thing walking, and couldn't care less.

But that's a big problem with me — I always try to suck up to whatever I think is hip at the time, and Pauline's judgment erased me. It was humiliating to realize that I hadn't related to what else she was saying; I had blocked where she said I wasn't "with it."

June 21, 1971

Two days ago I dreamed about Pauline, power, and sex. Pauline and I were making love to each other, though we weren't really making love at all — we were doing something hostile to each other (that was the feel of it, not the act of it). As we made love to each other, our clitori grew immense — that is, they didn't really look like pricks; more like small red hills, or mountains, or big tongues. We didn't reach a climax, and although I see the growth of the clitori as a growth of power and identity, which was positive, we were locked into a power struggle with each other and the whole thing was not pleasurable.

Then the dream switched; Pauline and Laura were sitting on a bed in each other's arms (that is, Laura was in Pauline's arms) and I was standing at the foot of the bed looking at them. Pauline was telling me that I had to come live on the back of her property, and I stood there feeling murderous. The dream drifted away at that point; I was awakened by the doorbell ringing.

Last night I dreamed of her again. The first part of the dream was a long series of "adventures" — I was in an enormous house, or maybe even castle, swinging from beams to escape something, or somebody — I was enjoying myself tremendously, despite the danger. Then the dream switched: Pauline and I were sitting and talking (again in a bedroom, but nothing sexual was going on). Pauline was telling me how she was going to make certain plans and do certain things for me — because she knew what was best for my own good. She looked malevolent, self-satisfied, and smug. My reaction was disbelief: I rejected her plans because she made the decisions without consulting me. That segment ended with Pauline smugly stating I was stupid to force her out of my life by refusing to see the wisdom of her plans and decisions.

The last segment of the dream was a long trip by car — with Pauline and several other unknown people — and included standing by a lake full of bugs and worms *talking to her again. This time it was positive, we were not struggling with each other, we were involved in this long trip together. There was also a deserted house, a dark forest. . . . The segment finished with Sid and me screwing. In the dream I wanted to fuck, but it came to no climax and was frustrating. I had to go off and masturbate to a climax in the dream, feeling abnormal in the process.*

I am uncomfortable putting this in the journal. I am exposing myself to Pauline, exposing weakness, vulnerability, impotence—as though I am conceding she has power over me, she has won, she always wins.

[E.N.]   June 28, 1971

Ho, ho, homosexual, the ruling class is ineffectual.
(Marchers at Christopher St. Liberation Day, 1971)

There is no such thing as liberation; one is in the struggle or one is not.
(Marta, from Rebecca's old consciousness-raising group)

The gay movement threatens not just America, but civilization.
(Rebecca Snow, during our weekly meeting)

Last weekend was the culmination of Gay Pride Week.

The "gay forum" was only a couple of hundred gay people but it was historic. That many of us came out, as gay people. Later, five of us and one gay man discussed being a gay revolutionary artist. (Who?) May was one of the women in gay arts discussion, and I like her better than before. I'd like her to be in the gay women's group that is shaping up. I've volunteered to do the initial getting together. There are about ten names now.

Putting first priority on gay women as reference group for my work is frightening. Can you believe I'm still evading this, after fifteen years? Mouth commitment to gay is one thing, from the safe vantage of my straight group and my straight job. Emotional, related, on-the-line-type commitment a different kettle of fish (ho, ho, homosexual).

I wasn't going to go to the gay march on Sunday, thinking the better part of valor was to skip it and go only to the "Gay-In" in Central Park, where I would be less likely to be photographed or spotted. You could be straight and just curious in the park, but couldn't be much else but gay in the march. But I had just breakfasted with a bunch of dykes who were going (including Laura) and at the last minute I couldn't back down. There were lots of gay people on the sidelines, too scared to join us. I could sympathize totally.

There was a human being in the march who I guess was a man (it was so hard for me to look at him that I couldn't be sure), swaddled up in some sheets and a floppy hat: he was as pale as the back ward of the state nut house. Around his neck was a sign saying "Pennsylvania Enema Society." He carried the most disgusting enema bag I've ever seen; the red color of a baboon's ass or an erect cock head. How did he prepare for the march? What was he thinking when he pulled the hat down over his eyes, or wrapped up the enema bag for the trip from Pennsylvania?

But the revolution is less authentic by every oppressed person it excludes. The enema man is no joke. He is my forbidden self twisted into human flesh, just as I am the twisted flesh of the straight woman's forbidden self. But what a dank smell these monstrous fantasies have when they walk! We need to air them.

Will the Real Lesbian Community

Please Stand Up?

1982/1998

Here [at the gay male baths] we are our naked selves, anonymous, wearing only our bodies, with no other identity than our bare skins, without estrangements of class or money or position. (Rumaker 1982)

There was, said Hollis, this whole mess of [lesbians] who were known to members of the community as people who came in from outer places like the army base and got drunk. When she first moved here it was a division that was acknowledged. She was told, "These are people we see at the bars who we don't bring into our homes." (Krieger 1983)

ALONG THE BIAS

Recently I met a white anthropology graduate student who told me she was doing an ethnography of "the lesbian community" in a southwestern city. "That's great," I said. "How did it go with the Chicana women?" She looked at me blankly. "Oh, I hardly have any Chicana informants," she said, revealing that in her mind, Anglos *were* "the community." Seeing my disapproval she explained defensively, "It's so hard to do this kind of work. I couldn't deal with Spanish too." It *is* hard. The few of us with the interest and nerve to do this kind of project lack resources and encouragement. But if we are unaware of our own limitations, we will naïvely reproduce them.

I came out in 1959 in working-class bars where most people were butch or femme and money was hard to come by. My lover comes from a working-class family; she used to run with a hard-drinking interracial crowd whose social life revolved around a lesbian bar and its softball team. Living in New York City, I know there are many Latin, black, Asian, Native American lesbians— I see them on the streets, in bars, at women's bookstores. Lately, their voices are being heard in newsletters and books.[1] Although as a white college professor who knows mostly other white intellectuals, my social world is more class and race segregated than I would like, lesbians of other races and classes are part of my conceptual model of the lesbian universe. Yet I have been forming a disturbing impression that new social science writing about lesbians is describing only white, middle-class women and asserting or implying that they are *the* lesbian community.

LESBIAN-FEMINISM CONSTRUCTS THE ANTHROPOLOGIST

My first take on this phenomenon was that even anthropologists and sociologists were victims of lesbian-feminist ideological hegemony. Since about 1970, a new breed of "political lesbian" has redefined "lesbian" to mean a genetic (because transsexual "women" are ruled out by the really pure) female who believes that a woman should give her primary emotional support and loyalty to other women, including (preferably) sexual loyalty, in the context of the feminist movement. Lesbian-feminists were generating most of the new fiction, poetry, and narratives,[2] and had an irritating tendency to call themselves "the community" and assert that nonfeminist lesbians, or lesbians who defined themselves as sexually (rather than ideologically) different, were a dying, if not extinct, species.[3] Knowing impressionistically that lesbian-feminists are primarily white and middle class, I set out to review the more recent literature on lesbians to see if it was as narrowly focused as I feared.

ON SAMPLES

Every quantitative study I found grossly overrepresented the proportion of white, college-educated women in the lesbian "community," if the "community" bears any resemblance whatever to the general population of women as described by the 1980 census.[4] The largest lesbian sample to date was the 1,500 women volunteers (all in couples) interviewed by Blumstein and Schwartz (1983). Their remarks on the sample population on which their generalizations are based (which rate only fine print in the appendix) are typical: "It would be misleading if our findings were applied to all groups within the country. For instance, a large number of our couples come from the New York, San Francisco, and Seattle areas . . . are primarily white and disproportionately well educated. We have more high salaries and prestigious occupations among our couples than would be found in the general population" (548).

This pattern is replicated in every sample, large and small; even the exceptions prove the rule. Hidalgo and Hidalgo-Christensen's (1976) important study on Puerto Rican lesbians overrepresents middle-class, college-educated women. The most ambitious sample is Bell and Weinberg's (1978) 340 lesbian respondents. Bell and Weinberg were explicitly trying for diversity (33). Their Kinsey backing allowed them to be far more resourceful about getting informants than anyone else. Of their lesbian sample, 28 percent were black (compared to 1.9 percent in Brooks's "big" study, and 1 percent in Jay and Young). But 74 percent of the blacks and 76 percent of the whites had some college education or more, compared to 28 percent of the total female population over twenty-five in the 1980 census.[5]

The ethnographic and quasi-ethnographic work I found (with two exceptions, mentioned below) yields a similar picture. The three ethnographies are explicitly limited to lesbian-feminist groups (Barnhart 1975; Wolf 1980; Krieger 1983). I expected these groups to be predominantly white, middle class in educational attainment, and downwardly mobile occupationally, and they were. Not only does the concentration on lesbian-feminist groups leave the impression that these ethnographies are describing *the* lesbian community, but the authors make only oblique attempts to situate their subjects in a broader context. Krieger, reviewing the same literature, believes that "there has been enough representation of other populations in these studies to suggest a broader mapping of lesbian diversity than is usually acknowledged" (1982:96). Calling a lesbian-feminist group under study "the [lesbian] community" follows native practice, but is a terrible error from the etic (observer's) point of view.[6]

Ponse's (1978) study, based on participant-observation and interviews, is different in that she reached both lesbian-feminists and covert, nonpolitical lesbians, but both groups were middle class and 96 percent of her respondents were white.[7] Only Nancy Lisagor's dissertation (1980) and Davis, Kennedy, and Michelson's (1981) paper on Buffalo lesbians significantly crossed the class and race barriers. During a year of participant-observation in Manhattan lesbian bars, Lisagor interviewed seventy-five women. By her estimate, 40 percent of her informants were working class and "not very highly educated as a group, with only thirty percent having completed a bachelor's degree" (96). One of the five bars she observed had an all-black clientele.

By contrast, 64 percent in Jay and Young's (1979) sample had a college degree, and 1 percent of their respondents were black. The correlation between class, race, and bars is indicated by the fact that only 2 percent of their questionnaires were obtained from gay bars (816).

GAY MALES

Why were the lesbian studies so class and race biased? I turned to studies of gay men to find out what model of "the gay community" is emerging there and who is included in it. The samples also suffer from similar class and race skewing,[8] but I found much more diverse ethnographic work and a lively discussion about what "gay community" means.[9] Humphreys proposes the term "satellite culture" instead of "subculture" because "there are a number of well-defined subcultures operating *within* the gay world: a diverse array that includes lesbian feminists, gay academics, suburban couples, street hustlers, drag queens and gay bikers" (1979:140).

Most of this literature remarks in passing that the gay male community is "more advance" or "developed" than the lesbian counterpart, but none linger on this question. It seemed to me that what gay men had more of (in addition to money and social power) was sex partners and institutions designed to facilitate sexual interaction. According to Harry and DeVall, "in the course of the development of gay institutions, the purely sexual ones of the restroom, the bar and the bath appear to be the first established" (1978:152).[10]

Working with sixty gay men in a "large Canadian city" in the 1950s Leznoff and Westley (1956) described a division in "the Homosexual Community" between "overt" and "covert" gay men which corresponded to class differences. Overts, "obvious" gays, had lower-status, often stereotypically gay jobs. Coverts, hidden gays, had more privileges to lose; they had better jobs and made more money. Despite bitter feelings, not only did both groups identify as "homosexuals" on the basis of a common (persecuted) sexual preference, they maintained social interaction and mutual knowledge through sexuality: "The homosexual community thus consists of a large number of distinctive groups within which friendship binds the members together in a strong and relatively enduring bond and between which *the members are linked by tenuous but repeated sexual contacts.* The result is that homosexuals within the city tend to know or know of each other, to recognize a number of common interests and common moral norms, and to interact on the basis of antagonistic cooperation. This community is in turn linked with other homosexual communities in Canada and the United States, chiefly through the geographical mobility of its members" (172–73; emphasis added). Leznoff and Westley point to the importance of public spaces and institutions that function as sexual facilitators: "specific bars, hotel lobbies, street corners, and lavatories" (172).

Even self-identified straights are linked to gays through sexual contacts (Nyberg 1976; Humphreys 1975). At least until the AIDS epidemic, the advent of gay liberation steadily amplified the number and variety of sexual institutions for gay men. Bars developed "back rooms" where sex could be had on premises, baths multiplied, gay publications devoted pages to sex ads, tearooms flourished, parks, though still patrolled by cops, seemed to be teeming (see Rechy 1977). All the comparative studies show that gay men tend to have many more sexual partners than do lesbians, and that these partners come from a much broader social spectrum than do lesbian partners. My impression is that race and class differences are not just ignored for sexual purposes, they are often prized and eroticized.[11] These liaisons involve momentary "tricks" but also sometimes deep commitments.[12] I also suspect that certain sexual institutions, particularly the baths, provide gay men with experiences of "communitas," the mystical sense of the community as indivisible whole, which powerfully reinforces broader group identity (Turner 1974).[13]

I am under no illusion that the gay male subculture is a classless, colorblind utopia. No amount of fellatio can dissolve social inequality. I am suggesting that via sexual interactions, ranging from cruising through tricking, prostitution, and even committed couples, gay men know about the existence of other gay men from widely disparate backgrounds and have opportunities to come in contact across social barriers.

What if, I began to ask myself, lesbians have not developed as complex a community or a broad sense of what is there because they lacked not only money—though its importance can't be underestimated—but, specifically, sexual institutions like "meat racks," baths, fuck bars, tearooms? The only quasi-sexual institution that lesbians had or have are the bars—and very few in comparison to those of gay men. Nancy Lisagor (1980:175) counted 5 lesbian to 135 gay male bars in New York City. What's more, she found that sex contacts were more talked about than accomplished, even in bars (135–221).[14] In any case, there is some evidence that (white, middle-class) lesbians mostly do not cross class and race lines for either sex or friendship.[15] In fact, class and race fragmentation is probably characteristic of the lesbian subculture, and social scientists, themselves middle class, are unwittingly representing selected white, middle-class lesbian-feminist groups as the whole.

A HISTORICAL PERSPECTIVE

The antecedents of modern "lesbianism" are markedly class- and race-divergent. Working-class ancestors included passing women and prostitutes (Katz 1976:209–80), whereas the institution of "romantic friendship" was genteel (Faderman 1981). By the beginning of this century, "invert" women of the upper class had taken elements of both traditions to form social groups in major American and European cities.

The Bulloughs (1977) report on a lesbian group in Salt Lake City during the 1920s and 1930s. Their twenty-five women were all white, from "middle-class backgrounds," and united (with only one exception) by "the drive for respect-

ability. . . . They were always conscious of the need to keep their lesbian identities hidden" (899, 901). On the other hand, the range of occupations was
wide, including a college teacher, two waitresses, and a farm laborer. There
seems to have been no lesbian bar in Salt Lake City during the 1920s and
1930s. Perhaps there was no comparable working-class group; maybe those
who could migrated to San Francisco. Any wealthy lesbians from Salt Lake
City probably fled to the larger cities or Europe.

Davis, Kennedy, and Michelson's (1981) breakthrough oral histories of the
Buffalo lesbian subculture during the 1930s, 1940s, and 1950s have revealed
a well-developed, primarily working-class life centered on bars (whites) and
bars and house parties (blacks); they found about fifteen bars by the 1940s
and 1950s. The bar life was organized around butch/femme roles, dressing
up, drinking, and increasingly in the 1950s, an aggressive stance toward the
straight world.

By the 1950s in San Francisco we can infer a professional sector that may
have overlapped with the really wealthy and is reported as shunning membership in Daughters of Bilitis (DOB), the first lesbian political organization:
"Women who have attained some measure of professional status," Martin and
Lyon reflected later, "zealously guard . . . their reputations. . . . Some root
for us from the sidelines and make infrequent donations of time or money.
Others damn us for bringing Lesbianism into the open, fearing that as the
public becomes more aware people might take a second look at them. And,
unfortunately, there are many whose attitude is, 'I've got it made. What can
DOB offer me?'" (D'Emilio 1983b:106).

The lower-middle-class group who made up the core of DOB membership
was as obsessed with respectability as the Salt Lake City group had been. The
founders were upwardly mobile strivers, who wanted to uplift lesbians as a
group. They also wanted to meet like-minded women, and founded DOB to
have an alternative to the bars. Members of the bar culture were going nowhere in class terms, drank and fought and were too "obvious." In the late
1950s, *The Ladder* "castigated lesbians who wore pants and kept their hair
short, suggesting that they begin to do a little 'policing' on their own. . . . Gay
women 'aren't barhoppers,' one [DOB] officer declared, 'but people with steady
jobs, most of them in good positions'" (D'Emilio 1983b:113).

How the "barhoppers" saw the lesbian community is harder to determine,
as first upper- and then middle-class women have dominated what little public expression lesbians have had. That lesbian groups of different races and
classes do not have equal power is not surprising. The same is true among gay
men, Italian Americans, and Baptists. But the lack of cross-cutting ties and

the way social scientists (more than historians, for some reason) have bought middle-class hegemonic claims constitutes a critical problem for lesbian sub-cultures and for scholars of them.

LESBIAN-FEMINISM REVISITED

Despite or because of the fact that the rhetoric of lesbian-feminism is univer-salist ("All women are sisters"), class and race antagonisms may have sharp-ened since 1970.[16] The lesbian-feminist segments descend from groups like the Salt Lake City lesbians and the early DOB, joined now, as then, by some disaffected or upwardly mobile members of the bar culture and by some professional women. They still abhor butch/femme roles, public sexuality, drinking, and the bars. Unlike the early DOB, lesbian-feminists are openly re-belling against many of the conventions of the straight world. But in differ-ent ways, both "political lesbians" and traditional middle-class women are still, in Erving Goffman's phrase, "normalizers." Lesbian-feminists insist that they are the healthy ones, and everyone else is sick or "unreal." Their politi-cal rhetoric about "egalitarian sexuality" emphasizes a traditionally female ideal (tenderness, affection, communication) and proscribes "male" genital sexuality (promiscuity, power relations, sexual excitement for its own sake).[17] Overt, respectable, middle-class lesbians, on the other hand, still want their sex lives to be seen as their only, and private, difference from heterosexuals.

Today's working-class lesbians are the descendants of femmes, bar dykes, bull daggers, and "blue-collar workers [who left] to form another social club" when DOB, early in its history, decided to model itself on the Mattachine Society (D'Emilio 1983b:103). Far from being the homogeneous little world portrayed in recent studies, the lesbian part of the gay "satellite culture" is very disparate and fragmented. When individuals attempt to cross over, severe social sanction may result.[18] A lot of what separates lesbian-feminist groups from other lesbians are class and race ignorance and antagonisms dressed in new, ideological clothes.

ON WOMEN AND SEXUALITY

Many have remarked the lower frequency of sexual activity and the absence from lesbian life of sexual institutions such as "fuck" bars, baths, tearooms, cruising areas, and all-male porn movie houses. But starting from the ques-tion, Why have recent ethnographies portrayed middle-class white groups as *the* lesbian community? I came to the conclusion that it is these sexual institutions, more than any other factor, that have given gay men more contact with other gays who were socially different, and enabled or forced them to have a more inclusive and perhaps more generous picture of their "community."

Does this type of contact exploit and objectify people from powerless groups? What is the role of objectification in sexual desire? Is it possible that powerless groups use their sexuality as a lever in negotiations with the more powerful?[19] Sexual contact clearly cannot, in itself, revolutionize fundamental power relations generated by the economy and the state. (If it could, heterosexual women wouldn't be oppressed.) But the question of whether sexual relations uphold or undermine power structures must be examined in each case. In that of gay men, such contact has been more conducive to crossing over class and racial divisions than not.

In any case, lesbians are not likely to become instant sexual adventurers, despite some new and fragile sexual institutions modeled on those of gay men (Patton 1985). The constraints are too entrenched. Our history is different and our path toward genuine community must be our own. But mutual awareness and a spirit of respect must come first. Scholars of the gay satellite culture have a crucial responsibility to hold up a mirror that reflects the true diversity of lesbian life.

AFTERWORD, 1998

Since the first draft of this essay in 1982, lesbian-feminism and its poetic and polemical representations have been forcefully challenged by the "pro-sex" feminists (including myself) during the "sex wars" dating from the 1982 Barnard Conference on Women's Sexuality and by the "difference feminism" articulated by lesbians of color.[20] Subsequently, lesbian enlistees in the fights against AIDS and the Republican right wing have bypassed separatism and have even been seduced into the gender-neutral term "queer."[21] Now we are getting white, middle-class, lipstick-lesbian images, primarily in the slick queer media and, to a lesser degree, on television.[22]

Although both lesbian-feminism and lipstick lesbianism appeal(ed) mostly to middle-class women, they are separated not only by time but by intent. Lesbian-feminism, the illegitimate offspring of the antiwar movement and radical feminism, was a grassroots, anarchistic social movement. Lesbian-feminism's raison d'être was radical political change: it was anticapitalist, rejected the established social order, and was downwardly mobile. Lipstick lesbianism, even if it exists more in media than in real life, does indicate social change among lesbians, for television's *Ellen* encapsulates the hope of acceptance and so is assimilationist, resolutely apolitical, and upwardly mobile.[23]

I first realized how much lesbian-feminist hegemony had fragmented in the late 1980s when an undergraduate student, cautioning beforehand on their exoticism, invited two "lesbian separatists" she had met at a women's music festival into my class on feminist theory at Purchase College. Most students saw these two plain, overalled women as bitter and out of touch as they went on about "patriarchy" and the need to sever all ties with men. To the extent that no graduate student today would make the mistake of calling just white lesbian-feminists the "lesbian community" of a multicultural city, the lesbian-feminist moment has passed.[24]

Meanwhile, despite continuing barriers in the academic and grant-giving worlds, some very important empirical research on lesbians has been published.[25] These works exhibit far greater sophistication about the historical, multiclass, multiethnic complexities of lesbian cultures than any of the literature I first reviewed.

Now, as then, there is far more empirical work about gay male communities.[26] Plummer (1998:608) remarks in his historical survey of gay and lesbian ethnographic work, "Curiously . . . lesbianism had been ignored," which is an exaggeration, as the work cited in this essay shows. Stephen Murray (1996:185) repeats his earlier remarks that lesbians exhibit the same features that define a community sociologically ("territorial concentrations," "institutional completeness/elaboration," "solidarity and collective action," etc.) as gay males, "albeit to a lesser extent." Yes, because gay and lesbian communities both have developed along the lines of the ethnic and racial minorities that are so American, but in several key respects lesbian communities are not just incompletely developed versions of gay male ones. Because of gay men's greater economic power and social freedom, including sexual freedom, lesbian communities are also different in kind, and I still think that one of these differences is the degree of racial and class segmentation.

I had a chance to explore these ideas in Cherry Grove, the American gay ghetto par excellence; if ever lesbians in the twentieth century might have developed cruising territories, it could have been there. Yet despite jokes about the "doughnut rack," the female counterpart of extensive male meat racks where promiscuous sexual encounters took place, nothing of the kind evolved. I also found that where gay men often eroticized class differences, with very few exceptions, lesbians of different classes viewed each other with suspicion and resentment; there was no intimate social mixing, even in this small compact community of under three hundred houses. Higher-class lesbians saw class difference as social catastrophe and/or threat to property values; lower-class lesbians resented these attitudes.[27]

Trying to understand these differences, I turned once again to Victor

Turner's (1974) well-known distinction between *communitas* and structure. Turner observed that either celibacy or promiscuity can be used to undermine gender differences and family structures to create a "massive extension of the sibling bond . . . aimed at homogenizing the group by 'liquidating' its structural divisions" (246). This is indeed a primary function that gay male promiscuity has served; Leznoff and Westley (1956) showed that socially diverse gay male friendship groups were already linked by "tenuous but repeated sexual contacts," which by the 1970s reached an apogee in the urban baths, fuck clubs, and meat racks. During this period the whole definition of what it meant to be gay, certainly in Cherry Grove and probably elsewhere, shifted from artistic taste and talent, which were gender-neutral but class-infected, to promiscuous male sexuality as an integral part of a new sense of gay nationalism.[28] This is why recent attempts by gay Jeremiahs Larry Kramer, Michelangelo Signorile, and Gabriel Rotello to reconfigure gay male identity around middle-class values (lesbian-type couples, tax paying, children) have been so controversial. But sexuality is not inherently linked to *communitas,* Turner wrote; it can also be manipulated to express the structural elements of sociality. Lesbians have typically used sex to establish and maintain couples; the notion of the couple as building block or Lego toy is apt, because many lesbian friendship circles are assembled from groups composed of couples and their ex-lovers. Because lesbians overwhelmingly choose partners of like class, race, age, and so on, this only reinforces social divisions.[29] The *communitas* orgy of the annual Michigan Women's Music Festival is not enough to counteract this tendency, and from what I understand, the Dinah Shore Golf Tournament does not encourage class mixing. The most varied lesbians that I have seen in recent years attend the New York Liberty women's basketball games in Madison Square Garden, where one sees lesbians from the working class to wealthy celebrities cheering on the home team. However, because ticket prices reproduce class hierarchy, we see each other mostly through binoculars.

PART III: BUTCH

Participant-observation: escorting "Ann Miller" to Cherry Grove's
Invasion of the Pines, 1986. Photo by Amber Hollibaugh

The Misunderstanding:

Toward a More Precise Sexual Vocabulary

with Shirley Walton, 1984

A sexual incident from our shared past suggested the topic for our workshop at the Barnard Conference. We are both committed feminists. We have written a book about our twenty-five-year friendship (Newton and Walton, *Womenfriends*, 1976), in which we thought we explored our differences as a lesbian and a heterosexual. Yet we recently discovered that we had completely misunderstood each other back in 1966.

We were both between relationships and wound up spending the summer together at the beach. All night we were hitting gay and straight bars. In this unstructured, experimental phase—in our middle twenties—Shirley propositioned Esther. Though officially straight, Shirley was titillated by lesbianism in general and Esther in particular. Shirley is attracted to men and to masculine women, and she likes them to be dark. Besides, she loved danger and risk.

Esther felt little sexual attraction, even though Shirley is a type—blonde, outgoing, and feminine—she is often drawn to. She couldn't explain this apathy to herself. But she felt used, and also feared damaging or even destroying their friendship. In fact, Esther had already deflected several previous passes. But this time, in a spirit of experimentation, she accepted.

We got into bed and began "heavy necking." Shirley remembers being queasy about Esther's genitals, because Esther was menstruating. Knowing that Esther was chary about having her breasts fondled, Shirley avoided that. Esther remembers that she tried to stimulate Shirley's genitals and that Shirley was unresponsive. Neither of us can remember exactly how, but the episode faltered into nothingness.

The next morning, Shirley felt like a failure. She recalls Esther implying that she (Shirley) was less than a hot lover. For her part, Esther remembers feeling exposed as a lesbian, assuming Shirley hadn't responded because she was "normal." Both of us were frightened about the possible disruption of our friendship. With virtually no discussion, the matter was dropped.

In the early 1970s, energized by feminism, we began keeping the journals that became *Womenfriends*. If lesbianism really boiled down to women-loving, why hadn't sexuality worked between us dedicated friends? Though we rehashed the episode briefly, we had no new insights. It was reestablished that Shirley was straight and that Esther hadn't been all that terribly attracted.

Then in the spring of 1982, we presented a workshop for "The Scholar and the Feminist ix Conference (On Sexuality)." Why were we interested in sexuality? For the very good reason that we were both frustrated.

Shirley, now long married, avoided intercourse because she was bored, irritated, and/or afraid of contraceptive devices. She preferred to have intercourse only when she initiated it and directed it. But to make these desires explicit would have made her an unacceptable wife in conventional terms. Cunnilingus was satisfying, but since fellatio had been implicitly condemned by feminism, Shirley had almost no sex life.

Esther had taken a parallel course. She had tried conscientiously to have the "egalitarian sex" demanded by feminism, without much success. Egalitarian sex is not easy to describe; it is fundamentally defined by what it isn't: any sexual interaction based on power such as the power men have over women. Egalitarian sex assumes functionally interchangeable partners and acts. But Esther kept wanting to control the sexual interchange. It was easy for her to fuck her lovers, not easy to be fucked. Sexual relationships weren't working, and just as Shirley was beginning to question her own sexual constriction, Esther found herself at a sexual dead end.

At this point, Esther read "What We're Rolling Around in Bed With" (Hollibaugh and Moraga 1981). She began to take another look at the question of butch and femme "roles." She also met some s/m lesbians and became familiar with their terminology (Samois 1983). One day, as she was struggling to describe a nascent idea she had about the difference between "erotic identity" and "erotic role," the light began to dawn in Shirley's mind:

"You know, I've always assumed — we've assumed — I'm a straight 'femme,' by definition, since I'm with a man. You know how I used to love dresses and makeup, before I made myself so drab to be politically correct."

"Right . . ."

"But Esther, in bed I always want to be dominant."

"You do?" Esther was stunned. Over the years as we discussed good and bad sex, we always assumed we knew what each other meant. "That means . . . you're a top!" Esther exclaimed.

Shirley said, "You are, too. No wonder we couldn't figure out what to do when we tried to sleep together. No wonder it was such an impasse! We're both tops—we both want to start, orchestrate, and complete the sexual event. We never had a chance."

"I just assumed," Esther replied, "if you are straight, you're femme. We just buried the whole thing under those labels."

Once we reached this insight we had to discuss the incident specifically and concretely, step by step, without our old assumptions. We found we needed at least four concepts to communicate with each other about sex, only one of which was familiar.

SEXUAL PREFERENCE

We started with the most easily defined concept. Sexual preference indicates from which gender you usually select your sexual partners.

EROTIC IDENTITY

Each human being's erotic identity—how one images oneself as erotic object—is unique. But the unique combination is necessarily modeled in public, that is, culturally shared, symbols (as are all aspects of mental life). Erotic identities are presented to Americans by the media (for example, Bette Midler and Brooke Shields) and, on a primary level, by our family and peer group.

Class is a crucial component of these images. Typically, working-class women are portrayed as trampish (Marilyn Monroe, Ava Gardner), middle-class as sexually neutralized (Doris Day, Jane Wyman), and upper-class as icy but desirable (Grace Kelly). But there are also "good" poor girls and "bad" rich ones. Erotic identities have strong racial and ethnic aspects, too. And male identities are equally altered by class (Marlon Brando versus James Mason). Some people may model themselves almost wholly on these cultural icons. Others have extremely complicated and idiosyncratic erotic identities.

Another crucial variable is where and how much each of us actually manifests our erotic identity. Some individuals and some groups wear their fantasies on their sleeves, so to speak. S/m gays have elaborated a symbolic code to communicate aspects of erotic identity. Erotic identity may be manifest in some contexts (the private party) and not in others (the office party). Many people's public personas may be nothing more than a mask of conventionality, designed to hide their erotic identity.

Obviously, the gender system is a key element in erotic identity. What is so confusing about (and for) straight people is that the conventional gender categories, "man" and "woman," are supposed to constitute erotic identities

in and of themselves. Like ritually demanded grief at a funeral, these culturally prescribed categories bear a deceptive relation to the real thing, that is,
how a person really images herself or himself as an erotic being.

Because of the severe restrictions on straight women's eroticism, their opportunity to consider erotic identity apart from rigid gender stereotypes was
virtually nil. And if a heterosexual woman perceived her erotic identity as
being somehow "unfeminine," for example, domineering, clumsy, or fat, she
was, almost by cultural definition, supposed to be a lesbian.

In the gay world, erotic identities polarized around gender appear arbitrary. The gay male drag queen is obviously "impersonating" Mae West, but
we do not think of Mae West as impersonating herself. Yet a drag queen's
erotic identity might be more organically tied to the image of Mae West than
Mae West's was. Gender categories are learned by all, and are "natural" to
none. The terms "butch" and "femme" refer to gay erotic identities, derived
historically from dominant gender categories but now distinct. Thus, "butch"
is a gay erotic identity in which symbols from the male gender category play
a significant part, and "femme" is the complementary gay identity drawing
on feminine gender symbols. The current predominance of the "clone" erotic
identity among gay men, which is a stylized butch image, masks the fact that
many men did and do play out erotic identities along gender differentials.

Gender, however, may not be a strong element in all erotic identities. Some
people may be very fluid in relation to gender symbols, their erotic identities
centering on their ability to slide through them. Others may see themselves
as animals or objects or entities that are not gendered at all.

EROTIC ROLE

In the straight world, and to a lesser extent in the gay one, how you look is
supposed to signal what you do once the sexual episode begins. Too much
suffering has been caused by this assumption. Your sexy persona (your erotic
identity) does not necessarily indicate what you imagine this sexy being doing
in partnered sex, which is what we mean by "erotic role." Nor does it dictate
whom you are attracted to. It is entirely possible that you see yourself as an
Ava Gardner who, when she gets Humphrey Bogart in bed, orders him to lie
back and submit. More subtly, she may allow him to be very active, all the
while confident she is controlling him and the entire sexual episode.

The conventional way of contrasting erotic roles—as "active" and passive"
—is misleading and inaccurate. We need to describe interactions, not physical activities. The terms that best describe the most common and inclusive
interpersonal polarity derive loosely from the terminology of s/m gays, "top"

and "bottom." We use these terms in a general sense, distinct from sadist/ masochist, which center on eroticized pain and cruelty, or dominant/submissive, which, though closer to our meaning, still refer to an exchange in which power is eroticized for its own sake. We regard both pairs as specialized types of the more global categories top/bottom.

In any given sexual exchange, the top is the person who conducts and orchestrates the episode, the one who "runs the fuck." The bottom is the one who responds, acts out, makes visible, or interprets the sexual initiatives and language of the top. How this exchange takes place is not a given. The top might not move much, only issuing verbal or subtle kinetic instructions. The bottom might be very expressive and physically active, rather than the inert being conjured up by the word "passive."

Some people may have very fluid erotic roles. They can be top or bottom, depending on the partner and the episode, or both in the same episode. Others are very rooted in a particular erotic role, always preferring to be either bottom or top. The common feminist assumption that everyone should be fluid and changeable seems entirely inappropriate to us. In sex, what works, what brings mutual pleasure, should be the criterion for "good." The problematic issue is consent, not whether my desire is better than yours.

The erotic roles of top and bottom transcend the gay/straight dichotomy underlying the idea of sexual preference and the gender dichotomy so often a part of erotic identity. That is, many gay and straight men and women have strong affinities for top and bottom erotic roles. Knowing someone's gender or sexual preference does not indicate whether that person usually is top or bottom. Biological males are not necessarily tops, nor are those who use male gender symbols. This applies to butch lesbians and gay men and, thousands of years of cultural mythology notwithstanding, to straight men.

EROTIC ACTS

These are particular acts that obsess, please, and turn you on either to do or to have done to you, to watch or to hear. Whereas erotic roles describe process and relation, erotic acts refer to content, such as body zones (anus, foot, penis), objects (shoes, leather, perfume), or specific scenes (rape, capture, schoolroom).

These concepts emerged from our dissection of our past sexual episode and helped us understand it. Once we realized we were both tops, we understood much more about why "nothing happened." Given that women are so sexually ignorant and restricted, it is not surprising we had so many unhelpful stereotypes and so little precision in communicating, even between best friends. What is more surprising, and very saddening, is that feminism, which purports to offer liberating concepts of gender and sexuality, didn't help us either. Rather, as feminists, we experienced a new kind of social pressure that limited exploration and understanding of our sexuality. Within the women's movement, the "politically correct" have led us to believe in and practice egalitarian sexuality, which we define as sexual partnering involving the functional (if not literal) interchangeability of partners and acts. Logically, there could only be one look and one role for all, which partly explains why lesbianism is assumed to be intrinsically more egalitarian than heterosexuality, and why lesbian feminists tend to look alike.

The underlying reasoning goes like this: men have power, women don't. Heterosexuality involves a man and a woman, hence an oppressor and a victim. Masculinity equals sexual power, femininity equals sexual powerlessness. Do away with heterosexuality and you do away with sexual oppression. Do away with masculinity and femininity and the residuum is egalitarian sexuality: open, honest, caring, and nonoppressive.

Unfortunately for this program, things are not so simple. Power and sexual desire are deeply, perhaps intrinsically connected in ways we do not fully understand and just can't abolish. Masculinity and femininity are entrenched, enduring aspects of personality, not just changeable styles. Rather than encouraging an open exploration of the meaning of sex and gender in women's lives, the movement intimidated women into silence and superficial compliance. Lesbian-feminists have toned down their butch or femme characteristics, and just don't talk about what they do in bed. Straight women are afraid to be sexy or attractive, on pain of displaying false consciousness and wanting to be oppressed as sex objects. They don't talk about what they do either; heterosexuality is by definition oppressive, so why bother?

It is true that men have more power than women in the sexual domain. But one cannot proceed directly from this fact to explain how sexuality works, any more than male domination of the art world, for example, explains aesthetic experience. Is "eliminating power" from sex a meaningful or realizable way of increasing women's autonomy and pleasure? Or has it led instead to a new version of "moral purity" based on our sexual conservatism and ignorance? In the fight against sexual oppression, the movement—to borrow an expression from the Chinese revolution—has "swept the floor out the door." Class prejudice and lesbian feminism have reinforced this trend.

The modern feminist movement has been dominated by white middle-class values, with their most visible manifestation in liberal, reformist organizations. But cultural feminism is also rooted in middle-class values. The sexual significance of middle-class predominance in the movement is that, historically, the middle class and the upwardly mobile working class have tended to be antisexual and antidifference. Tocqueville observed that Americans loved equality more than liberty, and for the middle class, "equality" has too often meant uniformity. Difference, whether of race, ethnic group, class, or gender, has been a barrier to opportunity and mobility. At the same time, the middle class has attributed hypersexuality to both the rich and the poor.

An old sociological "saw" expresses these ideas nicely. The joke in graduate school was that Americans betrayed their class by their automobile seating patterns. Working-class husbands ride together in front, wives in back (gender differences emphasized). In the middle class, couple A rides in front, couple B in back (gender difference is minimized, and sexuality is contained in the married couple). In the upper class, husband A rides in front with wife B, husband B in back with wife A (sexuality is emphasized).

While the reformist women's movement of the 1960s was predominantly middle-class, the old lesbian community was dominated (and stereotyped) by working- and upper-class images of hypersexuality and gender polarity manifested most dramatically in butch and femme roles. The founders of Daughters of Bilitis (the first lesbian political organization) urged lesbians to minimize roles to be more respectable and acceptable, in part for class reasons, but prior to 1969, DOB was a small part of lesbian life.

The old lesbian community was defined by a sexual difference. Lesbians were stereotyped as only sexual. It is understandable that many lesbians have reacted by counterdefining lesbianism as a political conviction. Nevertheless, sexual liberation was an important goal of early radical feminism. As the 1970s progressed, however, sexual liberation came to mean affection and tenderness with sex distilled out. As middle-class straight women joined up with those lesbians who hated the more extravagant and stigmatized aspects of lesbianism, lesbian-feminism and political lesbianism were born and invented a sexual "iron maiden" with which every dedicated feminist has had to live.

The "role playing" of the working and upper class was anathema to the new feminism. Working-class women, black, brown, and white, gay and straight, had "low consciousness" unless they "cleaned up their act," that is, became more middle class. Unfortunately, these were largely old class putdowns clothed in new political sanctity: the working class is too sexual and/or ignorant; the upper class is sexually decadent and elite. In reaction, most working-class women, gay and straight, have shied away from the movement. Working-class lesbians stayed in the bars and on softball teams. Working-class straight women went into occupational feminism (trade unions, neighborhood associations) or, we speculate, the New Right. The upper class was and is insulated from movement judgments.

The result of "sweeping the floor out the door" has been a very narrow sexual ideal, which can be schematized as follows:

Sexual preference: Lesbianism is seen as superior to heterosexuality or bisexuality, because the biological and presumed psychological/social sameness of the partners guarantees equality.

Erotic identity: Gone (from the movement) are the "trashy" butch and femme of yesteryear. The lesbian-feminist is a "dyke," interchangeable with all other "dykes." The dyke look is supposed to be androgynous, but leans toward masculine gender symbols: short hair, short nails, work boots, running shoes, overalls and jeans, flannel shirts. The dyke erotic identity is a modified butch look, we speculate, because femininity is the mark of difference and inferiority that must be eliminated. Paradoxically, the look is downwardly mobile. As for straight women, we are mystified as to what erotic identity they could adopt. Shirley suggests one option is to pattern oneself on the look of 1960s male radicals.

Erotic roles: Needless to say, the idea of top and bottom erotic roles are only acceptable if they are completely and immediately interchangeable. Most descriptions imply a kind of side-by-side or sibling sexual interaction for lesbians. An alternative is a nurturant, mother-child model, as long as these roles can be enacted by either partner. Straight women's role possibilities are rarely discussed in feminist circles. They should be assertive, but should they be dominant? Certainly, they should never be on the bottom.

Erotic acts: Any form of fetishism or sadomasochism is a male-defined no-no, as is any sex with too much emphasis on orgasm. Sexual interaction should not be genitally focused. More specifically, lesbians should not engage in any form of "hetero" sex. This includes both penetration, either by fingers or dildoes, and tribadism (rubbing the cunt against the partner's body), which can resemble the heterosexual missionary position.

If heterosexual women are not actually urged to refrain from penetration, the insistence that the clitoris is the only center of female sexual response implies that penetration is a superfluous "male trip." Certainly all acts that could be interpreted as submissive should be eliminated, such as cock-sucking.

By limiting discussion and imposing "standards," we have stifled diversity and exploration. The new feminist sexuality is too tied to old models of good-girl behavior and to old class prejudices. But to create a vision of sexual

With Shirley Walton on City Island, 1976. Photo by Esther Newton and Shirley Walton

liberation, we need to know more about sex. We can't assume we are all the same, or that we all mean the same thing by "good sex," "perversion," "attraction," or any other sexual concept. We need a more precise vocabulary to take us out of Victorian romanticism in sexual matters and toward a new understanding of women's sexual diversity and possibility. We suspect that when we know more, we will find that power exchange is a central part of sexuality. If so, women will not be freed by flattening sexual experience in the name of equality. Redistribution of power should be our goal, in sex as in society. But when old friends misunderstand one another, how can we overcome ignorance and dissension to build a strong, diverse feminist movement?

The Mythic Mannish Lesbian:

Radclyffe Hall and the New Woman

1984

I hate games! I hate role-playing! It's so ludicrous that certain lesbians, who despise men, become the exact replicas of them! (Quoted in Jay and Young 1979)

Thinking, acting, or looking like a man contradicts lesbian feminism's first principle: the lesbian is a "woman-identified woman."[1] What to do, then, with that figure referred to, in various times and circumstances, as the "mannish lesbian," the "true invert," the "bull dagger," or the "butch"? You see her in old photographs or paintings with legs solidly planted, wearing a top hat and a man's jacket, staring defiantly out of the frame, her hair slicked back or clipped over her ears; or you meet her on the street in T-shirt and boots, squiring a brassily elegant woman on one tattooed arm.

Out of sight, out of mind! "Butch and femme are gone," declares one lesbian author, with more hope than truth (S. Lewis 1979:40). And what about those old photographs? Was the mannish lesbian a myth created by "the [male] pornographic mind" (Dworkin 1981:219) or by male sexologists intent on labeling nineteenth-century feminists as deviant? Maybe the old photographs portray a few misguided souls—or perhaps those "premovement" women thought men's neckties were pretty and practical?

In the nineteenth century and before, individual women passed as men by dressing and acting like them for a variety of economic, sexual, and adventure-seeking reasons. Many of these women were from the working class.[2] Public, *partial* cross-dressing among bourgeois women was a late-nineteenth-century development. Earlier isolated instances of partial cross-dressing seem to have been associated with explicit feminism (e.g., French writer George Sand and American physician Mary Walker), although most nineteenth-century feminists wore traditional women's clothing. From the last years of the century, cross-dressing was increasingly associated with "sexual inversion" by the medical profession. Did the doctors invent or merely describe the mannish lesbian? Either way, what did this mythic figure signify, and to whom?

At the center of this problem is British author Radclyffe Hall (1880–1943).[3] Without question, the most infamous mannish lesbian, Stephen Gordon, protagonist of *The Well of Loneliness* (1928), was created not by a male pornographer, sexologist, legislator, or novelist, but by Hall, herself an "out" and tie-wearing lesbian. And *The Well*, at least until 1970, was *the* lesbian novel.[4] Why is it that *The Well* rather than all the other lesbian novels became famous?

Embarrassed by Radclyffe Hall but unable to wish her away, sometimes even hoping to reclaim her, our feminist scholars have lectured, excused, or patronized her.[5] Radclyffe Hall, they declare, was an unwitting dupe of the misogynist doctors' attack on feminist romantic friendships. Or, cursed with a pessimistic temperament and brainwashed by Catholicism, Hall parroted society's condemnation of lesbians. The "real" Radclyffe Hall lesbian novel, the argument frequently continues, the one that *ought* to have been famous, is her first, *The Unlit Lamp* (1924). Better yet, Virginia Woolf's *Orlando* (1928) *should* have been the definitive lesbian novel. Or Natalie Barney's work, or anything but *The Well*.[6]

Heterosexual conservatives condemn *The Well* for defending the lesbian's right to exist. Lesbian-feminists condemn it for presenting lesbians as different from women in general. But *The Well* has continued meaning to lesbians because it confronts the stigma of lesbianism—as most lesbians have had to live it. Maybe Natalie Barney, with her fortune and her cast-iron ego, or safely married Virginia Woolf were able to transcend the patriarchy, but most lesbians have had to face being called, or at least feeling like, freaks. As the Bowery bum represents all that is most feared and despised about drunkenness, the mannish lesbian, of whom Stephen Gordon is the most famous prototype, has symbolized the stigma of lesbianism (just as the effeminate man is the stigma bearer for gay men) and so continues to move a broad range of lesbians.[7] A second reason for *The Well's* continuing impact, which I explore briefly at the close of this essay, is that Stephen Gordon articulated a gender orientation with which an important minority of lesbians still actively identify, and toward which another minority is erotically attracted.

By "mannish lesbian" (a term I use because it, rather than the contemporary "butch," belongs to the time period in question) I mean a figure who is defined as lesbian because her behavior or dress (and usually both) manifests elements designated as exclusively masculine. From about 1900 on, this cross-gender figure became the public symbol of the new social/sexual category "lesbian." Some of our feminist historians deplore the emergence of the mannish lesbian, citing her association with the medical model of pathology. For them, the nineteenth century becomes a kind of lesbian Golden Age, replete with loving, innocent feminist couples.[8] From the perspective of Radclyffe Hall's generation, however, nineteenth-century models may have seemed more confining than liberating. I argue that Hall and many other feminists like her embraced, sometimes with ambivalence, the image of the mannish lesbian and the discourse of the sexologists about inversion primarily because they desperately wanted to break out of the asexual model of romantic friendship. Two questions emerge from this statement of the problem. First, why did twentieth-century women whose primary social and intimate interest was in other women wish their relationships to become explicitly sexual? Second, why did the figure of the mannish lesbian play the central role in this development?

The structure and ideology of the bourgeois woman's gender-segregated world in the nineteenth century have been convincingly described.[9] As British and American women gained access to higher education and the professions, they did so in all-female institutions and in relationships with one another that were intense, passionate, and committed. These romantic friendships characterized the first generation of "New Women"—such as Jane Addams, Charlotte Perkins Gilman, and Mary Wooley—who were born in the 1850s and 1860s, educated in the 1870s and 1880s, and flourished from the 1890s through the First World War. They sought personal and economic independence by rejecting their mothers' domestic roles. The goal of the battle to be autonomous was to stay single *and* to separate from the family sphere. They turned to romantic friendships as the alternative, and replicated the female world of love and commitment in the new institutional settings of colleges and settlement houses.

Whether or not these women touched each other's genitals or had orgasms together, two things seem clear: their relationships were a quasi-legitimate alternative to heterosexual marriage, and the participants did not describe them in the acknowledged sexual language—medical, religious, or pornographic—of the nineteenth century. Letters between romantic friends exhibit no shame in an era when lust was considered dirty and gross. On the contrary, the first generation had nothing to hide because their passionate outpourings were seen by others, and apparently by themselves, as pure and ennobling.

The bourgeois woman's sexuality proper was confined to its reproductive function; the uterus was its organ. But as for lust, "The major current in Victorian sexual ideology declared that women were passionless and asexual, the passive objects of male sexual desire."[10] Most bourgeois women and men believed that only males and déclassé women were sexual. Sex was seen as phallic, by which I mean that, conceptually, sex could occur only in the presence of an imperial and imperious penis. The low status of working women and women of color, as well as their participation in the public sphere, deprived them of the feminine purity that protected bourgeois women from males and from deriving sexual pleasure. But what "pure" women did with each other, no matter how good it felt, could not be conceived as sexual within the terms of the dominant nineteenth-century romantic paradigm. Insofar as first-generation feminists were called sexual deviants, it was because they used their minds at the expense of their reproductive organs.

The second generation of New Women were born in the 1870s and 1880s and came of age during the opening decades of the twentieth century. This was an extraordinarily distinguished group. Among them we count critics of the family and political radicals Margaret Sanger and Crystal Eastman; women drawn to new artistic fields, such as Berenice Abbot and Isadora Duncan; and lesbian writers such as Gertrude Stein, Willa Cather, Margaret Anderson, Natalie Barney, and Radclyffe Hall. For them, autonomy from family was, if not a given, emphatically a right. Hall's first novel, *The Unlit Lamp* (1924), is a sympathetic analysis of the first generation from the perspective of the second. The novel portrays a devouring mother using the kinship claims of the female world to crush her daughter's legitimate bid for autonomy.[11]

Hall uses the family in *The Lamp* to symbolize society, the imposition of traditional gender divisions, and the subjugation of female fulfillment to traditional bourgeois norms. The family stands for bourgeois proprieties: proper dress, stifling garden parties, provincial gossip. Fearful of alternatives, uncreative and unimaginative, the mother seeks to bind her daughter to an equally banal and confining life. Conversely, Hall uses a masculinized body and a strong, active mind to symbolize women's rejection of traditional gender divisions and bourgeois values. Joan Ogden, the protagonist, wants to be a doctor. Her mind is swift, intelligent, her body large, strong, healthy. Although Hall does not strongly develop male body and clothing imagery in *The Lamp,* in a momentous confrontation near the novel's conclusion, masculine clothing is unambiguously used to symbolize assertiveness and modernity. Second-generation women are described as "not at all self-conscious in their tailor-made clothes, not ashamed of their cropped hair; women who did things well, important things . . . smart, neatly put together women, *looking like well bred young men*" (emphasis added). When two such women see Joan, now faded and failed, they ridicule her old-fashioned appearance: " 'Have you seen that funny old thing with the short gray hair?' . . . 'Wasn't she killing? Why moiré ribbon instead of a proper necktie?' . . . 'I believe she's what they used to call a

New Woman,' said the girl in breeches, with a low laugh. 'Honey, she's a fore-runner, a kind of pioneer that's got left behind. I believe she's the beginning of things like me'" (1981 [1924]:284).

There is no explicit discussion of sexuality. Joan tells a male suitor, "I've never been what you'd call in love with a man in my life" (302) without a trace of embarrassment. Joan's passionate relationship with another woman is de-scribed in the traditional language of sentiment, never in a language of lust.

For many women of Radclyffe Hall's generation, sexuality—for itself and as a symbol of female autonomy—became a preoccupation. These women were, after all, the "sisters" of D. H. Lawrence and James Joyce. For male novelists, sexologists, and artists rebelling against Victorian values, sexual freedom be-came the cutting edge of modernism. Bourgeois women like Hall had a differ-ent relation to modernist sexual freedom, for in the Victorian terms of the first generation, they had no sexual identity to express. Women of the second gen-eration who wished to join the modernist discourse and be twentieth-century adults had to radically reconceive themselves.

That most New Women of the first generation resented and feared such a development I do not doubt. But many women of the second welcomed it, cautiously or with naïve enthusiasm. (One has only to think of Virginia Woolf's thrilled participation in Bloomsbury to see what I mean.) They wanted not simply male professions but access to the broader world of male opportunity. They drank, they smoked, they rejected traditional feminine clothing, lived as expatriates, and freely entered heterosexual liaisons, some-times with such disastrous results as alcoholism, mental illness, and sui-cide. Modernism and the new sex ideas entailed serious contradictions for women,[12] who, no matter what their hopes, could not behave like men on equal terms; unwanted pregnancy and "bad" reputations were only two of the hazards from which men were exempt. Yet many women eagerly took up the challenge. This was what first-generation women had won for the second: the tenuous right to try out the new ideas such as psychoanalysis and sexual freedom and participate in the great social movements of the day.

It was in the first two decades of the twentieth century in Britain, with perhaps a ten-year lag in the United States, that, due to external attack and internal fission, the old feminist movement began to split along the hetero-sexual/homosexual divide that is ancestral to our own. If women were to de-velop a lustful sexuality, with whom and in what social context were they to express it? The male establishment, of course, wanted women to be lusty with men. A basic tenet of sexual modernism was that "normal" women had at least reactive heterosexual desire.[13] The sex reformers attacked Victorian gender segregation and promoted the new idea of companionate marriage in which both women's and men's heterosexual desires were to be satisfied.[14] Easier association with men quickly sexualized the middle-class woman, and by the 1920s the flapper style reflected the sexual ambience of working-class bars and dance halls. The flapper flirted with being "cheap" and "fast," words that had clear sexual reference.

But what of the women who did not become heterosexual, who remained stubbornly committed to intragender intimacy? A poignant example is furnished by Frances Wilder, an obscure second-generation feminist (Claus 1977). Wilder had inherited the orthodox first-generation views. In a 1912 letter to the radical *Freewoman,* she advocated self-restraint, denouncing the new morality for encouraging the "same degrading laxity in sex matters which is indulged in by most of the lower animals including man." She herself, aged twenty-seven, had "always practised abstinence" with no adverse effects. But just three years later she was writing desperately to homosexual radical Edward Carpenter: "I have recently read with much interest your book entitled The Intermediate Sex & it has lately dawned on me that I myself belong to that class & I write to ask if there is any way of getting in touch with others of the same temperament" (930). Wilder was aware of the price tag on the new ideas. "The world would say that a physical relationship between two of the same sex is an unspeakable crime," she admits, but gamely reasons that, because of the "economic slavery" of women, *"normal sex"* is *"more* degrading" (930).

The New Woman's social field was opening up, becoming more complex, and potentially lonelier. Thus, along with their desire to be modern, our bourgeois lesbian ancestors had another powerful reason to embrace change. Before they could find one another in the twentieth-century urban landscape, they had to become visible, at least to each other. They needed a new vocabulary built on the radical idea that women apart from men could have autonomous sexual feeling.

"I just concluded that I had . . . a dash of the masculine (I have been told more than once that I have a masculine mind . . .)," Frances Wilder had confessed to Carpenter in 1915, explaining her "strong desire to caress & fondle" a female friend (Claus 1977:931). Like most important historical developments, the symbolic fusion of gender reversal and homosexuality was overdetermined. God Himself had ordained gender hierarchy and heterosexuality at the Creation. The idea that men who had sex with other men were like women was not new. But in the second half of the nineteenth century, the emerging medical profession gave scientific sanction to tradition; homosexual behavior, the doctors agreed, was both symptom and cause of male effeminacy. The masculine female invert was perhaps an analogous afterthought. Yet the mannish lesbian proved a potent persona to both the second generation of New Women and their antifeminist enemies. I think that her image came to dominate the discourse about female homosexuality, particularly in England and America, for two reasons. First, because sexual desire was not considered inherent in women, the lesbian was endowed with a trapped male soul that phallicized her, giving her active lust. Second, gender reversal became a powerful symbol of feminist aspirations, positive for many female modernists, negative for males, both conservative and modernist.[15]

It was Richard von Krafft-Ebing who articulated the fusion of masculinity, feminist aspirations, and lesbianism that became, and largely remains, an article of faith in Anglo-American culture.[16] Krafft-Ebing categorized lesbians into four increasingly deviant and masculine types.[17] The first category of lesbians included women who "did not betray their anomaly by external appearance or by mental [masculine] sexual characteristics." They were, however, responsive to the approaches of women who appeared or acted more masculine. The second classification included women with a "strong preference for male garments." By the third stage, "inversion" was "fully developed, the woman [assuming] a definitely masculine role." The fourth stage represented "the extreme grade of degenerative homosexuality. The woman of this type," Krafft-Ebing explained, "possesses of the feminine qualities only the genital organs; thought, sentiment, action, even external appearance are those of the man" (1886:262–64). Not only was the most degenerate lesbian the most masculine, but any gender-crossing or aspiration to male privilege was probably a symptom of lesbianism. In these pathological souls, "The consciousness of being a woman and thus to be deprived of the gay college life, or to be barred out from the military career, produces painful reflections" (264). In fact, lesbianism is a congenital form of lust caused by and manifested in gender reversal, as Krafft-Ebing makes clear in discussing one "case": "Even in her earliest childhood she preferred playing at soldiers and other boys' games; she was bold and tom-boyish and tried even to excel her little companions of the other sex. . . . [After puberty] her dreams were of a lascivious nature, only about females, with herself in the role of the man. . . . She was quite conscious of her pathological condition. Masculine features, deep voice, manly gait, without beard, small breasts; cropped her hair short and made the impression of a man in woman's clothes" (278–79). Krafft-Ebing was so convinced of his thesis that the woman's feminine feature—and the *only* indisputably biological one—"without beard" is lined up with the masculine traits as if they all prove the point.

Havelock Ellis simplified Krafft-Ebing's four-part typology, but retained an ascending scale of inversion, beginning with women involved in "passionate friendships" in which "no congenital inversion is usually involved" and ending with the "actively inverted woman" (1895:141–58). Ellis's discussion of the former was devastating; it turned upside down the value that first-generation feminists had placed on passionate friendships. A "sexual enthusiast," he saw these "rudimentary sexual relationships" as more symptomatic of female sexual ignorance and repression than of spiritual values.[18] At the same time, his inclusion of such friendships in a discussion of inversion inevitably marked them with the stigma of "abnormality."

When Ellis got to the hard-core inverts, he was confounded by his contradictory beliefs. He wanted to construct the lesbian couple on the heterosexual model, as a "man" and a woman invert. But his antifeminism and reluctance to see active lust in women committed him to fusing inversion and masculinity. What to do with the feminine invert? His solution was an awkward compromise:

> A class of women to be first mentioned . . . is formed by the women to whom the actively inverted woman is most attracted. These women differ in the first place from the normal or average woman in that they are not repelled or disgusted by lover-like advances from persons of their own sex. . . . Their faces may be plain or ill-made but not seldom they possess good figures, a point which is apt to carry more weight with the inverted woman than beauty of face . . . they are of strongly affectionate nature . . . and *they are always womanly* [emphasis mine]. One may perhaps say that they are the pick of the women whom the average man would pass by. No doubt this is often the reason why they are open to homosexual advances, but I do not think it is the sole reason. So far as they may be said to constitute a class they seem to possess a genuine, though not precisely sexual, preference for women over men.
> (1895:147–48)

This extraordinary mix of fantasy, conjecture, and insight clashes with Ellis's insistence that "the chief characteristic of the sexually inverted woman is a certain degree of masculinity" (152). No mention is made of "congenital" factors in regard to this "womanly" invert, and like most examples that do not fit pet paradigms, she is dropped. Gender reversal is not always homosexual, Ellis contends, exempting certain "mannish women" who wear men's clothes out of pragmatic motives, but the "actively inverted woman" always has "a more or less distinct trace of masculinity" as "part of an organic instinct" (148). Because of her firm muscles, athletic ability, dislike of feminine occupations, and predilection for male garments "because the wearer feels more at home in them," the sexually inverted woman, people feel, "ought to have been a man" (153).

Thus the true invert was a being between categories, neither man nor woman, a "third sex" or "trapped soul." Krafft-Ebing, Ellis, and Freud all associated this figure with female lust and with feminist revolt against traditional roles, toward which they were at best ambivalent, at worst horrified.[19] But some second-generation feminists, such as Frances Wilder, Gertrude Stein, and Vita Sackville-West, identified with important aspects of the "third sex" persona. None did so as unconditionally and—this must be said—as bravely as Radclyffe Hall did by making the despised mannish lesbian the hero of *The Well of Loneliness*, which she defended publicly against the British government. Hall's creation, Stephen Gordon, is a double symbol, standing for the New Woman's painful position between traditional political and social categories, and for the lesbian struggle to define and assert an identity.

Even newborn, Stephen's body achieves a biologically impossible masculinity: "Narrow-hipped and wide shouldered" (R. Hall 1950 [1928]:13). She grows and her body becomes "splendid," "supple," "quick"; she can "fence like a man"; she discovers "her body for a thing to be cherished . . . since its strength could rejoice her" (58). But as she matures, her delight degenerates into angst. She is denied male privilege, of course, in spite of her masculine body. But her physical self is also fleshly symbol of the femininity Stephen categorically rejects. Her body is not and cannot be male, yet it is not traditionally female. Between genders and thus illegitimate, it represents Every New Woman, stifled after World War I by a changed political climate and reinforced gender stereotypes. But Hall also uses a body between genders to symbolize the "inverted" sexuality Stephen can neither disavow nor satisfy. Finding herself "no match" for a male rival, the adolescent Stephen begins to hate herself. In one of Hall's most moving passages Stephen expresses this hatred as alienation from her body: "That night she stared at herself in the glass; and even as she did so, she hated her body with its muscular shoulders, its small compact breasts, and its slender flanks of an athlete. All her life she must drag this body of hers like a monstrous fetter imposed on her spirit. This strangely ardent yet sterile body. . . . She longed to maim it, for it made her feel cruel . . . her eyes filled with tears and her hate turned to pity. She began to grieve over it, touching her breasts with pitiful fingers" (187).

Stephen's difference, her overt sexuality, is also represented by cross-dressing. But if male writers used cross-dressing to symbolize and castigate a world upside down, and Virginia Woolf and other female modernists used it to express "gleeful skepticism" toward gender categories (Gilbert 1982:206), Stephen's cross-dressing asserts a series of agonizing estrangements. She is alienated from her mother as the New Woman often was, and as the lesbian was, increasingly, from heterosexual women. Unlike Orlando, Stephen is trapped in history; she cannot declare gender an irrelevant game. She, like many young women then and now, alternately rebels against her mother's vision of womanhood and blames herself for failing to live up to it. Preferring suits from her father's tailor, she sometimes gives in to her mother's demand that she wear "delicate dresses," which she puts on "all wrong." Her mother confirms Stephen's sense of freakishness: "It's my face," Stephen announces, "something's wrong with my face." "Nonsense!" her mother replies, "turning away quickly to hide her expression" (1950 [1928]:73). Cross-dressing for Hall is not a masquerade. It stands for the New Woman's rebellion against the male order and, at the same time, for the lesbian's desperate struggle to be and express her true self.

Hall, like the sexologists, uses cross-dressing and gender reversal to symbolize lesbian sexuality. Unlike the sexologists, however, Hall makes Stephen the subject and takes her point of view against a hostile world. Though men resent Stephen's "unconscious presumption," Hall defends Stephen's claim to what is, in her fictional universe, the ultimate male privilege: the enjoyment of women's erotic love. The mythic mannish lesbian proposes to usurp the son's place in the Oedipal triangle.[20]

Hall had begun to describe what I take to be a central component of lesbian orientation, mother-daughter eroticism,[21] several years earlier in *The Unlit Lamp,* where presumably the nonsexual framework of the novel as a whole had made it safe.[22] I write "eroticism" because sexual desire is distinct from either "identification" or "bonding." A woman can be close to her mother ("bond," "identify") in many ways and yet eroticize only men. Conversely, one can hate one's mother and have little in common with her, as did Radclyffe Hall, and yet desire her fiercely in the image of other women. In my view, feminist psychology has not yet solved the riddle of sexual orientation.

As bold as Hall was, she could not treat mother-daughter eroticism directly in *The Well;* instead, she turned it inside out. Stephen is strangely uncomfortable with all women, especially her mother. For her part, Stephen's mother gives her daughter only a quick goodnight peck on the forehead "so that the girl should not wake and kiss back" (1950 [1928]:83).

Instead, the Oedipal drama is played out with the maid standing in for the mother. At seven, Stephen's intense eroticism is awakened by Collins (who, as working-class sex object, never gets a first name) in an episode infused with sexual meaning. Collins is "florid, full-lipped and full-bosomed" (16), which might remind informed readers of Ellis's dictum that the good figure counts more with the "congenital invert" than does a pretty face. Thinking of Collins makes Stephen "go hot down her spine," and when Collins kisses her on impulse, Stephen is dumbfounded by something "vast, that the mind of seven years found no name for." This "vast" thing makes Stephen say, "I must be a boy, 'cause I feel exactly like one" (18, 20). In case the 1928 reader hasn't gotten the message, Hall shows Stephen's father reading sexologist Karl Heinrich Ulrichs and making notes in the margins. Later, Stephen reads Krafft-Ebing in her dead father's library and recognizes herself as "flawed in the making."

A high price to pay for claiming a sexual identity, yes. But of those who condemn Hall for assuming the sexologists' model of lesbianism I ask, Just how was Hall to make the woman-loving New Woman a sexual being? Despite Hall's use of words like "lover" and "passion" and her references to "inversion," her lawyer actually defended *The Well* against state censorship by trying to convince the court that "the relationship between women described in the book represented a normal friendship." Hall "attacked him furiously for taking this line, which appeared to her to undermine the strength of the convictions with which she had defended the case. His plea seemed to her . . . 'the unkindest cut of all' and at their luncheon together she was unable to restrain 'tears of heartbroken anguish'" (Brittain 1969:92).

How could the New Woman lay claim to her full sexuality? For bourgeois women, there was no developed female sexual discourse; there were only male discourses—pornographic, literary, and medical—about female sexuality. To become avowedly sexual, the New Woman had to enter the male world, either as a heterosexual on male terms (like Emma Goldman and eventually the flapper) or as a lesbian in male body drag (the mannish lesbian/congenital invert). Feminine women like Alice B. Toklas and Hall's lover Una Troubridge could become *recognizable* lesbians by association with their masculine partners.

Ideas, metaphors, and symbols can be used for either radical or conservative purposes.[23] By endowing a biological female with a masculine self, Hall both questions the inevitability of traditional gender categories *and* assents to it. The mannish lesbian should not exist if gender is natural. Yet Hall makes her the hero—not the villain or the clown—of her novel. Stephen survives social condemnation and even argues her own case. But she sacrifices her legitimacy as a woman and as an aristocrat. The interpersonal cost is high, too: Stephen loses her mother and her lover, Mary. *The Well* explores the self-hatred and doubt inherent in defining oneself as a "sexual deviant." For in doing so, the lesbian accepts an invidious distinction between herself and heterosexual women.

Heterosexual men have used this distinction to condemn lesbians and intimidate straight women. The fear and antagonism between us has certainly weakened the modern feminist movement. And that is why lesbian-feminists (abetted by some straight feminists) are fanatical about redefining lesbianism as "woman-identification," a model that, not incidentally, puts heterosexual feminists at a disadvantage.[24] Hall's vision of lesbianism as sexual difference and as masculinity is inimical to lesbian-feminist ideology.

Like Hall, I see lesbianism as sexual difference. But her equation of lesbianism with masculinity needs not condemnation, but expansion. To begin with, we need to accept that whatever their ideological purposes, Hall and the sexologists were describing something real. Some people, then and now, experience "gender dysphoria," a strong feeling that one's assigned gender as a man or a woman does not agree with one's sense of self.[25] This is not precisely the same thing as wanting power and male privilege—a well-paid job, abortion on demand, athletic prowess—even though the masculine woman continues to be a symbol of feminist aspirations to the majority outside the movement. Masculinity and femininity are like two dialects of the same language. Though we all understand both, most of us "speak" only one.[26] Many lesbians, like Stephen Gordon, are biological females who grow up thinking in and "speaking" the "wrong" gender dialect.

Obviously, the more narrow and rigid gender categories are, the more easily one can feel "out of role." And if there were no more gender categories, gender dysphoria would disappear (as would feminism). However, feminist critiques of traditional gender categories do not yet resolve gender dysphoria if only because we have made so little impact on child-rearing practices; it appears that individual gender identity is established in early childhood. Although gender dysphoria exists in some simple societies,[27] it may be amplified by the same sociohistorical processes—radical changes in the economy, in family structure and function, and in socialization—that have given rise to feminism. Why should we as feminists deplore or deny the existence of masculine women or effeminate men? Are we not *against* assigning specific psychological or behavioral traits to a particular biology? And should we not support those among us, butches and queens, who still bear the brunt of homophobia?

Hall's association of lesbianism and masculinity needs to be challenged not because it doesn't exist, but because it is not the only possibility. Gender identity and sexual orientation are, in fact, two related but separate systems; witness the profusion of gender variations (which are deeply embedded in race, class, and ethnic experience) to be found today in the lesbian community. Many lesbians *are* masculine; most have composite styles; many are emphatically feminine. Stephen Gordon's success eclipsed more esoteric, continental, or feminine images of the lesbian, such as Renee Vivien's *décadente*, Collette's bisexual, or Natalie Barney's *Amazone*. The notion of a feminine lesbian contradicted the congenital theory that many homosexuals in Hall's era espoused to counter demands that they undergo punishing "therapies." Though Stephen's lovers in *The Well* are feminine and though Mary, in effect, seduces Stephen, Hall calls her "normal," that is, heterosexual. Even Havelock Ellis gave the "womanly" lesbian more dignity and definition. As a character, Mary is forgettable and inconsistent, weakening the novel and saddling Hall with an implausible ending in which Stephen "nobly" turns Mary over to a man. In real life, Hall's lover Una Troubridge did not go back to heterosexuality even when Hall, late in her life, took a second lover.

Despite knowing Una, Natalie Barney, and others like them, Hall was unable to publicly articulate—perhaps to believe in—the persona of a *real* lesbian who did not feel somehow male. If sexual desire is masculine, and if the feminine woman wants to attract only men, then the womanly lesbian cannot logically exist. Mary's real story has yet to be told.[28]

Beyond Freud, Ken, and Barbie

1986

In one of many interesting passages in *Presentations of Gender,* Dr. Robert Stoller reveals how, in 1958, the problem of gender identity smacked him in the intellectual face. A new patient had been described to him as "a 'transsexual woman' (a biologic female who nonetheless considered herself a man). . . . Shortly before the appointment hour, I was approaching stupor at a committee meeting in a conference room with a glass wall that allowed us to see people pass. A man walked by; I scarcely noticed him. A moment later, a secretary announced my eleven o'clock patient. And to my astonishment, the patient was not what I expected—a woman who acted masculine and in the process was a bit too much, grimly and pathetically discarding her femininity. Instead it was a man, unremarkable, natural appearing—an ordinary man." A woman who *acts* masculine can be dismissed, but a person with a vagina who *is* masculine? From this incident, Stoller writes, grew his lifelong interest in gender identity. "[Psychoanalytic] generalizations . . . had, I felt, to give way to data—the realities of this patient's presence" (1985:4).

Exceptional people like Stoller's "patient" throw into question the way our world is divided into humans called "women" and those called "men," the situation that gave rise to feminism. Some feminist strategies, like the antipornography campaign, assume profound differences, perhaps biologically caused, between women and men. The Equal Rights Amendment campaign, in contrast, was based on the premise that no differences, if such exist, should be (legally) recognized. Unfortunately, these underlying assumptions are rarely made explicit. The interdisciplinary field of gender studies, which therefore has great significance for feminists, addresses questions raised by the fact that all known cultures sort people into categories that translate into English as "women" and "men."

There are roughly three orientations toward gender, each with both scholarly and political embodiments. The conservatives see maleness and femaleness as biological givens, the fabric of Mother Nature's raiment; any weak seams such as homosexuality or cross-dressing should be restitched. This position derives from traditional Judeo-Christian thinking; its politicos are currently running the Executive Branch. The radicals, who are often (but not always) influenced by Marxist historical perspectives, see masculinity and femininity as cultural, not biological creations. Our work on gender and sexuality is termed "social constructionist," meaning we analyze society, including how people have sex and who they are supposed to want to have it with, in terms of human beings' symbol-making activities.[1] Social constructionists have no power outside the feminist and gay movements. Straddled between the two persuasions are scholars like Stoller—liberals—who look to some mesh of biological and psychological and/or cultural forces to explain gender differences. This camp informs and in many cases controls liberal (including liberal feminist) policy on gender issues, from who shall get the "sex change" operation to whether or not preschool boys should be encouraged to play with dolls and whether lesbians make acceptable parents.

Robert Stoller is an eminent, prolific clinician who has devoted his career to theorizing about and "curing" people with "gender disorders," such as transsexuals and cross-dressers. One of his previous books, *Sexual Excitement* (1979), was as provocative and original as its title, so I approached *Presentations* with interest, despite the cover, which perhaps even as prestigious an author as Stoller does not control, showing Cranach's *Adam and Eve in the Garden*. Not an auspicious start for cutting-edge gender theory. Although it has some of the same virtues as *Sexual Excitement* (freedom from psychoanalytic mumbo jumbo, a personable style, and vivid case material), *Presentations* illustrates the contradictions in and dangers of the liberal position.

Feminists will note immediately that Stoller has mud from the nineteenth century on his feet. The most influential medical book on sex of that century, by Dr. William Acton, was called *Functions and Diseases of the Reproductive Organs*; the organs, however, were penises. *Plus ça change* . . . Despite his title—surely his own choice—Stoller's subject is not gender but rather how masculine gender identity can go haywire. His subjects are the mothers—fathers always refuse treatment—of little boys with "conditions" such as effeminacy, cross-dressing, transsexualism, and fetishism.

In a cross-cultural vein, Stoller examines the "cases" of two Native American "berdache," biological males who become a different gender (the meaning of the change is hotly debated by scholars) in adult life.[2] The penultimate chapter is frankly called "The Development of Masculinity: A Cross-Cultural Contribution," coauthored with anthropologist Gilbert Herdt and based on the latter's well-known fieldwork in New Guinea. Stoller begins in a way any social constructionist could live with: "Masculinity or femininity is defined here as any quality that is felt by its possessor to be masculine or feminine.

In other words, masculinity or femininity is a belief—more precisely, a dense mass of beliefs" (1985:11).

How surprising, then, that these beliefs are conjectured to result from a prenatal "biologic 'force,'" "biopsychic phenomena," and "sensations from the genitals" as well as "parental attitudes" and "sex assignment at birth." How can a "mass of beliefs" so culturally variable as those about masculinity and femininity be caused by fetal hormones? The answer lies not in nonexistent proofs—after a century of trying, no one has been able to prove any biological cause for any gender behavior or belief—but in unexamined assumptions; the "biologic 'force'" represents Stoller's heavy investment in the gender status quo. His original perception that "generalizations had to give way to data" is mostly all wind-up and no follow through. For one thing, the data never get off the couch. Twenty minutes in a gay bar would strike out the unsophisticated thesis that gay man = feminine man, for instance. But the heavy hitters in Stoller's ballpark are still Freud, Ken, and Barbie.

Nothing can take away from the fascination of the case material, which makes up the greater part of *Presentations*. Consider this mother's description of her three-and-a-half-year-old son: "He exhibits no femininity at all. That's not the problem. It's the pantyhose. He touches me or looks at me peculiarly lustful. . . . The other day, we were at the grocery store, and he saw, way down the aisle, the pantyhose advertised on TV. . . . He was giddy and laughing [and] he said, 'Let's buy pantyhose; let's buy pantyhose.' And I said, . . . 'You're a boy. You don't need pantyhose.' And he said, 'Oh no. I'm a girl.' And he kind of looked at me, and I just completely ignored that statement" (103).

Stoller's conclusions, however, have a frightening predictability: "too much mother and too little father [makes] for feminine boys" (8). The real villain is the mom who "gratifies" her infant son too much. It takes rough handling and paternal vigilance to create a rambo; Navy jet pilots are cited as outstanding masculine role models!

Because the "absent father" constellation has also been blamed for such disparate and unpopular phenomena as supermacho ghetto kids, rebellious youth movements of the 1960s, and the feminization of poverty, it should be dropped. "Absent father" is too imprecise a concept to explain a precocious turn-on to pantyhose. (To do Stoller justice, his analysis of this case is more subtle in the particulars; it's the generalizations that are banal.) It is also dangerous to treat a supposedly aberrant phenomenon in our culture like "absent father" as equivalent to cultural norms such as gender segregation and boys' initiation among the Sambia of New Guinea.

Mothers of feminine boys, Stoller asserts, have a sense of worthlessness about being female and tend to worship their sons. Happily, he was able to help one mother to "[become] peacefully and happily female," and today her son "is not a feminine or homosexual man" (78). This smug attitude strikes me as backward even by liberal standards. Stoller has grasped that some of us doubt the legitimacy of the boy/girl pecking order: "You may believe that, should he become a feminine man—homosexual or transsexual—such an outcome is bad only in the eyes of a sick society, that whether males are feminine or masculine is really a psychologically and morally neutral issue." But for him, the bottom line is, "Oedipal conflict . . . [is] . . . needed to produce the character structures, such as masculinity and femininity, that maintain the society" (78).

Dr. Stoller is so prominent in the field of gender studies that he must be considered an obstacle to more humane, if not revolutionary, gender policies until he reminds himself that power, privilege, and scholarship are deadly friends.

Psychologists Suzanne Kessler and Wendy McKenna (both colleagues of mine in women's studies at Purchase) see the same issues through radical and feminist glasses. *Gender: An Ethnomethodological Approach* (1985) was originally issued in a very expensive hardcover edition by Wiley in 1978. Although word of its virtues spread among the gender cognoscenti—Stoller's ignorance of their work is a mark of his total indifference to feminist scholarship—it never reached a wider audience. If you read only one book about how we become either women or men (but not both or neither), read this. It will teach you, in clear language accessible to the nonspecialist, what you need to know—and you do need to know it—about the range of issues in modern gender theory.

The authors go right for the jugular of the conservative thinking that dominates both science and everyday life: that "men" and "women" are biological entities. Influenced by such sociologists as Berger and Luckmann and Harold Garfinkel, they argue that the only objective fact is that all systems of truth, including science, are social constructions erected on "incorrigible propositions," unquestioned axioms: "The most basic incorrigible proposition is the belief that the world exists independently of our presence, and that objects have an independent reality and a constant identity" (1985:5). As it applies to gender, this means that "seeing two physical genders is as much a socially constructed dichotomy as everything else. . . . The element of social construction is primary in all aspects of being male and female" (6, 7).

It is a graduate school commonplace in anthropology that If people believe a thing to be true, that belief has real consequences. Take the following proposition: men have body hair; women don't. A moment's reflection will tell you this is not literally true. Nevertheless, millions of real dollars are made by Nair based on the fact that women's self-esteem, jobs, and relationships depend on their embodying this objectively false but culturally true proposition. The result — easily confirmed by watching any American movie — is that men have body hair; women don't.

For Kessler and McKenna, the statement "There are two sexes" is of the same order. In a lucid chapter on biology and gender, they show that gonads, genitals, hormones, and chromosomes don't necessarily have neat gender tags (all hormones, for example, are produced by both "sexes") or all line up in discrete male and female rows. Relegating the intersexed — people who are not clearly biologically male or female — to an "abnormal" category is another way of denying the fact that gender is continuous, not dimorphic. Kessler and McKenna estimate that chromosomally "intersexed" individuals are born about twice as often as Down syndrome babies. In addition, such configurations as androgen insensitivity syndrome cause xy babies to develop typically female bodies (these children develop "normal" female gender identity). This does not take into account the enormous "normal" range of variation in so-called secondary sex characteristics such as body hair, muscular development, and so on between genders and among races. By surgically "correcting" the intersexed and suppressing the physical, psychological, and cultural similarities among human beings, we create "opposite sexes." Just ask anyone who has ever blurred the line; behind the blandly "obvious" proposition "There are two sexes" lurks the menacing "There *must* be two sexes."

If gender is a social fact, how do people create it? The key process, Kessler and McKenna argue, is "gender attribution," the active (though usually unconscious) way we decide what gender a person is. Because the rules for gender attribution are unstated, the authors work to expose them: in non-Western cultures, where different rules throw ours into relief; in exceptional people like transsexuals, who confuse others about what gender to attribute; in the development of children who are actively learning the rules; and in ingenious tests for the visual cues used to decide whether an ambiguous figure is female or male.

Every chapter is original, relentlessly systematic, and thought-provoking. They argue, in an excellent discussion of the "berdache" phenomenon, that we are imposing our two-gender imperative on anthropological data; that Freud's theory about the primacy of genitals in gender-identity development is not borne out by children's drawings; and perhaps most controversially, that for Americans, "in the social construction of gender 'male' is the primary construction." Just as "men have body hair, women don't," the number one "incorrigible proposition" of gender attribution is that "men have penises; women don't."

Kessler and McKenna have succeeded (to my satisfaction) in casting doubt on the entire field of "sex role differences," for "biological, psychological, and social differences do not lead to our seeing two genders. Our seeing of two genders leads to the 'discovery' of biological, psychological, and social differences' (163).

What are the implications? The gender dichotomy, they say, must be eliminated because "Where there are dichotomies it is difficult to avoid evaluating one in relation to the other, a firm foundation for discrimination and oppression" (164). But must we be the same in order to be "equal"? Dichotomy need not lead to oppression as long as the two sides maintain a balance of power. Preindustrial cultures abound with such arrangements. The English and French see each other as opposites, but for all their efforts, neither has succeeded for long in oppressing the other. However, distinctions such as gender and race, supposedly unalterable, are incompatible with our society of mobility and "free choice." Perhaps gender dichotomy will still exist but be based on inclination and personality.

What remains is the necessity for sperm and egg to meet. Here Kessler and McKenna propose that there may be a biologically based ability to know "whether the other is similar or different from oneself" for purposes of reproduction. Perhaps with advances in reproductive technology, the status "sperm producer" and "egg carrier" would have no more impact than knowing your blood type does now. But then, why should the ability to "differentiate" genders be innate? There are certainly unresolved problems here.

All in all, though, *Gender* belongs in the ranks of social science "postmodernist" classics like David Schneider's *American Kinship* (1968) and "The Traffic in Women" (1975), Gayle Rubin's justly famous synthesis of Freud, Marx, and Lévi-Strauss. I can give no higher praise.

My Butch Career: A Memoir

1996

Gay, Laura thought to herself. Is that what they call it? *Gay?* She was acutely uncomfortable now. It was as if she were a child of civilization, reared among the savages, who suddenly found herself among the civilized. She recognized them as her own. And yet she had adopted the habits of another race and she was embarrassed and lost with her own kind. (Bannon 1983)

PROLOGUE: ALICE-HUNTING

I met Gertrude Stein in 1961, on the cover of a book. Inside were lots of facts and dates and witty sayings of hers but not the one thing I wanted most to know: Was Gertrude Stein a dyke?

So I ran out and found *The Autobiography of Alice B. Toklas,* thinking what a nervy idea to write someone else's autobiography, they must have been lovers, but it didn't say so any more than the first book had. It was all impersonal and too much about famous men, but there were many, many hints. And the more books and photographs I found the more I thought yes. But it's one thing to think yes and something else to know it.

Little by little this idea of being Gertrude began to grow inside my head. It wasn't yet about living in Paris or about writing, but about being accepted as an equal by men within a very small select circle, and of living in a happy domesticated couple with heaps of good food. So naturally, the big thing was to find an Alice.

But finding an Alice wasn't easy. At first it wasn't easy because some therapist said I should go out with men, and none of the men were at all like Alice. After several years I'd used up all the men and the therapist too, and was still as gay as ever. Just then I became one of a few women in a fancy graduate school, with lots of small select men who accepted me as an equal, so the time for Alice seemed right. But none of the women I met really deep down wanted to be an Alice. No matter how Alice they seemed, it always turned out that secretly they too wanted to be Gertrude, even if they'd never read anything about her. Unbelievable as it sounds, all those Alices wanted to use me as a model for becoming Gertrude themselves. And as they became more Gertrude, I fought with them more and desired them less.

This is because, speaking frankly, Gertrudes have a couple of faults— being bossy and being babies—and they like to be the only bossy baby in the house. And the aspiring Gertrudes—this is how I saw the situation—probably wanted Alices of their own or at least a more neutral sort of person than I was. And as for desire, I wanted to be the one who was doing something to an Alice who wanted something, not the other way around.

However, there was no giving up on this idea of Gertrude and Alice. Certainly I couldn't be Alice myself, and without an Alice I couldn't be Gertrude, which was for me the only way to be gay. And I was gay. So little by little I began to think that the reason why I couldn't find an Alice must be that I wasn't a genius. If only I could be a genius then absolutely Alice must appear. It was 1968.

Just then they showed the feminist protest of the Miss America contest on TV. Nothing had made me so excited since the day I'd first seen Gertrude's photograph, and I joined a consciousness-raising group. The other women had all been in the radical left and they were politically aware. And just as I was desperately longing to be Gertrude, these young women said that class privilege was wrong. I had been earning money on my first teaching job, and even though I still hadn't found an Alice, I'd been collecting good furniture and other things I thought a Gertrude sort of person should have in her home. And furthermore, my "sisters" most definitely didn't believe in "roles," meaning they were sick of having their boyfriends boss them around. They didn't approve of Gertrude and Alice's way of living either, which seemed to them just like a husband and wife.

Then I met Louise. At first she wore miniskirts and eye makeup. On our first date we went to see *King Kong* and afterwards Louise did a very funny imitation of Kong smelling Fay Wray's underpants. Because of her long blonde curls and sequined blouses, I never asked what it meant that Louise played King Kong. She could cook very well and made things like avocado and mushroom sandwiches, so I was thrilled and we moved in together.

But as time went on it got more and more mixed up who was really King Kong and who Fay Wray. Louise's hair got shorter and shorter. All the time we were going separately and together to feminist meetings, where it was always said that there were no more "roles," so there was no way to talk about our predicament. It was bad to be a "heavy" (meaning other people felt small because you were too big), and I was, and if Louise wanted to be King Kong in bed why couldn't I be Alice?

I began to doubt everything except being gay and wrote about all the doubts in a journal. Soon writing got to be more and more on my mind. And the more I liked doing it and having it on my mind, the more I began to feel Gertrude-like as a writer, just as I was rejecting her because what feminist wants to be accepted as an equal by men or be waited on by an Alice in a cozy couple surrounded by select fews? No, I was too Gertrude, that was the trouble. If only I were less Gertrude I'd meet someone who was less Alice and this would solve the problem.

MY BUTCH BODY

The butch is either the magical sign of lesbianism, or a failed, emasculated and abjected man. (Munt 1998)

Because of my chromosomes—xx as far as I know—and a reproductive biology, which is, or rather was, capable of giving birth, my sex is female. During my lonely childhood among the savages, I was stuck in the girl gender, which is linked, worldwide, to hard work, low pay, and disrespect, though this is not the only reason why for me, neither being female nor being a woman has ever been easy or unequivocal. Later, when I found gay life and started to become civilized, I was given a second gender.[1] This gay gender, butch, makes my body recognizable and it alone makes sexual love possible. But being butch has been problematic, too. How could it not be?

Butch is my handle and my collective name; a tribe, the late lamented writer Paul Monette called us gay people. My life's work has been inspired by and primarily written for these gay communities, entities that are no less powerful for being symbolic.

Remember that scene in *The Well of Loneliness,* where Stephen Gordon grieves over the reflection of her masculine body? Well, mirrors have always made me queasy, too. Maybe for the same reasons why I get anxious sometimes, even today, going around with other butches. Our forbidden looks are reflected back even bigger when butches hang out. In them I see what I look like, and how I look still has the power to shock me: sometimes because my masculine self-awareness, my ego body image is startled, for example, by the breasts or hips I see in the naked mirror; other times because I look so different from how, as a woman, I know I am supposed to look. In a documentary I once saw about dwarfs, a woman not much taller than a fire hydrant tells the impartial camera how at first she had recoiled from joining an association of little people because "I was horrified when I saw them. I had told myself, 'You don't look like that.'"

The other night I dreamed I came upon a brown bear surrounded by a boisterous crowd of street people. I approached the bear obliquely from the back; it was sitting upright and motionless in a hole, only the back of its torso and head were visible. The people were shouting at it and throwing garbage. I realized that they meant in the end to kill it and were only tormenting it for the fun of destroying a robust, beautiful animal who was hopelessly outnumbered. I woke in terror and threw myself into my girlfriend's arms. "It's you, the bear," she said. "But it's only a dream."

Is my butch body worth any more than the bear's, or is the hatred it inspires its only value? Certainly, butches have been the target of medical intervention to correct our grievous mistakes, our unshakable belief in how we should look and move. My body commits every one of these movement "mistakes"—for example, hands on hips, *fingers forward*—that are used to diagnose Gender Identity Disorder, a category of mental illness listed in the *DSM-IV*.[2] Luckily, when my friction of teenage misery burst into flames, I escaped the Thorazine and shock treatments others endured through the middle-class option of therapy to cure what still proved to be an intractable "case" of gender dysphoria and homosexual desire. But there is still a terror of calling attention to myself, of naming myself what is plain to see.

Child Monster

My child body was a strong and capable instrument somehow stuffed into the word "girl." I was the first kid up the jungle gym, as good as any of the boys at stoop ball. All my friends were boys; girls were dumb. I had nothing in common with them.

When I was about seven, a ten-year-old boy I idolized, a guy I was playing sex games with, thinking we were buddies and I could be him, showed me I was no boy by trying to use me as a sexual favor for his real buddies. My rage and shame over his betrayal threw me into a shock whose traumatic effects have proven to be lifelong. The guys had made me understand that they were the boys, and I was something other, a body to be used by them. Thus ended my life as a boy. But it didn't make me a girl. It made me an antigirl, a girl refuser, caught between genders.

Like "gay community," the female body is also an imaginary construct. Any body is shaped by being lived in. My own intrepid body and dominating (though needy) personality seemed to others—and to my child self—to be

The first kid up the jungle gym,
about 1946

masculine, and these perceptions (should they be called fears? convictions?)
bore out Oscar Wilde's dictum that life imitates art. My body ate masculinity
and thrived on it. Endless hours playing stickball, later tennis, basketball,
competitive physical games I loved. The horse books and baseball books that
appealed to me. All those dark Saturday mornings at the kids matinee in the
Superior Theater, the local movie house, dreaming myself into Tyrone Power,
Errol Flynn the buccaneer running his sword through villainous Basil Rathbone. This masculinity, my masculinity, is not external; it permeates and ani-
mates me. Nor is it a masquerade. In my own home, when no one is present,
I still sit with my legs carelessly flung apart.

I saw other female bodies: my mother's, the other girls' at summer camp
where my parents had sent me, hoping without saying so that somehow their
femininity would rub off on me, which it did not. But spending every summer
with girls made me feel more at ease with them, and showed me there were
ways of being a girl that might just work. There were counselors who were
physically confident and well coordinated like me, who could handle nervous
horses and slam tennis balls. For the first time I had tomboy friends and even
wound up liking regular, feminine girls more, despite their teasing because
even in my bunk I always wore that blue Brooklyn Dodgers baseball cap.

Eleven is supposed to be the age when girls lose confidence. That's how
old I was when my divorced mother dragged me to California. On the drive

cross-country, I spun around and around inside one desperate thought: that if I'd been a boy this exile from everything familiar in New York City could not have happened.

My Favorite Photo

In my favorite photo, the setting is urban: a kids' playground. In the background a 1940s baby carriage and a grim brick building, public toilets. My WASP mother and her little guy sit on a bench thigh to thigh. Her chestnut hair is braided around her head like a laurel wreath or a halo. She wears a plain cotton dress. She holds her legs together and smiles into the camera, but one knee is exposed. The edge of her skirt partly covers my thigh.

I must have been four or five. My mother thought bathing suit tops for little girls premature, a commercially motivated imposition of femininity, so I wear a boy's bathing suit. Little boots stuffed with socks beside me. My legs spread comfortably apart, feet swinging free. You can tell I'm a girl because my brown hair covers my ears. I am leaning into the crook of my mother's arm. Protectively, she circles my shoulders from behind. The outside hand pulls me into her; the closer one seems to ward off some danger to my chest. I stare out—unsmiling—as if to say, This is *my* spot.

Like my dark father, I am attracted to my mother's fair skin and light eyes. Is this a form of self-hate, a delicious eroticism, or both?

Desire among the Savages (Sue Wilson)

Palo Alto, California. By accident, Sue Wilson sat next to me in high school honors English. She was busty and inactive, the kind of girl that boys liked. Not that she showed what she had, like those so-called "cheap" Mexican girls. She was a "nice" white girl, neatly dressed in straight skirts and blouses with round collars, only the top button undone. Assured, easy in her body, Sue was definitely feminine.

What was it, to be feminine? I tried to learn. Inside the girls' clothing I loathed, inside the traitorous body that had grown into an alien shape, inside the suburban teenager who had to beg for an allowance and the use of the car, the me that was as free and big as Tyrone Power setting sail contracted to the vanishing point. I had understood, all over again, that there was no choice. I *had* to be a girl.

How did the girls do it? Practicing in front of the mirror, tugging the stiff crinolines this way and that, the rolled-down bobby sox, charm bracelets, flared skirts, straight skirts, Peter Pan blouses, Pendleton outfits . . . What was it? No clothing, no borrowed gesture ever performed the magic, made me right.

My favorite photo with my mother, Virginia Newton, about 1945.

The other girls just *were* it. Sue Wilson, for instance. The teacher read the best compositions aloud in class. Sue wrote that her father was in the Army. She'd been born in Turkey. I thought her writing was beautiful. Was there still something of Constantinople inside that WASPY blandness?

She asked me over to study for a test. Sue's room was right out of *Seventeen* magazine; her bed even had a canopy and stuffed animals on the pillow. We sat under the canopy. As she ran through a plot synopsis of *Cry, The Beloved Country,* I began to sweat. My eyes kept going to her blonde hair, and to her breasts, thick and fragrant as a rose bush I couldn't help but stick my nose into—because of the way just the top of her cleavage showed when she bent over the book. My body felt grotesque, bulky. Was I getting my period? There were no cramps. My ears were hot. My arms and hands seemed so huge and separate, almost out of control. I saw myself as a plague of locusts swarming all over her smooth creamy skin. Did Sue notice she was sitting next to a monster? I almost ran out of her house.

This fierce impulse to shake her up, to kiss her mouth, even to squeeze her breasts, it was sexual, it was how I imagined that men got turned on to women. Someone had passed me *The Well of Loneliness* in a brown paper bag, so I knew there had been a masculine girl like me in England. The kids called it "lesbian." It might as well have been "leper." No one in my high school wore green on Thursday for fear of being called one. That other lepers might be in Africa or even England was as good as saying there were none, here in the Bay Area.

I expected Sue would avoid me after that. I avoided everyone. Several weeks later, coming home from the dentist full of Novocain, I stared dispassionately in the bathroom mirror at my sullen, strong-jawed face. This face looked very ugly, very wrong. The big dark eyes scared me. What was inside there? Reaching into the medicine cabinet, I unwrapped a razor blade and cut a slash by the side of my mouth. "I can't feel anything," I said aloud as the blood dripped down my neck.

A WASP in Jew's Clothing

We are never simply women or men. Our American genders are always embodied as "races." These so-called races have a haphazard relation to biology, yet, like being queer, they are all too real, culturally speaking, in their consequences for individuals. My body was always definitely white when considered in relation to black people or Asian people. "White" was the given as I grew up, so I was not aware of how I became a white girl, of how the signs and smells of whiteness permeated me. Nor of all the perks and pleasures provided me within that dispensation.

My mother's coloring is fair. She came from old Yankee stock. All her ancestors but one had come over before the Revolution, one of them on the *Mayflower*. As I write this I am in Provincetown with my girlfriend, who is also, not coincidentally, a WASP; there is a plaque here dedicated to those same *Mayflower* Pilgrims who, in 1620, first landed in America. What possible leap of imagination connects me to my ancestor—his name was Peregrine White—without whom I would not exist? And why would I want to, except that our pasts must be owned? My WASP ancestors and people like them conquered the country, cheated the Indians and then disowned them, kept African slaves. They also bravely crossed the Great Plains in covered wagons, founded towns like Peoria, Illinois, freed slaves out of conviction, and gave birth in hard circumstances.

While my mother always talked proudly about her ancestors and relatives, I knew I was different from these people we hardly ever saw. Within whiteness there are subtleties and equivocations. Not all so-called white people are the same, or equal.

I was a red diaper baby. My mother had a thing for Jewish men. She met lots of them in the Communist Party she had joined out of a Depression-era liberal social conscience and to enrage her conservative father, a general in the U.S. Army. One of those left-wing Jews my WASP mother liked was my father, a man just as tyrannical as the general, and a womanizer who eventually had six wives. For a few years, until he tired of her, my father cast his erotic net over my mother and she didn't struggle. She had the hots for him. How intensely I resented that! He joined our circle late: while he had been away fighting Nazis I had been her little husband.

My father's parents were struggling immigrants from the Ukraine. He rejected Judaism right after his bar mitzvah—some mistreatment of his family by the local synagogue, he said, but really, the model of Jewish scholarly manhood repelled and shamed him. My father took up boxing in college—when I was six or seven, he tried to teach me never to telegraph my punches—and as a soldier he volunteered to be an artillery spotter, one of the most dangerous assignments. He was my masculine ideal.

When we lived in New York my parents sent me to one of those commie pinko progressive schools—anthropologist Margaret Mead was said to have been a founder—that believed in letting children "be themselves." As a nine-year-old, let's say, my everyday school outfit was sneakers, jeans, and a polo shirt, and for dress-up I was the Lone Ranger, whom I called the Long Ranger, so my father called me the Short Ranger.

Once when I was in my late thirties and had freed myself from his domination, my father and I had dinner near where he lived. As we stood on the corner of Broadway and 91st Street waiting for the light to change, I realized with a creepy shock that we were dressed nearly the same—running shoes, jeans, and plaid shirt—and were both standing with hands on our hips, *fingers forward,* a couple of tough Jewish guys.

My father was dark and, as luck would have it, I am too, though not as dark as he was. A mutt is what my students call us American mixed breeds. Recently I've begun to think of my butch self as bicultural and to appreciate my hybrid vigor. Because of growing up in New York among my father's Jewish relatives I'm at home among Jews, though ignorant of the religion. Because of being raised by my WASP mother, though, my sensibility is more akin to the WASPs I don't resemble. I came to understand that I wasn't as white as they were. My mother once corrected a hospital nurse who remarked on our resemblance as mother and daughter, "But her father was of a completely different race!"

Privilege Is Part of Me

Once [Ann Lister] inherits her uncle's estate, indeed, her social position actually protects her from the kind of disapprobation that she routinely undergoes as a masculine woman without her own income. (Halberstam 1998)

Most of my academic friends view my claiming butch as an eccentricity. They overlook it because they love me and they think I'm smart, which means, at least partly, that we move in the same intellectual circles. They prefer to understand my seeing myself this way as an offbeat and somewhat déclassé avocation, as if I followed mud wrestling or roller derby. They find my insistence that I am butch mildly titillating, but mostly embarrassing. This is even, or especially, true of professional women who themselves might be called butch behind their backs. It's sort of okay to *be* masculine as long as it's not named as such. I resent this lesbian version of Don't ask, don't tell.

If I were working class, there is more of a chance that my being butch might be taken for granted among my friends, and with luck, celebrated, as key to what is distinctive and maybe even good about me. Butch and femme have been central to working-class lesbian life at least since the 1950s.[3] My own research in Cherry Grove suggests that there was more working-class resistance to the total denigration of these identities under the influence of lesbian-feminist ideology in the 1970s and 1980s.

I was born in Manhattan, the privileged child of professional people. My butch body bears the marks of access, opportunity, and a life lived with papers and books. The confidence with which I usually enter stores and bureaucratic offices, my multisyllabic vocabulary, the intact teeth and gums that only lifelong dental work makes possible, all express the physical safety of my family's home, their comfortable income and good educations, and the fact that my own life has been lived approximately at their level.

What have I in common with working-class butches, then? My butch body recognizes the claims of our common tomboy origins and overlapping destinies. Yet privilege has always allowed me to get over in places where they mostly couldn't; it has always softened the edges of my butchness, because "masculinity" too is an abstract. In life, masculinity inhabits particular people with contrasting histories. Among men, the masculinity of most college professors looks effete compared to that of most plumbers. Yet no one debates that college professors are "men" (although who is "more of" a man or a "real" man is subject to debate), and to me, butch is a queer identity that cannot transcend but does cut across classes and races, thereby gaining immensely in resonance and richness. Most middle-class put-downs of butches and femmes are class stereotypes and prejudice, conscious or unconscious.

My class became a problem during freshman year in college, when I was seduced by Phyllis Green, a bohemian wildcat of an art student who knew how to find other gay people via New York City bar life. In the summer of 1959 I followed her into a world that thrilled and terrified me with its frankly erotic slow dancing, johns looking to pay lesbians for sexual "freak shows," pot smoking, and an edgy threat of violence. My girlfriend there was Nannette, a former synchronized swimmer turned chorus girl at the Club 82, a drag club on East Fourth Street. At 4 A.M. I'd pick my way through cigar-smoking gangsters to meet her after work. How glamorous she was in theatrical makeup, blue eye shadow-for-days and inch-long false eyelashes! Nannette was the first person I ever touched who dyed her hair—I vividly recall its orangy color and paperlike texture. A proud femme, Nannette boasted that no man had ever fucked her.

All the butches I met—one who was also dating Nannette threatened to carve up my college kid face with her knife—looked and mostly were tough. Their peroxided d.a. haircuts were slicked back into the same styles the hoody boys from the wrong side of the freeway had worn in my high school. Their most precious asset was pride. "I have no dignity left," my drag queen mentor and friend Skip Arnold told me, "but I do have my pride." Butch pride was expressed by short tempers, fists, and broken bottles. As much as I loved the flash of these butches, and admired their courage, their rugged masculinity and tough talk made me seem wimpish. And the truth is, those bar butches were incompatible with my life plans.

Professional is not the same as rich. I didn't have an independent income like Gertrude Stein, the painter Gluck, or Radclyffe Hall, women who, though not called butches or bull dykes, were the wealthy version of the same impulse, as Radclyffe Hall made perfectly clear in *The Well of Loneliness*. Their friends called them by men's names, they wore masculine clothing, and they paired with feminine women. That they got away with it and were called eccentric or even dashing was thanks to their refuge in bohemian artiness, made possible by money. These mannish wealthy women, like the bar dykes, functioned as the "magical sign of lesbianism" partly because their gender inversion made them so visible. Rich lesbians were not answerable to the work world's feminine gender code to keep a roof over their heads. They paid the price for their visibility in expatriatism and social ostracism. On the other hand, working-class butches paid the price of their visibility with unemployment, beatings, or having to pass as men, as Leslie Feinberg showed in *Stone Butch Blues*.

Middle-class women, floating between Radclyffe Hall's Stephen Gordon and Leslie Feinberg's Jess Goldberg, experience cultural and economic conditions that severely limit the expression of gender deviance. A woman of my class who was probably queer and wouldn't have a husband to depend on was going to have to work. It's important to be precise: for Americans, money and class are more taboo than sex. Slinging boxes onto a truck or waitressing: I was brought up to think that work like that wasn't for people like me. Even being a secretary, work my mother had done—it seemed like a life sentence to boredom, fake smiles, and bringing men coffee. More opportunities were opening up for college-educated women as the 1960s began. I clung tenaciously to my half-formed ambitions; someone who looked like a butch bar dyke, which is to say, someone who looked so obviously gay, could forget about a career.

I left the bars and returned to college, where I had kind of a breakdown. Out of panic I got engaged to a man with the unconscious intention of getting pregnant. An illegal abortion in Tijuana, Mexico, nearly finished me off. This negative limit proved my biological femaleness once and for all, and the moralistic lecture of the male doctor at Stanford Hospital who saved my life— "I hope you realize, young lady, that you brought this on yourself"—was perfectly consistent with the shame and disgust with which I had always perceived femaleness and femininity in relation to myself. I am never unaware of the vulnerability of this female body of mine.

I retreated in disarray, trying intermittently, with the "help" of a therapist, to be straight for the next seven years, years whose false starts and wasted efforts I regret bitterly. My butch self took refuge in a fantasy world dominated by the figure of Gertrude Stein, about whom I read everything I could find. Stein was to me a mannish ego ideal who had somehow created a domestic and intellectual life in a Parisian setting of dazzling appeal. Her story was like my favorite fairy tale or masturbation fantasy, the only version of butch that appealed to me in every way as I slogged my way through college and graduate school confused, conflicted, and in the closet.

Still, Nannette's friends, the femmes and butches who were strippers and post office clerks, had left their lipstick marks and their back slaps all over me. I saw those uptown ki-ki dykes through their resentful eyes. They made me smell and taste the smugness of women with money and education, and the bitterness of those without. And working-class bar dykes were the first to show me how to be butch, which means they showed me how to have a style. Postmodernism and consumerism have given style a bad name, it is not necessarily superficial. Adrift in a sea of hostility, drowning in shame, the strong little kid I was had grown into an angry, slump-shouldered lump of teenage flesh, and my secrets made me a loner even with friends. Being butch was the first identity that had ever made sense out of my body's situation, the first rendition of gender that ever rang true, the first look I could ever pull together. Butches may have been laughable to straight people and an embarrassment to the uptown dykes, but in the bar life they were citizens, they were menches, and they were hot.

Power, power: butch dykes had it, Gertrude Stein had it. Not power over femmes, who were as likely to be the seducers or to make more money or to lay down the law. And not worldly power, of course—we still don't have that. Of necessity butches used weapons of the weak, the terrorism of attitude and imagination. Butches had the confidence to take space from the straight world where none had existed, and the power of artists to make new forms out of cultural clay, the impact of the intended word and fabulous gesture. "I am a genius," Gertrude Stein declared, and I for one believed her.

A PERVERTED DESIRE

I spent much of my childhood trying to distinguish identification from desire, asking myself, "Am I in love with Julie Andrews, or do I think I am Julie Andrews?" (Koestenbaum 1993)

My butch body is more like a gay man's than a straight woman's in this respect: it is perverted, and I say that with pleasure. Many women who came out in the seventies via feminism think of themselves as having chosen, perhaps quite happily, to be lesbian, but not me. If women were like horses, I'd be a horse with stripes, a zebra, and the stripes go clear through me. Lifelong gender dysphoria and coming out ten years before Stonewall have made me into a pervert onto whom feminist convictions were successfully grafted. How lively and romantic—compared to girlhood—being a pervert was back in the fifties and sixties! Despite the self-hate, the lies. I told myself that if I could take a magic pill (that was the formulation) I'd choose to be "normal," of course. But try as I might to straighten out, my body always inclined like a landslide toward the valley of perverted desire.

I began to look at myself with some pleasure in the full-length mirror in the gym after my girlfriend Holly said she thought I looked sexy running on the treadmill. If I mention my girlfriends, past and present, a lot, that is partly because, from the days of Phyllis Green and Nannette, the impossible gender of my imagination was reflected back to me only in the lustful or loving gaze of the girly girl dykes to whom I was mostly attracted. I first saw what they saw—that is myself as a sex object—in a series of photographs taken by Nancy Smith, my first great love. Sophisticated and ten years older than me, Nancy, like many of my girlfriends, was a visual artist. Her painterly eye revealed an image the mirror had never shown me: that of a desirable pervert. In her photos my body was beginning to make sense as I stopped trying to be straight and gave up the attendant awkwardness and pretenses. When Picasso painted Gertrude Stein she objected that the portrait wasn't a good likeness. "It will be," he stated.

My girlfriends have told me I'm good-looking so often that, even though they are almost the only ones who say so, I'm finally starting to believe it. At the camp where my parents had sent me to become more feminine the girls had exclaimed, "Oh, you're so good-looking, you'd make such a good-looking boy! Just like Cornel Wilde." As a ten-year-old, what could I do with this? The question How do I look? transcends my own vanity and points toward what Sue-Ellen Case (1993) famously called, in an essay I both admire and critique, "a butch-femme aesthetic."

HELP FROM MY FRIENDS

Lived identities are complicated fictions essential to our social function.
(Munt 1998) [4]

Gradually evolving from 1950s stone butch to a 1960s graduate-student-in-the-closet, 1970s lesbian-feminist, and then, by the 1980s, back to a larger, more generous vision of being butch, I welded what inner strength I had onto the structures gay people had already built, to become a civilized human being.

With painter Louise Fishman, 1970.

What I mean is, like the song says, I did it *with a lot of help from my friends.* My butch career has been made possible by gay people who have fought to create an alternative vision, a freer cultural space for gender and sexuality. With the exception of my beloved anthropological mentor, the late David Schneider, the straight academic world has hindered me more than helped; respect has come to me mostly from queers without whom I would have published nothing and gone nowhere. Why do I claim this butch identity? Because, to paraphrase Stuart Hall, to claim an identity is to place oneself in a narrative of history. Or as anthropologist Edward Sapir put it: "The individual is helpless without a cultural heritage to work on. . . . Creation is a bending of form to one's will, not a manufacture of form *ex nihilo*" (1962:102).

Maybe you thought I wasn't going to acknowledge any of the antibutch insults and polemics. The one that suggests that the butch is nothing more than "a failed, emasculated, and abjected man." The one that asserts that butch-femme relationships are just pathetic imitations of heterosexuality. Or the more sophisticated apologias that press butchness into the service of some kind of "more interesting" theory, that might valorize butch as a tortured form of feminist protest, or as a masquerade or performance, or as a trans-vestic challenge to the social order. All of them flatten a lived identity into an abstract and imply that everyday butches in the gay community, who can be notoriously recalcitrant and rigid, are just too too . . . unhip.

I'll engage just one of the charges made against butches, the accusation that we are ugly, that in fact we epitomize the ugliness imputed to all lesbians. This charge of ugliness contains a partial truth, I think. Besides the ugliness stamped on us by the hatred we endure and the shame lodged in our own hearts, butches have the awkwardness of something partly formed, the rough edges of a work in progress.[5]

The terms of a different construction of gender also exist, in the margins of hegemonic discourses. (de Lauretis 1987)

Because we embody the contradiction of femaleness with masculinity, we stand for and are part of the evolution out of old-fashioned, biology-bound gender. Because our looks are read as obviously sexual, we symbolize and advance the modernist elaboration of nonprocreative desire.

Yet I am hostile to representations of queerness as antithetical to all order, to all categories, to queerness pressed into the service of romantic individual-ism. My queerness is for my own pleasure in loving and living, something that is impossible without being part of Communities (capital c), imaginatively connected via books and art, conferences and politics, and also community (small c) that comes to my birthday party or answers the telephone when I need someone. Being butch for me is all mixed up with everyday survival. As Wayne Koestenbaum put it, butch and femme and queenliness are "style[s] of resistance and self-protection, a way of identifying with other queer people across invisibility and disgrace."[6] Butch and femme are historic *and* present forms of queer culture, deeply meaningful to many, many lesbians.

Beauty and style give pleasure, and they are fundamental elements of queer ideas and queer art, which are among our most powerful resources (our ene-mies understood this in their campaign to surpress them). We lesbians must not allow our community sensibility to be anti-aesthetic, antisensual, or anti-sex. The better butches look—and I don't mean homogenized or slick or, worst of all, prettified versions, but rather masculine lesbians flush with affir-mation, verve, and the courage of our sexual convictions—the more we build the queer tribes, the more we affirm diversity and the bigger contribution we make to American culture's half-assed struggle to move into the twenty-first century.

CIVILIZED DESIRE (TONI)

Cops called me "boy," boys called me "sir," and the ladies . . . well,
the ladies just called me. (Hughes 1996)

While still in graduate school, I had the incredible good luck to meet a female impersonator named Skip Arnold who taught me many useful things and gave me the material for my doctoral dissertation and a book about gender in American culture called *Mother Camp*. Skip showed me a way of representing queenly being and queer desire that captured my fancy from the first time I saw his huge bejeweled form on stage.

It was in the gay resort of Cherry Grove, years later, that I was seduced by another drag queen in front of a cheering gay audience. I had gone to the Sunday night drag talent search as usual and found a seat pretty close to the front of the stage. There was a "guest hostess," a big tall queen named Toni in a sequined evening gown and strawberry blonde curls that doubled the volume of his head. I liked him right away, remembering meeting him on the dock on Friday, a middle-aged, obvious drag queen—swaying hips, wrists bent, shaved eyebrows—dragging hat boxes and bulky suitcases, and how he had stopped to admire my standard poodles.

When this maybe sweet but colorless person burst onto the stage as a towering dynamo of a sex goddess, the old thrill—what the hell is it?—shot through me. And he saw it. From the moment he came out for his second number, "And I Am Telling You I'm Not Going" from *Dreamgirls,* his eyes were on me. As he came down off the stage, I held out a dollar, but instead of taking it he pulled me onto the stage.

All I had to do was follow his lead—it was so easy. Bankston, the kid who videotaped it, said admiringly, "You weren't scared of him at all!" No, of course not. I wasn't afraid of him, because I loved *her*. She turned my back to the audience and forced me to my knees. I could have protested like I would have in real life, but on stage I didn't want to. At first her hand guided me. Later I was going with her so easily I couldn't say how I knew what I should do. People were sure we had rehearsed it. No. She had thought it all out and I followed her thought. On my knees looking up at her, the screams of the crowd behind my back—in real life, it happens something like this, between eye blinks or heartbeats, the look with which she appoints me her butch for a week or for years. Toni could back away then, sure of her conquest, the better to work the crowd: "I don't want to be free . . ." This was no dream. Watching the video later with Bankston, he said, "You looked so right, like the man I've always wanted!" Toni pushed me over on my back and lowered herself over me. Her whole gowned body was big and stiff, like a cardboard tube the size of a tree, because of the girdle and padding, but moving and hot. Above my face the lipsticked open mouth, close-set blue eyes, false lashes, makeup, and the strawberry blonde wig. Laughing, I threw my arms around her neck, and she laughed—the act was working—and we rolled around in a mutual bump and grind, she still mouthing the words to the song, "And you, and you, and youuuu're gonna LOVE me."

Then she turned me toward the screaming, cheering crowd. She curtseyed and I bowed. We were both still laughing and it was perfect, all that art or ritual should be and do in front of a queer crowd plugging right into the spectacle of a metafemme and a metabutch making it. We are hetero, homo, mother and son, father and daughter. This huge masterful mother who isn't really, who wanted me, recognized me, was hot for me like I dreamed she should be, had to be, never was. She who took over and made it all easy, who ran the show in which we starred as mutually adored and adoring: emblems of civilized desire.

Do what you want with me, I said to the queer audience and to Toni, to her. Just let me kiss you. And I did kiss her, and was kissed. Back home the mirror showed red marks of great big lips all over my face.

PART IV: QUEER ANTHROPOLOGY

With David Schneider and George (Moishe) the poodle, 1990.
Photo by Jane Rosett

DMS: The Outsider's Insider

1995

David Schneider and I both adored standard poodles. Back in the 1980s, terribly depressed after the death of his wife, Addy, David perked up at my suggestion that he get a dog. He'd always wanted one, it turned out. My two standard poodles won him over and I gave him the name of a breeder.

When David got to the breeder's place she trotted out a white female, who had been duly shampooed and blow-dried. But David was interested in a young black male who was hanging around the edges of the action. The breeder objected that the white one was much prettier, that the black one was matted and kind of a reject, but David knew his own mind. That black standard poodle became George, a credit to his breed, David's faithful associate for the last ten years of his life. David always had an eye for spotting and nurturing promising misfits, and his sympathies were always more drawn to the beast than to the beauty.

Anthropology ran on my father's side of the family. My father had buddies in anthropology like Johnny Murra who had been part of his Spanish Civil War days; my stepmother's father founded the University of Texas anthropology program, and as a young woman she had dated anthropologist Wally Goldschmidt. When I decided to follow this tradition, my father and stepmother called up Carl Withers, who, under the name of James West, had written an excellent ethnographic study of a Midwestern town, *Plainville, U.S.A.* (1971).

Over tea in his beautiful old Greenwich Village townhouse I told Withers I'd been accepted to Yale, Northwestern (with a full scholarship), and the University of Chicago. Which should I accept? Withers got on the phone with his pal, anthropologist Hortense Powdermaker, and they chewed it over while I sat there wondering if I would ever live in a house with beautiful books and wood paneling and have distinguished friends like Powdermaker. Fairly quickly they agreed: "Yale is too starchy, you won't like it. Northwestern is second rate. Go to Chicago. David Schneider has some interesting students." Actually, I think Withers added, "and he likes weirdos," because I decided to take his advice.

It was only at the end of my first year at Chicago, after I had passed my four field prelims, that David Schneider agreed to sponsor me, giving me a summer job coding data on what we students called "the kinship project," where I began to know a group of young people who were to varying degrees Schneider's students: Vern Carroll, Martin Silverman, Linda Wolf, Charley Keil, Cal Cottrell, and Liz Kennedy. (Later he also mentored my friends Harriet Whitehead, Sherry Ortner, Bobby Paul, and Ben Apfelbaum.) Linda Wolf eventually left anthropology. Ben Apfelbaum fled to Canada to avoid being drafted into the Vietnam War. And Cal died tragically and young. The rest of us became professional anthropologists.

The night after seeing a huge man in makeup and high heels mesmerize a bar full of laughing, shouting, clapping gay men, my mind raced with the idea of comparing drag queens to the blues singers that my friend Charley Keil (1966) was currently writing about as symbolic leaders of the black community. When I showed David some field notes and my excitement, he encouraged me to make female impersonators the subject of my doctoral dissertation, and followed that up with his support. He helped me to develop the intellectual tools to do the work, and just as important, he was prepared to back me up with his departmental clout.

Gays were then looked on within social science as the object solely of psychological, medical, or even criminological study. Our supposedly bizarre behavior was presumed to arise from abnormalities. To the degree that *Mother Camp* (along with Gayle Rubin's "The Traffic in Women"),[1] were foundational to gay and lesbian studies in anthropology, David Schneider was a key figure behind the paradigm shift that made the field possible. What he imparted to me, more in his office and his home than in the classroom, was that female impersonators (about whom he knew nothing more than what I told him) were a group of human beings and so necessarily had a culture worth studying.

The insight that gays were not just a category of sick isolates, but a group, and so had a culture, was a breathtaking leap whose daring is hard to recapture now, when the term "gay community" is familiar even to most straight people, but Schneider made it without any fuss. His impartiality toward homosexuality was later infused and informed by his deep affection for me and for a number of other gay people. His last essay (1997) suggested that homophobia be studied. "What do you think homophobia is about?" he asked me. "I don't get it." David's ideas, his example, and his influence stimulated later work in feminism and gender studies and in American field research, and helped create a multicultural, postcolonial anthropology.

On the face of it, David Schneider seemed an unlikely person to harbor such radical ideas.[2] He had himself successfully concluded non-Western field-work. There was certainly no outward indication that he would be sympathetic to "weirdos." The chair of an elite and conservative graduate department, long married to the same woman, father of two sons, he lived a conventional bour-geois life in a Chicago townhouse filled with Danish modern furniture. But the profoundly unruly and agnostic side of him was captured by a mutual friend's comment that if you could open David up you'd find an alien inside. This was the David who dryly exposed his own anti-Semitism by telling me he had named his dog George, rather than Moishe, which he confided was the poodle's "real" name. This was the acute, self-deprecating Jewish American double consciousness that produced, among other outstanding work, *American Kinship: A Cultural Account* (1968).

This combination of insiderhood with an iconoclastic temperament proved a blessing for those of his students like me who were marginal and offbeat, for in addition to the white males whom everyone thought would succeed, Schneider was attracted to students like closet gays and struggling women who could not easily attract the support of the powerful. I well re-call when Schneider reported to me on the year-end departmental review of my progress; the professors relayed to me through Schneider that my wear-ing pants manifested a lack of commitment to the anthropological vocation. I was very hurt and angry at this personal attack: why weren't they focusing on my work? Another advisor warned me that after all, it was important to be attractive and feminine and he thought the department had a point. Why did professional women have to try to be like men?

In the Schneiders' living room, by contrast, I was told that wearing dresses was neither here nor there on the ultimate scale of value and that Addy and David rather enjoyed my unconventionality (they did not know I was gay, though perhaps Addy suspected). But I had to play the game too, they said, urging me to wear a dress to my thesis defense in my own calculated inter-est. I did, and when the hearing date arrived, Schneider was there with his sleeves rolled up to take on the professors who said my thesis wasn't really anthropology.

Father-mentors were very necessary to professional women of my genera-tion. During ten years of higher education I never had a female professor. There was not one woman professor in the Chicago department then. My "role models" were all men, but most were not interested in helping women students develop as intellectuals and professional academics. Carl Withers and Hortense Powdermaker had not told me that Schneider was one of the few willing to mentor women students when they urged me to go to Chi-cago, but probably they knew it. Although Schneider was not exempt from sexist attitudes in those days before the second wave of feminism, most of his women students got much more help than aggravation.

What, besides their originality, are the qualities of really great scholarly mentors like David Schneider? Their own belief in the power of ideas and the value of an intellectual life inspires students. By refraining from gross forms of personal and intellectual exploitation they respect their students' integrity. They have clout within the profession and use it judiciously to protect and further their protégés. As you grow, your mentor lets you go without losing interest. In fact, David was so curious and so open he did not demand that his juniors echo his ideas, but allowed himself to be challenged by ours. And David had the gift of converting mentor-student relations into loving friendships.

In May of 1994 David told me: "I'm going out of the anthropology business. I don't want my books to wind up in secondhand bookstores. I'd rather my friends have them." He insisted that I take whatever I wanted from his huge personal library and, half-blinded by tears, I complied. We both knew he was saying he was getting ready to die. It was typical of his courage. He had come back from the heart attacks, the bypass surgeries, and even the stroke. "You're the bionic man," I used to tease him. But in the end, death conquered even *his* will to live. Good-bye, David. What goes around comes around. I want you to know that we who accepted your books value them as much as you did.

Too Queer for College: Notes on Homophobia

1987

For Kenneth W. Payne, anthropologist, fieldworker, scholar,
brilliant teacher, and my cherished gay colleague at Purchase
in the early 1980s, who never got a tenure-track job. Ken Payne
died of AIDS-related causes in 1988.

My wrist was broken in three places when I collided with the hardwood floor of a roller skating rink on a summer night six years ago. After six weeks in a cast and three months of physical therapy, my hand worked again, but not the way it had before. My right wrist—I am right-handed—is askew, thickened, and chronically painful.

That was the price for holding hands with another woman in public. As a lesbian who looks it, I hardly ever express affection where straight people might see. But this skating rink was in Greenwich Village, gay capital of the East Coast. I remember a young man shouting something angry at us. The words were blurred but the meaning was clear from his tone, his glower, and the girlfriend clinging to him. The next lap around the rink, something—I never saw what or who—felled me from behind.

The physical therapists were wonderful, but they dealt with physical trauma, and the mental shock proved even more intractable. I had to eat this man's anonymous hatred, accept the fact that, in a spiteful spasm, he could ruin my beautiful, capable hand. I could neither vomit the hatred back on him nor forgive, because I had not seen the attack. I couldn't even be certain it wasn't an accident. That would have been the more comforting explanation. Who wants to believe herself despised by total strangers? But if my assailant's hostility was impersonal, it was *my* wrist, not his, that was broken. The worst effect of homophobia, in the academic world or anywhere, is the damage done to lesbians and gay men. To a lesser degree, straight people are harmed by the lies they force us to tell.

Homophobia in the academic world is not the violent shove in the back. It occurs in a privileged context where hostility is rarely so "crudely" expressed. But it does break spirits, damage careers, ruin lives. Like my attacker at the

San Francisco Bay, with colleague and friend Kenny Payne, 1986.

skating rink, homophobia among academics is usually a sneak. It strikes in closed-door meetings of tenure-review and promotion committees and in secret letters of recommendation. Rejection and denial are almost always attributed to the victim's alleged personal and intellectual shortcomings. In twenty-eight years in higher education, the fact that I am a lesbian was never given as the reason for attacking me.

What little systematic data there are confirm that there's nothing exceptional or personal about discrimination against lesbians and gay men in higher education. The American Sociological Association's Task Group on Homosexuality surveyed two thousand sociology department heads about their attitudes toward gays and lesbians in academia. Based on the 640 responses, the ASA Task Group concluded: "Sociologists and students who are known as homosexuals or, even more so, as activists, run considerable risk, according to the perceptions of department heads and chairs, of experiencing discrimination in being hired or promoted in a sociology department. Hence the vast majority remain closeted within their colleagues. This, in turn, inhibits them from displaying interest in, and engaging in, research, advising, or teaching courses on, the topic of homosexuality" (Huber et al. 1982:165).

Academic homophobia first struck me in college, when the dean of women threatened me with expulsion because I had been seen in a phone booth with another woman. We were not lovers; we had simply been talking to a mutual friend. But the dean was rumored to be a lesbian herself; I knew she *knew*. She didn't say, I'm going to expel you because you're a lesbian. She said something about inappropriate behavior and not tolerating a bad attitude. Unlike the heroine of *Rubyfruit Jungle,* I cowered before the dean, and thanked my lucky stars when she decided to accept my story. I was left in that permanent state of fearfulness and vulnerability that is the fate of those with a dirty secret.

In 1965, when I was a graduate student in anthropology, I decided to write, or rather felt impelled to write, my thesis on female impersonators as symbolic leaders of the gay community. I was lucky to be at an elite graduate school, one that could afford to take chances on some students. Even so, my topic was widely viewed as an inappropriate dirty joke. Without the support of several powerful straight white male faculty members, my project would have been squashed. I dared not mention in my dissertation that my being a lesbian had anything to do with my choice of topic, my perspective, or the relative ease with which I had gained my informants' confidence.

In 1968, after I got my first job, I became a passionately committed feminist. People had always looked at me askance because I didn't smile enough, because my body language was all wrong, in short because I wasn't feminine. But now they could label me feminist as well as, or instead of, lesbian. The movement also attracted many straight women. Some have been staunch allies; others have capitulated under straight male pressure to get rid of the queer perspective my person and my work have represented.

I was denied tenure on my first job. The rejection felled me like a dumb ox. The process was secret, but privately and as a favor, the woman department head told me some people had trouble with my "personality." There was also a question about my "commitment to anthropology." It was like the menacing encounter I'd had with the college dean: You're doing something wrong and I won't say what, but we *know* about it.

In 1973, when I came up for tenure at my second job, I was more sophisticated. I had found my feet as a feminist teacher, and had a network of supporters. Also, my dissertation had been published (Newton 1972, 1979). My review committee split. The negative majority accused me of having a "feminist bias" and asserted, contrary to glowing student evaluations, that I was unfair to male students. My detractors were so confident that they committed these observations to paper. After a protracted campus struggle, the college president granted me tenure, with a one-year delay to make sure I didn't get overconfident. Neither my opponents nor my supporters ever said publicly that I was a lesbian. Most of my colleagues got tenure easily.

Colleague, friend, and leader of the feminist campaign for my tenure, the late Mary Edwards (standing far left) and the author (kneeling far right) with Purchase students, 1973.

Now that I had tenure, I "came out" on my job. I began to refer to my home life honestly among my colleagues and mentioned my homosexuality in class when *I* thought it appropriate. I also started to write about it. For instance, I added a section dealing with my graduate school experience in the closet to a paper I had written about life as an academic woman.[1] A feminist philosophy professor who was editing a book on women and work solicited my piece, commenting, "I'm surprised how much the inclusion of 'lesbianism' changes the tone of the essay—making it more serious, more moving, and in an odd way more seriously political." But the publisher saw it differently, and the professor was persuaded to drop my piece. It "assumed a feminist audience," she wrote in a subsequent letter, and was too focused on the academic world. Also, she said, her collection was now more about the relation of work to "mothering," not "personal relations," so the topic of lesbianism was inappropriate. She advised me that in revising the piece for publication elsewhere I should be more upbeat, lest people think that lesbians are bitter.

That article has never been published. The professor's book, which sold widely to feminists, included a bitter meditation on graduate school by a "straight" woman with whom I had had a clandestine affair. Not one author in that book on women and work, including several who are gay, mentions lesbianism.

Another paper of mine concerned the anthropological and feminist controversy over the existence of "primitive matriarchies." This work too was solicited and accepted by straight feminist editors, but in due course the publisher's reader expressed "disbelief that the paper was actually submitted for publication. It is bad. It is poorly written, poorly organized, poorly thought out and bereft of ideas of its own. . . . I could see a good visionary article that would revolve around some real things [such as] . . . total control of women over the reproductive process through chemical contraception and legal abortion; the shrinking of the family." These comments were sent on to me and my coauthor by the editors to justify their decision to "agree to drop [your paper] from the collection."[2] Like female impersonation, the vision of a female-dominated society was just not a legitimate topic, but phony "standards" were cited to strengthen the case. This kind of thing can drive you crazy. You end by distrusting everyone and shying away from the editorial help all writers need.

It took me a long time to get over a string of such rejections, but eventually a community of lesbian and gay scholars, primarily historians, provided the support and intellectual stimulation that enabled me to resume academic research. With fifteen years of outstanding teaching, one edited book and two authored ones, and a number of articles on gay and feminist topics, I had the nerve to propose myself for a promotion to full professor. Whether I had a "strong" enough publication record to make full professor at a major research university, I do not know. Obviously, previous rejections of my work didn't help. I do claim to be the equal of the full professors at my state college.

But my colleagues split again. The majority wrote that I hadn't published enough to merit promotion, and that eight lengthy favorable outside letters (many from full professors at major universities, some of whom called my first book a "classic" in urban anthropology) were outweighed by two cursory negative ones. One male member of the review committee reportedly dropped some of my work on the table with disdain, saying, "Have you *read* this?" In that atmosphere several more neutral colleagues, including a full professor who is a heterosexual feminist, found it more comfortable to vote against my promotion. Later, the feminist professor admitted disliking the irrational hostility of certain committee members toward me, but, she explained, she agreed with them about my lack of publications. "But I've written two books," I objected. "You were just promoted for editing one!" The insufficient publication note was also publicly sounded by a male administrator involved in my case. A colleague later reported my boss's off-the-record remark: "Can you imagine promoting someone who writes this shit?"

How have these experiences affected my career? On the face of it, I have been held back, paid less, disrespected by many of the people I work with. More profoundly, homophobia has forced me to frame my life by its imperatives. Without it, I would not identify so strongly with other gay people. My work might have been on Paleolithic arrowheads instead of on people who are marginal and different. I have found my intellectual voice in the silence society tried to impose on me. Although the kind of writing and teaching I do best—interdisciplinary, controversial—has been scorned by many of my colleagues, it has gained me the respect of others and the admiration of students, who continue to flock to my classes.

Now that I have job security, what I fear most is the bitterness that can trap you in a perpetual dance with the limits straight society sets. That is the inner wasteland from which Malcolm X emerged when, toward the end of his life, he saw that "white man" was a set of attitudes that might possibly, through hard political and spiritual action, be transformed. He was pushed to the floor of the skating rink a hundred times over, and turned that rage and that pain into his own growth, his own project. That is the kind of victory over homophobia I seek.

An Open Letter to "Manda Cesara"

1984

To: "Manda Cesara" (a.k.a. Karla O. Poewe)
From: Esther Newton
Date: February 16, 1984

I just read your book about your African fieldwork (Cesara 1982). I agreed with many of your ideas about research, and identified with your critical spirit toward social science. Your book is important because you are honest about how you worked in the field and thoughtful about what this means for anthropological knowledge. Early on, though, I was displeased to find you explaining to the Lenda that "in our [Western] society many are lonely, sexually frustrated because one man and one woman are each other's exclusive and private property. Some have even become perverse" (73). Because most Americans agree with this folk explanation of the causes of "perversity," my displeasure demands an explanation. In the spirit of self-examination and revelation you espouse (and courageously practice, except for using a pseudonym), I admit that I myself am a lesbian; naturally, I felt insulted. We perverts are insulted daily, of course, but I had not expected it from an author who writes (elegantly), "It is necessary that anthropologists assume an introspective attitude and dislodge from its hiding place those background assumptions to which he [sic], like *alle Menschen,* is subject" (12). The scholar in me was shocked too at your lack of intellectual sophistication. No one in the field of sex and gender accepts such a simplistic explanation for the causes of either homosexuality or heterosexuality these days, and that includes many who implicitly or even explicitly think homosexuality is undesirable.

Never mind, I told myself; sex isn't "Cesara's" field, but her book will show her developing interest and sophistication about it. So I read on, and behold, you seemed to realize that gender is a social construction. You quote Kessler and McKenna (1985) on the subject (210) and even describe lesbian-feminism as the "most radical" American solution to the problem of male dominance (186; a conclusion, by the way, with which I fervently disagree). Imagine my shock, then, to find a homophobic diatribe worthy of the Moral Majority in your conclusion, citing my work in support of your abuse! I quote your paragraph in full so that readers can see for themselves what I am upset about:

> Without . . . puzzling why, I tolerated homosexuality before I went to the field. While I tolerate it now, I agree with Newton's observation that gays "will always be traitors in the battle of the sexes" (1979: xii). I admired the ongoing "battle of the sexes" in Lenda. By contrast, I deplore the cultural principles which nourish American homosexuality, such as: (1) domination in sex; (2) obsession with youth; (3) obsession with extreme forms of masculinity and femininity; (4) commercialization of physical beauty; (5) egotism; (6) excessive status consciousness; (7) a flippant emotional freedom; (8) manipulation of sex-roles; (9) tendency to produce ersatz cowboys, imitation Hell's Angels, phony oppositions between make-believe men and make-believe women; and so on. American homosexuality is inauthentic. Worse still, in its ideology, it is everything many of us tried to leave behind in the sixties. It is at least as old as ancient Greece and as "primitive" as New Guinea culture. It is a form of sexual alienation every bit as inhumane as man's alienation from that social world whose history we should make. Indeed, it is alienation taken to its ultimate conclusion. At its best, American homosexuality appears to be, for all the above reasons, reactionary rather than forward looking. At its worst, homosexuals seem to grasp the worst American cultural premises and practices and bring them to their ultimate conclusion. Where homosexuals in Oman, for example, underline or bring into focus what Omanians consider to be the best in their culture, American homosexuals make the worst of American culture worse. (211)

Dear Ms. "Cesara," this just won't do, intellectually or morally. Space does not permit me to describe everything I object to in your paragraph, but here are the highlights. Your use of my words "gays will always be traitors in the battle of the sexes" to put gays down infuriates me. Isn't it good, from the feminist point of view, to be a traitor to male dominance? Doesn't it make gay men the potential allies of women? Whether you agree or not, that was *my* point. To the extent I was critical of gay men, I was arguing they should eschew s/m, not disappear. If you bothered to read past the introduction (which I plan to rewrite, retracting my attack on s/m), you saw that I was entirely sympathetic to "American homosexuality," if there is such an entity. And on the subject of the sexism we both hate, why do you imply in this diatribe that all homosexuals are men? Many homosexuals are women, including a good number of lesbian anthropologists who continue to be both intimidated and erased by attitudes like yours.

Mother Camp is one of a handful of books in all of social science literature that is sympathetic toward gays and seeks to understand homosexuality in cultural terms rather than to condemn it as a sickness. It represented a moral and intellectual step forward for anthropology, and has been important to gays inside and outside the field. I put my career on the line to write it (without a pseudonym, I might add). To see you misuse my book to denounce the group I was attempting to dignify—imagine how you would feel if someone used your descriptions of poverty and ignorance among the Lenda to "prove" that blacks are inferior—is a bitter, bitter irony. As a final insult, you omit my book from your bibliography; readers won't be able to check for themselves.

I respect your honest admission that you are heterosexual and that you found the Lenda so congenial in large part because they confirmed your preference. If more ethnographers and social scientists generally exposed their "background assumptions" and emotional investments, not just about sexuality, but more broadly, we'd have, I agree, a more powerful social science. But after we understand and expose our own investments, aren't we required to cast an even more scrupulous eye on the conclusions toward which they lead us? Where does this irrational hatred of homosexuality come from in you? What excuse do you have for indulging this shameful display of ignorance and vituperation?

All the accusations you make against gays—and I don't agree that "manipulation of sex-roles," for instance, is necessarily bad—are even more true in straight life. Isn't John Wayne an "ersatz cowboy" (my words, though you don't give me the credit), and what about superstraight Ronald Reagan? American heterosexuality is saturated with erotic domination that, unlike gay sex of any kind, is completely acceptable and even glorified. You would reply that you disapprove "excessive status consciousness," for instance, in straight life too. Why, then, is only homosexuality excoriated as "inhumane," "alienated," and "inauthentic"? How did you arrive at this judgment? Have you tried homosexuality lately? Have you ever done fieldwork with gays?

The truth is, you're indulging a vicious prejudice, secure in the knowledge that it's still okay to hate gays publicly. Meanwhile, despite your righteous anger at male power over women, you ignore the privileges being straight gives you over all gays, male and female. By your own admission, being straight helped you get along in the field, and it'll help you get along in anthropology. I'm not saying you're making it on the casting couch, but I am saying straight men run this world and they like women who prefer fucking them and men who think likewise.

Fortunately, there are women social scientists whose work on sex and gender is truly radical and free of bigotry. I refer you, for example, to Gayle Rubin's (1975) famous essay on the origins of the sex/gender system, to Kessler and McKenna's (1985) excellent book on gender, Blumstein and Schwartz (1983) on gay and straight couples, several essays in Ortner and Whitehead's (1981) outstanding collection, and, for the kind of criticism of "background assumptions" in social science to which you aspire, Carole S. Vance's (1983) funny article on the Kinsey Institute.

I hope you learn something from this letter, if only that a few of us "perverts" are now able to defend ourselves. In any case, I have set the record right regarding my own work.

Of Yams, Grinders, and Gays:

The Anthropology of Homosexuality

1988

Anthropologists, with a few lonely exceptions, contributed very little to our understanding of sexuality before the 1970s. Because sexuality is a taboo topic in our own culture, fieldworkers didn't ask other peoples about sex either, or if they did, they didn't write up what they saw and heard. Most of what *was* done in earlier years was marred by an all-male perspective, as male anthropologists conferred with male members of other cultures. Moral judgments and evasiveness such as "marital relations are unhappy" or "people indulge in sexual license" were the rule, if any mention of sex was made. Although in general we were supposed to interact with the "natives"—being there is the only way to learn another way of life—*sexual* contact was a no-no; we knew only by the rare confession or by professional gossip that it sometimes happens, regardless.

No, as hard as we anthropologists have tried, in politics or religion, to see past our own cultural noses, when looking "down there" we have shown the same ignorance and done the same name-calling as most other Westerners. We too are members of a society tied up in knots over everyone's "sex life," in which many people would literally rather let *others* die—they assume it will be others—than have certain sex words appear in public. Even the great chronicler of the Trobriand Islands, Malinowski—one of the few who took sex seriously enough before the 1970s to publish a scholarly book about it and who also recorded in a secret diary his sexual contact with the Trobriand women, whom he referred to as "niggers"—was accused by the French feminist scholar Briffault of being an "Adam and Eve" anthropologist for saying that "marriage is regarded in all human societies as . . . a sacred transaction establishing a relationship of the highest value to man and woman."[1] Marriage as we idealize it is no more universal than is man-on-top heterosexual intercourse.

GENDER AND DESIRE

To describe the shapes that marriage or desire takes in other traditions we have to take off our Judeo-Christian glasses. When missionaries decreed that masturbation was "immoral," they drove it underground but did nothing to understand other peoples' morality. Unfortunately, neither missionaries nor anthropologists see with the naked eye, but always through the lens of culture. The best we can do is a kind of correction, which means that Western words and concepts have to be extracted from their connotations before they can be packed in the anthropologist's intellectual luggage.

Development of a metacultural language—one that transcends our own time and place—is what the anthropological enterprise is all about. The early anthropologists found that some groups reckoned their close kin, for instance, only through women. So the idea of "kinship" had to be stripped of the assumption that English kinship names are simply biology writ large. An "aunt" can be our mother's sister, but she can also be our father's brother's wife. Other people don't have aunts, not even by another name, because "aunt" is an idea, not a biological link. As the French anthropologist Lévi-Strauss concluded, "Kinship does not consist in the objective ties of descent or consanguinity"—meaning genetic links—"between individuals. It exists only in human consciousness; it is an arbitrary system of representations" (1963:51).

Because anthropologists already accepted the necessity of suspending Western assumptions to look at the "respectable" areas of culture, when the energy of feminism and gay liberation propelled some of us toward previously submerged questions about sex and gender, we were a jump ahead.[2]

Desire, we began to think, is less like a heart, throbbing the same everywhere, and more like music, and every culture has its own—not only songs, but tonality, instruments, and occasions. To borrow a good metaphor from anthropologist Carole Vance, it is not our ears that compose symphonies, nor is it our genitals or our hormones that determine the erotic. Genitals, like ears, are just receptors. It is the brain that activates (or fails to activate) hormones that produce sexual excitement. This is not to say that sexual excitement can be created, or destroyed, on conscious command. Far from it. But desire, like music, is inscribed in a particular tradition: the medium from which our eroticism takes shape.

In *Sex and Temperament*, Margaret Mead showed that what is considered manly or womanly depends on which society is doing the considering. In "The Traffic in Women," an influential 1975 essay, Gayle Rubin proposed the idea of the sex/gender system, "a set of arrangements by which a society transforms biological sexuality into products of human activity and in which these transformed needs are satisfied" (159). By gender, anthropologists mean cultural categories to which infants are assigned when adults first inspect the child's genitals. In our hospitals, when the genitals are ambiguously sexed, the baby is called a girl or a boy anyway and nature is surgically altered to fit. Biology is even less the determinant of human sexual response; it is not flesh, in itself, that "makes people hot," as we say, but flesh infused with beliefs and ideas. In the domain of the erotic, actions, fantasies, pictures, games, rituals, or simply words lead, or are supposed to lead, to genital arousal. Anthropologists and historians who share this approach call ourselves "social constructionists."

When we try to find out what other people's sexual beliefs and actions really are, as opposed to supposing they are like or at least a reflection— "primitive" or "liberated"—of ours, the results are unsettling. Let me give you an example from the Mehinaku people, forest-dwelling Amazonian Indians. Mehinaku men told this story:

The Wandering Vagina

In ancient times, all the women's vaginas used to wander about. Today, women's vaginas stay in one place. One woman of ancient times, Tukwi, had a vagina that was especially foolish. While Tukwi slept, her vagina would crawl about the floor of the house, thirsty and hungry, looking for manioc porridge and fish stew. Creeping about snail-like on the ground, it found the porridge pot and slid the top off. One of the men awoke and listened: "Aah, nothing but a mouse," he said, and he went back to sleep. But as the vagina slurped up the porridge, another man awoke and took a brand from the fire to see what was happening. "What is this?" he said. To him it looked like a great frog, with a nose and an immense mouth. Moving closer, he scorched the vagina with his torch. Oh, it scurried back to its owner, slipping right inside her. She cried and cried, for she had been burned. Then Tukwi called all the women and lectured them: "All you women, don't let your genitals wander about. If they do, they may get burned as mine were!" And so, today, women's genitals no longer go wandering about.

Recorded by anthropologist Thomas Gregor in *Anxious Pleasures* (1985:72) an extraordinary book about the sexual life of the Mehinaku, this story exemplifies the "thick" descriptions we need most; not simply international Kinsey reports—"x percent of Mehinaku have masturbated by age ten"—but acts embedded in their significance.

In medieval Europe, heterosexual intercourse was seen as agricultural: the male peasant plowing a female field and sowing seeds to harvest crop children. Such metaphors both reflect and guide action—in this case, the correct position for intercourse, its legitimate purpose, and the right relation of the genders. The Mehinaku see intercourse as being like food preparation and eating. Intercourse is said to resemble the process by which women prepare the manioc root for cooking; both sex and scraping are done in a squat. Male and female genitals are also likened to mouths, and at orgasm a man is said to "vomit" semen. It is hungry genitals that seek intercourse; babies are made from semen and a vagina has to "eat" a lot of it. How do women and men experience desire when the penis is a mouth or edible rather than a tool or a gun? When vaginas go adventuring at night, even if they are punished for it, what notion of women's sexual initiative is supposed? If heterosexuality means genital contact between biological males and females, this is an example, but not as we know it.

HOMOSEXUAL DESIRE

There are too few studies like Thomas Gregor's. And if the evidence on sexuality in general is scanty and distorted by moral judgments, that on homosexuality is worse. Edgar Gregersen's 1983 update on the pioneering cross-cultural work of Clellan Ford and Frank Beach (1951) found anthropological sex data on 294 societies. (Out of a possible 3,000, that's a measly 10 percent.) Of these, about half mention male homosexuality and one third female homosexuality, though in most cases, there was no information on the culture's attitude toward it. The usual combination of taboo, male anthropologist, and male informant has left lesbian behavior so unexplored that all generalizations are provisional only.

But what *do* we know? Homosexual relations take a profusion of shapes that fall into four main types suggested by Gregersen and Barry Adam (1986), which may or may not eventually fit lesbian behavior. (The fact that no such preliminary classification has been done on heterosexuality worldwide shows just how taken for granted, hence unknown, heterosexuality is.) First, many groups practice *juvenile* homosexuality, sex play among children and youth. This tends to be premarital, casual, and generally not a cause of great social consternation. Even our homophobic, sexually anxious culture has the "circle jerk," the "schoolgirl crush," and playing "house" or "doctor."

Second, there is *age-structured* homosexuality. A younger partner, usually a preadolescent or adolescent, has sexual relations with an older partner or partners of the same gender. Many or all members of a society may be involved, but generally at a defined stage of life. Age-structured homosexuality was legitimate for men and some women in classical Greece; these were essentially student-teacher bonds, as celebrated in Plato's *Symposium* and in Sappho's poetry. It is also common among Australian aborigines and the tribes of New Guinea, for men and perhaps for women. Boys are initiated into manhood over a period of years by elaborate rituals, among them, "eating" the semen of older males, in some societies by fellatio, in others by anal intercourse, or absorbing sperm through cuts in the skin. Like the Mehinaku—whose passion is male-male wrestling but who shun homosexual relations—the New Guineans equate semen and saliva. Yams are smeared with saliva to make them grow big, just as boys are "fed" semen. The sexuality is a ritual vehicle. This work done on Melanesia by Kenneth Read (e.g. 1965), Gil Herdt (e.g., 1984), and a number of others, by the way, is wonderfully rich and sophisticated, and calls into question every preconceived notion we have about sexual orientation. Boys spend years fellating their elders, further years being fellated by juniors, and still wind up, as expected, married fathers. In Greece, Melanesia, and Japan, male homosexuality was associated with masculinity: in varying degrees with masculine beauty, core identity, or martial valor. There are two well-documented instances of age-structured homosexuality among women, and in both cases, women are relatively powerful and autonomous. In southern Africa, women from the Basotho tribe form what are called "mummy-baby" relationships—sexual, sensual, and supportive—with adolescent girls (Gay 1986). The older partner is generally married, but husbands work as migrant laborers and are away for long periods of time. There are also socially accepted lesbian couples and social groups among Muslim Africans in Mombasa, even though all girls must marry young. Writes their ethnographer, Gil Shepherd, "The word in Swahili glossed as 'lesbian' is *msagaji*—'a grinder.' The verb *kusaga* [to grind] is commonly used for the grinding of grain between millstones, but the close interplay between the two usages is illustrated, perhaps, by the fact that the upper and lower millstones are known as *mwana* and *mama* respectively: 'child' and 'mother,' strictly speaking, or simply 'young woman' and 'older woman'" (1987:254). Of course, all these relationships obey a culture-specific logic. Whereas in New Guinea male-male sexual relations are an aspect of interaction between kinship groups and so are forbidden between certain types of kin and expected between others, in Lesotho a "mummy" may have several "babies," but a "baby" only one "mummy." In age-structured relations, it is usual for the former baby/student/initiate to become the mummy/teacher/initiator as an adult, in addition to marrying.

A third homosexual context is transgender or *gender bending*, in which ordinary men or women can appropriately have sex only with special people belonging to variant genders, which often have a supernatural dimension. We know of instances in Africa, Siberia, Polynesia, Indonesia, and Brazil. Especially well documented are gender benders among North American Indians (see Williams 1986) and an East Indian caste, the Hijras. In Hindu tradition, the Hijras are born males or, in rare cases, hermaphrodites who live in urban communes under a guru and devote themselves to the worship of Bahuchara Mata, a mother goddess. The Hijras tell this story about their origins:

> In the time of the Ramayana, Ram . . . had to leave Ayodhya (his native city) and go into the forest for 14 years. As he was going, the whole city followed him because they loved him so. As Ram came to . . . the edge of the forest, he turned to the people and said, "Ladies and gents, please wipe your tears and go away." But these people who were not men and not women did not know what to do. So they stayed there because Ram did not ask them to go. They remained there 14 years and snake hills grew around them. When Ram returned . . . he found many snake hills. Not knowing why they were there he removed them and found so many people with long beards and nails, all meditating. And so they were blessed by Ram. And that is why we hijras are so respected in Ayodhya. (Nanda 1986:37)

The dharma or caste obligation of the hijras is to castrate themselves and live an ascetic, asexual life devoted to the goddess Bahuchara. However, alongside their ritual duties and religious discipline they sometimes prostitute themselves to and/or marry men. Not surprisingly, different people put forward different explanations for this apparent contradiction. Some hijras say they are driven to prostitution only by desperate poverty. Others insist that boys become hijras just to have sex with men. The older hijras bitch that the conduct of some young *chelas* or disciples brings a bad name on the caste. Their ethnographer, Serena Nanda, adds that Hindu culture is more flexible than ours; asceticism and sexuality are not necessarily opposites in the Hindu way of thinking.

Although once again, information on women is much scantier, we know of female gender benders among North American Indians and Brazil cult worshippers and of so-called female husbands in certain African tribes.

The fourth and most familiar type of homosexual relation, *homophilia*, is distinguished from the others by involving adults of approximately the same age and social status. Homophilia is primarily modern and Western, although we do know, for instance, of lesbian marriage resisters who worked in the silk factories in Southern China (Sankar 1986). Lesbianism in the West sometimes has a gender-bending aspect ("roles"), and male homosexuality has both gender-bending ("drag") and age-graded elements, but the ritual and spiritual dimensions found in so many other cultures are lacking here. On the other hand, only in the West has a large articulate community developed around a supposed exclusive homosexual orientation. Which of the non-Western, traditional contexts will merge with the Western-oriented gay subculture remains to be seen. We know that some of the gender benders, such as the American Indian berdache, are beginning to think of themselves as "gay." Both berdache and gays have special life-shaping identities that set us apart from other people.

THE SOCIAL CONSTRUCTION OF HOMOSEXUAL IDENTITIES

So what can anthropology tell us about homosexuality? Clearly, homoeroticism is not just a product—decadent or liberating, depending on your point of view—of Western culture, but occurs among many peoples with an infinite range of meaning. On the other hand, anthropological evidence contradicts the notion that hetero- and homosexual, concepts that were only invented in 1869, are actors everywhere on the world stage. Western lesbian and gay anthropologists, for the most part, have not run around the world looking for other lesbians and gay men. Instead, we have taken the lead in comparative studies of gender and especially of sexuality. Among us, there really is no essentialist position on sexuality, no notion that people are born with sexual orientations. The evidence, fragmentary as it is, all points the other way.

There is an anthropological axiom that says that, if people believe a thing to be real, that belief has real consequences. Our society is certain that heterosexual orientation is human nature. For contradicting, or flouting, that "law," gays are hated. Our defense against being called unnatural is to make our own appeal to nature. Either we were born gay—so gays must be born everywhere—or homosexuality is a universal form of desire that others have repressed. To my mind neither of these arguments is necessary to justify a profound identification with gayness and the gay community.

No American group has members in all other societies, and none, with the exception of Jews, existed two thousand years ago. Even Jews, with one of the most seductive claims to exist in nature, not just nurture, and a glorious and durable history, also anxiously scan the mirror of the past when it gives back no likeness. A recent *New York Times* article (1 October 1987) quoted the intense interest felt by Midwestern Jews in Ezekiel Solomon, the first Jewish man to settle Michigan and the Northwest Territories. "It's amazing just to imagine his being here," said a Jewish lawyer who spent last July at the site of Solomon's eighteenth-century house, "bringing some small touch of 'yiddishkeit' to what must have been such a strange world." Like gays who expect to find gay liberationists in the past, or must know for sure if two famous women friends actually had sex, the contemporary Jews were disappointed because "not a single artifact reflecting Mr. Solomon's religious faith has yet been found." Even Jewish identity is a complex mosaic, fragile, contested, changing, and fuzzy around the edges. Only Eastern European Jews among the world's Jews would be looking for *yiddishkeit,* and Ezekiel Solomon married a Catholic girl. They had five children, who in the absence of a larger Jewish community most probably ceased to be Jews. The truth is, all identities have to be created and recreated by us, the living.

I am writing a history of the gay community of Cherry Grove, on Fire Island. The Grove, a small but notorious and wonderful colony of summer houses, has had gay settlers since the mid-1930s and has been almost exclusively gay since the late 1940s. One of my most useful models has been anthropologist Barbara Myerhoff's *Number Our Days* (1978) a fascinating study of a Southern California Jewish senior citizens center, which, like Cherry Grove, draws adults from a larger world of members. Like me, Myerhoff was both a member of and an outsider to the community. At the heart of her work is the question of identity: What is *yiddishkeit?* What does it mean to be a Jew in America? The lives of old people in the senior citizens center, like those of gays, have not turned out as expected. Their children are Americanized, apolitical, and mostly absent. If anything, in Cherry Grove, which represents traditional orthodoxy in the spectrum of modern gay life, identity issues are more taken for granted, less up for grabs.

Humans are social animals. From inside our darkest closets to the most routine chores of daily living, we exist and can only exist in a dense web of connectedness. Who shares our web determines what values we hold sacred, which in turn shapes our connectedness. The process is the same whether we are Jewish, Mehinaku, or gay. My students often say that "labels are limiting." Using the word *labels* shows that they feel these identities—gay, Jewish, whatever—as external to themselves, glued on. This is partly an American illusion they share with their elders, that freedom means no limits, no definition. But it also signals their powerlessness as young people. Identities *are* limiting if you play no active role in relation to them, if they are simply received. Legs must be limiting if you simply drag them around in a wheelchair or on crutches; but if you can walk, what sense does it make to say legs restrict us? We will never grow wings, so we must use what makes us human. Our identities are more than metaphorical legs, they are our psychic and moral bodies, which explains why people are willing to give birth and to kill in order to preserve them.

This aspect of our human nature has its dangers in an interdependent world. As an antidote to all excessive nationalisms, we must recognize that no identity is a given, by god or nature—while defending our right to be who we are here and now, and to organize for communal survival. The gay community is a proud creation, worth running great risks—even dying—for. Half a million people, including some who were gravely sick, traveled to Washington last October and stood for hours in the cold, to affiliate with and show their allegiance to the gay community. More than nine hundred people defied arrest to protest the homophobic actions of the Supreme Court. As a people, we gays have special gifts—of resilience, of humor, of sexual expression, of sensibility. The causes we embody (the right to be different without being persecuted, the right to a greater measure of sexual freedom and choice, and the challenge we pose to rigid gender systems) have meaning beyond today's circumstances.

Recently, Toni Morrison was asked if she saw herself "simply" as a writer or as a black woman writer. Did she resent those labels? She replied that what others called limitations—African or Southern roots, a history of slavery, a female perspective—were the very elements of her creative vision. Far from seeking to escape them or explain them away, she wanted to explore and shape their meaning. So too for me as a gay woman anthropologist. History has placed gay people *here;* from here we are making history.

Lesbian and Gay Issues in Anthropology:

Some Remarks to the Chairs of Anthropology

Departments

1993

I address you today as people who are in a position to do something about two related problems: discrimination against lesbians, gay men, and bisexuals, and the challenges and opportunities that a more diverse and multicultural society pose to our profession.

As anthropologists, you pride yourselves, I presume, on being flexible and open-minded. Most likely you support the ideal of equal rights, and you don't intend to discriminate against any aspiring or worthy anthropologists. If so, your department might be similar to Oberlin College, where a sociological study revealed this paradox: although most heterosexuals expressed positive attitudes toward equality for gays and lesbians (for example, 89 percent of Oberlin employees said they would not oppose hiring someone gay, and 80 percent professed to feel comfortable socializing with someone they knew to be gay), gays and lesbians on campus experienced pervasive discrimination, ranging from assault to job discrimination to insulting jokes and graffiti. In addition, 40 of gay Oberlin employees had not revealed their sexual orientation to any supervisor (Norris 1992).

What accounted for this contradiction? Sociologist William Norris suggested that the majority of heterosexuals were torn between an abstract belief in equal rights and a competing adherence to "heterosexual orthodoxy," which "implicitly links heterosexuality to job performance, student roles, athletic performance, and community participation" (1992:117). Elements of this orthodoxy, wrote Norris, were the widespread desire not to discuss *any* sexual matters, which were believed to be private; adherence to traditional gender roles, which assume heterosexuality, in all aspects of campus life; and the influence of religious doctrines. The majority of straight people were actually uncomfortable with gay and lesbian issues, and some gays feared the spotlight that gay rights advocacy could shine into their own closets. Widespread am-

Commission on Lesbian and Gay Issues in Anthropology meeting at American Anthropological Association headquarters, October 1994; l. to r. Bill Leap and the author, cochairs; Jack Cornman, executive director of AAA; Liz Kennedy; Deb Amory. Photo by Sue-Ellen Jacobs

bivalence abetted by a lack of leadership from Oberlin's administration created a vacuum. This silence gave the green light to "a segment of the Oberlin employees and students (certainly not all and probably not even half) [who] do not approve of homosexuality, do not want it discussed, and harass and insult [lesbians, gays, and bisexuals] or people perceived in some way to be sympathetic to or interested in their issues" (116). Over 90 percent of gays on campus had not reported such incidents to authorities.

How can I encourage you to try to make your departments more hospitable for us despite whatever nagging doubts are perhaps lingering in many of your hearts? In advocating more inclusiveness, I won't try to sell you the liberal nostrum that the open presence of gays and lesbians would change nothing. For in addition to what we straights and gays have in common as intellectuals and professional educators in a world that doesn't value us much, lesbians and gays *are* also different, and as all anthropologists know, genuine difference can be a shock. Gay rights is about so much more than the defense of what some of you may see as unorthodox sex practices. For reasons that are specific to Western culture, lesbians and gay men form a vital but submerged and embattled subculture. Our sexuality, but also our friendships, families, finances, health problems, and creativity are commanded to remain private and hidden so that the majority's can appear to be natural and universal. At first, many of you might be uncomfortable as open gays reveal more of ourselves and as some closeted people come out. But when you defend gay people's rights and freedom, you are defending everyone's freedom to be different (including that of gay people of color to be doubly different), everyone's scholarly, artistic, and popular freedom of expression, everyone's freedom to love whom we choose, and the need we all share to define family however we are living it.

Supporting gay presence and gay rights also directly benefits anthropology. Gay activists are among the most dynamic players in the fight for multiculturalism on campus and in society. Lesbians and gays have been at the leading edge of modernism throughout this century, which is why we have been and are now, more than ever, a prime target of religious and cultural conservatives. If you don't want to wind up teaching creationism and Christian values instead of evolution and cultural relativism, support gay rights. Inclusiveness toward gays and other marginalized groups is crucial if anthropology is to regain its leadership in the movement toward a culturally diverse twenty-first century. Cultural differences have become a matter of national debate, and where is anthropology?

I put into action the sentiments expressed at crowded sessions on multiculturalism at last year's annual meetings by teaching a freshman seminar whose title is "Multiculturalism." Half my students are whites and the other half are black and Latino. One out of three of these freshman students identify themselves as gay, lesbian, or bisexual. I am trying to persuade them that anthropology can help them survive and thrive. But currently many of the brightest gay students go into literary criticism and media studies, believing their interests and careers will be supported in those departments. Gay inclusion is not only morally right, it also has the potential to increase your undergraduate enrollments. Courses in multiculturalism both attract students and fulfill diversity requirements. Departments that offer supervision on sexuality-related research get bright and promising graduate students. And a gay-inclusive atmosphere strengthens the commitment of gay professionals to anthropology and to the American Anthropological Association. But you *must* begin to change the ways in which you knowingly and unknowingly coerce us into silence.

What specifically can you do? The most important first step is inexpensive: in public announcements, catalogue copy, and speeches you can include us by name. Vague references are not enough. For example, the report on a four-day Wenner-Gren conference charged with exploring critical issues facing the discipline, as reported in AAA *Newsletter* (1993), decries the lack of complete equality of opportunity in all fields of anthropology and continues, "For intellectual, practical and ethical reasons, anthropology cannot afford to and ought not limit anyone's contribution to the discipline because of gender or *lifestyle;* scientific rigor, quality of work and importance of findings should be the tests" (emphasis added).

To be lesbian or gay is not a "lifestyle." There are suburban, inner-city, and rural gays; black, Latina, Native American, and Asian gays; working-class gay truck drivers and soldiers, scholarly bisexuals and opera-loving corporate lesbians. We are drawn toward members of our own gender as intimate companions, and because of this society has punished us; it is this history of oppression and resistance that we all share. The Wenner-Gren statement leaves the impression, however unintentionally, that although discrimination against us is bad, actually naming us is worse. To change the climate of your departments, you must explicitly include lesbians, gay men, and bisexuals as part of the audience you address in your speeches and public announcements— and especially when the topic is discrimination. Some of the other things you can do or advocate in areas under your purview to create a more gay-friendly environment are these:

— *Reseach Topics*: When a graduate student suggests sexuality-related or specifically gay and lesbian research topics, it is not wrong to point out that this may make career advancement more difficult, but you should also evaluate the proposal on the merits and assure the student you will be supportive if he or she decides to go ahead.

— *Faculty Hiring and Promotion*: One of the strongest symbols of a department's willingness to support gay and lesbian students is through fair treatment for gay faculty already in your department and through hiring and promoting openly gay scholars. Studies have shown that homophobic attitudes and discrimination are directed especially at faculty who do gay-related research and/or play any kind of activist role on campus, so they are especially vulnerable. They are also valuable to anthropology: lesbian and gay studies are at the cutting edge of scholarship in a number of disciplines in the humanities and social sciences.

— *Curriculum*: Encourage the inclusion of some of the outstanding work that has been done on what Kath Weston (1993b:177) termed "transcultural studies of sexuality and gendering" in your department's courses and try to have your department offer at least one course devoted to this field. And although AIDS is not an inherently gay course topic, it is obviously of special concern to gays, yet homophobia prevents anthropologists from taking more leadership in AIDS education and research.

— *Funding for Research:* So far there has been no study of discrimination in funding, but everyone I know assumed that during the Reagan-Bush era, no gay-oriented projects (except perhaps for those directly connected to AIDS) would be funded by either the federal government or by private sources. In the early stages of my research on the lesbian and gay resort of Cherry Grove, a gay colleague urged me only half-jokingly to write it up as a study of beach erosion to try to get funding. Scholars interested in diverse sexualities and gendering assume we will not be funded, and as far as I know we hardly ever are if we are frank about our intentions, as I was. You can recommend students and colleagues with good projects to funding agencies, and no matter how government and private funders respond, you may be able to fund bright students from departmental block grants.

— *Institutional Diversity Initiatives:* Make sure that lesbians, gays, and bisexuals are included on committees devoted to developing curriculum, policies, mission statements, and so on whose goal is to make your university more inclusive. And follow the lead of Stanford and the University of Chicago in instituting domestic partner benefits.

The Executive Committee of the AAA has just created the Commission on Lesbian and Gay Issues in Anthropology. This means a lot to us gay anthropologists, who have sweated hard and lonely miles to survive and achieve visibility through SOLGA, the Society of Lesbian and Gay Anthropologists. Let your friends, colleagues, and students know that the Commission on Lesbian and Gay Issues in Anthropology exists. Let your actions show that you think its mission is timely and worthwhile by working with us, your fellow anthropologists, when we come knocking on your office door.

My Best Informant's Dress:

The Erotic Equation in Fieldwork

1992

MALINOWSKI'S "SEX-SICKNESS"

"Aren't there any anthropologist jokes?" asked a doctor friend of my mother's who had just entertained a table of lunch buddies at their retirement community with a series of doctor gags. To my mother's disappointment, I couldn't think of even one. I do have a poor memory for jokes, but a quick survey of my peers revealed that we are not given to either wit or thigh-slapping when it comes to the practice of our trade. The only anthropologist to deliver was my friend and former mentor David Schneider, who came up with this one: "A postmodern anthropologist and his informant are talking; finally the informant says, 'Okay, enough about you, now let's talk about me.' "[1]

Retelling this joke, I realized one reason that it struck me as funny was its similarity to a recent television advertisement. A young man and woman, postmodern-looking in their tight black clothes and spiked hair, are chatting at a party, and she says to him, "Okay, now let's talk about you; what do you think of my dress?"

Not only did Schneider's joke suggest a certain absurdity in the so-called reflexivity discourse, but its kinship with the suggestive commercial also inspired me to wonder why the postmodern scrutiny of the relation between informant, researcher, and text is limited to who is talking or even what is said. What else is going on between fieldworker and informant? Is "the romance of anthropology" only a manner of speaking?

In their germinal article contrasting postmodernism and feminism in anthropology, Mascia-Lees, Sharpe, and Cohen see "a romantic yearning to know the 'other' " behind the reflexive "turn" (1989:25–26). But rather than leading on to the obvious erotic possibilities, they circle back within the metaphor: "Traditionally, this romantic component has been linked to the heroic quests, by the single anthropologist, for 'his soul' through confrontation with the exotic 'other' . . . in turning inward, making himself, his motives, and his experience the thing to be confronted, the postmodernist anthropologist locates the 'other' in himself."

Following Mascia-Lees, Sharpe, and Cohen's suggestion to be "suspicious of relationships with 'others' that do not include a close and honest scrutiny of the motivations for research" (1989:33), I am going to ask an embarrassing question. Is all this romance totally sublimated in fieldnotes and language learning only to emerge in texts as a metaphor for the "heroic quest by the single anthropologist," or does the erotic ever make a human gesture? If so, what might be the significance of the erotic equation in fieldwork and its representation or lack thereof in ethnographic texts?

Rarely is the erotic subjectivity or experience of the anthropologist discussed in public venues or written about for publication. If this omission is not due to any plot or conspiracy, neither is it incidental. In the dominant schematic that has set the terms of discourse, the distanced neutral observer presented in traditional anthropological texts is at the opposite pole from the sexually aroused (repelled? ambivalent?) fieldworker. By not "problematizing" (dreadful word, but none other works as well here) *his* own sexuality in his texts, the anthropologist makes male gender and heterosexuality the cultural givens, the unmarked categories. If straight men choose not to explore how their sexuality and gender may affect their perspective, privilege, and power in the field, women and gays, less credible by definition, are suspended between our urgent sense of difference and our justifiable fear of revealing it.

In graduate school in the early 1960s I learned—because it was never mentioned—that erotic interest between fieldworker and informant didn't exist, would be inappropriate, or couldn't be mentioned, I had no idea which. The anthropologist was pictured as a man who would ideally bring his wife to the field as company and helper. That she would absorb his sexual interests was, I suppose, understood. I knew that Margaret Mead and Ruth Benedict had done fieldwork, of course, but the former seemed to always be married to another anthropologist and the latter, whose "private" life was opaque, to have spent little time there.[2] If single male fieldworkers were thought by our male professors to engage in, or even refrain from engaging in, sexual activities, these were never discussed in front of me. This being the case, how could the sexuality of female fieldworkers ever emerge as an issue?

The black hole enveloping this nonsubject in most anthropological writing invites one of two conclusions: either desire is to be firmly squelched—even though many anthropologists are (or were) young, unattached, and living in lonely, isolated situations for months at a time—or it should be satisfied away from the glare of the published account, cordoned off from legitimate ethnography. A recent comprehensive guide to conducting fieldwork (Ellen 1984) has no index heading under "sexuality." From Casagrande's groundbreaking collection *In the Company of Man* (1960) to *In the Field* (Smith and Kornblum 1989), when a fieldworker writes in the first person, she or he thinks and sometimes feels but never actually lusts or loves. Most guides ward off desire with vague warnings against getting "too involved," hardly daring to admit that fieldworkers and informants do and must get involved emotionally.[3]

Between the lines lurk certain shadowy givens. The straight male anthropologist's "best informants" are likely to be, or at least to be represented as, male, presumably minimizing the danger of these key relationships becoming eroticized.[4] On the other hand, a veil of professional silence covers the face of indulgence toward men's casual sex with women in the field. For instance, the fieldwork guide mentioned earlier with no index heading for "sexuality" may allude to it coyly in a discussion of why anthropologists tend to "get so much more out of their first than out of subsequent fieldwork." Among other factors is the suggestion that "when anthropologists first go into the field they are often single" (Ellen 1984:98).

Most reflexive anthropology, which explicitly spotlights how ethnographic knowledge is produced, has rendered sex and emotion between ethnographers and informants more abstract than before. The exceptions show a pattern: Briggs (1970) and Myerhoff (1978), who do make their subjectivity gendered and grounded, are women; of three men who come to mind, Murphy (1987) was disabled and Rosaldo (1989) is Chicano. So far the only white, able-bodied, and, one is led to infer, heterosexual male who writes as if he knows this affected his fieldwork is Michael Moffatt (1989).[5]

Generally, practitioners of "new ethnography" have used metaphors of emotion and sexuality to express their ethnographic angst. Vincent Crapanzano (1980:134) likens his quest for knowledge of the Moroccans to a "belief in total sexual possession" and acknowledges that "passion" and "science" "are not in fact so easily separable," without grounding this observation in flesh.[6] And despite James Clifford's (1986:13, 14) observation that "excessive pleasures" and "desire" have been absent from traditional ethnography, these topics remain equally absent from the chapters in *Writing Culture* (Clifford and Marcus 1986). Why are emotion and sexuality less important or less implicated in what Clifford calls the "relations of production" of ethnography (13) than are race or colonialism? And if the absence of odor, which played a large part in travel writing (Clifford 1986:11), leaves ethnography at best stale and at worst deodorized, what does the absence of an erotic dimension do?

Historian John Boswell (1992) has advocated the contemplation of social margins both for their own beauty—he invoked the medieval manuscript page—and to advance our knowledge of the text. In anthropology, *only* the margins—marginal texts, the margins of more legitimate texts, or the work of socially marginal members of the profession—can tell us why we signify or squelch the erotics of fieldwork. By looking at *who* has written about sexuality in the field and *how* they have written about it, I ask why the erotic dimension is absent from the anthropological canon and, after offering an example from my own fieldwork, I will argue for its future inclusion.

As far as I know, only two white heterosexual men belonging to what Geertz (1988:73–101) termed the "I-Witnessing" literary genre of ethnography have problematized themselves as "positioned [sexual] subjects" by writing about sexual encounters with women in the field.[7] The revered ethnographer Bronislaw Malinowski was one of the few anthropologists to write *about* the sexuality of a non-Western people (1955), and in his private diary, in Polish (1967), he detailed his *own* sexual subjectivity, a persistent and painful struggle against "lewd" and "impure" fantasies about Trobriand and missionary women, whom he "pawed" and perhaps more (the *Diary* was censored by Malinowski's widow before publication).

Not only was an exemplary "competent and experienced ethnographer" (Geertz 1988:79) caught with his pants down, so to speak, but if anthropology's historic political agenda has been "to secure a recognition that the non-Western is as crucial an element of the human as the Western" (Mascia-Lees, Sharpe, and Cohen 1989:8), why was Malinowski thinking of Trobrianders, including objects of his ambivalent lust, as "niggers"?

The anthropological honchos who reviewed the *Diary* defended, dismissed, or gloated over it within a common and familiar frame of reference: "These diaries do not add in any significant way to our knowledge of Malinowski as a social scientist. They do, however, tell us a good deal about Malinowski as a person" (Gorer 1967:311).[8] Malinowski's sexuality, his physical health, his bigotry toward the Trobrianders, and his insecurity as a fieldworker were private matters subsumed in the concept "person," which had, or should have had, nothing to do with Malinowski the public social scientist. Underlying all the reviews is the belief that human beings can be sorted into "lower" and "higher" parts corresponding to self-consciousness and consciousness, emotions and intellect, body and soul. Of course, Malinowski shared these same assumptions: Geertz (1967) noticed a resemblance between the *Diary* and the "Puritan tract," and Geoffrey Gorer (1967:311) compared Malinowski to "the desert Fathers, [who are] tempted by devils" and likened the *Diary* to "spiritual confessions, with the same person being both the penitent and the priest." The hostile and dismissive reaction of the reviewers suggests even less tolerance in scientific dualism for the "lower" aspects of human experience than there had been in its Christian version. Ian Hogbin (1968) fumed that the

Diary was concerned with nothing but "trivia" and should never have been published.

At the time, only Clifford Geertz realized the profound significance of the *Diary* for the anthropological enterprise.[9] The gap between Malinowski the "person" and Malinowski the "social scientist" revealed by the *Diary* was indeed "shattering" to the "self-congratulatory" image of anthropology (1967: 12). But for Geertz, Malinowski was all the more admirable because, "through a mysterious transformation wrought by science" (13), he had heroically transcended his bad attitude and lack of empathy toward the Trobrianders to become a "great ethnographer."

Twenty years later Geertz looked backward and saw in the publication of this "backstage masterpiece" the first signs of the profound disquiet revealed in "new ethnography" and "the breakdown of epistemological (and moral) confidence" (1988:75, 22) in postmodern anthropology. Although Malinowski had turned his cultural pockets inside out in a diary he could bring himself neither to publish nor to destroy, the postmodernists have made I-Witnessing central to their legitimate texts. But the unpleasantly corporeal body in Malinowski's diary has become, in deconstructionist thought, a more comfortable "metaphor of the body" (Bordo 1990). Admitting that there is no objective location outside the body from which to transcend culture, postmodernists in and out of anthropology have conceived the body as a "trickster" of *"indiscriminate sex and changeable gender"* (Smith-Rosenberg 1985a:291; emphasis added) whose "unity has been shattered by the choreography of multiplicity. . . . Deconstructionist readings that enact this protean fantasy are continually 'slip-slidin' away'; through paradox, inversion, self-subversion, facile and intricate textual dance, they . . . *refuse to assume a shape for which they must take responsibility*" (Bordo 1990:144; emphasis added).

Postmodern anthropologists are taking upon themselves one part of the white man's burden—the power to name the "other"—but they still do not want to shoulder the responsibility for their erotic and social power in the field, possibly, as Mascia-Lees, Sharpe, and Cohen (1989) have argued, because they are not enthusiastic about the insights of feminism. Paul Rabinow, who has explicitly rejected a feminist perspective (Mascia-Lees, Sharpe, and Cohen 1989:18), published, although not in his principal ethnography, an account of his one-night stand with a Moroccan woman thoughtfully provided by a male informant (1977:63–69). Most of Rabinow's description is disingenuously off-handed and is made to seem—despite the unexplored admission that this was "the best single day I was to spend in Morocco"—primarily about validating his manhood to male Moroccans while fending off "haunting super-ego images of my anthropologist persona."

Several women anthropologists have told me they read Rabinow's account as a boasting admission about what is really standard operating procedure for male fieldworkers. Very likely, one of the models for the "haunting super-ego images" that interfered with Rabinow's pleasure was that of his mentor, Clifford Geertz. In his brilliant analysis of postmodern texts by (male) anthropologists, Geertz specifically interprets the episode as part of Rabinow's literary strategy to show himself as a "pal, comrade, companion" type of field-worker.[10] Just in case we might hope that Geertz's thinking had evolved beyond Malinowski's in the sexual department, he dismisses the woman involved as a "wanton" (1988:93).

Progressives who want to transform the cruel, oppressive, Judeo-Christian sexual system and the correlated "objectivist" power grid that both entraps and privileges white heterosexual men should not condemn Malinowski or Rabinow for writing explicitly about the sexual subjectivity they struggled against or indulged, because coercive silence regarding the unwritten rules of the sex and gender system makes changing them impossible. As the issues crystallize out of our history, anthropologists must begin to acknowledge eroticism, our own and that of others, if we are to reflect on its meaning for our work and perhaps help alter our cultural system for the better.

Changing the gender and/or sexual orientation and probably the race of either fieldworker or informant modifies the terms of the erotic equation.[11] The sexuality of heterosexual men, however much a puzzle or pain on a personal level, is the cultural "ego," the assumed subjectivity, and it is predictable that women and gays, for whom matters of sexuality and gender can never be unproblematic, have begun to address these issues for the discipline as a whole.[12]

Quite a few women anthropologists of undisclosed sexual orientation have written about *not* having sex with men where apparently even being seen as (hetero)sexual meant losing all credibility, risking personal danger and the catastrophic failure of their fieldwork projects. As Peggy Golde put it, women anthropologists have felt compelled to "surround [themselves] with symbolic 'chaperones'" (1970:7). Working in South America, Mary Ellen Conaway restricted her freedom of movement and wore "odd-looking, loose-fitting clothing, no makeup, and flat-soled shoes" to prevent the local men from getting any wrong ideas (1986:59, 60). Maureen Giovanni warded off Sicilian men by "dressing conservatively and carrying a large notebook whenever I left the house" (1986:110).

"Manda Cesara" (Karla O. Poewe) is the only woman I know about who has written for publication, although under a pseudonym and not in an ethnographic text, about having sex with male informants. Unlike the male anthropologists, she neither retreated into abstraction nor narrated her erotic experience as a casual notch on the bedpost: "To lay hold of a culture through one's love of one individual may be an illusion, but there can be no doubt that love became a fundamental relation of my thoughts and perceptions to both, the world of the Lenda and myself" (1982:59). "Douglas opened for me the gate to Lenda. I don't mean that he introduced me to his friends. I mean that he opened my heart and mind" (61).

The male Africans' so-called natural attitude toward heterosexual intercourse and extramarital affairs buttressed Cesara's doubts about the Judeo-Christian system. And in the midst of a long reflection beginning with "sexuality is a cultural system" (1982:146) but veering off into a discussion of what is wrong with Western culture as measured by the prevalence of male homosexuality, she adds, "The Lenda, thank heaven, and I am speaking selfishly, are beautifully heterosexual" (147). Although Cesara's homophobia upset me enough to write her an open letter (Newton 1984b) — straights are still holding gays accountable for the decline of the Roman Empire — I do hope to read more bold papers and books like hers in which the erotic dimension of power and knowledge is acknowledged openly.

For years the pages of *SOLGAN,* formerly the *ARGOH Newsletter,* the quarterly publication of the Society of Lesbian and Gay Anthropologists, have been enlivened by accounts of (mostly male) homosexuality in far-flung parts of the world. Many of these brief accounts include a note on the fieldworker's sexual orientation, and a few have implied participation.[13] Walter Williams, in *The Spirit and the Flesh* (1986), was clear that his being gay gave him access to the Plains Indian "berdaches" (105) and suggests that intimate relations enabled his knowledge (see especially 93).[14]

The anthropologist who has most lyrically expressed eroticism toward the "other" is Kenneth Read in his work on the Gahuku-Gama of New Guinea.[15] In *Return to the High Valley* (1986), Read, in hot pursuit of honesty about fieldwork and that illusive emotional dimension to ethnographic texts, scales the barbed wire fence between emotion and ethnography: "I have the greatest affection for [the Gahuku-Gama]," he writes, adding, "I have never known why this admission generates suspicion" (ix, x). That this attraction is or borders on homoerotic desire is signaled in code words that are understood by both gay and straight: "Lest anyone begin to feel uneasy at the possibility of being exposed to embarrassment, I assure the more sensitive members of my profession that I will not *flaunt this personal ingredient like a banner*" (x; emphasis added).[16]

Yet such is the intensity of Read's attachment, and so insistent, that he winds up doing a kind of literary striptease, first putting out disclaimers to alert the "more sensitive members of my profession," then revealing what had just been hidden. Read's "best informant" and the man who "may be said to have invited me there" (1986:11) was Makis, "an influential man in the tribe." Although Read reassures his readers that "propriety restrains me from revealing the full depth of my affective bond to him" (12), he throws propriety to the winds, it seems to me, in his subsequent description of remembering, thirty years after the fact, Makis coming into his (Read's) room: "Emerging with a marvelous physical solidity into the circle of light cast by my lamp, all the planes of his chest, his face, his abdomen and thighs chiseled from black and shining marble, his lips lifted upward with the natural pride of an aristocracy owing nothing to the accidents of birth, and his eyes holding mine with the implications of at least a partial understanding neither of us could express in words" (75).[17]

Following in Read's footsteps (but with banners flying), I offer an account — perhaps the first to describe a relationship between a lesbian anthropologist and her female "best informant"—of the emotional and erotic equation in my own recent fieldwork.[18]

KAY

My fieldwork experience has been fraught with sexual dangers and attractions that were much more like leitmotifs than light distractions. To begin with, the fact that I am a gay woman has disposed *me*—the great majority of gay anthropologists work with heterosexuals and avoid sexual topics—toward working with other gay people (a correspondence that heterosexuals observe more often than gays do, albeit with the unexamined privilege of the powerful).[19] I was not looking for sexual adventure in the field. Cultural, political, and psychological factors more than eroticism have determined my affinity for gays as research subjects; for one thing, I have worked more with gay men than women. Looking back, I used my first fieldwork among gay people, mostly male, to consolidate a fragile and imperiled gay identity. Prospective dissertation projects in East Africa and Fiji—again I stress I am not speaking *for* gay fieldworkers but *as* one—presented unknown dangers that scared me off. Most closeted gay people, as I then was, manage information and stress in America by retreating to private or secret "gay zones" where, alone and with other gays, we can "be ourselves." No African or Fijian village would offer such refuge, I figured, and what if they found me out? Bringing my then-lover to an exotic field locale was never imaginable, and the prospect of living for months without physical and emotional intimacy was too bleak.[20]

So, by the "erotic dimension," I mean, first, that my gay informants and

Kay in Cherry Grove in the 1950s. Collection of Esther Newton

I shared a very important background assumption that our social arrangements reflected: that women are attracted to women and men to men. Second, the very fact that I *have* worked with other gays means that some of the
people who were objects of my research were also potential sexual partners.
Partly because of this, my key informants and sponsors have usually been
more to me than an expedient way of getting information, and something different from "just" friends. Information has always flowed to me in a medium
of emotion, ranging from passionate—although never consummated—erotic
attachment through profound affection to lively interest, that empowers me
in my projects and, when it is reciprocated, helps motivate informants to put
up with my questions and intrusions.

I had thought of writing an ethnohistory of the gay and lesbian community
of Cherry Grove several months before I met Kay, having become attached to
the place—a summer resort on Fire Island, about forty-five miles from New
York City—during the previous summer. Career pressures and political commitment were behind the initial decision. I needed a second big field experience and book to advance professionally. From the outset I also intended to
write for New York's huge gay communities in whose evolution Cherry Grove
had, I suspected, played a starring role.[21]

But not everyone who sets sail keeps afloat—or catches the wind. A great
deal of the lift one needs in the field when one is becalmed or swamped came

through my love for two elderly Grove women, and because of them the work was suffused with emotion and meaning. Two years after starting fieldwork I described them in my notes as "the sun and the moon of my love affair with Cherry Grove—without them there would be neither heat nor light in me to pursue and embrace my subject." Peter (Ruth) Worth became my Grove cicerone, my close friend, and my confidant; I was in love with Kay.[22]

Kay was an old-timer I should meet, Grovers said. After several weeks I matched the name with a dignified and classy-looking old woman who rode around the boardwalks in an electric cart. Like most able-bodied people, I had looked through her out of misplaced politeness and because of her advanced age. When I did introduce myself, I received more than I had hoped for: a warm and impulsive invitation for a drink at her cottage. That evening I wrote about my first encounter:

> Kay lives in a tiny charming white house, the deck full of potted flowers. I found her shuffling (she moves precariously by advancing each foot a few inches ahead of the other) to get me a drink of juice and complaining that her hair wasn't done—she hates that. Despite wrinkles and thinning hair, she still pulls off a look.
>
> She told me unsentimentally how infirm she was: the hearing aid, the contact lenses, the inability to read, a slipped disk she was too old to have fixed, and how she hated to be one of those complaining elderly. . . . Emphysema makes her wheeze painfully with every movement. (She still smokes: "I don't inhale, dear. Please—it's my only vice, the only one I have left.")
>
> Was it because I liked her cottage which still had the charm of an earlier Cherry Grove, because I found her beautiful and her suffering poignant, or because her allusions to past vices intrigued me? Or was it because she called me "dear" that I came away enchanted?[23]

Several hours after writing my fieldnotes, too elated to sleep, I wrote to David Schneider: "The more I get into the history, the harder hold Cherry Grove has on my imagination. . . . I'm embarking, and thrilled about it." And then I plunged on, far more confident and confiding than I had been as his closeted graduate student when I was doing fieldwork with female impersonators and my "best informant" was a gay man (whom I also adored).[24] "This morning," I wrote, "I introduced myself to a woman of eighty plus whom I'd been wanting to meet, as she rolled toward me in her electric cart. Not only was she receptive, she clasped my arm in an intimate embrace and practically pulled me into her lap while we talked . . . and my heart quite turned over. Such are the perils of fieldwork."

After that I went by Kay's cottage every day, and as I talked to other community members, my fascination with her grew. I discovered that her powers of seduction were legendary. As one Grove woman told me: "Kay was the first one to walk into the Waldorf and say, 'Send me a bottle and a blonde.' She's a law unto herself; don't think you can compare her to the average lesbian. She could walk into the Taj Mahal and people would think she was the owner." That triggered this reflection, only weeks after our first meeting: "Seeing Kay now, crippled and gasping for breath, I still can imagine it, remembering how her ex-lover Leslie came in and threw her arms around Kay saying, 'Oh Kay, we had some great times on this couch!' and Kay's enormous blue eyes light up to go with the smile—the expensive dentures gleaming—the gesture of a devilish flirt."

The work progressed around and through my crush on Kay. She helped me organize a group of old-timers to reminisce about the Grove, and I followed up in a burst of energy with individual interviews. And despite her often expressed fear that my book would reveal to an unsuspecting world that the Grove was a gay haven, she became ever more helpful. Six weeks later, "We had an intense five minutes of smiling at each other. On my way out I gave her my number out here and said 'If there's ever a problem, don't hesitate to call me,' and she seemed very pleased, and asked if she could do anything for me. I said yes, 'Show me your pictures, tell me about the people.' She agreed."

That winter I returned to my teaching job. I spoke to Kay by telephone, and in April I picked her up at her Park Avenue apartment for a lunch date. By then our pattern of flirtation and teasing was established. "Back then, Kay, did you get who you wanted?" I asked, as she was insisting on paying for our pricey meal with her American Express gold card. "Yes," she smiled, "and lots of them." She told me that she still got sexual urges but just waited for them to pass. We both flirted with the idea of making love. "Someday I'm going to surprise the hell out of you and really kiss you back," she said once gleefully.

Two summers after I met Kay the fieldwork project was cresting, and although it was tacitly settled that her physical pain and chronic illness precluded sex and we would not actually become lovers, our daily visits were affectionate and full of erotic by-play. On July 11, 1988, I wrote, "I don't remember now when I used to sit *facing* Kay across the round coffee table. Probably even that first summer I began to sit next to her on the Naugahyde (so practical for the beach) orange couch, partly because she generally hears me if I speak about six inches from her right ear, and mostly just to get closer. In the last weeks my visits have taken a new pattern. I arrive, I kiss her quickly on the lips and find out what she needs from the store—then I return. Now comes the real visit."

During the "real visit," when she felt up to it, Kay repeated stories about her past life, her many lovers, her marriages, and about the major and minor characters in Cherry Grove's history. I sat enthralled as she recited verses from poems of Edna St. Vincent Millay—she had known the poet—which I guessed had been part of her seduction repertoire. And although I could never persuade her to leave her letters and papers to a university library, she did allow me to copy many valuable photographs and newspaper clippings. She also continued to help me gain access to other old-timers. When I asked Kay to tell one Grover who had resisted an interview that I was a "good guy," she answered smiling, "Oh I tell that to everybody." I later wrote in my field-notes, "Millions couldn't buy this goodwill. No one's word means more than Kay's to the old-timers here, and she has given me her trust freely. I know Kay's affection has never been compelled or bought. She just likes me, and the beauty of it is I adore her even though I need her and have ulterior professional motives."

Kay never had to say "Now let's talk about me" because she rarely asked me about my life. She was used to being the entertaining center of attention, even though she was acutely and painfully aware that her friends, me included, sometimes found her conversation boring because she didn't remember what she had told to whom, couldn't get out, didn't hear gossip, and was so preoccupied with her physical problems. But even on days when Kay had no new story, no information or photograph to offer, I enjoyed being with her: "What's deep about her is almost all nonverbal. It's her bodily presence, bearing—still—and that emotional force, crushing and liquid like an ocean wave. . . . Kay once told me that driving out to the Grove with two other lesbians on a cloudy day she had raised her arms to the sky and intoned 'Clouds Go Away, Sun Come Out' several times. Within minutes the clouds split and the sun came out. Kay showed me how the other two women turned around and looked at her incredulously from the front seat. In another culture Kay would have been some kind of priestess." Her stories and our mutual pleasure in each other constantly led me back to the work: "The more I think about Kay allowing herself to be seduced in the girls' school the more her life connection to the history I am helping to construct excites me. Kay's beauty and presence would have made me crazy in her younger days, but I wonder if—because she was a party girl rather than an intellectual—I could have loved her deeply. But now, instead of *having* ideas she *embodies* ideas. Kay spans almost the entire period from 'smashing' and romantic friendship to the age of AIDS. When I kiss her I am kissing 1903."

My love affair with Kay and with Cherry Grove culminated in 1988 celebrations around her eighty-fifth birthday, which also marked her fiftieth summer as a Grover. At her small birthday party I was proud that her hand on my knee proved she could still attract women. I was her escort at a Cherry Grove theater performance dedicated to "Kay, our national institution." Until the day a year later when Kay had what quickly proved to be a fatal heart attack, our loving relationship continued. To Grovers, Kay's death symbolized the end of an era; to many of us, her loss was also a personal one. My fieldwork suddenly felt more finished than it had before, and I decided not to return another summer.

"ALL POEMS ARE LOVE POEMS"

This would have been a very different chapter had I set out to "decide" whether ethical and/or strategic considerations should constrain anthropologists from having sexual relationships with informants. If we are to believe that only those who publicly confessed to it are tempted, then, Manda Cesara aside, women fieldworkers' vulnerability as women rules out (hetero)sex. In print, and probably much more so in life, the men feel freer. Malinowski struggled to keep *himself* pure, and Rabinow saw no ethical difficulty in his sexual behavior in the field. Yet it is hard to see why, if our power as anthropologists to name the subordinated "other" poses an ethical problem, the power to screw them doesn't. Most of our English sexual vocabulary implies domination to begin with. I doubt that a way out of this problem will be found so long as it is posed in these terms. But if "the burden of authorship cannot be evaded," as Geertz suggests (1988:140), then neither can the burden of being, and being seen as, an erotic creature.

In my own case, there was no higher status to take advantage of to buy or attract sexual partners. Almost all my informants were, like me, American, white, and at least middle class. Though some Grovers were apprehensive about what I might write, few were impressed by my being a scholar, and many Grove men considered themselves my superior because of my gender. Far from my being above Kay, in Cherry Grove's lexicon she was a wealthy homeowner and longtime community icon, while I was a passing blip, a newcomer and lowly renter. Unquestionably, her regard enhanced my status far more than the reverse. Because our loving relationship never became defined as an affair, my strategic anxieties about possible complications from becoming sexually involved with a beloved member of a small face-to-face community were never put to the test. Those fears did advise caution (as did the fact that we both had somewhat absent longtime companions—that is another story), but for Kay, too, the fact of sexual attraction was more compelling than "having sex" and much safer than "having an affair."

As a child who was more comfortable with adults than with other kids, I've often been attracted to older people as friends, advisors, and in adulthood, as lovers, so it's predictable that the work of writing gay history seduced me and kept me enchanted through Kay, who had lived and created it. If Kay had not existed, I might have had to invent her. For me, intellectual and creative work, including fieldwork and the writing of ethnography, has always been inspired by and addressed to an interior audience of loved ones like informants and mentors. The most intense attractions have generated the most creative energy, as if the work were a form of courting and seduction.

What Kay got was an admirer forty years younger who could run errands, set up appointments, move garden furniture, bring friends by, flirt, and who genuinely wanted to know and hear who her friends had been and what their common experience had meant to her. Kay had other devoted friends who helped with some of the problems old age brings. Perhaps my unique gift was erotic admiration, which must have brought her vital powers back into focus amid the dissolution caused by failing mental and physical strength. Eroticism energized the project—which caught Kay's imagination—of giving her old age shape and meaning by recording the journey of her generation in Cherry Grove and seeing it as connected to my own life.[25]

This manner of working poses the danger of "uncritically adopting Kay's point of view," as one of the *Cultural Anthropology* readers and two colleagues who had read drafts of *Cherry Grove, Fire Island* (1993), my ethnohistory of the Grove, have warned. But until we are more honest about how we feel about informants we can't try to compensate for, incorporate, or acknowledge desire and repulsion in our analysis of subjects or in our discourse about text construction. We are also refusing to reproduce one of the mightiest vocabularies in the human language.

Philosophy, psychology, and literature have reflected on how creativity may be powered and shaped by Eros—I invoke both the glorious and the terrible powers of the winged god, not the debased sweetness of the cuddly Cupid—even if anthropology has not. "The lover is turned to the great sea of beauty," Diotina tells Socrates in that touchstone of Western meditation on Eros, the *Symposium*, "and, gazing upon this, he gives birth to many gloriously beautiful ideas and theories, in unstinting love of wisdom" (Plato 1989:58). Freud's theory of sublimation reinterprets Plato's encomium of Eros, albeit darkened by Judeo-Christian pessimism. And in a novel by May Sarton the lesbian protagonist declares, "When I said that all poems are love poems, I meant that the motor power, the electric current is love of one kind or another. The subject may be something quite impersonal—a bird on a window sill, a cloud in the sky, a tree" (1965:123).

The subject might also be a culture, a people, or a symbolic system. Of course, ethnographic texts are not poems, and neither are they diaries. Whatever motivates them, their purpose should be "enabling conversation over societal lines—of ethnicity, religion, class, gender, language, race—that have grown progressively more nuanced" (Geertz 1988:147). The erotic dimension intersects with those lines. To follow Malinowski's lead by including the sexuality of "our" people among the topics worthy of publication, anthropologists will have to surpass him and describe not just in Polish but also in English—in I-Witnessing or any other authorial style of "being there"—where we anthropologists, as encultured individuals like all other humans, are "coming from." [26] In the age of Anita Hill and AIDS, can we do less?

From the Appendix to Mother Camp: *Field Methods*

This essay is from *Mother Camp: Female Impersonators in America,* reprinted by permission of the University of Chicago Press, copyright 1972, 1979 by Esther Newton.

1 This happened toward the end of my first stay in Kansas City. It took about three weeks to establish a good working rapport with the performers. I considered such incidents as being urged to perform and invitations to spend time with performers during the daytime indicative, but most conclusive was the gradual relaxation of linguistic usage in my presence, especially the unselfconscious use of feminine pronouns and names. (As with so many stigmatized groups, terms that are slanderous and insulting from an outsider are self-identifying from an insider.) Finally, in the last week of the first trip, one of the performers offered me what I considered to be a full "courtesy stigma" (Goffman 1963:28–31). When asked by a visiting impersonator who I was, he replied casually, "Oh, she's my husband."

It seems to me that I had relatively little difficulty establishing rapport. I assume this was due to the influence of my sponsor, but some peculiarities of my status and personality must be taken into account. My status as a bookish female enabled me to present myself as a relatively asexual being, which was helpful. Although my own background is middle class, alienated perspectives are congenial to me. Because of this, I may have erred on the side of "unconventional sentimentality" (Becker 1965). However, the respect and liking that I had for many of the performers may have been decisive. Impersonators, like members of other stigmatized groups, are extraordinarily sensitive to contempt.

Role Models

This essay is from *Mother Camp: Female Impersonators in America,* reprinted by permission of the University of Chicago Press, copyright 1972, 1979 by Esther Newton.

1 In two Broadway plays (since made into movies) dealing with English homosexuals, *The Killing of Sister George* (lesbians) and *Staircase* (male homosexuals), drag played a prominent role. In *George,* an entire scene shows George and her lovers dressed in tuxedos and top hats on their way to a drag party. In *Staircase,* the entire plot turns on the fact that one of the characters has been arrested for "going in drag" to the local pub. Throughout the second act, this character wears a black shawl over his shoulders. This item of clothing is symbolic of full drag. This same character is a camp and, in my opinion, George was a very rare bird, a lesbian camp. Both plays, at any rate, abounded in camp humor. *The Boys in the Band,* another recent play and movie, doesn't feature drag as prominently but has two camp roles and much camp humor.

2 This concept was developed and suggested to me by Julian Pitt-Rivers.

3   Even one feminine item ruins the integrity of the masculine system; the male loses his caste honor. The superordinate role in a hierarchy is more fragile than the subordinate. Manhood must be achieved, and once achieved, guarded and protected.

4   The middle-class idea tends to be that any man who has had sexual relations with men is queer. The lower classes strip down to "essentials," and the man who is "dominant" can be normal (masculine). Lower-class men give themselves a bit more leeway before they consider themselves to be gay.

5   It becomes clear that the core of the stigma is in "wrong" sexual object choice when it is considered that there is little stigma in simply being effeminate, or even in wearing feminine apparel in some contexts, as long as the male is known to be heterosexual, that is, known to sleep with women or, rather, not to sleep with men. But when I say that sleeping with men is the core of the stigma, or that feminine behavior logically corresponds with this, I do not mean it in any causal sense. In fact, I have an impression that some homosexual men sleep with men *because* it strengthens their identification with the feminine role, rather than the other way around. This makes a lot of sense developmentally if one assumes, as I do, that children learn sex-role identity before they learn any strictly sexual object choices. In other words, I think that children learn they are boys or girls before they are made to understand that boys *only* love girls and vice versa.

6   The role of the "pretty boy" is also a very positive one, and in some ways the camp is an alternative for those who are not pretty. However, the pretty boy is subject to the depredations of aging, which in the subculture is thought to set in at thirty (at the latest). Because the camp depends on inventiveness and wit rather than on physical beauty, he is ageless.

7   This phrase is used by Kenneth Burke in reference to poetry and is used by Keil in a sociological sense.

8   Today I would say that the main problem is heterosexuals, just as the main problem for blacks is whites.

9   I don't want to pass over the implication here that female impersonators keep up with Susan Sontag. Generally, they don't. I had given him Sontag's "Notes on 'Camp'" (1964) to see what he would say. He was college educated and perfectly able to get through it. He was enraged (justifiably, I felt) that she had almost edited homosexuals out of camp.

10   Informants said that many ideas had been taken over by straights through the mass media, but that the moment this happened the idea would no longer be campy. For instance, one man said that a queen he knew had gotten the idea of growing plants in the water tank of the toilet. But the idea is no longer campy because it is being advertised through such mass media as *Family Circle* magazine.

How to defend *any* symbols or values from the absorbing powers of the mass media? Jules Henry (1963) was one of the first, I believe, to point to the power of advertising to subvert traditional values by appropriating them for commercial purposes. But subcultural symbols and values lose their integrity in the same way. Although Sontag's New York avant-garde had already appropriated camp from homosexuals, they did so in the effort to create their own aristocracy or integrity of taste as against the mass culture.

11   It is clear to me now (1971, e.g., post-Stonewall) how camp undercuts rage and therefore rebellion by ridiculing serious and concentrated bitterness.

12 It would be worthwhile to compare camp humor with the humor systems of other oppressed people (Eastern European Jewish, Negro, etc.).

13 Speed and spontaneity are of the essence. For example, at a dinner party, someone said, "Oh, we forgot to say grace." One woman folded her hands without missing a beat and intoned, "Thank God everyone at this table is gay."

14 It's important to stress again that camp is a pre- or proto-political phenomenon. The anticamp in this system is the person who wants to dissociate from the stigma to be like the oppressors. The camp says, 'I am not like the oppressors.' But in so doing he agrees with the oppressors' definition of who he is. The new radicals deny the stigma in a different way, by saying that the oppressors are illegitimate. This step is only foreshadowed in camp. It is also interesting that the lesbian wing of the radical homosexuals have come to women's meetings holding signs saying "We are the women your parents warned you against."

15 The "bitch," as I see it, is a woman who *accepts* her inferior status but refuses to do so gracefully or without fighting back. Women and homosexual men are oppressed by straight men, and it is no accident that both are beginning to move beyond bitchiness toward refusal of inferior status.

16 Many impersonators told me that they got tired of being camps for their friends, lovers, and acquaintances. They often felt they were asked to gay parties simply to entertain and camp it up, and said they did not feel like camping offstage, or didn't feel competent when out of drag. This broadens out into the social problems of all clowns and entertainers or, even further, to anyone with a talent. He will often wonder if he is loved for himself.

Preface to the Phoenix Edition of Mother Camp

This essay is from *Mother Camp: Female Impersonators in America,* reprinted by permission of the University of Chicago Press, copyright 1972, 1979 by Esther Newton.

1 I denote here the whole spectrum of political activities whose minimum goal is the toleration of the gay community as a minority group. Within the gay pride movement, a few groups have what would properly be called gay liberation as a goal: the end of state-enforced heterosexual hegemony and male domination and a consequent disappearance of the gay/straight opposition as we know it. Besides, the word "liberation" implies a socialist coloration that at present is rather pale. If the distinction seems invidious, perhaps I must plead guilty. But if even the more limited goals of the gay pride movement could be realized in my lifetime, it would make me proud of my native land.

2 Passing by my local (working-class) French movie theater, I find they are featuring *Outrageous*, with the subtitle *Un amour "different"* beside pictures of the starring impersonator and the female lead gazing tenderly at each other. Not all forms of co-optation are so blatant.

3 I see the transsexual phenomenon as a variant of this struggle. If you don't like being a man, get out. America: Love it or leave it.

4 That is, among urban, white males. There is a possibility that black and Hispanic gays (and poor whites?) have retained the effeminate drag style.

Theater: Gay Anti-Church—More Notes on Camp

This essay was originally written in 1992 and was to have been part of my 1993 ethnohistory of Cherry Grove (*Cherry Grove, Fire Island,* Beacon Press, Boston), but was left unfinished when the book manuscript proved too long. In the Grove book I included a few sections about theater in general and Grove theater in particular that I first wrote for this essay, which are reproduced here courtesy of Beacon Press. In 1998 I reorganized the essay to make it clearer and got significant editorial help from Holly Hughes, David Román, and from Liz Kennedy's reading for Duke University Press. Space and time limitations preclude me from fully integrating material from a fine group of new books on gay/lesbian/queer theater that only reinforce my central thesis: that queers and theater have a special relationship. See de Jongh (1992), Clum (1994), Solomon (1997), Román (1998), Schanke and Marra (1998), and Hughes and Román (1998). A word of caution: the historical sections that constitute the background leading up to the twentieth century are aimed at the general reader; theater historians who may be familiar with scholarship on antitheatricalism might want to turn to the middle of the essay, in which the twentieth-century models of Grove theater are discussed.

And finally, a note on my use of the word "gay" in both the title and elsewhere in the text. I have lived long enough to shed a more doctrinaire attitude I once held toward signifiers. Though I am fiercely attached to what is being signified—linked networks and communities of gender deviants who generally prefer the intimate company of their own gender—I can be gay, lesbian, or queer, depending on the context.

1   No less a personage than W. H. Auden begged to differ with Sontag's interpretation, according to Grover and theatrical writer Irving Drutman (1976:264): "When Susan Sontag published her lengthy, humorless explication of 'camp' [W. H. Auden] the master of that effervescent (and evanescent) form said commiseratingly, 'Poor dear, she got it all wrong.'"

Although he criticizes some of Sontag's assertions, Mark Booth makes the same mistake, albeit more explicitly. Booth specifically and homophobically disallows the idea that camp is the special sensibility of gay men. "Troglodytes sometimes confuse camp with homosexual [but] . . . camp's origins are far from being so humble." In fact, he continues, "camp people tend to be asexual rather than homosexual," and "while it may be true that many homosexuals are camp, only a small proportion of people who exhibit symptoms of camp behavior are homosexual" (1983:20). Ross (1989) repeats and amplifies Sontag's error of minimizing the gay role in camp. For a more balanced and nuanced appraisal of camp, see Bergman (1993). Analysis of how elites and advertisers appropriate subcultural styles is a different project.

2   Quoted in Clarke 1988:146.

3   The dissertation that became *Mother Camp* (1972, 1979) was finished in 1968. See "Appendix" and "Role Models" in this volume.

4   The Grove is less theatrical now (1990s) because of the influx of lesbians, who have a complex relationship to the community in which they've always been a minority; see "Dick(less) Tracy," this volume. For a description of the early theatricals and theme parties leading to the formation of the Arts Project by theater-crazy Grovers, see

Newton (1993:48) and other sections of *Cherry Grove* tracing the sixty-year history of Grove productions.

5   "This *is* my church," exclaimed Kiki, whose drag persona is a bitter and witty over-the-hill lounge singer, during a campy "Christmas Special" Off-Broadway on Christmas Eve 1998 (the theater, P.S. 122, was packed to capacity with queers, including the den mother of queer theory, Eve Kosofsky Sedgwick).

6   I always thought this phrase was invented by Larry Gross, but Michael Bronski (1984) uses it on the back cover of his book, *Culture Clash* and Larry Gross thinks it was first used by Christopher Isherwood. It *does* describe my experience of the relentless heterosexual presumption whose intent is to asphyxiate queer desire and personhood, by violence or otherwise.

7   For a full discussion of the ways that butch-femme and camp have and have not been connected, see " 'Dick(less) Tracy," this volume.

8   At first I termed this the "egalitarian/realistic" perspective, but I ultimately adopted Jeff Escoffier's concept of authenticity as more descriptive of the sensibility in opposition to camp. See Escoffier (1998:15–18) for a somewhat different use of the concept of authenticity.

9   A somewhat similar and much lengthier analysis of gay sensibility can be found in Bronski 1984:1–88.

10   Kennedy and Davis (1993) have made a parallel assertion about the importance of working-class butch-femme bar culture as the antecedent of the lesbian-feminist liberation movement.

11   An invaluable resource is Curtin's (1987) play-by-play discussion of gay and lesbian themes and characters on the American stage and the critical response to them in *We Can Always Call Them Bulgarians*. A shorter and somewhat more analytical treatment is in Bronski (1984:110–32). Wayne Dynes (1987:268–76) nodded at the importance of theater in gay history in his research guide.

12   It cannot be answered because most gays are still in the closet. In a survey of the impact of AIDS on the New York theater world, Michael Lasalle notes, "AIDS has claimed the lives of hundreds, if not thousands, of theater professionals, from megastar producer-director-choreographer Michael Bennett (*A Chorus Line, Dreamgirls*) to the unknown kids backstage and the boys in the band. Everyone in this closely knit, rather insular population has been affected by the epidemic" (1991:70). Yet Lasalle thinks the stereotype of gays being concentrated in the arts is just that, a stereotype, and no more true than the idea that only gays get AIDS. He quotes designer William Ivey Long as saying, "You know, AIDS is universal. . . . You keep hearing 'theater, theater, theater,' but there are straight people in Uganda dying, straight people. This thing has hit all mankind.' [Rodger] McFarlane [executive director of Broadway Cares, an AIDS service organization for theater professionals] makes a rather different point in the same article. 'If you look at the AIDS diagnosis figures by profession,' he says, 'you find that the per capita incidence among dancers, actors, or stagehands is not different from teachers, lawyers, government workers, or auto workers. The difference is that show biz lives are led in public. There are more famous actors than famous lawyers or auto workers' " (Lasalle 1991:73). However, this is far from being the only difference between gay artists and gay auto workers. Bronski (1984:142) argues more subtly that "because of the historical development of gay sensibility . . . the arts permit and reinforce gay male visibility."

13 Laurence Senelick (1990) cites an English sociological study that purported to find a "prevalence of male homosexuality" in modern English theater. The authors attributed this to "poor economic remuneration, low occupational prestige (among the rank and file), unpredictable and unstable employment, and geographic instability." Of course, if this were all, casual labor would also encourage homosexual participation. Perhaps it does, but the relationship I am claiming between theater and homosexuality is far more significant. The English authors, summarized by Senelick, continue: "Moreover, activities such as dancing, let's pretend, making-up, and wearing costumes are associated in the public mind with women. These conditions, says the study, militate against men forming conventional, socially sanctioned relationships, such as marriage or single-partner liaisons; whereas actresses (except for down-market strippers) tend to be glorified by the stage and can 'reach higher levels of the stratification system.' Hence, it concludes, the theater both promotes and fosters same-sex relationships among men" (41).

Senelick rightly criticizes the Ashworth and Walker (1972) study's "narrowly deterministic character" and adds, "It neglects the historical role of the theatre as a safehouse for the depiction of gender ambiguities and mystery within restrictive societies, although with the potential for personal expression through impersonation." He asserts that all professional theaters have been havens for homosexual desires: "If the London stage was not populated to a large degree by sodomites, it would have differed remarkably from professional theatre in every culture from the Korean *namsadang* and the Roman *mimi* on" (41).

14 Although the Jewish ghettos, the protected and restrictive settlements of Eastern Europe, make an obvious parallel, an even stronger analogy might be made to the role, both constraining and nurturing, of Protestant churches in the lives of American slaves. Despite many obvious differences between the situation of slaves prior to 1865 and gays prior to 1969, there are two striking similarities. First, both slaves and gays were severely restrained in their ability to socialize or to act in concert to promote their own interests. Second, both groups were subjected to a process of "symbolic annihilation" (Gross 1991), meaning they were never allowed to represent themselves from a subjective viewpoint, and when they were represented in mainstream venues (minstrel shows, plays, cartoons, radio, television), they were "minstrelized"—portrayed as figures of fun for others to laugh at—or, more lately, "normalized"—supposed, despite their wildly divergent history and situation, to be no different from people in the groups that oppressed them (the latter two terms are from Goffman, 1963). The predominance that churches, in the case of slaves and their descendants, and theater, in the case of gays and lesbians, came to hold over the imaginations and efforts of the respective populations is partly explained, then, by two factors: the attempted "symbolic annihilation" of both groups and the successful interdiction against political or economic action by them.

Because Christian sentiments were all that were publicly permitted (and could not be denied) to slaves, they accepted and elaborated what was inherently congenial, healing, and morale building in the Christian message. Moses' escape from slavery in Egypt, the repeated condemnations of the rich and powerful, the glorification of the weak, and the consolation of a better life in the hereafter all had intrinsic appeal to people who were enslaved. More directly, African American theater history makes a fascinating comparison with the material at hand. See, for example, the survey by Gates (1997) of the recent Wilson–Brustein debate and his account of the all-black Chitlin Circuit.

15   See Lisa Duggan's (1993) account of Annie Hindle (a mid-nineteenth-century male impersonator) and of the Alice Mitchell case, where Alice and Freda both were "stage struck."

16   To add to the queer double entendre, the actress Nance O'Neil was an outspoken feminist who had been dogged by rumors of an affair with Lizzie Borden (Jones 1998). A "nancy boy" was a widely known term for a gay man. Even the relatively provincial Gerrodette family of Cherry Grove knew and used the term (Newton 1993:32).

17   Perhaps the fact that this identity is based on a human faculty as central as desire gives it the weight that ethnic identities have by virtue of coming through childhood socialization. The only representation of this in a heterosexual context that I know about appeared in the film *Europa Europa*, where an adolescent Jewish boy masquerades first as a young communist and then as a Nazi cadet. The necessity to hide his circumcised penis frustrates desire, which must be squelched or completely hidden on pain of death.

18   Tennessee Williams put it best in the words of a character in *The Glass Menagerie:* "Yes, I have tricks in my pocket, I have things up my sleeve. But I am the opposite of a stage magician. He gives you illusion that has the pleasant disguise of truth. I give you truth in the pleasant disguise of illusion" (quoted in Bronski 1984:114).

19   According to R. Baker (1968:52), there was strong opposition to women on stage: "When a French troupe that included actresses did once venture onto the London stage in 1632, the women were jeered and pelted with apples" and "the arch-Puritan William Prynne called them 'unwomanish and graceless.'" In *Histrio-mastix: The Players Scourge, or Actors Tragedie* (1633–1974), Prynne "inveighed widely against both women on the stage, and the performances of the boys. His work was interpreted as an insult to the theatre-loving [Queen] Henrietta Maria and for his pains Prynne lost his ears" (R. Baker 1968:68).

20   R. Baker (1968:52) insists, "There were no sly remarks or lecherous sneers, no passing moments of distaste or laughter, when a comely boy recited a feminine protestation of love or of deflowering. The boys and young men were accepted as representatives of the female sex." Baker, whose agenda seems to be to legitimize female impersonation by showing it was once acceptable, does not address whether there were homosexual relations in the theater nonetheless. Both Bray (1982) and Senelick (1990) believe there were. Senelick, noting both the frequency of the accusation of sodomy against the all-male Elizabethan stage and the reluctance of historians to investigate the charge (n. 7), thinks there was fire behind the smoke: "The Renaissance English theatre, with its boy-players portraying young women, must have accepted an androgynous ideal of beauty and been permeated to some degree with homophilic feeling, acceptably neutralized by performance conventions" (38).

21   On the distinctive forms of homosexuality in the London theater, see Bray 1982:54–55. On the boy troupes, see R. Baker 1968:61, 68–75.

22   As Bray's (1982) examination of Renaissance England showed. Also on this point for Western Europe generally, see Saslow (1989:93). Both Saslow and Bray say the prevailing Renaissance model of male homosexual relations was superior/subordinate, usually with a significant age gap. The same pattern prevailed in the theater.

23   The phrase is Saslow's (1989:95), although he connects this development with generalized urban life and with all the arts, not particularly theater. The primary markers
of such subcultures are the shift toward group homosexual arrests and the existence
of organized male prostitution. These began first in Venice in the 1400s. In England
prostitution seems to have existed before group arrests, the first recorded of which
was in 1699 (Bray 1982:92).

24   For a more recent summary of what little is known about Renaissance and early
modern lesbianism, see Traub (1992:107–13).

25   For more detail on female-to-male cross-dressing on stage, see Straub (1991) and
"Dick(less) Tracy," this volume.

26   Barish (1981), the historian of antitheatricalism, misses the link with homophobia
(there is no index entry for either sexuality or homosexuality), although he notes
that the Puritan Prynne—he whose ears were shorn (see n. 19 above)—was obsessed
with "sexuality and effeminacy, as though to underscore the author's fearful aversion
to anything—dancing, love-making, hair-curling, elegant attire—that might suggest
active or interested sexuality, this being equated with femininity, with weakness,
with the yielding to feeling, and consequently with the destruction of all assured
props and boundaries." Compare this to Bray's (1982) analysis of the place of homosexuality in Christian cosmology as evidenced in the Adam and Eve story: homosexuality, just because it is *not* mentioned when God ordered the world during creation, stands for chaos. Prior to the seventeenth century, according to Bray, attacks
on homosexuality were attacks on disorder, not on an organized gay community or
even networks.
      Saslow (1989:100–104) mentions drama, although he primarily discusses paint-
ing and sculpture, as reflecting increased homosexual awareness during the Renaissance.

27   Quoted in Saslow 1989:97.

28   The same conflation between sodomy and heresy is explored by Saslow (1989:100):
"Perhaps the Church's ancient linkage of sodomy and heresy, though overdrawn,
intuited a more subtle reality: Some of those who are defined as deviant will, to retain
a measure of self-respect, become 'conceptual traitors' capable of deconstructing the
official symbols and values that deny their worth and wholeness."
      Trumbach (1989:130–31) has shown how a small circle of aristocratic Restoration
"libertines" lived out the connections between sexual licence, including prostitution
and sodomy, and a general skepticism toward authority: "It is as though sodomy
were so extreme a denial of the Christian expectation that all sexual acts ought to
occur in marriage and have the potential of procreation, that those who indulged in
it were likely also to break through all other conventions in politics and religion."

29   Jeremy Collier, *Short View of the Immorality and Profaneness of the English Stage* (1698);
"Collier's central argument is for the moral end of drama. . . . The first chapter at-
tacked 'immodest and obscene language'; the second, 'profanity and blasphemy'"
(Carlson 1984:123).

30   And maybe more than four hundred years. Specifically Christian inveighing against
theater begins with Tatian's denunciations of the Roman arena, ca. A.D. 160. Impersonation is an evil in itself and one of the worst is to portray sodomy. Tatian was
one of those fanatic early Christians, an "unbalanced spirit, exponent of a heretical
asceticism that viewed all sexual activity as impure and the eating of meat as a sin—

the first, then, in a long succession of Christian moralists to denounce the theater mainly because, like sexual activity and the eating of meat, it gave pleasure" (Barish 1981:44).

31 Senelick (1990:33) notes that with regard to sodomy, the popular stage has a "split personality": "It entertains by presenting normative material and reinforcing public opinion; at the same time, it is often regarded as a subversive fringe phenomenon, harboring behavior inadmissible within society itself." Therefore, the homo-erotic desires of theater people must be "disguised, neutralized, or manipulated so that they seem to endorse accepted norms. Since sodomy, by definition, implies the legal and religious injunctions that criminalize a recurrent and ubiquitous human practice, the Western stage, itself subject to similar injunctions, has had to proceed gingerly in exploiting it as dramatic material."

32 R. Baker's (1968:17) definition follows Eric Partridge in *The Dictionary of Slang and Unconventional English*. It derives from "the drag of the dress, as distinct from the non-dragginess of the trouser." Baker writes, "Partridge dates the reference back to at least 1850."

33 Quoted in Bray (1982:87).

34 See Senelick (1990:58–64) for an account of this affair; Bickerstaff, though never tried for sodomy, fled to France.

35 Quoted in Mordden 1981:66. Yet the old suspicions against the secular theater lingered. The diatribe of a protagonist in a nineteenth-century French novel, *Le désespère*, by Léon Bloy, makes all the connections I am pointing to here among impersonation, homosexuality, and antitheatricalism: "I regard the state of an actor as the shame of shames. . . . The vocation of the theater is, in my eyes, the basest misery in the abject world, and passive sodomy is, I believe, slightly less infamous. The male whore, even when venal, is obliged to confine his debauchery to cohabitation with a single other person, and can still—in the midst of his frightful ignominy—preserve a certain freedom of choice. The actor abandons himself, without choice, to the multitude, and his industry is not less ignoble because it is his body which serves as instrument of the pleasure given by his art" (quoted in Barish 1981:321–22).

36 Craig was the son of Ellen Terry, the actress to whom Wilde dedicated his first play, and architect and stage designer Edward Godwin (Ellman 1988:119).

37 In the peak season of 1927–1928, Broadway productions alone numbered 264 (Clurman 1983:314).

38 Leonard Spigelgass, quoted in Curtin 1987:57.

39 See ibid. Le Gallienne was acknowledged to be a lesbian by the *New York Times* at her death, aged ninety-two; see her obituary (June 5, 1991). Le Gallienne had already been "outed" in 1930 by the scandal sheets when "a socialite sued his actress wife, Josephine Hutchinson, because, in his words, she preferred to be with Le Gallienne 'morning, noon and night'" (quoted in Curtin 1987:53). The *Times* obituary referred to above tactfully omits the scandal. Le Gallienne was awarded the National Medal of the Arts by President Ronald Reagan in 1986. For Le Gallienne, see Schanke (1998); for Lunt and Fontanne, see Abel (1998); and for Cornell and McClintic, see Ferris (1998).

40 Bronski (1984:111) claims that the reality on Broadway was "far different" from the toleration supposed to exist in "common perception" because the ratio of gays in theater to the number of gay plays and plays with gay sensibility was very high. This is

certainly true, but the picture Grove narrators present foregrounds gay affinity with theater and the tremendous tolerance relative to other professions and businesses, where one had to hide everything, all the time.

41 Cole is not mentioned in the index to Cronyn's memoir, *A Terrible Liar* (1991), but he was always so accurate in theatrical matters that I could check that I have no reason to doubt him here.

42 Interview with Kathleen Mulqueen by Kaier Curtin (1987:252).

43 In Robin Maugham, *Somerset and All the Maughams* (New York: New American Library, 1966:201), quoted in Curtin (1987:21).

44 For a description of the scene and the critics' reaction to the play, see Curtin 1987: 25–41. The controversy over this play makes fascinating reading. Rabbi Silverman, though hostile to all "deviation," was perhaps especially upset by *God of Vengeance* because all the characters, including the lesbians, were Jewish. Sholom Asch, the play's author, reacted strongly to the hostility that American Jews such as Silverman directed toward it: "*God of Vengeance* is not a typically 'Jewish Play.' A 'Jewish Play' is a play where Jews are especially characterized for the benefit of the Gentiles. I am not such a 'Jewish' writer. . . . Jews do not need to clear themselves before anyone. They are as good and as bad as any race" (program for the Broadway production of *God of Vengeance*, p. 18, quoted in Curtin 1987:34). The pressure to create what are now called "positive role models" builds up for any minority artist when her or his group begins to represent itself.

45 William M. Hoffman, introduction to *Gay Plays: The First Collection* (New York: Avon Books, 1979), xvi, quoted in Curtin 1987:80. Although Curtin believes that the subject of gay men was more threatening to the establishment than was lesbianism, *The Well of Loneliness* was banned in England and nearly banned in the United States in 1928 and 1929. It may have been the element of gays speaking for themselves and from their viewpoint that was most threatening.

46 "The War on Unclean Plays," *New York Evening Post*, 18 February 1927, quoted in Curtin 1987:18.

47 "Captive Immoral, Mahoney Decides," *New York Times*, 9 March 1927, quoted in Curtin 1987:63.

48 "Banton Abandons Play Jury System," *New York Evening Post*, 1 February 1927, quoted in Curtin 1987:82.

49 Robert Littell, "The Play," *New York Evening Post*, 2 October 1928, quoted in Curtin 1987:135.

50 Curtin 1987:188. For a full discussion of these plays, see 170–90.

51 For an account of these women, see Newton 1993:203–20.

52 Cris did not want her last name to be printed in the Grove book. Fred Koester's companion and Libby Holman had the same manager, Bud Williams, who said, "You guys have to see Fire Island" and introduced them to realtor Bob Munnell, who rented them a house owned by Mary Hecht, the department store heiress.

53 There are, of course, more modern versions of dissociation. The most disingenuous is to claim that some gay or lesbian painting, photograph, novel, play, or film "isn't a lesbian movie," as I heard director Lisa Choderenko recently (1998) say of her wonderful lesbian movie, *High Art*, on National Public Radio. Choderenko continued that her movie is *really* about the art world. Fortunately lesbian film critic Ruby Rich followed up with the explanation that directors had a lot to lose by having their work

categorized as "lesbian," that is, mainstream (heterosexual) audiences who have the ticket-buying power to assure that the director can make another movie.

54   The "little theater" movement was actually inaugurated in Chicago by another Englishman and Craig disciple, Maurice Brown. "Little theater" at first meant not New York and not Broadway (Mordden 1981:58, 60–61).

55   See Freedley and Reeves (1968:59) and Durham (1987:377–79).

56   In his obituary of Thomas Farrar, Freedley (June 15, 1951) wrote, "Ever since I was an assistant to wonderful Kate Drain Lawson, technical director of the Theater Guild, when I first hit New York, I've known Tommy and admired him."

57   Crawford is a lot franker about being masculine than she is about being gay: at Smith College, "As a freshman I played in various one-acts. My low voice and the ability to ape men, learned from my brothers, always won me male roles" (1977:15). For more detail about Crawford's closeted life in the theater, see Plum (1998).

58   Calling Ruth Norman a "friend" (Crawford 1977:169) was common practice among gays at the time, but in the context of the book it is totally misleading.

59   She mentions touring Rome in 1949 with Natalia Murray, a Grove friend, as her guide (171).

60   For the progressive era in theater, see especially Clurman 1983:279, 289.

61   See Erenberg 1981, especially chapter 7; and about the birth of the revue form in cabarets, see 206–30.

62   Ibid.: 227 n. 2 for references on the origin of the revue.

63   Ibid.: 220, quoting from *Variety*.

64   For Drutman's summary of the revues, less scholarly but more vivid than Erenberg's—Drutman was an eyewitness—see 1976:61–67.

65   Quoted in Bradshaw 1985:49. For a description of *The Green Hat* and the critical reaction to it, see Curtin 1987:118–21.

66   The best of the intimate revues, in Irving Drutman's opinion, was *The First Little Show of 1929*, starring the young Fred Allen, Clifton Webb (who was gay), and torch singer Libby Holman, later a visitor to and booster of the Grove (Drutman 1976:64). Several early Grove revues were called *The First Little Show of . . .*

67   The only time such a realist play was performed by the Arts Project in the 1970s, it was purportedly a total flop.

68   Chauncey 1989:302, and see esp. 296–302.

69   See Duggan (1992), Smith-Rosenberg (1989), and "The Mythic Mannish Lesbian," this volume.

70   Savoy "was equally uninhibited off-stage: when the block-long Saks–Fifth Avenue was being erected, he rode past it in an open touring car shouting, 'I don't care, he can build it for me but I'll *never* live in it!'; he met his death when he was struck by lightning in Long Beach, just after sneering, 'Listen to Miss God carrying on!' which, perhaps in Divine Reproach, turned out to be the last words he was ever able to utter" (Drutman 1976:63).

71   Mae West in *Parade*, September 1927, quoted in Curtin 1987:84.

72   "Mae West Defies Police, Continues to Present Play," *New York World*, 3 October 1928, quoted in Curtin 1987:133.

73   The only other public manifestation was at the public drag balls at Halloween from the late 1920s into the 1940s; see Chauncey (1994) and Bérubé (1990:74).

74   See Bérubé 1990:67–97 for a thorough discussion of the soldier drag shows.

75 By the 1973–1974 season the total dropped to forty-eight (Clurman 1983:314).

76 Nor were gays as free in New York–based radio and television. Bob Adams could never tell his bosses at the radio station that he came to Cherry Grove in the fifties and sixties: "Nobody ever told his boss where they were going. Unless they were in the theater, I think it was easier there. Some of their bosses were probably out there at the time, I'm sure they were" (interview with author).

77 Sources for this revue are the program, interviews by me, and a number of photographs in my collection. To my great regret, the book (script and stage directions) to *Berthe* has not surfaced, but may be in a collection of George Freedley's papers at the New York Public Library that could not be accessed when I looked in the early 1990s. Freedley, or Ed Burke after Freedley's death, made sure that two copies of the program for *Berthe of a Nation* were preserved among Freedley's papers at the Lincoln Center Library for the Performing Arts (which he founded and directed). One copy was produced from somewhere by a sympathetic librarian. Had I not already found one in the Grove, this would have been a treasure indeed. Subsequently, I found another copy occupying pride of place in a scrapbook (Lincoln Center, MWEZ + n.c. 16754).

78 Two sources, both clippings: Freedley is quoted in the program for "Mr. T. C. Jones and Mask and Gown" (n.d.:34), and an article in "Mask and Gown" (n.d.:17, 47, 48), both in Lincoln Center Library of the Performing Arts MWEZ + n.c. 17480.

79 No one in recalling this revue mentioned the racist character of the film. Either white Grovers saw the movie as a campy gloss of American history and thus not deserving of serious criticism or else the racism was not seen as relevant to the project of announcing the birth of gay nationalism.

80 Maggie MacCorkle, interview with author.

81 Another photograph from *Berthe* shows the cast standing under red, white, and blue bunting from which depends an escutcheon of a cocktail glass above a bunch of cherries—presumably the emblems of the new nation.

82 The most important of these venues, argues Gordy (1998), was *Caffe Cino*. The quote is from Mordden 1981:257. See also Helbing (1981) and Brecht (1986).

Dick(less) Tracy and the Homecoming Queen: Lesbian Power
Representation in Gay Male Cherry Grove

This essay first appeared in *Inventing Lesbian Culture in America*, edited by Ellen Lewin. Copyright 1996 by Ellen Lewin, reprinted by permission of Beacon Press, Boston.

Holly Hughes, to whom this essay mysteriously led me, had an insider's knowledge of the performance scene and a clarity that deepened my understanding and gave me confidence in my interpretation.

A much shorter version of this essay was presented in the INQueery, INTheory, INDeed Conference at the University of Iowa in November 1994; at the Annual Meetings of the American Anthropological Association in Atlanta in December of the same year; and at the first annual Performance Studies Conference: The Future of the Field, at New York University in March 1995. Audience response at those meetings helped me to refine my arguments.

I am very much indebted to Jill Falzoi, who whetted my preexisting appetite for lesbian performance and theater, deluged me with many books and articles by performance theorists I had not known about, and commented on a draft of this essay. Lisa Duggan's astute and friendly reading helped me sort out the issues and do the last difficult revisions.

1   My work on female impersonators, who are known in the gay world as drag queens, was originally published in *Mother Camp: Female Impersonators in America* (1972/ 1979). In that book I defined "drag" as "the clothing of one sex when worn by the other sex (a suit and tie worn by a woman also constitute drag)" (3). Sarah Murray's (1994:345) definition is more developed: "a tradition of enacting the essential characteristics of the opposite gender through cross-dressing and use of other symbols and gestures strongly associated with that gender. I distinguish between cross-dressing as an individual practice, drag as a theatrical convention, and drag as a developed theatrical genre."

2   See Elizabeth Drorbaugh, 1993.

3   According to Drorbaugh (1993:133), Stormé's performance was "seldom if ever" mentioned in newspaper reviews, even though she was the emcee and the only male impersonator.

4   Murray emphasizes what she thinks are collective psychological differences between men and women that make drag more satisfying to men, and also the difficulties of sending up masculinity, lines of argument I do not engage here. What our approaches share is grounding in ethnography and a concern with how power shapes representation.

5   I follow Gayle Rubin (1992:467) in defining butch as "a category of lesbian gender that is constituted through the deployment and manipulation of masculine gender codes and symbols."

6   This point has been made by performance theorist Kate Davy 1992.

7   Kath Weston (1993a:6) cites an earlier example by Marilyn Frye in 1983 that conflates butch-femme with gay male drag in the term "queer role-playing," which she contrasts favorably to heterosexual gender performance, as the latter lacks the former's humor and theatricality. However, it was Case's piece along with Judith Butler's work that seem to have stimulated the current flutter in performance studies over butch-femme.

Murray and I aren't the first anthropologists to engage with the performance theorists' ideas about butch-femme. Although they refer only briefly to Case's essay, Davis and Kennedy (1992:63) specifically compare "the role of the butch with that of the queen" in order to "illuminate this puzzling *lack* of camp" (62; emphasis added) in the butch-femme system of the 1940s and 1950s. I am in substantial agreement with their conclusions, including that "No cultural aesthetic seems to have developed around male impersonation" (75).

Kath Weston's essay (1993a) is a more direct challenge to performance theory. Her formulation, with different data, was similar to mine: "How do recent attempts to retheorize gender in literary studies, theater/film criticism, and philosophy stack up against an ethnographic analysis that examines what lesbians of different backgrounds and political persuasions have been doing and saying while scholars debate gender's fate?" (1). Deb Amory (1996) also calls for ethnographic siting of gender "performance." For two attempts to take a broader view of the relationship between social theory and performance theory, see Lisa Duggan (1992) and Michael Warner (1993).

In a 1995 e-mail response to this essay that I quote with her permission, Sue-Ellen Case herself agreed that "Toward . . ." should have been more embodied: "There was a 'king' in San Francisco in North Beach from the early 1970s on. So 'history' is local. I don't think B[utch]-F[emme] [in San Francisco] is anything like what they describe in upstate New York, for example. So, I think S[an] F[rancisco] had a different sense of it, and you're right—'I should have said at Mauds' in the 1970s in S[an] F[rancisco] this is the way I saw it [but] I agree with much of what you said."

8   The logical opposition/attraction between (lesbian) butch and (gay male) queen has been enacted theatrically by Peggy Shaw and Bette Bourne, who played Stanley Kowalski and Blanche DuBois, respectively, in the 1991 Bloolips production of *Belle Reprieve;* see Alisa Solomon (1993a:153).

9   Even when the term "queer" is not used, I notice an increasing disinclination to distinguish gay male experience from lesbian experience. For instance, "Gay men and lesbians are the people of drama. . . . From the moment of that first entry into 'the community' or 'the life,' we're embedded in a legendary network of gossip, taletelling, and multiple interpretations of the same events. . . . Identity becomes an art form at times, a pastiche of meanings, affiliations, and self-parody that can be baroque" (L. Hall 1993:229). For a critique of the tendency toward genderless queers, see Biddy Martin (1994). For essays that both exhibit and "interrogate" the lesbian attraction toward queer, see the A. Stein collection (1993) and two other essays: Cathy Griggers (1993) and Lauren Berlant and Elizabeth Freeman (1993).

10   On this point Case and I agree. She specifically complains about "heterosexual feminist critics" who disappear historical butches and femmes into concepts of cross-dressing and "carnivalesque" (1993:299). Eve Kosofsky Sedgwick, one of the foremost partisans of the "queer" concept, makes the same observation: "One of the most striking aspects of the current popular and academic mania for language about cross-dressing is its virtual erasure of the connection between transvestism and— dare I utter it—homosexuality" (Sedgwick and Moon 1993:220).

11   It seems to me that in gay bar life in the 1950s and 1960s, "drag butch" was a term occasionally used for a masculine lesbian who was passing as a boy or man on the street (not necessarily the same as a "stone butch," who would not have her genitals touched by her partner), whereas a "drag queen" was a gay man who was either hustling on the street in female clothing or performing for an audience, wearing any permutation of feminine clothing. In Kennedy and Davis's (1993) history of the Buffalo lesbian community, there is no index heading for "butch drag" or "drag butch," despite detailed descriptions of butches' masculine dress (154–67).

12   Of course, Susan Sontag (1964) first appropriated camp for modernism by "disappearing" gay men, a move elaborated by Andrew Ross for postmodernism (1989: 135–70).

13   This dissatisfaction was not limited to the younger generation (or even to lesbians), as is often asserted. Indeed, the majority of the planners of and participants in the 1982 Barnard Conference on Sexuality (I was both), which first made opposition to antipornography feminism so visible, were heterosexual and verging on middle age. I well remember Ann Snitow's coming to one of the Barnard planning meet-

ings waving a manuscript copy of Gayle Rubin's essay "Thinking Sex" (1984) and exclaiming, "I'm holding revolutionary work in my hand; after this essay we'll never think about sex the same way!"

14   Very preliminary income data *not* based on advertising hype indicate the average lesbian makes $22,397 per year compared to the average gay man's $28,432, a difference that intuitively seems understated (*Beyond Biased Samples* 1994).

15   Lisa Duggan (1992:18) believes that "Any gay politics based on the primacy of sexual identity defined as unitary and 'essential,' reading clearly, intelligibly and unalterably in the body or psyche, and fixing desire in a gendered direction, ultimately represents the view from the subject position '20th-century Western white gay male.'"

16   Needless to say, the "she" to whom Skip Arnold alludes is a gay man (Newton 1979:110).

17   For more on this community, see my ethnohistory, *Cherry Grove, Fire Island: Sixty Years in America's First Gay and Lesbian Town* (1993). For the origins of the queen role, see Randolph Trumbach (1989). Gay men in the Grove, like gay men in general before Stonewall, called each other "she," and many had effeminate names.

Carole-Anne Tyler (1991) expresses amazement that people like Vito Russo and Jack Babuscio would actually appeal to the notion of gay sensibility to contextualize drag and camp. But if there is any such thing as a sensibility, a gay male one exists. Jill Falzoi, a graduate student in performance studies at New York University, also advised me, in some alarm, to drop this passé term "sensibility," but if so, how to describe coherent aesthetic perspectives associated with social groups? Why would some other word be better? To those who doubt the existence of a critter such as camp humor, I say get out from behind your e-mail and go meet some gay men, or at least go to the movies, to see, for example, *Unzipped*, the documentary film about gay fashion designer Izaac Mizrahi.

18   For more detail about prominent Grove fag hags, see Newton 1993:24, 81–82.

19   To avoid confusion, Grove names and pronouns that refer to gay cross-gender identities are italicized the first time they occur.

20   From the beginning of this episode Joan's narrative has been consistent in newspaper interviews and in informal Grove conversations. These quotes are from Sidebottom (1994:19).

21   In lighter moments Joan was willing to play with some subthemes about the meaning of her performance in ways that might please performance theorists. Once, when Joan was dressed as Queen Scarlet Ooh, I remarked that she had every qualification for the position except one, and I pointed to her crotch. "You never know," she cautioned, laughing, "you never know."

22   For example, in the fifties Natalia Murray had attended a theme party as "Europa" in a female body suit, riding a male "bull." Though this is a variant on the Grove trope of the drag queen being carried by bearers, no one referred to Natalia as a "drag queen" or "drag king."

23   The possibility that lesbian femmes might want to be or perhaps *were* some kind of drag queens was first suggested in print by Lisa Duggan (1988). In a spirited defense of feminism and femmeness, Biddy Martin (1994:112) seconds Duggan.

24   The only reference to lesbian sexuality I recall was late in the eighties, made by a drag queen named *High Camp*, who played a lesbian lip-synching a song by lesbian comic Lynn Lavner.

25   During the years that *Candy* Stevens was the Ice Palace Disco emcee, *she* brought in any number of black drag queens, some pathetic and some amazingly talented. One of the latter was Paris Dupree, the namesake of Jenny Livingston's acclaimed documentary film, *Paris Is Burning.* Paris ultimately declined to appear in Livingston's film and is seen only in silhouette in the breathtaking opening moments. See Phillip Brian Harper (1994); Harper's essay is a devastating critique, based on objections similar to mine, of the voluntarist approach to gender found in so much performance theory.

26   Performance artist Holly Hughes, encased in a giant lobster costume, had lip-synched "It's Not the Meat, It's the Motion" to a Maria Muldaur cover of the original Andrews Sisters song (perhaps the same recording used by the Jersey Girls) back in 1982 or 1983, proving once again that artists are ahead of the curve. This was part of Hughes's first production, titled *Shrimp in a Basket,* at the wow Café in New York City (personal communication). As to the crowd's spontaneous enthusiasm for the butchest Jersey Girl, Amber Hollibaugh has long maintained in conversations that, culturally speaking, the butch is the central object of lesbian eroticism. This interesting subject is beyond the scope of my essay, but see Alisa Solomon's (1993b:42) excellent essay on butchness, especially her description of butches Leslie Feinberg and Peggy Shaw dancing together in an Off-Broadway performance.

27   Whether this is cause and effect, as some suspected, is open to question. More likely, there were many factors involved in the shift.

28   See Newton (1993, chap. 6) for a fuller discussion of ethnic, racial, and class discrimination among Grovers. In the late eighties and early nineties many white male Grovers were upset, primarily about lesbians coming to the Grove to buy, rent, and day-trip, but also about groups of African American day-trippers. Prior to this time, African Americans had come mostly as individual workers or partners of whites.

29   Weston (1993a:16), in an all-lesbian context, also raised this question: "What about the power relations embedded in my own presence as a lesbian ethnographer who found herself simultaneously 'natived' and 'othered,' desiring and desired, observing and observed? How to depict my participation?" Also see my discussion of the problems of being a lesbian fieldworker in the Grove in "My Best Informant's Dress: The Erotic Equation in Fieldwork," in this volume.

30   Lorraine's butch appearance raised what I considered to be interesting questions about Joan's willingness to portray a drag queen, but Grovers did not comment on it in my hearing. There was, however, gossip about the fact that Joan and Lorraine formed the second apparently butch-butch relationship among prominent Grove lesbians in recent years.

31   *Peter* Worth, nearing eighty, was approached by one of Joan's lesbian supporters to bless Joan as Homecoming Queen at the tea, presumably to symbolize continuity between the lesbian generations. Peter declined, explaining it was too drafty at Cherry's and she's not a "public person." I reminded her that Kay, the grandest of all Grove "lady" lesbians, "would have loved to do it!" Peter agreed. "Kay was the one person who *could* have done it, but she's no longer with us."

32   "A First for Cherry Grove" 1994:3 ran in the *New York Times;* Wasserman 1994b ran in *Newsday.* Wasserman did a follow-up article after the Invasion: "Cherry Grove Queen Proves She's No Drag" (1994a).

33   Panzi said the number of cross-dressers going over on the ferry had peaked at about

170 eight or nine years previously, then decreased for several years, and increased
to about 175 in 1994.

34 Davy (1993) goes on to write that lesbians, like women in general, are still defined
by what they are not; that is, they cannot be "phallic signifiers." It is just this construction that Holly Hughes, and the Jersey Girls, were contesting by performing,
as lesbians, "It's Not the Meat, It's the Motion" (lyrics that were perhaps originally
intended as sex advice for men). Despite Davy's attacks on the work of Hughes and
of the Five Lesbian Brothers (especially their play *Voyage to Lesbos*) as essentially too
male-identified, in my view their work does just what Davy advocates: "The challenge for lesbian and feminist theater, it seems to me, is to devise strategies for
not only foregrounding the ways in which female sexuality is denied access to the
phallus, as signifier of desire, but for seizing the phallus, as it were, and forcing it
to function representationally in the service of an autonomous female sexuality"
(1994:153). See also Carr 1993a. In any case, it seems to me that Davy, the performance artists, and I are all contesting Audrey Lorde's famous dictum "The master's
tools will never dismantle the master's house."

As I wrote this section, I was watching the televised celebration for Martina Navra-
tilova's retirement at the Virginia Slims Tournament (November 15, 1994). Martina,
more than any other public lesbian, attained the status of mainstream phallic signifier when she became the first woman in history to have her banner raised to
the roof of Madison Square Garden. On this occasion she was also given a black
silver-studded motorcycle while the song "Born to Be Wild" blasted over the p.a.
system.

35 Besides works already cited, see Hart (1993:119–37) and H. Harris (1993:257–76).
For an article by a self-described femme that critiques the "emphasis on the visible"
in lesbian culture, see Lisa M. Walker (1993).

36 Some lesbians were so acutely aware of male fears of exclusion that one woman suggested that Joan should have been escorted to the tea at Cherry's by a gay male escort
dressed as a man rather than by her partner dressed in a tux.

37 The concept of "gay gender" in regard to butch-femme was first suggested to me
by Amber Hollibaugh in the early eighties. "Nellie"—an adjective, not a noun—is
the gay male concept that corresponds to lesbian femme. It has become somewhat
disused.

38 Kate Davy thinks male impersonation can never serve lesbians the way female impersonation has served gay men, for Lacanian and also historical reasons. But she
still thinks that "the tools that camp provides—artifice, wit, irony, exaggeration—
are available to butch-femme gender play separate from the ways in which they are
inscribed by camp as a historically marked phenomenon" (1992:243). Although I
agree that lesbians can (and do) use camp, I disagree on three fundamental points:
first, that lesbians cannot use drag; second, that camp or drag as practiced by gay
men is *intrinsically* either misogynist or some kind of sellout; and third, that lesbians could use drag or camp in a separatist historical vacuum. These points have
been addressed with a different emphasis and in a somewhat different context by
José Esteban Muñoz (1995) in an appreciation of the Cuban American lesbian performer Carmelita Tropicana, whom he sees as successfully practicing both drag and
camp to create a persona who is a queer "hybrid diasporic subject."

39 It is ironic, as Kath Weston (1993a:8) has pointed out, that "femme- and butch-*iden-*

tified lesbians" have been marginalized just as performance theory has reclaimed butch-femme *performances* as subversive. Alisa Solomon (1993b:45) makes a related point: "Because it subverts male privilege, butchness can be the most dangerous queer image—and that's exactly why it is increasingly invisible even as gays and lesbians find ourselves in the news for good or ill. And that's why when it does appear, it's tamed, even commodified."

40   Judith Butler (1993a:22) has more recently tried to counter the postmodern tendency to think of gender as something like a clothing style: "Gender performativity is not a matter of choosing which gender one will be today. Performativity is a matter of reiterating or repeating the norms by which one is constituted: it is not a radical fabrication of a gendered self." Although I believe genders *are* psychosocially created, that does not mean they are fluid or easily changeable, on either the macro (social) or micro (subjective) levels.

41   Quoted in Kakutani 1994.

42   For Carmelita Tropicana, see Muñoz 1995, and Dolan 1985:26–32.

43   In her 1994 piece, Davy softens her repudiation of gay male camp, but still worries about "the shift away from gender and feminism, [and] the simultaneous move toward the sensibilities of gay male sexuality. In the same breath that feminism was disavowed [at the 1991 Rutgers Queer Studies Conference], gay male practices, aesthetics, and representational strategies were hailed as sites not only of new alliances, but of new ways of imagining and imaging lesbian sexuality" (143).

44   Davy (1992:234) quotes Peggy Shaw as saying, "When lesbians make it to Off-Broadway, it's the boys who are doing it," referring to Charles Busch's long-running show *Lesbian Vampires of Sodom*. For an overview of the development of lesbian and feminist theater, see Sisley (1981). For descriptions of the wow Café, besides her other articles, see Davy (1985); Chansky (1990); Solomon (1993a, 1985); and Carr 1993b.

According to Holly Hughes (personal communication), several wow performers have now received Obies and respectful reviews in the *New York Times* and have performed in Off-Broadway venues. However, only Lisa Kron's 1994 solo monologue, *101 Humiliating Stories*, has broken through to receive a Drama Desk nomination and three reviews in the *Times*. None of the lesbian work, Hughes told me, has "anywhere near" the recognition that gay male theater work now routinely gets.

45   In a later phone conversation, Murray and I agreed that the recent flourishing of lesbian drag and camp is based more than anything on increasing confidence and power. Shane Phelan (1993:779) makes a very similar point: "Lesbians have been denied the right to be heard not just by forced silence but also by having 'lesbian' voices and words deprived of authority. So the first need for our politics is the guarantee that these will be heard."

High School Crack-up

This essay was originally published in 1973 in Phillis Birkby et al., eds, *Amazon Expedition: A Lesbianfeminist Anthology* (Times Change Press, Washington, NJ). I have shortened it, especially the first section on women and insanity, which seems embarrassingly simplistic now—though there is still power in the central insight.

1   As I recall, we budding feminists would read the same group of books at the same time—often as soon as they came out, as this sentence implies.

2   Although Palo Alto was already the home of Hewlett-Packard in the 1950s, "Silicon Valley" was still in the future. Palo Alto was then a plushy, sleepy suburb, the most excitement provided by Stanford University football games and the local drive-in restaurant.

3   That the "John" referred to here was the son of prominent California attorney Melvin Belli, and that another major crush was the son of David Packard (the cofounder of Hewlett-Packard) gives an impression of the social class we are talking about. Neither of these boys was in the popular caste, however; boys' popularity did not exactly replicate the social class of the parents.

Marginal Woman/Marginal Academic

This essay was originally written as a keynote speech delivered at Women's Week Conference, March 21, 1973, at the State University College at Oneonta, New York. As noted in the essay "Too Queer for College," this piece was rejected for inclusion in a collection on women and work as "too bitter." I have revised the essay, but only to make it read more smoothly.

1   My committee consisted of David M. Schneider, who was the department chair, Clifford Geertz, and Julian Pitt-Rivers. Schneider became my lifelong friend, as the essay "DMS" shows. The essay "My Best Informant's Dress" was in some ways a dialogue with Geertz. Pitt-Rivers, who was personally very helpful to me at Chicago, moved back to Europe and I saw him again only once. These men influenced my thinking about anthropological issues profoundly.

2   Women's International Terrorist Conspiracy from Hell (WITCH). There were several different groups of this name; the one I joined was called Upper West Side WITCH.

3   I have never understood why I came up for tenure three years ahead of time. It was explained to me by then department chair Sydel Silverman as some quirk of the union contract.

4   The departmental tenure committee had actually recommended my tenure, three to two, but it was axiomatic that candidates with split committees were fired by the administration.

5   The group included a number of women who went on to become successful anthropologists, for example Sherry Ortner, now at Columbia University, Judith Friedlander, now a dean at the New School for Social Research and Bambi Schiefflen, at NYU. As a closeted lesbian, I was actually quite uncomfortable in the Ruth Benedict Collective, but was afraid to mention that in this essay, at the time.

6   This house and land were owned, as far as I know, by the writer Jill Johnston, who was the de facto leader of the group that produced the collection of essays *Amazon Expedition,* which consisted of me and my then lover, the painter Louise Fishman (the only one who did not work on editing the book), Jill's then lover Jane O'Wyatt, the late architect Phyllis Birkby and her then lover novelist Bertha Harris. When the group fell apart in the early 1970s, shortly after this piece was written, I never visited the house again. Some of these alternative feminist schools such as the Feminist Art Institute, where my current partner Holly Hughes studied for a while when she first came to New York, and Sagaris, the women's writing school, were quite influential for brief periods of time, but all eventually fizzled out for lack of money and institutional stability.

The Personal Is Political: Consciousness Raising and Personal Change in the Women's Liberation Movement

This paper was originally presented to the symposium "Anthropologists Look at the Study of Women" chaired by Brooke Grundfest Schoepf, at the Annual Meetings of the American Anthropological Association, November 19, 1971.

1   For descriptions of informants and groups, see the appendix. We have not reproduced the questionnaire, as so many questions are described in the body of the essay.

2   Quotes from different informants are separated by asterisks.

3   Because our data were limited in crossing class lines (we have virtually no working-class women) or racial boundaries (only one group contained a black woman, who was middle class and professional), we cannot make statements about the general c-r group as anything but an effective institution for middle-class, relatively well-educated white women. Nor can it be said that the general c-r group can function for severely neurotic or psychotic women, as women with these problems were dropped out of every group relatively early in the group's history.

4   In this section we used Gerlach and Hine's terminology (1970:110) to describe the commitment process.

5   Clifford Geertz (1963:16–17) integrates both the social and individual preconditions for the growth of ideology in his discussion of the "strain" theory.

6   From the perspective of 1998, it seems obvious that the tremendous successes of both the c-r movement and 12-step movements modeled on Alcoholics Anonymous sprang from common features of American culture, for example, the dislike of hierarchy and the power of personal testimony.

7   Such core and buffer zones are a common structural characteristic of movements of social transformation, according to Gerlach and Hine (1970:157).

Excerpt from Womenfriends

In 1976, having failed in several attempts to get a publisher, Shirley Walton and I self-published (as Friends Press, New York) a book called *Womenfriends,* a dual journal in the form of letters to each other. When we began the project, in the fall of 1970, I was closeted at work and Shirley wanted to protect her family, so I used the pseudonym "Pauline Basket" (although my memory for Gertrude Stein trivia is not what it was, I believe that Pauline was one of her cars, and both of her white standard poodles were definitely named Basket). Shirley used the pseudonym "Rebecca Snow." Other people we wrote about also got pseudonyms.

Shirley and I had been close friends since being randomly assigned as roommates during our freshman year at the University of Michigan. *Womenfriends* is the chronicle of our struggles with each other, a gay woman and a straight woman, in the crucible of feminist transformation and the gay liberation movement, from 1971 through 1972 in New York City. When this excerpt begins, both Shirley and I belonged to the Ruth Benedict Collective, a consciousness-raising group made up largely of young women anthropologists, although Shirley was and is a journalist. I was living with "Laura," and Shirley had married "Sid" a few years previously. Shirley had just announced that she was pregnant with her first child. My (Pauline's) journal entries are in roman type; Shirley's (Rebecca's) are in italics.

1   The original reference was to this piece as it appeared in *The Village Voice* in 1971. The piece has since been reprinted (Johnston 1998:24–31), and although I cannot find the exact quote, the sentiment is still there.

Will the Real Lesbian Community Please Stand Up?

Originally titled "Sex and Sensibility: Notes on Politics and Ethnography," the first draft of this essay was read at the Annual Meetings of the American Anthropological Association, 1982. A second draft was read at the Sex and the State Conference, Toronto, Canada, 1985. For this version, the earlier drafts were lightly edited rather than revised, and an afterword added in 1998. Strangely enough, Arlene Stein's 1997 book on similar issues has the same title as my original one, though neither of us was aware of it.

1   For example, *Sage; Asian Lesbians of the East Coast; Between Ourselves: Women of Color Newspaper;* work in the magazine *Conditions;* Moraga and Anzuldúa 1981; Cornwell 1983; Hull, Scott, and Smith 1982; and B. Smith 1983.

2   In fact these, along with polemics by such authors as Andrea Dworkin and Susan Griffin, are the major forms of lesbian-feminist writing, as Bonnie Zimmerman (1984) has pointed out. Her essay, looking at the writings produced from within lesbian-feminism rather than at descriptions of it, deals with many of the same issues of identity and diversity that I raise here.

3   "There are lesbians, and there are gay women," my lover was told by a "political lesbian" just the other day. "Lesbians love and respect women. Gay women just sleep with them."

4   Tanner 1978; Ettore 1980; Moses 1978; Brooks 1981; Cotton 1975; Blumstein and Schwartz 1983; Nyberg 1976; Jay and Young 1979.

5   Education is a better indicator of class among women than is income because the income spread is so small compared to men. Occupation is better, but still confusing. A more thorough study of the quantitative work should be done but would, I am convinced, only confirm the bias.

6   It is better to write "a lesbian community" as Barnhart does, but not sufficient because it is precisely the "lesbian-feminism" that distinguishes it from other lesbian groups. As to "a women's community" (Kreiger), that is what the natives call themselves, but its relationship to other women and other self-identified lesbians should be specified. Obviously I am siding with Sandoval's (1984) trenchant criticism of Krieger's review of the literature.

7   Because all these studies are primarily urban, their low proportion of minority informants is even more misleading of the total universe.

8   Jay and Young 1979; Bell and Weinberg 1978; Harry and DeVall 1978; Weinberg and Williams 1974; and Blumstein and Schwartz 1983 are the major samples. Weinberg and Williams's sample is international. Harry and DeVall (26–27, 155–64) remark on the high proportion of college-educated men and low proportion of blue-collar workers in their and others' samples. Dismissing the probability of sampling bias, they speculate that gay men hedge against discrimination by becoming well educated and avoid "macho" blue-collar jobs because masculine values are repugnant. My objections to this are that no clear distinction is being made between homosexual identity and behavior (fewer working-class homosexual behavers may iden-

tify as gay but still might participate in the community: as hustlers, tearoom participants, etc.), that many gay men are not repulsed by traditional masculinity as lingering sexism and fashion trends among gay men have shown, and that Harry and DeVall's argument fails to explain the similar bias in lesbian samples. Given the parallel white overrepresentation, class sampling bias must still be considered the primary problem. Only when this is explored will we know if the existing samples' college and service occupation bias has significance in light of Weeks's (1977), D'Emilio's (1983a), and others' thinking that capitalist development is the driving force in the creation of gay (and other sexual communities), and that gays and modernism are linked.

9   Examples of notable ethnographic work are on middle-class gays (Warren 1974), bar patrons (Read 1980), tearoom participants (Humphreys 1975), drag queens (Newton 1979), the leather subculture (Weinberg and Kamel 1983, several essays in Levine 1979). For discussion of the concept of gay community, see Harry and DeVall (1978:151–54), Levine (1979), Humphreys (1979), Stephen Murray (1979), and Altman (1979:155–58).

10 "Sex is the gay man's speciality, the game in the Olympics that's reserved for him," says gay writer Richard Goldstein (1985).

11 The gay male organization Black and White Men Together includes, I am told, a number of interracial couples and deals explicitly with the political and social implications of interracial eroticism. The lesbian counterpart, Dykes Against Racism Everywhere, is basically a white "support group."

12 The *New York Times* (4 November 1984:79) recently ran a story about a gay college dean, active in conservative Orange County politics, whose "life mate" of ten years is a hairdresser.

13 Rumaker (1982) poetically expresses his sense of self as an entity stripped of social structure in the liminal atmosphere of the baths (see quote heading this paper). Bell and Weinberg (1978:239–40) also remark on the absence of everyday social stratification markers and relations at the baths. The baths fit Turner's (1974:243) formulation of "cultural—and hence institutionalized—expressions of communitas . . . as a potentially dangerous but nevertheless vitalizing moment, domain, or enclave." Rumaker's bath odyssey is close to Turner's concept of "a situation which is temporally liminal and spatially marginal [in which] the neophytes or 'passengers' in a protracted *rite de passage* are stripped of status and authority. . . . Much of what has been bound by social structure is liberated, notably the sense of comradeship and communion, in brief, of communitas" (258–59). See also Delph (1978:27–28): "When he enters a setting for sex, the homosexual leaves behind the social self of everyday society and its indices of prestige, status, and moral values. . . . The simple shutting of a toilet door, a ride on a ferryboat between 'straightsville' and Fire Island, or crossing the street from or to a notorious park serve as 'rites of passage' that transform one moral reality into another."

14 Lesbians (at least the white, middle-class women who have been studied) may have a lower frequency of any sexual activity than either gay men or heterosexuals (see Blumstein and Schwartz 1983), but it's not clear how this relates to their fewer number of partners.

15 Wayne Cotton (1975) found that although both gay men and women in his sample chose friends of like status (in terms of age, ethnicity, religion, race, class), gay men

tended to choose lovers of unlike status (86 percent of the time!), whereas lesbians chose *both* friends and lovers with like status. Only 36 percent of lesbian relationships involved *any* status difference, mostly age (147). Bell and Weinberg (1978) found the same pattern.

16 Not without some public protest, for example, the following statement by Zulema, a black women's collective in San Francisco: "Many white women have the mistaken notion that there is only one women's community and that its needs and goals are a reflection of white society" (quoted in Gibbs and Bennett 1980:4). Or, "The social definition of Lesbian separatism has gotten pickier and pickier. I remember a time when a woman was considered a separatist if she made it a point not to socialize with men. Then that alone wasn't good enough, she couldn't associate with straight women either, and finally, many separatists weren't even friendly with other *Lesbians* who hobnobbed too much with straight women or with men. . . . The barrier these women had so systematically constructed served as often as not to sever women from other women and even divided Lesbians up into castes, each more-separatist-than-thou (and therefore holier). With each successive purer caste came the hidden question in dollars and cents: how many people could you *afford* to 'do without' simply because of who their friends were?" (McCandless 1980:111).

17 For more on this, see "The Misunderstanding," in this volume.

18 In an incident reported by Blumstein and Schwartz (1983:482–83), one woman's lesbian-feminist collective nearly beat her up to prevent her forming a relationship with a working-class butch. Krieger (1983) writes about similar social pressure.

19 This idea was suggested to me by Dorothy Allison.

20 See n. 2 above. A lot of this work of complicating the picture of a lesbian community has been self-representation coming from *outside* academia, which is where a lot of the early white ethnography and history came from too—that is, the Lesbian Herstory Archive, the San Francisco Oral History Project, and such independent scholars as Allan Bérubé and Jonathan Katz. Already in 1979 the black feminists of the Combahee River Collective stated: "We reject the stance of lesbian separatism because it is not a viable political analysis or strategy for us" (1998:523). But the difficulties disadvantaged lesbians had in representing themselves are illustrated in the self-publication in 1987 of *Compañeras: Latina Lesbians* (Ramos 1994). According to Romo-Carmona (1997:37), Juanita Ramos began work on *Compañeras* in 1980, but most people who wanted to participate "didn't feel they could write. And these were precisely the women she wanted to have in this book." Ramos resorted to the same interviewing techniques that have been used successfully in anthropology.

21 Arlene Stein (1998) gives an excellent overview of the "decentering" of lesbian feminism, which, however, has not occurred without some justified handwringing; on feminist objections to "queer," see Biddy Martin 1994 and Susanna Danuta Walters 1994.

22 The upward skewing of samples apparent in the earlier social science surveys was purposely replicated in the late 1980s and 1990s by magazines such as the *Advocate* and picked up by gay marketers to appeal to advertisers. For a scientific and political critique of this process, see Badgett (1997), who, along with Stephen Murray (1996), reference the far more representative samples that are possible now. For essays about how queerness and class intersect, see Raffo (1996). For a more analytical approach, see essays in Duberman (1997:465–546).

23   When Ellen DeGeneres came out on TV and in real life in 1997, I was briefly teaching
      in Michigan. Most of my white Middlewestern lesbian and gay students at Kalama-
      zoo College were exultant over Ellen. Here was someone like them, a "mainstream,"
      nonbutch, nonthreatening figure they could relate to. The real Ellen, however, seems
      to have burst the lipstick case to become more militant and political as a result of
      her mistreatment by the executives at ABC.

24   One caveat: the pace of change has been uneven. During the six-month stint alluded
      to above in Kalamazoo, Michigan last year (1997), my partner and I discovered that
      two lesbian-feminist separatist faculty members and their allies had convinced most
      lesbian students that pornography was the root cause of "patriarchy" and that no
      joint political actions should be undertaken with gay men.

25   Having served for the past five years on the Commission on the Status of Lesbian,
      Gay, Bisexual and Transgender issues in Anthropology of the American Anthropo-
      logical Association, I have explored the barriers to queers in the discipline in depress-
      ing detail. The report of the Commission will be published by the American Anthro-
      pological Association in spring 1999. See also Roscoe 1996 and Weston 1997. For
      sociology, see Plummer 1998.

      The most important research studies are *Families We Choose*, about lesbian and
      gay networks in the Bay Area (Weston 1991); *Boots of Leather, Slippers of Gold*, about
      the Buffalo working-class lesbian community (Kennedy and Davis 1993), which in-
      cludes an extensive discussion of the historical relationship between working-class
      lesbians and lesbian-feminism; *Lesbian Mothers* (Lewin 1993); *Cherry Grove, Fire
      Island*, about gays and lesbians in that summer resort (Newton 1993); *Recognizing
      Ourselves*, about gay and lesbian commitment ceremonies (Lewin 1998); and essays
      in Beemyn (1997) and Lewin and Leap (1996). From England there is *Urban Ama-
      zons* (S. Green 1997), an ethnohistory of a lesbian-feminist community in London.

26   For recent summaries, see Stephen Murray 1996 and Plummer 1998.

27   See Newton 1993, esp. chaps. 8 and 9.

28   I have elaborated these ideas in my book on Cherry Grove (Newton 1993:110, 180–
      201). Clearly, what Turner meant by *communitas* is a core element of what Benedict
      Anderson (1983) termed the "imagined communities" of nation-states and, I would
      add, nationalistic groups, whether ethnic or gay.

29   Stephen Murray 1996:169 n. 8. Though a lesser majority of gay male couples also
      appear to be socially homogeneous, the effect is counteracted by casual sexual and
      social contacts, as stated earlier. Even in choosing a partner, white gay men were less
      likely to pick someone of the same social position: 55 percent compared to 68 per-
      cent for lesbians (Bell and Weinberg 1978:314).

The Misunderstanding: Toward a More Precise Sexual Vocabulary

This essay was originally printed in Carole Vance, ed., 1984. *Pleasure and Danger:
Exploring Female Sexuality* (Boston: Routledge Kegan Paul).

The Mythic Mannish Lesbian: Radclyffe Hall and the New Woman

This essay first appeared in *Signs* vol. 9, no. 4 (1984). That in turn emerged from
a very different earlier paper entitled "The Mythic Lesbian and the New Woman:

Power, Sexuality and Legitimacy," written with Carroll Smith-Rosenberg and presented by us at the Berkshire Conference on the History of Women, Vassar College, June 16, 1981. A revised version of that paper has appeared in French under the title "Le Mythe de la lesbienne et la femme nouvelle" in *Strategies des femmes* (Paris: Editions Tierce, 1984). Smith-Rosenberg's further use of this material appeared as "The New Woman as Androgyne: Social Disorder and Gender Crisis, 1870–1936, in *Disorderly Conduct: Visions of Gender in Victorian America* (New York: Knopf, 1985). Ultimately, revisions of both of our essays appeared in Martin Duberman et al., eds., *Hidden from History* (New York: New American Library, 1989); that is the version reprinted here.

Developing the Radclyffe Hall material independently, I drew conclusions that do not represent Smith-Rosenberg's thinking and for which she is not responsible. I am in her debt for all I learned from her as a historian and as a friend for the two years that we worked jointly. I am also indebted to the members of the Purchase women's studies seminar, particularly Mary Edwards, Suzanne Kessler, and Louise Yellin, who read drafts and made helpful suggestions, as did David M. Schneider, Carole Vance, Wendy McKenna, and especially Amber Hollibaugh. I thank the Lesbian Herstory Archives in New York, where I did early research, and Jan Boney for technical help. And for another kind of insight and support, without which this paper might never have been written, I thank the women of the в. group.

1   Two key texts are Radicalesbians 1973 and Rich 1983. The best analysis of how these ideas have evolved and of their negative consequences for the feminist movement is Echols 1983.

2   On passing women, see San Francisco Lesbian and Gay History Project 1989 and Katz 1976:209–80.

3   Since I wrote this essay, a useful biography of Radclyffe Hall has appeared (M. Baker 1985), along with a biography of Hall's lover (Ormrod 1985). Although these works contain fascinating material I had not seen before (in 1984), they did not impel me to modify the ideas expressed here (1989). See my review, ". . . Sick to Death of Ambiguities" (1986).

4   "Most of us lesbians in the 1950's grew up knowing nothing about lesbianism except Stephen Gordon's swagger," admits Blanche Wiesen Cook, herself a critic of Hall (1979:719–20). Despite Stephen Gordon's aristocratic trappings, her appeal transcended geographic and class barriers. We know that *The Well* was read early on by American lesbians of all classes (personal communication with Liz Kennedy from the Buffalo Oral History Project [1982]; and see Bullough and Bullough 1977:895–904, esp. 897). *The Well* has been translated into numerous languages. According to Una Troubridge (1961), in the 1960s it was still steadily selling over a hundred thousand copies a year in America alone; Troubridge was still receiving letters of appreciation addressed to Hall almost twenty years after Hall's death. Even today, it sells as much as or more than any other lesbian novel, in straight and women's bookstores (personal communication with Amber Hollibaugh [1983], who has worked at Modern Times Bookstore, San Francisco, Djuna Books, and Womanbooks, New York City).

5   Hall deserves censure for her possible fascist sympathies, but this is not the focus of feminist attacks on her. In any case, such sympathies developed after she wrote *The Well;* see Troubridge 1961:118–24.

6   For the anti-*Well* approach, see Cook (1979); Faderman and Williams (1977:31–41); Stimpson (1982); Faderman (1981:322–23); Gornick (1981). Only Inez Martinez (1983), whose approach is quite different from mine, defends Hall.

7   Many lesbians' connection to the mannish lesbian was and is painful. The relation of any stigmatized group to the figure that functions as its symbol and stereotype is necessarily ambiguous. Even before lesbian-feminism, many lesbians hastened to assure themselves and others that they were not "like that." Lesbians who could pass for straight (because they were married or appeared feminine) often shunned their butch sisters. I have dealt with these concepts at length in *Mother Camp* (1979).

8   See esp. Faderman 1981. The pro-romantic friendship, anti–Radclyffe Hall line of thought has recently led to its logical absurdity in the encyclopedic *Women of the Left Bank*. Shari Benstock (1986), arguing, correctly, that Natalie Barney's vision of lesbianism was different from Hall's, concludes that Barney and Vivien were almost different species from Hall and a long list of other women who formed a "later generation, one that had been liberated to dress, talk, smoke, and act like men" (307). Unfortunately for this hypothesis, Barney and Vivien were only four and two years older than Hall; Una Troubridge, supposedly one of the mannish ones, hardly ever dressed or acted like a man, despite Romaine Brooks's famous portrait. Benstock continues, "Barney was democratic enough to encourage the participation of both types of women [in her salon], just as she invited men" (307). As Barney had affairs with many of the mannish women Benstock mentions, I wonder how "democratic" her motives were.

9   See Smith-Rosenberg 1975 and Faderman 1981. On the contradictions within the romantic friendship system, see Vicinus 1982a.

10 Chauncey 1982–1983:114–45, esp. 117. Chauncey argues that even if some doctors began to assert a female sexual subjectivity in the last third of the nineteenth century, this remained a minority opinion until the twentieth (see 118 n. 6). He has reached the same conclusion I have regarding the "necessary" masculinity of the early lesbian persona.

11 For a related approach, see Carolyn Burke (1982). Gertrude Stein shared the second generation's frustrations with "daughters spending a lifetime in freeing themselves from family fixations" (223).

12 Among the many examples: the heterosexual misery of Jean Rhys's heroines; Emma Goldman's love problems as documented in Alice Wexler's (1984) recent biography; the suffering documented by Trimberger (1983) among Greenwich Village sex radical women.

13 See Robinson 1976:2, 3, and chap. 1.

14 See Simmons 1979.

15 Sandra Gilbert (1982) has developed this idea in the context of modernist literature.

16 Chauncey (1982–1983) argues that medical opinion began to shift in the 1930s from an exclusive focus on "inversion" as gender reversal to "homosexuality" as deviant sexual orientation. The change has had only limited effect on popular ideology.

17 I am most indebted here to Carroll Smith-Rosenberg, who developed the prototype of this section on the sexologists. See "The New Woman as Androgyne" (1985b).

18 See Robinson (1976) for a balanced appraisal of Ellis's radicalism in sexual issues versus his misogyny.

19 Freud's analysis was by far the most sophisticated. He rejected the trapped-soul

paradigm and distinguished between "choice of object" and "sexual characteristics and sexual attitude toward the subject." However, his insights were distorted by his antifeminism and his acceptance of a biological base for gender. See esp. Freud 1963:133–59.

20   My use of Freud's concepts indicates my conviction that they do begin to explain sexual desire, at least as it operates in our culture. Hall rejected or ignored Freud, presumably because of the implication, which so many drew from his work, that homosexuality could be "cured" (see Faderman and Williams 1977:41 n.11).

21   Ruth-Jean Eisenbud (1982:85–109, esp. 99) asserts that "primary lesbian choice" occurs at about age three, resulting from the little girl's "precocious eroticism" directed toward a mother who is excluding her. Martinez (1983), whose theme is the mother-daughter relationship in Hall's two novels, ignores the concept of mother-daughter eroticism, rejecting any relevance of the psychoanalytic model.

22   See especially the vivid passage in R. Hall 1981:75.

23   The sexologists' discourse, itself hostile to women, "also made possible the formation of a 'reverse' discourse: homosexuality began to speak in its own behalf, to demand that its legitimacy or 'naturality' be acknowledged, often in the same vocabulary, using the same categories by which it was medically disqualified" (Foucault 1980:102).

24   Superficially, cultural feminism reunites lesbians and straight women under the banner of "female values." As Echols (1983:41) points out, hostility still surfaces, "as it did at the 1979 Women Against Pornography conference where a lesbian separatist called Susan Brownmiller a 'cocksucker.' Brownmiller retaliated by pointing out that her critic 'even dresses like a man.'"

25   Sexologists often use the concept of "gender dysphoria syndrome" synonymously with "transsexualism" to describe the "pathology" of people who apply for gender reassignment surgery. Of course, the effort to describe and treat transsexualism medically has been awkward because gender is a cultural construct, not a biological entity. My broader use of "gender dysphoria" is in agreement with some sexologists who limit the designation "transsexual" to people who actually have had surgery to alter their bodies. Gender dysphoria, then, refers to a variety of difficulties in establishing conventional (the doctors say "adequate" or "normal") gender identification; intense pain and conflict over masculinity and femininity is not limited to people who request reassignment surgery (see Meyer and Hoopes 1974:447). Female-to-male transsexuals appear to share many similarities with lesbian butches. The most impressive difference is the rejection or acceptance of homosexual identity. Compare *The Well* to the lives described in Pauly (1969). Gender dysphoria could very fruitfully be compared with anorexia nervosa, a more socially acceptable and increasingly common female body-image problem. As feminists, we need a much more sophisticated vocabulary to talk about gender. Sexologists are often appallingly conservative, but they also deal with and try to explain important data. See, e.g., Money and Ehrhardt 1972. For a radical scholarly approach, see Kessler and McKenna 1985. One of the best recent pieces on gender reversal is Califia 1983.

26   See Money and Ehrhardt 1972:18–20.

27   There is a long and complicated debate within anthropology about this. See H. Whitehead (1981:80–115); Williams (1986); several articles in Blackwood (1985); and Allen (1989).

28   Two impressive beginnings are Joan Nestle (1981) and Amber Hollibaugh and Cherríe Moraga (1981). The latter has been reprinted in Snitow, Stansell, and Thompson (1983:394–405).

Beyond Freud, Ken, and Barbie

This essay was originally published as a book review in *The Women's Review of Books,* October 1986, and titled "Closing the Gender Gap."

1   For examples of the social constructionist perspective in feminism, see Vance 1984.
2   The literature on the berdache is large and growing. For a sophisticated treatment, see Harriet Whitehead 1981.

My Butch Career: A Memoir

I wrote this essay to be given as the David R. Kessler Lecture, December 6, 1996, at the Center for Lesbian and Gay Studies at the Graduate Center of the City University of New York. The "Alice-Hunting" section is reproduced from Sally Munt, ed., 1998, *butch/femme: inside lesbian gender,* by permission of Cassell, Wellington House (125 Strand, London, WC2R OBB, England). My thanks to Jeffrey Escoffier, whose idea the title was; to Holly Hughes and Gerry Gomez Pearlberg, for being the best audience ever; and to Jane Rosett and Jean Carlomusto, for feedback and for the indispensable help they, and especially Jane, gave me with the many slides that made this essay so evocative as the Kessler Lecture.

1   "Secondary genders" is the term used by anthropologist Jennifer Robertson (1998: 11), who writes about the Japanese all-woman *Takarazuka Revue* troupe that includes both "female" and "male" players. Incoming students are assigned which gender they will play "based on both physical (but not genital) and socio-psychological criteria; namely, height, physique, facial shape, voice, personality, and to a certain extent, personal preference."
2   The American Psychiatric Association's *Diagnostic and Statistical Manual of Mental Disorders,* 4th ed. As listed in a recent exposé of gender correctional programs aimed at children (P. Burke 1996:29).
3   See Kennedy and Davis 1993.
4   "However seemingly intransigent, however poignantly experienced, lived identities are complicated fictions essential to our social function. Pragmatically speaking, this means an equivocal response to identity is required: that we tender our theoretical skepticism with an unaffected respect for the way individuals have negotiated their own desire through the swamp of sexual uncertainty" (Munt 1998:83).
5   "The stone butch has made the roughness of gender into a part of her identity. Where sex and gender fail to match (female body and masculine self), where appearance and reality collide (she appears masculine and constructs a real masculinity where there should be a 'real' femininity), this is where the stone butch emerges as viable, powerful, and affirmative" (Halberstam 1996:7).
6   Koestenbaum 1993:85. "Geraldine Farrar dared to tell Arturo Toscanini, 'You forget, *maestro,* that I am the star.' One need not be a star to relish Farrar's concise way of gathering a self, like rustling skirts, around her. . . . No single gesture, gown, or haughty glissando of self-promotion will change one's actual social position: one is

fixed in a class, a race, a gender. But against such absolutes there arises a fervent belief in retaliatory self-invention; gay culture has perfected the art of mimicking a diva—of pretending, inside, to *be* divine—to help the stigmatized self imagine it is received, believed, and adored" (133).

DMS: The Outsider's Insider

A version of this paper was read at the annual meetings of the American Anthropological Association in San Francisco, November 1992, and another version became a eulogy for David M. Schneider at the annual meetings in 1995.

1   The title of my dissertation, which became the book *Mother Camp* (1972), is *The Drag Queens: Female Impersonators in America* (1968); for "The Traffic in Women," see Rubin 1975. Rubin says that *Mother Camp* did not influence "Traffic" but was "crucial to my later work" (personal communication).

2   For a delicious collection of Schneider's thoughts on his life in anthropology, see Richard Handler's edited collection (Schneider 1995).

Too Queer for College: Notes on Homophobia

A version of this paper was first read at the Modern Languages Association, December 1986. It has since been printed, in different forms, in the *Gay Studies Association Newsletter* (March 1987); the *ARGOH Newsletter* (Anthropological Research Group on Homosexuality of the American Anthropological Association) (May 1987); and the *Sociologists' Gay Caucus Newsletter* (of the American Sociological Association) (July 1987). An abridged and edited version was published under the title "Academe's Homophobia: It Damages Careers and Ruins Lives," in the *Chronicle of Higher Education*, March 11, 1987. This essay could be considered a sequel to "Marginal Woman/Marginal Academic," this volume.

1   This was "Marginal Woman/Marginal Academic," this volume.

2   My coauthor was Paula Webster. The essay had been published in a small feminist literary magazine (Newton and Webster 1973); we were seeking broader readership. Later, we were asked to revise the piece for publication, but I was living in France then and had lost heart, so I gave her permission to revise it alone. See Webster 1975.

An Open Letter to "Manda Cesara"

Originally published in *ARGOH* (Anthropology Research Group on Homosexuality) *Newsletter* (spring 1984). Karla Poewe has since made a friendly gesture, and although I was furious at the time I wrote this, I reprint it here as a general example of how homophobia can divide feminist anthropologists.

Of Yams, Grinders, and Gays: The Anthropology of Homosexuality

This paper was read at the "Gays, Lesbians and Society" lecture series at the 92nd Street YMHA, New York City, October 17, 1987, and revised for *Outlook: National Gay and Lesbian Quarterly*, 1 (1988).

1   Quoted in Montagu 1956:37.

2   Two overview articles on the new thinking in anthropology are Barry D. Adam (1986) and Pat Caplan (1987:1–30). A summary of the lesbian material can be found in Blackwood (1986:1–18).

Lesbian and Gay Issues in Anthropology: Some Remarks
to the Chairs of Anthropology Departments

This speech was written when, as a representative of the Society of Lesbian and Gay Anthropologists, I was asked by the Executive Board of the American Anthropological Association to address the assembled department chairs at the Annual Meetings of the Association in Washington, D.C., November 19, 1993.

My Best Informant's Dress: The Erotic Equation in Fieldwork

An earlier version of this paper was read at the "Lesbian/Gay Identity" session, annual meeting of the American Anthropological Association, December 1, 1990, New Orleans. It is reproduced by permission of the American Anthropological Association from *Cultural Anthropology* 8 (February 1993): 1–23. Without the support of my colleagues in SOLGA (Society of Lesbian and Gay Anthropologists) who loved the earlier draft, I wouldn't have had the nerve to try for publication. I also thank Julie Abraham, two anonymous readers for *Cultural Anthropology*, Amber Hollibaugh, Morris Kaplan, Ellen Lewin, Sherry Ortner, Jane Rosett, David M. Schneider, Kath Weston, and Peter Worth, all of whom read drafts of this essay and made helpful suggestions. "Sex Sickness!" is Marvin Harris's term for his review of Malinowski's *A Diary in the Strict Sense of the Term* (1967).

1   One of my informants, Peter Worth, was shocked by reading here the word "informant" in reference to herself and her friends. I explained that in all my published work on Cherry Grove I intended to use the word "narrator" for those whom I had interviewed, but in this essay, I was addressing an anthropological audience for whom the historical importance of the word informant recommended its use.

   David Schneider said he had heard the postmodern anthropologist joke from Marshall Sahins. Later, Kath Weston pointed out that Judy Stacey (1990:272) had quoted a slightly different version, attributing it to Sahlins (1991).

2   I think it was only in the later 1960s that I heard rumors that Mead lived with another woman who was thought to be her lover. Partly I doubted it because she had been so publicly and often married, and partly the news had less impact because, being more confidently lesbian, I needed role models less. Much more important to my survival—I mean that quite literally—from high school on was the forceful advocacy for human variation, gender and otherwise, in both Mead's and Benedict's work.

   In the acceptance speech upon receiving the Margaret Mead Award at our 1991 annual meetings of the American Anthropological Association, Will Roscoe (1992) expressed the hope that if Benedict and Mead were still living they would not have to hide their sexuality to be credible public advocates for greater tolerance.

3   "Personal interactions and relationships are the stuff of field data collection," asserts sociologist Carol A. B. Warren (1977:105) in an excellent article on fieldwork in the male gay world, but, she ends mysteriously, "They only become a problem when they block access to certain parts of the data." She astutely discusses how the researcher

may be stigmatized as gay by "normals" and so lose credibility, how the fieldworker trying to establish trust may be grilled by informants about her own sexual orientation, and even the need for "reflective subjectivity" by the fieldworker (104), all without ever tipping her own hand. This is the same elusiveness to which I resorted in my early work on gay men (Newton 1979).

4   Only one of the male anthropologists in *In the Company of Man* chose to write about a female informant, a prepubescent girl (Conklin 1960).

5   Jean Briggs (1970) made her own anger and frustration central to her Eskimo ethnography; Barbara Myerhoff's (1978) elderly Jewish informants got under her skin in a rich variety of ways; Robert Murphy's (1987) account of how becoming paralyzed changed his identity and propelled him toward studying the disabled moved me deeply; Renato Rosaldo (1989) explored how his wife Shelly's death helped him grasp the rage motivating Ilingot head-hunting; and Michael Moffatt (1989) constructs a narrative about college students with himself as a very present participant-observer (whatever one thinks of his initial ethical lapse in fooling the students about his identity). All three of the men's texts do begin to construct the sexuality of the author as a subject, especially Moffatt's, perhaps because he writes extensively about the student's sexuality.

6   Quoted in Geertz 1988:98.

7   Geertz (1988:90) actually observes that in this genre the authorial voice is somehow configured as "an object of desire," but apparently only by reading and from afar. The term "positional subject" is Rosaldo's (1989:19), and I think he wouldn't mind my adding "sexual" because he alone of the new ethnographers includes sexual orientation as a meaningful axis of difference that can help dismantle "objectivism" and add richness to ethnographic accounts (see esp. 190–93).

8   See also Geertz (1967), Greenway (1967), Harris (1967), and Hogbin (1968).

9   Recently, I was discussing the *Diary* in a class of undergraduates. One woman student said indignantly, "Knowing about the *Diary*, why should I read Malinowski's ethnographies?" and another added after thinking about it, "Maybe if you could put the *Diary* together with *Sex and Repression* you'd have good ethnography."

10 Of those who could be considered in the I-Witnessing school of ethnography, the only woman to rate a mention from Geertz is Barbara Myerhoff in a footnote (1988: 101–15). Not comparing Cesara's *Reflections of a Woman Anthropologist* (1982) to Rabinow's *Reflections on Fieldwork in Morocco* (1977) is disappointing to say the least. Note that comparing titles, Rabinow can just be in the field, but Cesara has chosen to accept and acknowledge being in the marked category.

11 For the perspective of an African American man working in the Caribbean, see T. Whitehead (1986). For the perspective of a black lesbian anthropologist working in Yemen, see Delores K. Walters (1996).

12 Of course, the majority of gay and lesbian anthropologists are in the closet, which by definition precludes them from publicly acknowledging their orientation and generally from even writing about sexuality. And is it necessary to add that in my review of the literature in this essay, the work done on gay *culture* is not mentioned unless it deals specifically with erotic issues and systems? An article about a gay community center, for instance, is not necessarily any more (or less) about sexuality than one on a small-town Elks Club.

13 For an interesting, odd (and perhaps fabricated) account that actually centers on

the homoerotic relations between Amazonian Indians and a Western observer-adventurer, see Schneebaum 1969.

14   In a conversation at the 1990 AAA convention in New Orleans, Walter Williams confirmed that this was the case and that, although he had written more explicitly about it in his manuscript, friends had advised him to "tone it down" before publication lest too much frankness jeopardize his tenure, which he has since gotten, though only after a struggle.

15   Perhaps emboldened by Read, other anthropologists have followed in his New Guinea trail with important (although less evocative) work on (homo)sexuality (Herdt 1981, 1984).

16   The authorial presence in Read's (1980) ethnography of a gay bar is far more tortured and dissembling than in the New Guinea work.

17   The diffuse homoeroticism, even in Read's (1965) first ethnography on the Gabuku-Gama, did disturb at least one "sensitive" anthropologist, Clifford Geertz (1988:86), who in an appreciation of Read's "brilliantly realized" I-Witnessing style can neither give his discomfort plain speech nor restrain a snide remark about Read's description of the farewell hug he had shared with Makis.

18   After I began this essay, Kath Weston sent me her "Requiem for a Street Fighter," which is about her relationship with a young woman who would have been an informant had she not committed suicide. My fieldwork was conducted in Cherry Grove, Long Island, New York, from the summer of 1985 through the summer of 1989 (Newton 1993).

19   A welcome exception is Serena Nanda's (1990) fascinating work on the gender-variant Indian *hijras*, which received SOLGA's Ruth Benedict Prize in 1990.

20   Gay and lesbian anthropologists have discussed these problems in a series of recent panels at the annual meetings of the American Anthropological Association; many of these groundbreaking and silence-breaking papers are in Lewin and Leap (1996).

21   I agree with Mascia-Lees, Sharpe, and Cohen (1989:33) that the way anthropologists should work against power imbalance between themselves and their subjects is to make conscious choices to write for them too and to be attentive to research questions they want answered.

22   Kay asked me not to publish her last name. A different version of this narrative is embedded in Newton (1993:3-7).

23   This and all subsequent quotes in this section are from my unpublished fieldnotes, except for the letter to Schneider.

24   The categories "gay" and "straight," no matter how fateful and socially real, cannot be taken literally to mean that people so identified are never, as individuals, sexually interested in whichever gender is supposed to be erotically null. Even at the time of my dissertation fieldwork with female impersonators in the mid-1960s, I recognized that, improbable as it seemed, my then "best informant's" considerable charms, which included his dresses, or rather his persona in dresses, had a certain erotic component for me. But here I allude to a complex subject beyond the scope of this essay.

25   Even when we gays are teachers, as many of us are, our identity is the one thing about which most of us can never teach the young. Many gay people do not have children who could give them personal and intimate access to succeeding generations and cannot share their lives even with nieces and nephews. Kay, for instance,

was childless, and in the name of "discretion" never discussed her homosexuality—all of her living, that is, that formed the substance and subject matter of our friendship and was the reason why she had lived in Cherry Grove for fifty summers—with any of her family. Because of the enforced secrecy in which we live, older gays have trouble transmitting our culture to younger ones.

26   Although our cupboard is nearly bare, it isn't empty. In addition to the articles and books previously referred to, Gregersen (1983) has done a quirky follow-up of Ford and Beach's (1951) early cross-cultural work. For American culture, there is Rubin's (1984) article on the hierarchical stratification of sexual practices, Vance's (1983) witty essay on the Kinsey Institute, my effort to develop a more precise sexual vocabulary (Newton and Walton 1984), Thompson (1984, 1990) on teen girls, and Davis and Kennedy's (1989) pioneering work on the sexuality of lesbians in Buffalo. For non-Western cultures, there is the "berdache" controversy (Callender and Kochems 1983; Roscoe 1991; H. Whitehead 1981; Williams 1986), the essays in Blackwood (1985), and three monographs: Thomas Gregor's (1985) account of the heterosexual Mehinaku, Gilbert Herdt and Robert Stoller's (1990) collaboration on the Sambia, and Richard Parker's (1991) Brazilian work, the winner of SOLGA's 1991 Benedict Prize.

BIBLIOGRAPHY

Abel, Sam. 1998. "Staging Heterosexuality: Alfred Lunt and Lynn Fontanne's Design for Living." In *Passing Performances: Queer Readings of Leading Players in American Theater History*, ed. Robert A. Schanke and Kim Marra. 175–96. Ann Arbor: University of Michigan Press.

Adam, Barry D. 1986. "Age, Structure, and Sexuality: Reflections on the Anthropological Evidence on Homosexual Relations." In *Anthropology and Homosexual Behavior*, ed. Evelyn Blackwood. 19–34. New York: Haworth.

Albro, Joyce, and Carol Tully. 1979. "A Study of Lesbian Lifestyles in the Homosexual Micro-Culture and the Heterosexual Macro-Culture." *Journal of Homosexuality* 4: 331–44.

Allen, Paula G. 1989. "Lesbians in American Indian Cultures." In *Hidden from History: Reclaiming the Gay and Lesbian Past*, ed. Martin B. Duberman, Martha Vicinus, and George Chauncey. 106–17. New York: New American Library.

Altman, Dennis. 1979. *The Homosexualization of America*. Boston: Beacon Press.

American Anthropological Association. 1993. *Newsletter* (September):68.

Amory, Deborah P. 1996. "Club Q: Dancing with (a) Difference." In *Inventing Lesbian Cultures in America*, ed. Ellen Lewin. 145–60. Boston: Beacon Press.

Anderson, Benedict. 1983. *Imagined Communities: Reflections on the Origin and Spread of Nationalism*. London: Verso.

Ashworth, A. E., and W. M. Walker. 1972. "Social Structure and Homosexuality: A Theoretical Appraisal." *British Journal of Sociology* (23):146–58.

Badgett, M. V. L. 1997. " 'Thinking Homo/Economically.' " In *A Queer World: The Center for Lesbian and Gay Studies Reader*, ed. Martin Duberman. 467–76. New York: New York University Press.

Baker, Michael. 1985. *Our Three Selves: The Life of Radclyffe Hall*. New York: William Morrow.

Baker, Roger. 1968. *Drag: A History of Female Impersonation on the Stage*. London: Triton Books. Reprinted 1994, New York: New York University Press.

Bannon, Ann. 1983. *I Am a Woman*. Tallahasse, FL: Naiad Press.

Barish, Jonas A. 1981. *The Antitheatrical Prejudice*. Berkeley: University of California Press.

Barnhart, Elizabeth. 1975. "Friends and Lovers in a Lesbian Counterculture Community." In *Old Family, New Family*, ed. Nona Glazer-Malbin. 90–115. New York: Van Nostrand.

Becker, Howard. 1965. *The Other Side: Perspectives on Deviance*. New York: Free Press.

Beemyn, Brett, ed. 1997. *Creating a Place for Ourselves: Lesbian, Gay, Bisexual and Community Histories*. New York: Routledge.

Bell, Alan P., and Martin S. Weinberg. 1978. *Homosexualities: A Study of Diversity among Men and Women*. New York: Simon and Schuster.

Belote, Deborah, and Joan Joesting. 1976. "Demographic and Self-Report Characteristics of Lesbians." *Psychological Reports* (39):21–22.

Benstock, Shari. 1986. *Women of the Left Bank: Paris, 1900–1940*. Austin: University of Texas Press.

Berger, Peter, and Thomas Luckmann. 1967. *The Social Construction of Reality*. New York: Anchor Books.

Bergman, David, ed. 1993. *Campgrounds: Style and Homosexuality*. Amherst: University of Massachusetts Press.

Berlant, Lauren, and Elizabeth Freeman. 1993. "Queer Nationality." In *Fear of a Queer Planet: Queer Politics and Social Theory*, ed. Michael Warner. 193–229. Minneapolis: University of Minnesota Press.

Bérubé, Allan. 1990. *Coming Out Under Fire: The History of Gay Men and Women in World War II*. New York: Free Press.

Beyond Biased Samples: Challenging the Myths on the Economic Status of Lesbians and Gay Men. 1994. Pamphlet published by the National Organization of Gay and Lesbian Scientists and Technical Professionals and the Institute for Gay and Lesbian Strategic Studies.

Birkby, Phillis, Bertha Harris, Jill Johnston, Esther Newton, and Jane O'Wyatt, eds. 1973. *Amazon Expedition: A Lesbian Feminist Anthology*. Washington, NJ: Times Change Press.

Blackwood, Evelyn. 1986. "Breaking the Mirror: The Construction of Lesbianism and the Anthropological Discourse on Homosexuality." In *Anthropology and Homosexual Behavior*, ed. Evelyn Blackwood. 1–18. New York: Haworth.

———, ed. 1985. *Anthropology and Homosexual Behavior*. New York: Haworth.

Blumstein, Philip, and Pepper Schwartz. 1983. *American Couples: Money, Work, Sex*. New York: William Morrow.

Booth, Mark. 1983. *Camp*. London: Quartet Books.

Bordo, Susan. 1990. "Feminism, Postmodernism, and Gender-Skepticism." In *Feminism and Postmodernism*, ed. Linda J. Nicholson. 133–56. New York: Routledge.

Boswell, John. 1992. "Same Sex Marriages in Medieval Europe." Paper presented at State University of New York College at Purchase.

Bozzone, Barbara. 1994. "Homecoming Queen Is a Woman." *Fire Island Tide* (1 July):12.

Bradshaw, Jon. 1985. *Dreams That Money Can Buy: The Tragic Life of Libby Holman*. New York: William Morrow.

Bray, Alan. 1982. *Homosexuality in Renaissance England*. London: Gay Men's Press.

Brecht, Stefan. 1986. *Queer Theater*. New York: Methuen.

Briggs, Jean. 1970. *Never in Anger: Portrait of an Eskimo Family*. Cambridge, MA: Harvard University Press.

Bristow, Ann R. 1984. "Comment on Krieger's 'Lesbian Identity and Community: Recent Social Science Literature.'" *Signs* 9(4):729–32.

Brittain, Vera. 1969. *Radclyffe Hall: A Case of Obscenity?* New York: A. S. Barnes.

Bronski, Michael. 1984. *Culture Clash: The Making of Gay Sensibility*. Boston: South End Press.

Brooks, Virginia R. 1981. *Minority Stress and Lesbian Women*. Lexington, MA: Lexington Press.

Brown, Judith. 1989. "Lesbian Sexuality in Medieval and Early Modern Europe." In *Hid-

den from History: Reclaiming the Gay and Lesbian Past, ed. Martin Duberman, Martha Vicinus, and George Chauncey. 67–75. New York: New American Library.

Bull, Chris. 1994. "Stonewall Celebrations." *Advocate* (26 July):19.

Bullough, Vern, and Bonnie Bullough. 1977. "Lesbianism in the 1920s and 1930s: A New-found Study." *Signs* 2(4):895–904.

Burke, Carolyn. 1982. "Gertrude Stein, the Cone Sisters, and the Puzzle of Female Friend-ship." In *Writing and Sexual Difference,* ed. Elizabeth Abel. 221–42. Chicago: Univer-sity of Chicago Press.

Burke, Phyllis. 1996. *Gender Shock: Exploding the Myths of Male and Female.* New York: Doubleday.

Burns, Elizabeth. 1973. *Theatricality: A Study of Convention in the Theatre and in Social Life.* New York: Harper and Row.

Butler, Judith. 1993a. "Critically Queer." *GLQ* 1:22.

———. 1993b. "Imitation and Gender Insubordination." In *The Lesbian and Gay Studies Reader,* ed. Henry Abelove, Michele A. Barale, and David M. Halperin. 307–20. New York: Routledge.

———. 1990. *Gender Trouble: Feminism and the Subversion of Identity.* New York: Rout-ledge.

Caldwell, Mayta, and Letitia Anne Pelau. 1984. "The Balance of Power in Lesbian Re-lationships." *Sex Roles* 10 (April):587–99.

Califia, Pat. 1983. "Gender-Bending: Playing with Roles and Reversals." *Advocate* (15 Sep-tember).

Callendar, Charles, and Lee M. Kochems. 1983. "The North American Berdache." *Current Anthropology* 24(4):443–70.

Caplan, Pat. 1987. Introduction. In *The Cultural Construction of Sexuality,* ed. Pat Caplan. 1–30. London: Tavistock.

Carlson, Marvin. 1984. *Theories of the Theatre.* Ithaca, NY: Cornell University Press.

Carr, C. 1993a. "The Lady Is a Dick: The Dyke Noir Theater of Holly Hughes." In *On Edge: Performance at the End of the Twentieth Century.* 132–37. Hanover, NH: Wesleyan University Press.

———. 1993b. "The Queer Frontier." In *On Edge: Performance at the End of the Twentieth Century.* 84–87. Hanover, NH: Wesleyan University Press.

Casagrande, Joseph, ed. 1960. *In the Company of Man: Twenty Portraits by Anthropologists.* New York: Harper and Brothers.

Case, Sue-Ellen. 1993. "Toward a Butch/Femme Aesthetic." In *The Lesbian and Gay Studies Reader,* ed. Henry Abelove, Michele A. Barale, and David M. Halperin. 294–306. New York: Routledge.

Cesara, Manda (Karla O. Poewe). 1982. *Reflections of a Woman Anthropologist: No Hiding Place.* New York: Academic Press.

Chansky, Dorothy. 1990. "wow Cafe: A Stage of Their Own." *Theatre Work* (September): 39–41.

Chauncey, George, Jr. 1994. *Gay New York: Gender, Urban Culture, and the Making of the Gay Male World, 1890–1940.* New York: Basic Books.

———. 1989. "Christian Brotherhood or Sexual Perversion? Homosexual Identities and the Construction of Sexual Boundaries in the World War I Era." In *Hidden from His-tory: Reclaiming the Gay and Lesbian Past,* ed. Martin Duberman, Martha Vicinus, and George Chauncey. 294–317. New York: New American Library.

———. 1982–1983. "From Sexual Inversion to Homosexuality: The Changing Medical Conceptualization of Female 'Deviance.'" *Salmagundi* (58–59):114–45.

Chopin, Kate. 1972 [1899]. *The Awakening*. New York: Avon Books.

Clarke, Gerald. 1988. *Capote: A Biography*. New York: Simon and Schuster.

Claus, Ruth F. 1977. "Confronting Homosexuality: A Letter from Frances Wilder." *Signs* 2(4):928–33.

Clifford, James. 1986. "Introduction: Partial Truths." In *Writing Culture: The Poetics and Politics of Ethnography*, ed. James Clifford and George E. Marcus. 1–26. Berkeley: University of California Press.

Clifford, James, and George E. Marcus, eds. 1986. *Writing Culture: The Poetics and Politics of Ethnography*. Berkeley: University of California Press.

Clum, John M. 1994. *Acting Gay: Male Homosexuality in Modern Drama*. New York: Columbia University Press.

Clurman, Harold. 1983. *The Fervent Years*. New York: Da Capo Press.

Combahee River Collective. 1998. "A Black Feminist Statement." In *Social Perspectives in Lesbian and Gay Studies*, ed. Peter M. Nardi and Beth E. Schneider. 521–26. London: Routledge.

Committee on Discrimination, SOLGA (Society of Lesbian and Gay Anthropologists). 1992. *Proposal to the American Anthropological Association for the Creation of a Task Force on Discrimination against Lesbians and Gay Men in Anthropology*.

Conaway, Mary Ellen. 1986. "The Pretense of the Neutral Researcher." In *Self, Sex, and Gender in Cross-Cultural Fieldwork*, ed. Tony Larry Whitehead and Mary Ellen Conaway. 52–63. Urbana: University of Illinois Press.

Conklin, Harold C. 1960. "Mailing, a Hanunoo Girl from the Philippines." In *In the Company of Man: Twenty Portraits by Anthropologists*, ed. Joseph Casagrande. New York: Harper and Brothers.

Cook, Blanche Wiesen. 1979. "Women Alone Stir My Imagination: Lesbianism and the Cultural Tradition." *Signs: Journal of Women and Society* 4(summer):719–20.

Cornwell, Anita. 1983. *Black Lesbian in White America*. Tallahassee, FL: Naiad Press.

Cotton, Wayne L. 1975. "Social and Sexual Relationships of Lesbians." *Journal of Sex Research* 11(2):139–48.

Crapanzano, Vincent. 1980. *Tuhami, Portrait of a Moroccan*. Chicago: University of Chicago Press.

Crawford, Cheryl. 1977. *One Naked Individual: My Fifty Years in the Theatre*. Indianapolis: Bobbs-Merrill.

Cronyn, Hume. 1991. *A Terrible Liar: A Memoir*. New York: Morrow.

Curtin, Kaier. 1987. *"We Can Always Call Them Bulgarians": The Emergence of Lesbians and Gay Men on the American Stage*. Boston: Alyson.

Davis, Madeline, and Elizabeth L. Kennedy. 1992. "'They Was No One to Mess With': The Construction of the Butch Role in the Lesbian Community of the 1940s and 1950s." In *The Persistent Desire*, ed. Joan Nestle. 62–80. New York: Alyson.

———. 1989. "Oral History and the Study of Sexuality in the Lesbian Community: Buffalo, New York, 1940–1960." In *Hidden from History: Reclaiming the Gay and Lesbian Past*, ed. Martin Duberman, Martha Vicinus, and George Chauncey. 426–40. New York: New American Library.

Davis, Madeline, Elizabeth Kennedy, and Avra Michelson. 1981. "Buffalo Lesbian Bars:

1930–1960." Paper read at Berkshire Conference on Women's History, Vassar College.

Davy, Kate. 1994. "Visibility Troubles and Literate Perverts." *Women and Performance: A Journal of Feminist Theory* 7(1):141–57.

———. 1993. "From Lady Dick to Ladylike: The Work of Holly Hughes." In *Acting Out: Feminist Performances*, ed. Lynda Hart and Peggy Phelan. 55–84. Ann Arbor: University of Michigan Press.

———. 1992. "Fe/Male Impersonation: The Discourse of Camp." In *Critical Theory and Performance*, ed. Janelle G. Reinelt and Joseph R. Roach. 231–47. Ann Arbor: University of Michigan Press.

———. 1985. "Heart of the Scorpion at the wow Cafe." *TDR: The Drama Review* 29(1): 52–56.

Delph, Edward W. 1978. *The Silent Community: Public Homosexual Encounters*. Beverly Hills, CA: Sage.

D'Emilio, John. 1983a. "Capitalism and Gay Identity." In *Powers of Desire: The Politics of Sexuality*, ed. Ann Snitow, Christine Stansell, and Sharon Thompson. 100–113. New York: Monthly Review Press.

———. 1983b. *Sexual Politics, Sexual Communities: The Making of a Homosexual Minority in the United States, 1940–1970*. Chicago: University of Chicago Press.

de Jongh, Nicholas. 1992. *Not in Front of the Audience: Homosexuality on Stage*. New York: Routledge, Chapman and Hall.

de Lauretis, Teresa. 1987. *Technologies of Gender: Essays on Theory, Film and Fiction*. Bloomington: Indiana University Press.

Dolan, Jill. 1998. "Foreword." In *Passing Performances: Queer Readings of Leading Players in American Theater History*, ed. Robert A. Schanke and Kim Marra. ix–xii. Ann Arbor: University of Michigan Press.

———. 1993. "Desire Cloaked in a Trenchcoat." In *Acting Out: Feminist Performances*, ed. Lynda Hart and Peggy Phelan. 105–18. Ann Arbor: University of Michigan Press.

———. 1985. "Carmelita Tropicana Chats at the Club Chandelier." *TDR: The Drama Review* 29(1):26–32.

Drorbaugh, Elizabeth. 1993. "Sliding Scales: Notes on Stormé DeLarverie and the Jewel Box Revue, the Cross-Dressed Woman on the Contemporary Stage, and the Invert." In *Crossing the Stage: Controversies on Cross-Dressing*, ed. Lesley Ferris. London: Routledge.

Drutman, Irving. 1976. *Good Company: A Memoir, Mostly Theatrical*. Boston: Little, Brown.

Duberman, Martin, ed. 1997. *A Queer World: The Center for Lesbian and Gay Studies Reader*. New York: New York University Press.

Duberman, Martin Bauml, Martha Vicinus, and George Chauncey Jr., eds. 1989. *Hidden from History: Reclaiming the Gay and Lesbian Past*. New York: New American Library.

Duggan, Lisa. 1993. "The Trials of Alice Mitchell: Sensationalism, Sexology and the Lesbian Subject in Turn of the Century America." *SIGNS* 18(4):791–814.

———. 1992. "Making It Perfectly Queer." *Socialist Review* 22(1):11–31.

———. 1988. "The Anguished Cry of an 80s Fem: 'I Want to Be a Drag Queen.'" *Out/Look* 1:63–65.

Durham, Weldon B. 1987. *American Theatre Companies: 1888–1930*. New York: Greenwood.

Dworkin, Andrea. 1981. *Pornography and Silence: Culture's Revenge against Nature*. New York: Harper and Row.

Dynes, Wayne R. 1987. *Homosexuality: A Research Guide*. New York: Garland Publishing.

Echols, Alice. 1983. "The New Feminism of Yin and Yang." In *Powers of Desire: The Politics of Sexuality*, ed. Ann Snitow, Christine Stansell, and Sharon Thompson. 439–59. New York: Monthly Review Press.

Eisenbud, Ruth-Jean. 1982. "Early and Later Determinates of Lesbian Choice." *Psychoanalytic Review* 69(1):85–109.

Ellen, R. F., ed. 1984. *Ethnographic Research: A Guide to General Conduct*. London: Academic Press.

Ellis, Havelock. 1895. "Sexual Inversion in Women." *Alienist and Neurologist* (16):141–58.

Ellman, Richard. 1988. *Oscar Wilde*. New York: Vintage Books.

Erenberg, Lewis A. 1981. *Steppin' Out: New York Nightlife and the Transformation of American Culture, 1890–1930*. Westport, CT: Greenwood Press.

Escoffier, Jeffrey. 1998. *American Homo: Community and Perversity*. Berkeley: University of California Press.

Ettore, E. M. 1980. *Lesbians, Women and Society*. London: Routledge and Kegan Paul.

Faderman, Lillian. 1981. *Surpassing the Love of Men: Romantic Friendship and Love between Women from the Renaissance to the Present*. New York: William Morrow.

Faderman, Lillian, and Ann Williams. 1977. "Radclyffe Hall and the Lesbian Image." *Conditions* 1(1):31–41.

Ferris, Leslie. 1998. "Kit and Guth: A Lavender Marriage on Broadway." In *Passing Performances: Queer Readings of Leading Players in American Theater History*, ed. Robert A. Schanke and Kim Marra. 197–220. Ann Arbor: University of Michigan Press.

"A First for Cherry Grove." 1994. *New York Times*, Long Island section (19 June): 3.

Ford, Clellan S., and Frank A. Beach. 1951. *Patterns of Sexual Behavior*. New York: Harper and Brothers.

Foucault, Michel. 1980. *The History of Sexuality*, Vol. 1: *An Introduction*. New York: Vintage Books.

Freedley, George. 1954a. "Off Stage—And On." *New York Morning Telegraph*. (? July). Folder MWEZ+NC 16107, George Freedley 1947–1955. Lincoln Center Library of the Performing Arts, New York.

———. 1954b. "Off Stage—And On." *New York Morning Telegraph* (8 January). Folder MWEZ+NC 16107, George Freedley 1947–1955. Lincoln Center Library of the Performing Arts, New York.

———. 1951a. "Off Stage—And On." *New York Morning Telegraph* (17 October). Folder MWEZ+NC 16107, George Freedley 1947–1955. Lincoln Center Library of the Performing Arts, New York.

———. 1951b. "Off Stage—And On." *New York Morning Telegraph* (15 June). Folder MWEZ+NC 16107, George Freedley 1947–1955. Lincoln Center Library of the Performing Arts, New York.

———. 1948a. "The Community Theatre." Folder MWEZ+NC 16107, George Freedley 1947–1955. Lincoln Center Library of the Performing Arts, New York.

———. 1948b. Typed manuscript. Folder MWEZ+NC 16107, George Freedley 1947–1955. Lincoln Center Library of the Performing Arts, New York.

Freedley, George, and John A. Reeves. 1968. *A History of the Theatre*. New York: Crown.

Freedman, Estelle. 1982. "Sexuality in Nineteenth-Century America: Behavior, Ideology and Politics." *Reviews in American History* 10(4):196–215.

Freedman, Estelle, Barbara C. Gelpi, Susan L. Johnson, and Kathleen M. Weston, ed. 1985. *The Lesbian Issue: Essays from Signs.* Chicago: University of Chicago Press.

Freud, Sigmund. 1963. "The Psychogenesis of a Case of Homosexuality in a Woman." In *Freud: Sexuality and the Psychology of Love,* ed. Philip Rieff. 133–59. New York: Collier Books.

Gates, Henry L., Jr. 1997. "The Chitlin Circuit." *The New Yorker* (February 3):44–55.

Gay, Judith. 1986. " 'Mummies and Babies' and Friends and Lovers in Lesotho." In *Anthropology and Homosexual Behavior,* ed. Evelyn Blackwood. 97–116. New York: Haworth.

Geertz, Clifford. 1988. *Works and Lives: The Anthropologist as Author.* Stanford: Stanford University Press.

———. 1967. "Under the Mosquito Net." *New York Review of Books* (September 14):12–13.

———. 1963. "Ideology as a Cultural System." In *Ideology and Discontent,* ed. David Apter. New York: Free Press.

Gerlach, Luther P., and Virginia H. Hine. 1970. *People, Power, Change: Movements of Social Transformation.* Indianapolis: Bobbs-Merrill.

Gibbs, Joan, and Sara Bennett, eds. 1980. *Top Ranking: A Collection of Articles on Racism and Classism in the Lesbian Community.* New York: Come! Unity Press.

Gilbert, Sandra. 1982. "Costumes of the Mind: Transvestism as Metaphor in Modern Literature." In *Writing and Sexual Difference,* ed. Elizabeth Abel. 193–220. Chicago: University of Chicago Press.

Giovanni, Maureen. 1986. "Female Anthropologist and Male Informant: Gender Conflict in a Sicilian Town." In *Self, Sex, and Gender in Cross-Cultural Fieldwork,* ed. Tony Larry Whitehead and Mary Ellen Conaway. 103–16. Urbana: University of Illinois Press.

Goffman, Erving. 1963. *Stigma: Notes on the Management of Spoiled Identity.* Englewood Cliffs, NJ: Prentice-Hall.

Golde, Peggy, ed. 1970. *Women in the Field: Anthropological Experiences.* Chicago: Aldine.

Goldstein, Richard. 1985. "Kramer's Complaint." *Village Voice* (2 July):20–22.

Gordy, Douglas W. 1998. "Joseph Cino and the First Off-Off-Broadway Theater." In *Passing Performances: Queer Readings of Leading Players in American Theater History,* ed. Robert A. Schanke and Kim Marra. 303–23. Ann Arbor: University of Michigan Press.

Gorer, Geoffrey. 1967. "Island Exorcism." *The Listener* (7 September):311.

Gornick, Vivian. 1981. "The Whole Radclyffe Hall: A Pioneer Left Behind." *Village Voice* (10–16 June).

Gramick, Jeannine. 1984. "Developing a Lesbian Identity." In *Women-Identified Women,* ed. Trudy Darty and Sandee Potter. 31–44. Palo Alto, CA: Mayfield.

Green, Hannah. 1964. *I Never Promised You a Rose Garden.* New York: Henry Holt.

Green, Sarah F. 1997. *Urban Amazons: Lesbian Feminism and Beyond in the Gender, Sexuality and Identity Battles of London.* New York: St. Martin's Press.

Greenway, John. 1967. "Malinowski Unbuttoned." *World Journal Tribune* (26 March).

Gregersen, Edgar. 1983. *Sexual Practices: The Story of Human Sexuality.* New York: Franklin Watts.

Gregor, Thomas. 1985. *Anxious Pleasures: The Sexual Lives of an Amazonian People.* Chicago: University of Chicago Press.

Griggers, Cathy. 1993. "Lesbian Bodies in the Age of (Post)Mechanical Reproduction." In

Fear of a Queer Planet: Queer Politics and Social Theory, ed. Michael Warner. 178–92. Minneapolis: University of Minnesota Press.

Gross, Larry. 1991. "Out of the Mainstream: Sexual Minorities and the Mass Media." *Journal of Homosexuality* 21(1–2):19–46.

Halberstam, Judith. 1998. *Female Masculinity*. Durham, NC: Duke University Press.

———. 1996. "Lesbian Masculinity, or Even Stone Butches Get the Blues." *Women and Performance: A Journal of Feminist Theory* 8(2).

Hall, Lisa K. C. 1993. "Bitches in Solitude: Identity Politics and Lesbian Community." In *Sisters, Sexperts, Queers: Beyond the Lesbian Nation*, ed. Arlene Stein. 218–29. New York: Plume.

Hall, Radclyffe. 1981 [1924]. *The Unlit Lamp*. New York: Dial Press.

———. 1950 [1928]. *The Well of Loneliness*. New York: Pocket Books.

Harper, Brian P. 1994. "'The Subversive Edge': *Paris Is Burning*, Social Critique, and the Limits of Subjective Agency." *Diacritics* 24(2–3):90–103.

Harris, Hilary. 1993. "Toward a Lesbian Theory of Performance: Refunctioning Gender." In *Acting Out: Feminist Performances*, ed. Lynda Hart and Peggy Phelan. 257–76. Ann Arbor: University of Michigan Press.

Harris, Marvin. 1967. "Diary of an Anthropologist." *Natural History* 76:72–74.

Harry, Joseph, and William B. DeVall. 1978. *The Social Organization of Gay Males*. New York: Praeger.

Hart, Lynda. 1993. "Identity and Seduction: Lesbians in the Mainstream." In *Acting Out: Feminist Performances*, ed. Lynda Hart and Peggy Phelan. 119–37. Ann Arbor: University of Michigan Press.

Helbing, Terry. 1981. "Gay Plays, Gay Theatre, Gay Performance." *The Drama Review* 25(1):35–46.

Henry, Jules. 1963. *Culture against Man*. New York: Random House.

Herdt, Gilbert H., ed. 1984. *Ritualized Homosexuality in Melanesia*. Berkeley: University of California Press.

———. 1981. *The Sambia: Ritual and Gender in New Guinea*. New York: Holt, Rinehart and Winston.

Herdt, Gilbert, and Robert J. Stoller. 1990. *Intimate Communications: Erotics and the Study of Culture*. New York: Columbia University Press.

Hidalgo, Hilda. 1984. "The Puerto Rican Lesbian in the United States." In *Women-Identified Women*, ed. Trudy Darty and Sandee Potter. 105–15. Palo Alto, CA: Mayfield.

Hidalgo, Hilda, and Elia Hidalgo-Christensen. 1976. "The Puerto Rican Lesbian and the Puerto Rican Community." *Journal of Homosexuality* 2(winter):109–21.

Hogbin, Ian. 1968. "Review of *A Diary in the Strict Sense of the Term* by Bronislaw Malinowski." *American Anthropologist* 70:575.

Hollibaugh, Amber, and Cherríe Moraga. 1981. "What We're Rollin' Around in Bed With." *Heresies Sex Issue 12*, 3 (4):58–62.

Hooker, Evelyn. 1967. "The Homosexual Community." In *Sexual Deviance*, ed. John H. Gagnon and William Simon. 167–84. New York: Harper and Row.

Huber, Joan, et al. 1982. "Report of the American Sociological Association's Task Group on Homosexuality." *The American Sociologist* 17 (August):164–180.

Hughes, Holly. 1996. *Clit Notes: A Sapphic Sampler*. New York: Grove Atlantic.

Hughes, Holly, and David Román, eds. 1998. *O Solo Homo: The New Queer Performance*. New York: Grove Press.

Hull, Gloria, Patricia B. Scott, and Barbara Smith. 1982. *All the Women Are White, All the Blacks Are Men, But Some of Us Are Brave*. New York: Feminist Press.

Humphreys, Laud. 1979. "Exodus and Identity: The Emerging Gay Culture." In *Gay Men: The Sociology of Male Homosexuality*, ed. Martin P. Levine. 134–47. New York: Harper and Row.

———. 1975. *Tearoom Trade: Impersonal Sex in Public Places*. New York: Aldine.

James, William. 1902. *The Varieties of Religious Experience*. New Hyde Park, NY: University Books.

Jay, Karla, and Allen Young. 1979. *The Gay Report: Lesbians and Gay Men Speak Out about Sexual Experiences and Lifestyles*. New York: Summit Books.

Johnston, Jill. 1998. *Admission Accomplished: The Lesbian Nation Years (1970–75)*. New York: Serpent's Tail.

Jones, Jennifer. 1998. "Rebels of Their Sex: Nance O'Neill and Lizzie Borden." In *Passing Performances: Queer Readings of Leading Players in American Theater History*, ed. Robert A. Schanke and Kim Marra. 83–103. Ann Arbor: University of Michigan Press.

Kakutani, Michiko. 1994. "The Rise of a Self-Proclaimed Phenomenon." *New York Times* (15 November):C19.

Katz, Jonathan N. 1976. *Gay American History: Lesbians and Gay Men in the U.S.A.* New York: T.Y. Crowell.

Keil, Charles. 1966. *Urban Blues*. Chicago: University of Chicago Press.

Kennedy, Elizabeth L., and Madeline D. Davis. 1993. *Boots of Leather, Slippers of Gold: The History of a Lesbian Community*. New York: Routledge.

Kessler, Suzanne J., and Wendy McKenna. 1985. *Gender: An Ethnomethodological Approach*. Chicago: University of Chicago Press.

Koestenbaum, Wayne. 1993. *The Queen's Throat: Opera, Homosexuality and the Mystery of Desire*. New York: Poseidon Press.

Krafft-Ebing, Richard von. 1886. *Psychopathia Sexualis*. Trans. Franklin S. Klaf. New York: Bell.

Krestan, Jo-Ann, and Claudia Bepko. 1980. "The Problem of Fusion in the Lesbian Relationship." *Family Process* 19(3):277–89.

Krieger, Susan. 1984. "Reply to Sandoval and Bristow and Pearn." *Signs* 9(4):732–33.

———. 1983. *The Mirror Dance: Identity in a Women's Community*. Philadelphia: Temple University Press.

———. 1982. "Lesbian Identity and Community: Recent Social Science Literature." *Signs* 8(1):91–108.

Laing, R. D., and Aaron Esterson. 1970. *Sanity, Madness and the Family: The Families of Schizophrenics*. Harmondsworth, England: Penguin.

Lanternari, Vittorio. 1963. *Religions of the Oppressed*. New York: Mentor Books.

Lasalle, Michael. 1991. "Broadway Loses Talent to AIDS." *Advocate* (Los Angeles) (8 October):70–75.

Lesbofile. 1994. *Deneuve* 4(4):48.

Lessing, Doris. 1969. *The Four-Gated City*. New York: Knopf.

Levine, Martin. 1979. "Gay Ghetto." In *The Sociology of Male Homosexuality*, ed. Martin Levine. 182–204. New York: Harper and Row.

Lévi-Strauss, Claude. 1963. *Structural Anthropology*. New York: Basic Books.

Lewin, Ellen. 1998. *Recognizing Ourselves: Ceremonies of Lesbian and Gay Commitment*. New York: Columbia University Press.

———. 1993. *Lesbian Mothers*. Ithaca, NY: Cornell University Press.

———, ed. 1996. *Inventing Lesbian Cultures in America*. Boston: Beacon.

Lewin, Ellen, and William L. Leap, eds. 1996. *Out in the Field: Reflections of Lesbian and Gay Anthropologists*. Urbana: University of Illinois Press.

Lewis, Draper. 1989. "Sand in My Pumps." *Advocate* (5 December):36–38.

Lewis, Sasha Gregory. 1979. *Sunday's Women: A Report on Lesbian Life Today*. Boston: Beacon.

Leznoff, Maurice, and William A. Westley, 1956. "The Homosexual Community." *Social Problems* 3(4):257–63.

Lipton, Eunice. 1971. "The Invisible Woman." Unpublished manuscript.

Lisagor, Nancy L. 1980. *Lesbian Identity in the Subculture of Women's Bars*. Ann Arbor, MI: University Microfilms International.

Maggenti, Maria. 1993. "Wandering through Herland." In *Sisters, Sexperts, Queers: Beyond the Lesbian Nation*, ed. Arlene Stein. 245–55. New York: Plume.

Malinowski, Bronislaw. 1967. *A Diary in the Strict Sense of the Term*. London: Routledge.

———. 1955. *Sex and Repression in a Savage Society*. Cleveland, OH: World Publishing.

Martin, Biddy. 1994. "Sexualities without Genders and Other Queer Utopias." *Diacritics* 24(2–3):104–21.

Martin, Del, and Phyllis Lyon. 1972. *Lesbian/Woman*. New York: Bantam.

Martinez, Inez. 1983. "The Lesbian Hero Bound: Radclyffe Hall's Portrait of Sapphic Daughters and Their Mothers." *Journal of Homosexuality* 8(3–4):127–37.

Mascia-Lees, Frances E., Patricia Sharpe, and Colleen Ballerino Cohen. 1989. "The Post-modernist Turn in Anthropology: Cautions from a Feminist Perspective." *Signs: Journal of Women in Culture and Society* 15(1):7–33.

McCandless, Cathy. 1980. "Some Thoughts about Racism, Classism and Separatism." In *Top Ranking*, ed. Joan Gibbs and Sara Bennett. New York: Come! Unity Press.

McCoy, Sherry, and Maureen Hicks. 1979. "A Psychological Retrospective on Power in the Contemporary Lesbian-Feminist Community." *Frontiers* 4(3):65–69.

Meyer, Jon K., and John T. Hoopes. 1974. "The Gender Dysphoria Syndromes." *Plastic and Reconstructive Surgery* (54).

Milford, Nancy. 1970. *Zelda Fitzgerald: A Biography*. New York: Harper and Row.

Moffatt, Michael. 1989. *Coming of Age in New Jersey: College and American Culture*. New Brunswick, NJ: Rutgers University Press.

Money, John, and Anke A. Ehrhardt. 1972. *Man and Woman, Boy and Girl*. Baltimore: Johns Hopkins University Press.

Montagu, M. F. A., ed. 1956. *Marriage, Past and Present: A Debate between R. Briffault and B. Malinowski*. Boston: Porter Sargent.

Moraga, Cherríe, and Gloria Anzaldúa. 1981. *This Bridge Called My Back: Writings by Radical Women of Color*. Watertown, MA: Persephone Press.

Mordden, Ethan. 1981. *The American Theatre*. New York: Oxford University Press.

Moses, Alice E. 1978. *Identity Management in Lesbian Women*. New York: Praeger.

Muñoz, José Esteban. 1995. "Choteo/Camp Style Politics: Carmelita Tropicana's Performance of Self-Enactment." *Women and Performance: A Journal of Feminist Theory* 7:2(14–15):39–52.

Munt, Sally R. 1998. *Heroic Desire: Lesbian Identity and Cultural Space*. New York: New York University Press.

Murphy, Robert. 1987. *The Body Silent*. New York: Henry Holt.

Murray, Sarah. 1994. "Dragon Ladies, Draggin' Men: Some Reflections on Gender, Drag and Homosexual Communities." *Public Culture* (6):343–63.

Murray, Stephen O. 1996. *American Gay*. Chicago: University of Chicago Press.

———. 1979. "The Institutional Elaboration of a Quasi-Ethnic Community." *International Review of Modern Sociology* 9 (July):165–77.

Myerhoff, Barbara. 1978. *Number Our Days*. New York: Simon and Schuster.

Nanda, Serena. 1990. *Neither Man nor Woman: The Hijras of India*. Belmont, CA: Wadsworth.

———. 1986. "The Hijras of India: Cultural and Individual Dimensions of an Institutionalized Third Gender Role." In *Anthropology and Homosexual Behavior*, ed. Evelyn Blackwood. 35–54. New York: Haworth.

Nardi, Peter M., and Beth E. Schneider, eds. 1998. *Social Perspectives in Lesbian and Gay Studies*. London: Routledge.

Navasky, Victor. 1980. *Naming Names*. New York: Viking.

Nestle, Joan. 1981. "Butch-Fem Relationships." *Heresies Sex Issue* 3(12):21–24.

Newton, Esther. 1996a. "Dick(less) Tracy and the Homecoming Queen: Lesbian Power and Representation in Gay Male Cherry Grove." In *Inventing Lesbian Cultures*, ed. Ellen Lewin. 162–93. Boston: Beacon.

———. 1996b. "My Best Informant's Dress: The Erotic Equation in Fieldwork." In *Out in the Field: Reflections of Lesbian and Gay Anthropologists*, ed. Ellen Lewin and William Leap. 212–35. Urbana: University of Illinois Press.

———. 1993. *Cherry Grove, Fire Island: Sixty Years in America's First Gay and Lesbian Town*. Boston: Beacon.

———. 1986. ". . . Sick to Death of Ambiguities." *Women's Review of Books*, October.

———. 1984a. "The Mythic Mannish Lesbian." *Signs: Journal of Women in Culture and Society* 9(4):557–75.

———. 1984b. "An Open Letter to 'Manda Cesara.'" *Anthropology Research Group on Homosexuality Newsletter* (spring).

———. 1979. *Mother Camp: Female Impersonators in America* (with a new introduction). Chicago: University of Chicago Press.

———. 1972. *Mother Camp: Female Impersonators in America*. New York: Prentice Hall.

Newton, Esther, and Carroll Smith-Rosenberg. 1984. "Le Mythe de la lesbienne et la femme nouvelle." In *Strategies des femmes*. Paris: Editions Tierce.

Newton, Esther, and Shirley Walton. 1984. "The Misunderstanding: Toward a More Precise Sexual Vocabulary." In *Pleasure and Danger: Exploring Female Sexuality*, ed. Carole S. Vance. 242–50. Boston: Routledge and Kegan Paul.

———. 1976. *Womenfriends*. New York: Friends Press.

Newton, Esther, and Paula Webster. 1973. "Matriarchy as Women See It." *Aphra, the Feminist Literary Magazine* 4 (3).

Norris, William. 1992. "Liberal Attitudes and Homophobic Acts: The Paradoxes of Homosexual Experience in a Liberal Institution." *Journal of Homosexuality* 22(3/4):81–120.

Nyberg, Kenneth L. 1976. "Sexual Aspirations and Sexual Behaviors among Homosexually Behaving Males and Females: The Impact of the Gay Community." *Journal of Homosexuality* 2(1):29–38.

Ormrod, Richard. 1985. *Una Troubridge: The Friend of Radclyffe Hall*. New York: Carroll and Graf.

Ortner, Sherry B., and Harriet Whitehead, eds. 1981. *Sexual Meanings: The Cultural Construction of Gender and Sexuality*. Cambridge, England: Cambridge University Press.

P. A. [Patti Ann]. 1994. "Talk of the Grove." *Fire Island Tide* (17 June):34.

Palmer, R. R. 1960. *A History of the Modern World*. New York: Knopf.

Parker, Richard. 1991. *Bodies, Pleasures and Passions: Sexual Culture in Contemporary Brazil*. Boston: Beacon.

Patton, Cindy. 1985. "Brave New Lesbians." *Village Voice*, (2 July):24–25.

Paul, William, James D. Weinrich, John C. Gonsiorek, and Mary E. Hotvedt, eds. 1982. *Homosexuality: Social, Psychological, and Biological Issues*. Beverley Hills, CA: Sage.

Pauly, Ira B. 1969. "Adult Manifestations of Female Transsexualism." In *Transsexualism and Sex Reassignment*, ed. Richard Green and John Money. 59–87. Baltimore: Johns Hopkins University Press.

Peplau, Letitia Anne, Susan Cochran, Karen Rook, and Christine Padesky. 1978. "Loving Women: Attachment and Autonomy in Lesbian Relationships." *Journal of Social Issues* 34(3):7–27.

Phelan, Shane. 1993. "[Be]Coming Out: Lesbian Identity and Politics." *Signs: Journal of Women and Society* 18(4):779.

Plato. 1989. *Symposium*. Trans. Alexander Nichamas and Paul Woodruff. Indianapolis: Hackett.

Plum, Jay. 1998. "Cheryl Crawford: One Not So Naked Individual." In *Passing Performances: Queer Readings of Leading Players in American Theater History*, ed. Robert A. Schanke and Kim Marra. 239–61. Ann Arbor: University of Michigan Press.

Plummer, Kenneth. 1998. "The Past, Present, and Futures of the Sociology of Same-Sex Relations." In *Social Perspectives in Lesbian and Gay Studies*, ed. Peter M. Nardi and Beth E. Schneider. 605–14. London: Routledge.

Ponse, Barbara. 1978. *Identities in the Lesbian World: The Social Construction of Self*. Westport, CT: Greenwood.

President's Select Committee for Lesbian and Gay Concerns. 1989. *In Every Classroom*. New Brunswick, NJ: Rutgers University Press.

Prynne, William. 1633/1974. *Histrio-mastix: The Players Scourge, or Actors Tragedie*. New York: Garland.

Rabinow, Paul. 1977. *Reflections on Fieldwork in Morocco*. Berkeley: University of California Press.

Radicalesbians. 1973. "The Woman-Identified Woman." In *Radical Feminism*, ed. Anne Koedt, Ellen Levine, and Anita Rapone. 240–45. New York: Quadrangle.

Raffo, Susan, ed. 1996. *Queerly Classed: Gay Men and Lesbians Write about Class*. Boston: South End Press.

Ramos, Juanita, ed. 1994. *Compañeras: Latina Lesbians, an Anthology*. New York: Routledge.

Read, Kenneth E. 1986. *Return to the High Valley*. Berkeley: University of California Press.

———. 1980. *Other Voices: The Style of a Male Homosexual Tavern*. Novato, CA: Chandler and Sharp.

———. 1965. *The High Valley*. New York: Scribner's.

Rechy, John. 1977. *The Sexual Outlaw*. New York: Dell.

Rich, Adrienne. 1983. "Compulsory Heterosexuality and Lesbian Existence." In *Powers of Desire: The Politics of Sexuality*, ed. Ann Snitow, Christine Stansell, and Sharon Thompson. 177–205. New York: Monthly Review Press.

Riddle, Dorothy, and Barbara Sang. 1978. "Psychotherapy with Lesbians." *Journal of Social Issues* 34(3):84–100.

Roberts, J. R. 1981. *Black Lesbians: An Annotated Bibliography.* Tallahasse, FL: Naiad Press.

Robertson, Jennifer. 1998. *Takarazuka: Sexual Politics and Popular Culture in Modern Japan.* Berkeley: University of California Press.

Robinson, Paul. 1976. *The Modernization of Sex.* New York: Harper Colophon.

Román, David. 1998. *Acts of Intervention: Performance, Gay Culture, and AIDS.* Bloomington: Indiana University Press.

Romo-Carmona, Mariana. 1997. "Latina Lesbians." In *A Queer World: The Center for Lesbian and Gay Studies Reader,* ed. Martin Duberman. 35–38. New York: New York University Press.

Rosaldo, Renato. 1989. *Culture and Truth: The Remaking of Social Analysis.* Boston: Beacon.

Roscoe, Will. 1996. "Writing Queer Cultures: An Impossible Possibility?" In *Out in the Field: Reflections of Lesbian and Gay Anthropologists,* ed. Ellen Lewin and William L. Leap. 200–211. Urbana: University of Illinois Press.

———. 1992. "Comments on Receiving the Margaret Mead Award." *Society of Lesbian and Gay Anthropologists Newsletter* 14(1):11–12.

———. 1991. *The Zuñi Man-Woman.* Albuquerque: University of New Mexico Press.

Ross, Andrew. 1989. "The Uses of Camp." In *No Respect: Intellectuals and Popular Culture.* 135–70. New York: Routledge and Kegan Paul.

Rubin, Gayle. 1992. "Of Catamites and Kings: Reflections on Butch, Gender, and Boundaries." In *The Persistent Desire: A Femme-Butch Reader,* ed. Joan Nestle. 466–82. Boston: Alyson.

———. 1984. "Thinking Sex: Notes for a Radical Theory of the Politics of Sexuality." In *Pleasure and Danger: Exploring Female Sexuality,* ed. Carole S. Vance. 267–319. Boston: Routledge and Kegan Paul.

———. 1975. "The Traffic in Women." In *Toward an Anthropology of Women,* ed. Rayna Reiter. New York: Monthly Review Press.

Rumaker, Michael. 1982. *A Day and a Night at the Baths.* San Francisco: Grey Fox Press.

Russo, Vito. 1987. *The Celluloid Closet: Homosexuality in the Movies.* New York: Harper and Row.

Sahlins, Marshall. 1991. "The Return of the Event, Again." In *Clio in Oceania,* ed. Aletta Biersack. Washington, DC: Smithsonian Institution Press.

Samois, ed. 1983. *Coming to Power.* 2d ed. Boston: Alyson.

Sandoval, Chela. 1984. "Comment on Krieger's 'Lesbian Identity and Community: Recent Social Science Literature.'" *Signs* 9(4):725–29.

San Francisco Lesbian and Gay History Project. 1989. "'She Even Chewed Tobacco': A Pictorial Narrative of Passing Women in America." In *Hidden from History: Reclaiming the Gay and Lesbian Past,* ed. Martin B. Duberman, Martha Vicinus, and George Chauncey. 183–94. New York: New American Library.

Sankar, Andrea. 1986. "Sisters and Brothers, Lovers and Enemies: Marriage Resistance in Southern Kwangtung." In *Anthropology and Homosexual Behavior,* ed. Evelyn Blackwood. 69–82. New York: Haworth.

Sapir, Edward. 1962. "Culture, Genuine and Spurious." In *Edward Sapir: Culture, Language and Personality,* ed. D. G. Mandelbaum. Berkeley: University of California Press.

Sarton, May. 1965. *Mrs. Stevens Hears the Mermaids Singing.* New York: Norton.

Saslow, James. 1989. "Homosexuality in the Renaissance: Behavior, Identity, and Artistic Expression." In *Hidden from History: Reclaiming the Gay and Lesbian Past,* ed. Martin Duberman, Martha Vicinus, and George Chauncey. 90–105. New York: New American Library.

Schanke, Robert A., and Kim Marra, eds. 1998. *Passing Performances: Queer Readings of Leading Players in American Theater History.* Ann Arbor: University of Michigan Press.

Schneebaum, Tobias. 1969. *Keep the River on Your Right.* New York: Grove Press.

Schneider, David M. 1997. "The Power of Culture: Notes on Some Aspects of Gay and Lesbian Kinship in America Today." *Cultural Anthropology* 12(2):23–31.

———. 1995. *Schneider on Schneider: The Conversion of the Jews and Other Anthropological Stories.* As told to Richard Handler. Durham, NC: Duke University Press.

———. 1968. *American Kinship.* Englewood Cliffs, NJ: Prentice-Hall.

Schwartz, Helen. 1994. "Homecoming Queen Is a Woman." *Fire Island Tide* (1 July):12.

Sedgwick, Eve Kosofsky, and Michael Moon. 1993. "Divinity." In *Tendencies,* ed. Eve Kosofsky Sedgwick. 215–51. Durham, NC: Duke University Press.

Senelick, Laurence. 1990. "Mollies or Men of Mode? Sodomy and the Eighteenth-Century London Stage." *Journal of the History of Sexuality* 1(1):33–67.

Shepherd, Gill. 1987. "Rank, Gender and Homosexuality: Mombasa as a Key to Understanding Sexual Options." In *The Cultural Construction of Sexuality,* ed. Pat Caplan. 240–70. London: Tavistock.

Sidebottom, Jeanne. 1994. "Homecoming Queen Overcomes Furor in the Grove." *Sappho's Isle* (August):19.

Simmons, Christina. 1979. "Companionate Marriage and the Lesbian Threat." *Frontiers* 4(3):54–59.

Simon, William, and John H. Gagnon. 1967. "The Lesbians: A Preliminary Overview." In *Sexual Deviance,* ed. John H. Gagnon and William Simon. 247–81. New York: Harper and Row.

Singer, Milton. 1955. "The Cultural Pattern of Indian Civilization." *Far Eastern Quarterly* 15:23–36.

Sisley, Emily L. 1981. "Notes on Lesbian Theatre." *The Drama Review: Sex and Performance Issue* 25(1):47–56.

Smith, Barbara, ed. 1983. *Home Girls: A Black Feminist Anthology.* New York: Kitchen Table/Women of Color Press.

Smith, Carolyn D., and William Kornblum, eds. 1989. *In the Readings on the Field Research Experience.* New York: Praeger.

Smith-Rosenberg, Carroll. 1989. "Discourses of Sexuality and Subjectivity: The New Woman, 1870–1936." In *Hidden from History: Reclaiming the Gay and Lesbian Past,* ed. Martin B. Duberman, Martha Vicinus, and George Chauncey Jr. 264–80. New York: New American Library.

———. 1985a. *Disorderly Conduct: Visions of Gender in Victorian America.* New York: Knopf.

———. 1985b. "The New Woman as Androgyne: Social Disorder and Gender Crisis, 1870–1936." In *Disorderly Conduct: Visions of Gender in Victorian America.* New York: Knopf.

———. 1975. "The Female World of Love and Ritual." *Signs* 1(1):1–30.

Snitow, Ann, Christine Stansell, and Sharon Thompson, eds. 1983. *Powers of Desire: The Politics of Sexuality.* New York: Monthly Review Press.

Solanis, Valerie. 1971. *The Scum Manifesto*. London: Olympia Press.

Solomon, Alisa. 1997. *Re-Dressing the Canon: Essays on Theater and Gender*. New York: Routledge.

———. 1993a. "It's Never Too Late to Switch: Crossing toward Power." In *Crossing the Stage: Controversies on Cross-Dressing*, ed. Lesley Ferris. 144–54. London: Routledge.

———. 1993b. "Not Just a Passing Fancy: Notes on Butch." *Theatre* (November):35–46.

———. 1985. "The wow Cafe." *TDR: The Drama Review* 29(1):92–101.

Sontag, Susan. 1964. "Notes on Camp." *Partisan Review* (fall):515–30.

Stacey, Judith. 1990. *Brave New Families*. New York: Basic Books.

Stein, Arlene. 1998. "The Decentering of Lesbian Feminism." In *Social Perspectives in Lesbian and Gay Studies*, ed. Peter M. Nardi and Beth E. Schneider. 551–63. London: Routledge.

———. 1997. *Sex and Sensibility: Stories of a Lesbian Generation*. Berkeley: University of California Press.

———, ed. 1993. *Sisters, Sexperts, Queers: Beyond the Lesbian Nation*. New York: Plume.

Stein, Gertrude. 1971. *Fernhurst, Q.E.D., and Other Early Writings*. New York: Liveright.

Stimpson, Catherine R. 1982. "Zero Degree Deviancy: The Lesbian Novel in English." In *Writing and Sexual Difference*, ed. Elizabeth Abel. 243–60. Chicago: University of Chicago Press.

Stoller, Paul. 1989. *The Taste of Ethnographic Things: The Senses in Anthropology*. Philadelphia: University of Pennsylvania Press.

Stoller, Robert. 1985. *Presentations of Gender*. New Haven: Yale University Press.

———. 1979. *Sexual Excitement*. New York: Pantheon.

Straub, Kristina. 1991. "The Guilty Pleasures of Female Theatrical Cross-Dress and the Autobiography of Charlotte Charke." In *Body Guards: The Cultural Politics of Gender Ambiguity*, ed. Julia Epstein and Kristina Straub. 142–66. New York: Routledge.

Stroud, Irene E. 1994. "The Best of Times, the Worst of Times." *Women's Review of Books* 7(2).

Study Committee on the Status of Lesbians and Gay Men. 1991. *From Invisibility to Inclusion: Opening the Doors for Lesbians and Gay Men*. Vol. 1. Affirmative Action Office, University of Michigan.

Tanner, Donna M. 1978. *The Lesbian Couple*. Lexington, MA: Lexington Books.

Thompson, Sharon. 1990. "Putting a Big Thing into a Little Hole: Teenage Girls' Accounts of Sexual Initiation." *Journal of Sex Research* 27(3):341–61.

———. 1984. "Search for Tomorrow: On Feminism and the Reconstruction of Teen Romance." In *Pleasure and Danger: Exploring Female Sexuality*, ed. Carole S. Vance. 350–84. Boston: Routledge.

Traub, Valerie. 1992. *Desire and Anxiety: Circulations of Sexuality in Shakespearean Drama*. New York: Routledge.

Trimberger, Ellen K. 1983. "Feminism, Men, and Modern Love: Greenwich Village, 1900–1925." In *Powers of Desire: The Politics of Sexuality*, ed. Ann Snitow, Christine Stansell, and Sharon Thompson. 131–52. New York: Monthly Review Press.

Troubridge, Una. 1961. *The Life and Death of Radclyffe Hall*. London: Hammond.

Trumbach, Randolph. 1991. "London's Sapphists: From Three Sexes to Four Genders in the Making of Modern Culture." In *Body Guards: The Cultural Politics of Gender Ambiguity*, ed. Julia Epstein and Kristina Straub. 112–41. New York: Routledge.

———. 1989. "The Birth of the Queen: Sodomy and the Emergence of Gender Equality in Modern Culture, 1660–1750." In *Hidden from History: Reclaiming the Gay and Lesbian Past*, ed. Martin Duberman, Martha Vicinus, and George Chauncey. 129–40. New York: New American Library.

Turner, Victor. 1974. *Dramas, Fields, and Metaphors: Symbolic Action in Human Society.* Ithaca, NY: Cornell University Press.

Tyler, Carole-Anne. 1991. "Boys Will Be Girls: The Politics of Gay Drag." In *Inside/Out: Lesbian Theories, Gay Theories*, ed. Diana Fuss. 32–70. New York: Routledge.

Tyler, Parker. 1963. "The Garbo Image." In *The Films of Greta Garbo*, ed. Michael Conway, Dion McGregor, and Mark Ricci. 9–31. New York: Citadel Press.

Vance, Carole S. 1983. "Gender Systems, Ideology, and Sex Research" In *Powers of Desire: The Politics of Sexuality*, ed. Ann Snitow, Christine Stansell, and Sharon Thompson. 371–84. New York: Monthly Review Press.

———, ed. 1984. *Pleasure and Danger: Exploring Female Sexuality.* Boston: Routledge and Kegan Paul.

Vicinus, Martha. 1982a. "One Life to Stand beside Me: Emotional Conflicts of First-Generation College Women in England." *Feminist Studies* 8(3):602–28.

———. 1982b. "Sexuality and Power: A Review of Current Work in the History of Sexuality." *Feminist Studies* 8(spring):147–51.

Vida, Ginny, ed. 1978. *Our Right to Love: A Lesbian Resource Book.* Englewood Cliffs, NJ: Prentice-Hall.

Walker, Lisa M. 1993. "How to Recognize a Lesbian: The Cultural Politics of Looking Like What You Are." *Signs: Journal of Women in Culture and Society* 18(4):866–90.

Wallace, Anthony F. C. 1961. *Culture and Personality.* New York: Random House.

Walters, Delores K. 1996. "Cast among Outcastes: Interpreting Sexual Orientation, Racial and Gender Identity in the Yemen Arab Republic." In *Out in the Field*, ed. Ellen Lewin and William L. Leap. Urbana: University of Illinois Press.

Walters, Susanna D. 1994. "From Here to Queer: Radical Feminism, Posmodernism, and the Lesbian Menace (Or, Why Can't a Woman Be More Like a Fag?)." *Signs* 21(4):830–69.

Ward, Mary J. 1946. *The Snake Pit.* New York: Random House.

Warner, Michael. 1993. Introduction. In *Fear of a Queer Planet: Queer Politics and Social Theory*, ed. Michael Warner. vii–xxxi. Minneapolis: University of Minnesota Press.

Warren, Carol A. B. 1977. "Fieldwork in the Gay World: Issues in Phenomenological Research." *Journal of Social Issues* 33(4):93–107.

———. 1974. *Identity and Community in the Gay World.* New York: Wiley.

Wasserman, Elizabeth. 1994a. "Cherry Grove Queen Proves She's No Drag." *Newsday* (5 July).

———. 1994b. "This Queen Crosses Some on Fire Island." *Newsday* (16 June).

Webster, Paula. 1975. "Matriarchy, As Women See It." In *Toward an Anthropology of Women*, ed. Raina Reiter. New York: Monthly Review Press.

Weeks, Jeffrey. 1977. *Coming Out: Homosexual Politics in Britain, from the Nineteenth Century to the Present.* London: Quartet Books.

Weinberg, Martin S., and Colin J. Williams. 1974. *Male Homosexuals: Their Problems and Adaptations.* New York: Oxford University Press.

Weinberg, Thomas, and G. W. Levi Kamel. 1983. *S&M: Studies in Sado-Masochism.* Buffalo, NY: Prometheus Books.

West, James [Carl Withers]. 1971. *Plainville, U.S.A.* Westport, CT: Greenwood Press.

Weston, Kath. 1997. "The Virtual Anthropologist." In *Anthropological Locations*, ed. Akhil Gupta and James Ferguson. 163–84. Berkeley: University of California Press.

———. 1993a. "Do Clothes Make the Woman? Gender, Performance Theory, and Lesbian Eroticism." *Genders* 17 (fall).

———. 1993b. "Lesbian/Gay Studies in the House of Anthropology." *Annual Review of Anthropology* 22:157–85.

———. 1991. *Families We Choose: Gays, Lesbians and Kinship*. New York: Columbia University Press.

Wexler, Alice. 1984. *Emma Goldman in America*. Boston: Beacon.

Whisman, Vera. 1993. "Identity Crises: Who Is a Lesbian, Anyway?" In *Sisters, Sexperts, Queers: Beyond the Lesbian Nation*, ed. Arlene Stein. 47–60. New York: Plume.

Whitehead, Harriet. 1981. "The Bow and the Burden Strap: A New Look at Institutionalized Homosexuality in Native North America." In *Sexual Meanings: The Cultural Construction of Gender and Sexuality*, ed. Sherry B. Ortner and Harriet Whitehead. 80–115. Cambridge, England: Cambridge University Press.

Whitehead, Tony Larry. 1986. "Breakdown, Resolution, and Coherence: The Fieldwork Experiences of a Big, Brown, Pretty-Talking Man in a West Indian Community." In *Self, Sex, and Gender in Cross-Cultural Fieldwork*, ed. Tony Larry Whitehead and Mary Ellen Conaway. 213–39. Urbana: University of Illinois Press.

Williams, Walter. 1986. *The Spirit and the Flesh: Sexual Diversity in American Indian Culture*. Boston: Beacon.

Wolf, Deborah Goleman. 1980. *The Lesbian Community*. Berkeley: University of California Press.

Zimmerman, Bonnie. 1984. "The Politics of Transliteration: Lesbian Personal Narratives." *Signs* 9(4):663–82.

INDEX

Note: EN in index refers to Esther Newton

and 1960s, 64–65, 160; terms used in, 272 n.11
Butch men: erotic identity of, 170; and socioeconomic class, 20, 260 n.4
Butler, Judith, 65, 89, 271 n.7, 276 n.40; EN's influence on, ix–x

Camp: authentic self in, x, 66, 86–87; ethos/themes of, 23–29, 260 n.8, 260–61 nn.10–16; and gay pride, 31; humor in, 23, 26, 27–28, 35, 64, 260 n.11, 261 nn.13, 16; incongruity in, 22–24, 27, 35, 64; influence of revues, 53–57; inside-outside oppositions in, 19; in mass culture, 23, 24–25, 26–27, 31, 34, 259 n.1, 260 n.10, 261 n.2; misinterpretations of, 23, 34, 260 n.9, 262 n.1; origins of, in English theater, 36, 40, 42, 265 n.20; suppression of, on Broadway, 47–48; theatricality in, 23, 24–27, 35, 64, 260 n.11; and victimhood, 62. See also Lesbian camp
Camp queens: characteristics of, 27–29, 68, 261 nn.13–14, 16; vs. drag queens, 22–23, 28–29, 261 n.16; vs. "pretty boys," 260 n.6
Cannon, Hallye, 50
Capezio, Salvatore, 48
Capote, Truman, 34–35
Captive, The, 47, 51
Carlson, Marvin, 41, 226 n.29
Carpenter, Edward, 36, 181
Carpenter, Louisa, 49
Casagrande, Joseph, 245
Case, Sue-Ellen: on butch-femme aesthetic, 64–65, 67, 70, 88, 89, 208; on feminist view of butch-femme, 67, 272 n.10; on regional differences in camp, 271–72 n.7
Censorship: of alternatives, in American theater, 44–48, 51, 56–57, 268 n.44; of books, 186, 268 n.45; in Cherry Grove, 55, 59; by Nazis, 2; and subcultural bonding, 41
Cesara, Manda (Karla O. Poewe), 225–28, 248–49, 289 n.10
Charles II, 42

Cherry Grove, Fire Island (Newton): fieldwork for, 79, 236
Cherry Grove: the Meat Rack, 72, 78; racism in, 77, 274 n.28; real estate/home ownership in, 35, 68, 72, 78; socioeconomic profiles/issues in, 56, 68, 71–72, 81, 85; theatricality of, 35, 36–37, 39, 44, 262 n.4
Cherry Grove—gay male/lesbian dynamics: and lesbian marginalization, 72–78, 85–86, 273 n.24, 274 n.27, 275 n.34, 275–76 n.39, 276 nn.45–46; lesbians as empty signifiers in, 85–86, 275 n.34; lesbians in queenly/"ladies" roles in, 69, 71–72; in Queen Joan controversy, 70, 78–85, 86, 87, 273 n.21, 274 nn.30–32, 275 n.36
Cherry Grove—Homecoming Queen/Invasion of the Pines: Empress of the Invasion, 82; EN escorting "Ann Miller" to, 165; meaning of Invasion, 69–70; Queen Joan and the Invasion, 71, 82–85; Queen Joan as camp/campy, 70, 80, 81, 82, 84, 86–87; Queen Joan election and controversy, 70, 78–82, 86, 87, 273 n.21, 274 nn.30–32, 275 n.36; Queen's duties, 69–70; Queen Shapiro, 85; Queen Vera, 77, 83
Cherry Grove—theater: Arts Project antecedents of, 53–58, 69, 269 n.66, 270 n.76; and Arts Project founders/founding, 35, 50, 52, 58, 69; and Arts Project membership, 85; and Arts Project thirtieth-anniversary ball, 75; and Berthe of a Nation project, 57, 59–60, 270 nn.77, 79, 81; and Broadway connections/influences, 48–50, 57, 268 n.52; censorship in, 55, 59; and community theater movement, 58; and EN and Toni on stage, 211–12; first nonlocal performer at, 85; lesbians in, 75–77, 85, 87, 273 n.24, 274 n.26, 275 n.34, 276 n.44; and Off-Broadway connections/influences, 50–52, 58, 62, 269 n.56; Off-Off-Broadway, Grove influence on, 62; predominance in Grove life, 39; realistic treatment of

Esther Newton is Professor of Anthropology at State University of New York at Purchase. She is the author of *Cherry Grove, Fire Island: Sixty Years in America's First Gay and Lesbian Town* (1993) and *Mother Camp: Female Impersonators in America* (1972).

Library of Congress Cataloging-in-Publication Data

Newton, Esther.

Margaret Mead made me gay: personal essays, public ideas / Esther Newton.

p.   cm. — (series Q)

ISBN 0–8223–2604–3 (cloth : alk. paper) —

ISBN 0–8223–2612–4 (pbk. : alk. paper)

1. Gays—United States.   2. Lesbians—United States.   3. Lesbian feminism—United States.   4. Homophobia in anthropology—United States.   5. Newton, Esther.   6. Lesbian anthropologists—United States—Biography.   7. Anthropologists—United States—Biography.

I. Title.   II. Series.

HQ76.3.U5 N49   2000

305.9'0664—dc21   00-029400